WAYS *of* BEING, WAYS *of* READING

WAYS *of* BEING, WAYS *of* READING

Asian American Biblical Interpretation

Mary F. Foskett
Jeffrey Kah-Jin Kuan
EDITORS

CHALICE
PRESS
ST. LOUIS, MISSOURI

Cover and interior design: Elizabeth Wright

Visit Chalice Press on the World Wide Web at
www.chalicepress.com

10 9 8 7 6 5 4 3 2 1   06 07 08 09 10

Library of Congress Cataloging–in–Publication Data

Ways of being, ways of reading : Asian American biblical interpretation / Mary F. Foskett and Jeffrey Kah-Jin Kuan, editors.

    p. cm.

Includes bibliographical references.

ISBN-13: 978-0-8272-4254-8

ISBN-10: 0-8272-4254-9

1. Bible–Criticism, interpretation, etc.–Asia. I. Foskett, Mary F., 1961- II. Kuan, Jeffrey K. III. Title.

BS511.3.W39 2006

220.6095–dc22

                    2006023311

Contents

Contributors

John Ahn is adjunct professor of Hebrew Bible at Hartford Seminary. Currently, he is ABD in Hebrew Bible/Old Testament in the department of religious studies at Yale University. The title of his dissertation is "Exile, Literature, and Theology: The Literary and Socio-Theological Impact of the Forced Migrations of the Southern Kingdom of Judah," under the direction of Prof. Robert Wilson. He is a second-generation Korean American.

Samuel Cheon is professor of Old Testament at Hannam University in Daejon, South Korea. He received his Ph.D. from the Graduate Theological Union and is the author of *The Exodus in the Wisdom of Solomon* (1997).

Philip P. Chia is adjunct professor of Old Testament at the Divinity School of Chung Chi College, The Chinese University of Hong Kong. He received his Ph.D. from The University of Sheffield and is the author of *Truth & Absurdity* (1996) and *Conflicting Interpretation* (1997), both published in Chinese. He is a Malaysian residing in Hong Kong and has taught Old Testament at various institutions in Southeast Asia, Taiwan, Hong Kong, and China.

Mary F. Foskett is associate professor of religion at Wake Forest University in Winston-Salem, North Carolina. She is an ethnic Chinese and an Asian American adoptee. She is the author of *A Virgin Conceived: Mary and Classical Representations of Virginity* (2002) and a contributor to *The Bible in Asian America* (2002). Her current research and teaching interests include New Testament Apocrypha, gospels, and contextual biblical interpretation.

Jean K. Kim is assistant professor of New Testament at Moravian Theological Seminary in Bethlehem, Pennsylvania. She is the author of *Woman and Nation* (2004) and several articles on John and Paul.

Uriah Yong-Hwan Kim is professor of Hebrew Bible at Hartford Seminary in Hartford, Connecticut. His first book, *Decolonizing Josiah: Toward a Postcolonial Reading of the Deuteronomistic History,* is forthcoming from Sheffield Phoenix Press. He is also a contributor to *The Bible in Asian America* (2002). He is a Korean American and a member of the steering committee of the Asian and Asian American Hermeneutics Group of the Society of Biblical Literature.

Jeffrey Kah-Jin Kuan is associate professor of Old Testament at Pacific School of Religion and the Graduate Theological Union in Berkeley, California. Originally from Malaysia, he is an associate editor of *The New Interpreter's Dictionary of the Bible* and the author of *Neo-Assyrian Historical Inscriptions and Syria-Palestine* (1995). His current research and teaching interests include contextual biblical interpretation, ancient Near Eastern history, the books of Job and Joshua, and pedagogies for teaching the Bible in the local church.

Andrew Yueking Lee is a minister at the Oversea Chinese Mission in New York City. In addition to the pastoral ministry, he has also been involved in seminary teaching and administration, most recently at New Brunswick Theological Seminary. His Ph.D. emphasis is in the Old Testament.

Lai Ling Elizabeth Ngan is associate professor of Christian Scriptures at George W. Truett Theological Seminary, Baylor University, in Waco, Texas. She is a native of Hong Kong and came to the United States in her late teens. She is the author of the "Amos" commentary in *The IVP Women's Bible Commentary* (2002) and *The Global Bible Commentary* (forthcoming). Also, she was a member of the Committee on Underrepresented Racial and Ethnic Minorities in the Society of Biblical Literature.

Devadasan N. Premnath, a native of India, is academic dean and associate professor of biblical studies at St. Bernard's School of Theology and Ministry in Rochester, New York. He is the author of *Eighth Century Prophets: A Social Analysis* (Chalice Press, 2003).

Henry W. Morisada Rietz is associate professor of religious studies at Grinnell College in Grinnell, Iowa, where he also received his B.A. He received his M.Div. and then Ph.D. in biblical studies from Princeton Theological Seminary. His work on articulating a contextual biblical interpretation from his multiethnic, or *hapa,* perspective has been published in *Semeia* and the *Union Seminary Quarterly Review.* His monograph, entitled *Time in the Sectarian Dead Sea Scrolls,* is forthcoming.

Mai-Anh Le Tran is assistant professor of religious education and Asian American cultures at Pacific School of Religion in Berkeley, California. She is also the faculty administrator of the Represent-to-Witness Youth Leadership Project at the Institute for Leadership Development and Study of Pacific and Asian North American Religion. She identifies herself as a 1.5–generation Vietnamese American.

Sze-kar Wan is John Norris Professor of New Testament Interpretation at Andover Newton Theological School in Newton Centre, Massachusetts. A 2001–2002 Henry Luce III Fellow in Theology, he is the author of *Power in Weakness: Conflict and Rhetoric in Paul's Second Letter to the Corinthians* (2000), editor and part translator of a Chinese translation of Philo's *De opificio mundi* and *Legum allegoriae,* and co-editor of *The Bible in Modern China: The Literary and Intellectual Impact* (1999). He is editing a volume of essays on May Fourth Chinese Protestant writers and working on an introductory text to the New Testament.

Frank M. Yamada is assistant professor of Old Testament at Seabury Theological Seminary in Evanston, Illinois. He is a Sansei–third-generation Japanese American. With interests in hermeneutics, ethics of reading, and culturally contextual interpretation, his two most recent articles are: "Shibboleth and the Ma(r)king of Culture in Judges 12: Judges 12 and the Monolingualism of the Other," in *Derrida's Bible* (2004); and "Dealing with Rape (in) Narrative (Genesis 34): Ethics of the Other and a Text in Conflict," in *The Meanings We Choose* (2004).

Gale A. Yee is professor of Hebrew Bible at Episcopal Divinity School in Cambridge, Massachusetts. She is the author of *Poor Banished Children of Eve: Woman as Evil in the Hebrew Bible* (2003), and of the "Commentary on Hosea" in *The New Interpreter's Bible*. She has also edited *Judges and Method: New Approaches in Biblical Studies* (1995). She is Chinese American.

John Yueh-Han Yieh is associate professor of New Testament at Virginia Theological Seminary in Alexandria, Virginia. Originally from Taiwan, he received his Ph.D. in religious studies (New Testament) from Yale University. He is the author of *A Concise Greek-Chinese Dictionary of the New Testament* (1989) and *One Teacher: Jesus' Teaching Role in Matthew's Gospel Report* (2004) and has published essays, articles, and reviews in the areas of gospel studies, Chinese biblical interpretation, and cross-cultural hermeneutics.

Acknowledgments

We wish to acknowledge the many people who have contributed to the production of this volume. We would like first of all to acknowledge all our authors for allowing us to publish their essays in this volume. We thank them for their pioneering work as well as their collaboration and cooperation in the editorial process. Our thanks go also to Trent Butler and Pablo A. Jiménez of Chalice Press for their encouragement and guidance in the editorial process. We want to express our gratitude to Jon Berquist, formerly of Chalice Press, without whose initiative and invitation this volume would not have happened. We thank, too, the institutions that have supported us along the way. The Institute for Leadership Development and Study of Pacific and Asian North American Religion (PANA) funded a collaborative meeting of all our authors in 2003, and our respective schools, Wake Forest University and Pacific School of Religion, have provided ongoing and significant support of our work in Asian American biblical hermeneutics.

We are also profoundly grateful to our spouses, J. Scott Hudgins and Valentine Poh-Gaik Toh, who have supported our endeavors in countless ways through their encouragement, understanding, and love.

Finally, we dedicate this volume to our children, Daniel Tran Foskett Hudgins, Valene Min-Lin Kuan, and Janene Min-Mei Kuan, whose lives continually bless and enrich our own and who will carry on the legacy of constructing and negotiating their identities as Asian Americans. It is for them and their generation that we do this work.

Foreword

Since the dawn of liberation theology in the 1960s, contextual theology has gained a strong foothold in the academic disciplines. Begun in Latin America, contextual liberation theologies soon manifested themselves in, for example, Black Theology both in the African continent and in North America, Minjung Theology in Asia, and Feminist Theology in North America. While earlier Asian theologians and biblical scholars were not completely ignorant and inattentive to the significance of social and cultural contexts in their theological thinking and biblical interpretation, liberation theology helped bring the significance of interpreters' contexts to the fore. Asian theologians soon began producing works on contextual theology, of which two of the most significant were *Waterbuffalo Theology* by Kosuke Koyama and *Third-eye Theology: Theology in Formation in Asian Settings* by Choan-Seng Song.[1] The latter, in particular, with a strong background in biblical studies, dealt with biblical interpretation from a contextual perspective in his theological writings. Following Song's lead, a number of Asian biblical scholars soon began approaching biblical interpretation from a contextual perspective in the 1980s, among whom were Archie C.C. Lee, and Carlos H. Abesamis.[2] Since then, Asian biblical scholars working from the methodological approach of contextual hermeneutics have multiplied manifold, to the extent that it is no longer uncommon to find younger Asian biblical scholars writing their dissertations from such a perspective.

Over the last decade and a half, following the lead of their Asian colleagues as well as African American scholars and others examining the significance of social and cultural location in biblical interpretation, Asian American[3] biblical students and scholars have been formally exploring and constructing what is now generally known as Asian American biblical interpretation. Staking out new territory in the field, the task has been both exciting and daunting. Such work in part should be credited to the founding of the Asian and Asian-American Biblical Studies Consultation in 1995. The consultation provided a formal and ongoing context for the exploration of Asian American biblical interpretation. In the ensuing dialogues between Asian and Asian American biblical scholars, the latter, while acknowledging the common heritage and traditions they share with the former, became more cognizant of the significance of their particular social and cultural contexts in North America. Asian American scholars began examining how these contexts impact the ways in which Asian Americans read and construct meaning as they engage the Bible, and by necessity, the specific issues that they, as Asian Americans, address in their biblical scholarship.

An example, which is also a dominant theme that a number of the authors in this volume pursue, is that of the construction of Asian American identity and the dialogical interaction of identity with biblical interpretation. While Asians for the most part have not felt the need to deal explicitly with the construction of racial and ethnic identity and related issues, Asian Americans as a minority group have had to address it for survival and empowerment.

As editors of this volume, we recognize the distinctiveness of our Asian American context and seek to show through the essays the interplay between our Asian American social and cultural contexts and biblical interpretation. Nonetheless, as Asian Americans we are indebted not only to the work of our Asian colleagues but also to the common heritage and traditions for which we are all by-products. Hence, we chose to root our volume within the contours of Asian biblical interpretation, both its history and issues. As readers, we hope that you will see the threads that have come into Asian American biblical interpretation as well as the new trajectories that Asian American biblical scholarship is heading toward.

We want to draw your attention to another issue that biblical scholars have been embroiled in, namely, that of the relationship between *Wissenschaft* (primarily the historical-critical methodology) and contextual hermeneutics. The essay by Sze-kar Wan addresses this issue succinctly. Almost every single biblical scholar in this volume is trained in *Wissenschaft*, which in large part still dominates biblical scholarship. Nonetheless, as we begin to be more sensitive to our Asian American social and cultural contexts, the historical-critical approach is not able to answer all the questions we bring to the texts as readers. This has led many of us in the direction of contextual and cultural hermeneutics and caused us to engage new interpretive lenses in our contributions to biblical scholarship. In addition, many of us have begun engaging the field of Asian American studies as dialogue partners. As readers, you will find that even as we move in the direction of contextual and cultural hermeneutics, many of us, while acknowledging the limitations of the historical-critical methodology have chosen not to abandon it completely. Rather, many of the authors in this volume have engaged historical-critical methodology insofar as it helps us answer the particular questions we bring to the texts.

An illustration will suffice to show the move many of us have made toward Asian American biblical interpretation. At the 1994 annual meeting of the Society of Biblical Literature in Chicago, Ill., Gale Yee, a contributor to this volume, declared: "How my Asian-American identity affects my scholarship is a difficult question for me at this point... I suppose that just as the early biblical feminists entered strange, hostile waters to explore the Bible from a woman's perspective, so will I as an Asian-American enter new territory in studying the Bible from an Asian-American perspective... Wish me luck in this new adventure and ask me this question in five years."[4]

Nine years later, Yee was able to articulate her work as an Asian American biblical interpreter as examination of the dynamics that she "had already experienced in real life: that there are insidiously complex interconnections among religion–based on the biblical text–and the 'isms': sexism, racism, classism, colonialism, heterosexism, fundamentalism, and so forth."[5] Not alone in her task, Yee's voice is but one among a growing number of voices in biblical studies. The purpose of this collection of essays is to illustrate for readers, especially advanced undergraduate and graduate students in religious studies, the range of approaches that Asian American scholars now articulate and exercise in the work of Asian American biblical hermeneutics.

Although persons in a variety of fields (Asian American studies, sociology, theology, etc.) engage biblical interpretation and the Bible's role in Asian North America, the essayists in this volume represent a cross-section of the work formally being done in the area of biblical studies. Contributors to this volume have been trained in the multiple disciplines that constitute the field and represent a range of religious affiliations (including, but not limited to, Christian tradition).

As Asian Americans, we are scholars working in the United States and Canada with ethnic and racial identities that tie us to the cultures and histories of East, Southeast, and South Asia; and the Pacific Islands. Sometimes the ties are quite direct, as in the case of persons born, raised and educated in Asia who come to North America to study or teach; sometimes such ties are experienced and negotiated in the context of second-, third-, or fourth-generation Asian communities in North America; sometimes the ties are partially obscured or even more difficult to negotiate, as in the case of the increasing population of adoptees born in Asia and raised in North America by non-Asian (mostly white) families, or the growing numbers of bi- or multi-racial ("hapa") persons in North America. With such multiplicity assumed, the designation "Asian American" refers not to a single culture, history, or experience. Instead, it signals the experience of living in North America as a member of a constellation of racial/ethnic minority communities. As such, "Asian American" is more a social and political designation than a cultural identifier.

Since its inception, Asian American biblical interpretation has emerged not as a single method or approach but as a discourse that acknowledges both the multicultural and trans-generational infrastructure of Asian America and the social and political dynamics at play in the Asian American experience. This discourse can be loosely organized along three trajectories: cultural hermeneutics, cultural studies, and postcolonial interpretation. Each of these is represented in the current volume.

As we have already noted, the development of cultural hermeneutics (that is, culturally contextualized readings of the bible) as a mode of Asian

American biblical interpretation is rooted in Asian biblical interpretation. Asian American interpretation as a form of cultural studies is, in some sense, an Asian North American adaptation of the liberationist perspectives practiced in Asia by Asian biblical scholars. In the Asian North American context, liberationist agendas have merged with the aims and practices of Asian American studies, feminist hermeneutics, and the analysis of gender, race, and class. The result is a complex discourse wherein the construction of identity, race/ethnicity, gender, and class either "in" the biblical text or "in the act of reading the text" is in central focus.

R.S. Sugirtharajah and Kwok Pui-lan are two of the leading proponents of postcolonialism in Asian biblical and theological studies. In the North American scene, Fernando Segovia has argued for the connection between diasporic interpretation and postcolonial studies. In recent years, Asian American biblical interpreters have pursued this particular trajectory, with some examining the experience of diaspora as the context for reading the bible and others focusing on the relevance of postcolonial notions of hybridity, heterogeneity, and identity as fluid and multiply-constructed for Asian American biblical interpretation. In other words, postcolonial perspectives have been used to shape both the trajectories of cultural hermeneutics and cultural studies in Asian American biblical studies.

The key issues and themes that the authors in this volume deal with are multiple and varied. We wish only to highlight a few here. First, because we trace our ancestry to the continent of Asia, we have, as Asians and Asian Americans, inherited many common religio-cultural traditions, values, and practices. As biblical interpreters, these traditions, values, and practices often impinge upon our readings of the biblical texts. Thus, Asian biblical scholars have pointed to the practice of the contextualization or indigenization of the gospel and Christianity. (See the essays of D.N. Premnath, John Yieh, and Samuel Cheon.) This is done often through the use of Asian religious and philosophical categories in understanding the biblical texts and the Christian gospel. For example, Yieh points to the practice of referring to Jesus as a Confucian sage in Chinese biblical interpretation, while Premnath talks about Jesus as an *avatar* (divine incarnation) in Indian biblical interpretation. Rooted within the similar framework of contextual hermeneutics, Asian American biblical scholars have continued to incorporate religio-cultural categories of their ancestry in their engagement with biblical texts. Such readings, however, are more nuanced than the earlier contextual readings to which Yieh and Premnath refer. For instance, Frank Yamada challenges the notion that Japanese cultural values and beliefs tend to dissipate with the later generations of Japanese Americans, arguing instead that these later generations are constantly reformulating and reconstituting their cultural identity. Thus, culture continues to play a role in his biblical interpretation. Mai-Anh Tran, on the other hand, uses a cultural story to engage the stories of two biblical women in a dialogical reading.

A second issue, the politics of identity, is dealt with in many of the essays. Our writers come at the issue of identity from several angles. Andrew Lee, Uriah Kim, and Lai Ling Ngan tend to think of the Asian American identity in terms of "marginality" and "liminality," namely, an existential experience on the margins of the dominant society and in a state of "in-betweenness," that is, in between two or more socio-cultural constructs. Yamada, on the other hand, prefers the categories of "hybridity" and "heterogeneity" to describe the Asian American identity. For Yamada, later generations of Asian Americans are attempting to complicate the notions of Asian-ness and American-ness in the construction of their cultural identity in order to render the essentialized inscription of Asian American identity by the dominant society problematic. (Philip Chia also uses the category of hybridity in describing the cultural identity of Southeast Asians.) Henry Rietz stresses the importance of thinking about the Asian American cultural identity in terms of "particularity." He argues that too often in identity construction, similarities are emphasized to the extent that particularities are ignored and erased. He shows how emphasizing particularities in his own cultural identity as a *hapa* has enabled him to construct new meanings in the biblical texts he reads.

A related issue in the politics of identity is the use of the hyphen in categorizing or describing the "Asian American" identity. This is still a debated issue in the Asian American communities. There is, on the one side, people like Bharati Mukherjee, a writer of South Asian descent, who has said, "I am an American, not an Asian-American. My rejection of hyphenation has been called race treachery, but it is really a demand that America deliver the promises of its dream to all its citizens equally."[6] On the other side are Americans of Asian descent for whom identity is a self-inscription for the purpose of political empowerment as a minority group. What began as a hyphenated inscription eventually generated concerns that a hyphenated identifier would imply that people belonging to such group are less fully members of a society than those of unhyphenated identities. The convention in scholarly publication is to eliminate the hyphen. Likewise, the Asian American magazine *Hyphen*, which as the name suggests acknowledges the Asian American identity as hyphenated, adopts the convention of not using the hyphen. However, as editors we subscribe to the view that identity is a self-inscription. Hence, we have allowed the essayists to use or not use the hyphen. Wan's article, in particular, is a play on the "hyphen" as a hermeneutical lens.

Third, a number of essays deal with women's issues. Most of these include efforts to reread the biblical texts, particularly in relation to women characters and stories, as Asian American women scholars. (See the essays by Lai Ling Ngan, Jean Kim, Mai-Anh Tran.) These authors challenge older (and often patriarchal) construction of meanings in these texts by rereading and reinscribing the characters in the texts from their social and cultural location, toward the view of empowering the characters and other Asian American women. Mary Foskett, on the other hand, focuses on the intersection between the experience of (mostly women) Asian adoptees in search of origins and the concern for origins in New Testament and early Christianity studies.

A final issue addressed by many of the authors is best framed as a question: What constitutes an Asian American biblical interpretation? The essays by Lai Ling Ngan, John Ahn, Sze-kar Wan, and Gale Yee take the question head-on and offer their preliminary thoughts on the issue. While there is agreement by the authors that their cultural identity as Asian Americans, in part, renders their work as Asian American biblical interpretation, readers will nonetheless realize that there is little agreement beyond that in what they say about what constitutes Asian American biblical interpretation. Yee's work, in particular, is an attempt to problematize the simple notion of Asian American biblical interpretation as interpretation based primarily on ethnicity.

In closing, we commend to you *Ways of Being, Ways of Reading: Asian American Biblical Interpretation,* and invite you to share in the experiences, the journeys, and the "ways of being" of the authors, and to engage in dialogue their "ways of readings."

1

Biblical Interpretation in India

History and Issues

DEVADASAN N. PREMNATH
St. Bernard's School of Theology and Ministry
Rochester, New York

This is an attempt to provide a historical sketch of biblical interpretation in India and in that process generate some critical issues pertaining to the discipline. These twin foci (history and issues) will be set forth as the two broad sections of this paper. The historical section is further divided into subsections, on the basis of important periods, which have produced significant contributions to biblical scholarship. The organization is as follows:

1. The Origins
2. Early Roman Catholic Missions
3. Early Protestant Missions
4. Pioneers of Indigenous Christianity
5. Pre-Independence (Pre-1947)/National Freedom Movement and
6. Post-Independence (Post-1947)

The second part is devoted to raising some critical issues in relation to biblical interpretation in India.

At first glance the task may seem deceptively simple. Nothing could be farther from the truth. For anyone attempting to present a history of biblical interpretation in India, the bewildering variety of cultures, communities, and languages presents a tremendous challenge. A general treatment such as this cannot begin to do justice to the complex picture.

Therefore, my strategy is to limit the survey to publications in English. This makes the undertaking a bit more manageable. However, I regrettably have left out of consideration vast amounts of indigenous materials in various Indian languages. Also, an exhaustive cataloguing and discussion of all the works written in English is beyond the scope of this treatment. Only a sampling of key works that have made significant contributions methodologically is possible. The section on the last historical period is organized around distinct issue/approach-oriented categories. This is one way of getting a handle on the various publications.

History of Biblical Interpretation in India

The Origins

The origin of Christianity in India is generally traced back to the arrival of Thomas the apostle to South India around 52 C.E. As the tradition goes, Thomas came to Cranganore in Kerala, preached to the Hindus, and converted them to Christianity.[1] The tradition also attributes to the apostle the work of organizing a community of Christians in Malabar and erecting places of worship. Thomas is also believed to have suffered martyrdom and to have been buried in Mylapore, Chennai. We have little information pertaining to this period other than fragments in support of the mission of Thomas and the existence of the Christian community and its worship places.

In the succeeding centuries the relation between the Christian community in India and the East-Syrian Church grew to such an extent that the latter's influence began to shape the ecclesiastical, liturgical, and theological aspects of the community in India.[2] The positive aspect of this dependence on the East-Syrian Church was that it enabled the Indian community to maintain a strong Christian tradition. Part of this tradition was the ancient Peshitta version of the Bible going back to the very early days of the Christian Church.[3] Yet the Bible probably remained a closed book to ordinary believers. The negative aspect was the failure of the Christian community in India to emerge as a truly indigenous church in theology, polity, and ecclesial practice. This is a familiar theme in the history of Christianity in India, the effects of which can be seen even today.

The impact of the sixteenth-century Reformation in Europe ushered in a new era. An important result was the accessibility of the Bible to the laypeople due to availability in vernacular and large-scale printing. The Bible was held to be the key to the entire system of faith and belief.

The Early Roman Catholic Missions

The practices of the early Roman Catholic missionaries also reflected the impact of the Reformation and the Counter-Reformation. Even though they had no clearly discernible scriptural and hermeneutical tradition, they still made some pioneering attempts at indigenous theologizing.

A well-known example is the work of Robert De Nobili, a Jesuit missionary. The Jesuit mission under the patronage of the Portuguese crown was set up in Madurai, South India. Soon after his arrival in 1606, De Nobili quickly adapted himself to the local ways of the high caste Brahmins, living and dressing like them. This approach was quite revolutionary for that time because the typical attitude of the missionaries was to look down on the local cultures and peoples. Once settled in an ashram, a renewal or retreat center normally located in a secluded area, he started learning Tamil, Telugu, and Sanskrit to be able to read and master various religious and philosophical writings. His ultimate aim was to learn insights from Indian religious traditions and reformulate his own Christian beliefs in categories and thought patterns that were familiar to the indigenous people.

For instance, recognizing the popularity of the Puranas (lengthy versified texts of legends concerning gods) among the Hindus, De Nobili composed a Christian Purana narrating some of the stories from the Bible in colloquial Marathi language.[4] His earnest attempt to identify with the lifestyle of the natives, his interpretation of the Christian message using Hindu terminology and theological categories, and his ability to coin new Indian theological vocabulary were unique.[5] He used them as a missionary strategy even though he drew criticism and opposition from his superiors.[6]

Another key example is from a time closer to the end of that century. Constanzo Beschi (1680–1747) came to India around 1710. He attempted to emulate the work of De Nobili. He was adept at many languages, particularly Tamil. His command over Tamil was so superb that he was able to produce what became one of the greatest works in Tamil literature for all times, *Thembavani.* This was a Christian epic on the life and message of Joseph. It is a masterful presentation of a Christian subject matter using Puranic traditions and techniques.[7] Beschi deftly intersperses discussions of Christian doctrines, theological explanations, and argumentation with heroic acts from the stories of the Old and New Testaments. This marvelous epic poetry weaves as many as 120 episodes from the Old Testament alone. Even though one may not see here a radical theologizing or biblical hermeneutics, the creative attempt at such presentation itself is an unparalleled achievement. The superior literary quality of the work has earned him an undisputed and unique place in Tamil literary history and the honorable title *Viramamunivar* (literally meaning, the most courageous hermit).

The Early Protestant Missions

The history of the Protestant missions in India begins with the arrival of the two famous Lutheran missionaries, Ziegenbalg and Plutschau in Tranquebar, South India, in 1706. The early Protestant missions held the Bible as central to their faith. Hence the Protestant missionaries were also the first ones to translate the Bible into an Indian language, Tamil.[8] The

Bible was used as a tool in the evangelistic undertakings of the missionaries. Ziegenbalg's translation was very much functional in that it was colloquial and devoid of any literary flourish—so much so that the Italian Jesuit Beschi ridiculed it as "horrid gibberish."[9] Ziegenbalg was genuinely sympathetic to Indian religious traditions, much to the chagrin of his superiors. He wrote: "one will find here and there such teachings and passages in their writings which are not only according to human reason but also according to God's word."[10]

Fabricius, another Lutheran missionary from the Tranquebar Mission, produced a much superior translation. Fabricius came to India in 1740. What is interesting is the process he adopted in preparing the translation. In the first stage Fabricius finished a rough translation and reviewed it himself for mistakes. Then he gathered a select group of people from different castes—Brahmins, Sudras, and Pariahs (the last two were considered low castes)—under a tree in front of his house. The catechist who assisted the missionary in the evangelistic work read aloud the translated portions, then asked the group for input for improving the translations. Fabricius gathered all the comments and discussed them with a native scholar in Tamil language. Only then was the translation finalized.[11]

The Serampore Mission in Calcutta, founded by William Carey (1793–1834), undertook translation projects on a much larger scale. They set up a printing factory with different language departments. This resulted in the Bible being available in as many as thirty Indian languages. Each of these translations grappled with linguistic problems that raised theological and hermeneutical issues. Words in any language convey familiar connotations and meanings for the native speakers. The Bible translators in India had to deal with the problem of rendering the texts in terms that could evoke totally different connotations among native speakers. A case in point is the initial reluctance of the translators to use the word *svarga* (a logical choice) for heaven on the grounds that its meaning was limited to the sensual realm of the Hindu god, Indra. Translators opted, instead, for a more neutral term *devaloka* (world of the god).

For the missionaries of this period, the Bible was a powerful tool for evangelism and conversion. For a more creative articulation, we have to look to the last part of the eighteenth century. Interestingly, this did not come from Christians but from Hindus and converts to Christianity from Hinduism. We now turn to some of these pioneers of "Indian" Christianity.

Pioneers of Indigenous Christianity

The first Indian to write on Christian theological themes was not a Christian but a Bengali Brahmin, Raja Ram Mohan Roy (1772–1833). He is well known in the history of modern India as a pioneering social reformer in bringing about the abolition of *Sati* (burning of the widow). One of the sources of inspiration for this was the teachings of Christ as recounted in the gospels. Ram Mohan Roy undertook a serious study of the Bible, learning Hebrew and Greek. His well-known book *The Precepts of Jesus,* published in 1820, gravitates toward moral teachings. Ram Mohan Roy showed very little interest in the gospel of John. For the great social reformer in him, the synoptic gospels were more attractive with their practical and moral import.[12] His main purpose was to persuade and urge other Hindu intellectuals in the task of moral reform of the country. He also held unorthodox views on some fundamental Christian doctrines, a discussion of which is beyond the scope of this paper.[13]

A more novel approach to the Bible came from those who saw Christianity as a fulfillment of the prophecies and longings in Hinduism. A good representative of this approach was Krishna Mohan Banerjea (1813–1885). Also a convert from Hinduism, Banerjea spent most of his life teaching theology in Bengal. After retirement he wrote a book entitled *The Arian* (sic) *Witness,* showing striking parallels between the Old Testament, especially Genesis, and the Vedas.[14] Banerjea's purpose was to show that the Bible fulfilled some of the Hindu prophecies. He finds parallels between the biblical account of creation and the serpent section of the *Mahabharatha.*[15] He also argues that the names Manu and Noah have the same etymological root. As a parallel to the flood story he cites the story of the big fish saving Manu in *Satpatha Brahmana.*[16] Banerjea expounds the similarity between Genesis and the Vedas with particular reference to the sacrificial system.[17] In the Vedic idea of the primeval Purusha as the cosmic sacrifice[18] he finds an obvious pointer to the cross of Christ.[19]

Pre-Independence (1947)/National Freedom Movement

The next group of writers to be considered in this section wrote in the context of the national struggle for freedom. Foremost among these voices were P. Chenchiah, V. Chakkarai, and A.J. Appaswamy.

For P. Chenchiah (1886–1959), the only absolute in Christianity was "the raw fact of Christ."[20] Jesus and the new creation in Christ form the essence of Christianity. The primary value of the gospels is that they contained information about the life and teaching of Jesus. Next in importance were the letters. Of all the New Testament writers, he only credited John and Paul with an understanding of Jesus that surpassed the limitations of their time.[21] Even though the Old Testament figures were rather low in the scheme of Chenchiah's theology, he does acknowledge the usefulness of the theme of the exodus in the context of the national struggle against the British imperialism and also the contribution of the Psalms and the prophets to world religion. However, he does not see the Old Testament as an essential component of Christian theology because the basis for Christian theology is the experience of communion with the living Christ. This experience does not depend on one accepting Moses and the prophets.[22]

The starting point for V. Chakkarai's (1880–1958) theology was christology. Chakkarai uses the Hindu concept of the *Avatar* (incarnation) with the only difference that Jesus is the permanent and dynamic incarnation of God.[23] His theology is far more biblically based than his brother-in-law's, Chenchiah. Chakkarai grants supreme place to the Bible. This conviction is based on his own personal experience of coming to Christ through the reading of the Bible. He also upholds the value of the Old Testament for moral action and social justice concerns. He resonates with the *bhakti* (piety/devotion) of the psalms.[24] His interpretation of the Bible tends to be more mystical or spiritual rather than historical-critical.[25]

Both Chenchiah and Chakkarai emphasize the need for a continuous contact and communion with the living Christ. However, the Bible has a more central place in Chakkarai than Chenchiah. In fact, the point of departure for Chakkarai was the Christian *Sruti* (a word used for the Hindu Vedas, which he uses to designate the Bible) and the *anubhava* (experience) of Christ.[26] If one were to give the pride of place to one's own *anubhava* (experience), subjective experience becomes final. There are no checks to our fantasies as we have in the form of the Scriptures and the Church.[27]

Another notable figure in this period was Bishop A.J. Appaswamy, who was very much influenced by the Bhakti movement of Hinduism. He provides an Indian reading of the gospel of John.[28] He finds a close affinity between its teachings and the core of the Bhakti movement, which is love/devotion.[29] He also sees this as the primary emphasis of the inner spirit of Christianity and Hindu religious thought.[30] Using this approach, Appaswamy is able to offer interesting insights into the text of the gospel. For instance, his interpretation of the *gnosis* (knowledge) in John as personal relationship of *bhakti* rather than the *jnana-marga* (way of knowledge) is intriguing.

Post-Independence Period to the Present

This period has seen a tremendous renewal in biblical hermeneutics. A few general observations may be in order. First, Vatican II played an important role in contributing to the surge in biblical studies in the Roman Catholic circles. Second, in light of the volume of output, only a sampling of representative works is possible in this short treatment. Third, by way of getting a handle on the diverse works, I choose works with a distinctly "Indian" approach or a concern that speaks to an aspect of the Indian reality under the following categories: liberation perspectives, ecological, religiocultural, and artistic. These are offered as a convenient way of organizing a wide range of publications.

1. Liberation perspectives

This rubric groups a wide variety of works with a distinctly liberation perspective. They are further divided into the following subheadings: dalit, tribal, feminist, socioeconomic and postcolonial.

A. DALIT

Proponents of dalit theology trace the etymology of the word *dalit* to both Sanskrit and Hebrew (*dal*), meaning broken, downtrodden. It is a self-designation of a group of oppressed peoples who fall outside the traditional four-caste system. Marginalization from the caste structure may well be the cause of their economic deprivation. Thus, the liberation thrust in this movement has a specifically Indian character, namely caste. The history of the dalits has two facets involving their history in general and in relation to the history of Christianity in India.[31] Serious theologizing on the plight of the dalits began to emerge in the 1980s. Over the years there has emerged a body of literature with a Christian focus.[32] Some writings specifically incorporate treatment of biblical materials.[33]

Arvind Nirmal finds tremendous implications for dalit theology in Deuteronomy 26:5–12. He offers insightful commentary on the passage.[34] Nirmal argues that the ancient creedal statement of the Hebrews has paradigmatic value for dalit theology. First, there is a recognition of the roots–being "Aramean." Then comes the nature of their identity–being "few in number." This is followed by consciousness of the "affliction." Then comes the reference to "terror." Nirmal may be suggesting here an active struggle that may entail the use of force. Finally comes "the land flowing with milk and honey." This is only the result of the act of liberation.[35] The most important task/goal is freedom from bondage. In this connection, Nirmal also draws on the ideal of the "image of God" (Gen. 1:26) as the goal for the dalits, that is, to realize "our full humanness or conversely our full divinity."[36] On the basis of the suffering servant image in Isaiah 53:2–12, Nirmal portrays Jesus as a truly dalit deity. It is in the dalitness of Jesus that the dalits ought to recognize the mystery of their "exodus." He insists that "a non-dalit deity cannot be the God of the Dalits."[37]

B. TRIBAL

The tribal reality in India is multifaceted and pervasive, yet much neglected. The term "tribal" designates a category of diverse groups/communities who are classified as "scheduled" (a technical term used for backward communities under the policy of the government of India). These communities are present in almost all the states. Nirmal Minz finds in the biblical models of the covenant a theological principle to interpret the tribal reality.[38] The covenant with Noah (Gen. 9:8–19), which embraces the whole earth, resonates with the tribal vision of the human-nature-Spirit continuum.[39] The Abrahamic covenant (Gen. 12:1–4) is seen as a story of the process of adaptation of how a people learns to relate itself with others.[40] The tribals in India have shown tremendous adjustment and adaptation after being displaced by the Aryans. The Mosaic covenant (Ex. 19:1–24) has two bearings on the tribal reality. First, unlike the Hebrew slaves in Egypt in a foreign land, the tribals are under the yoke of different Pharaohs in their *own* homeland. As a result, the tribals have been subject to the dominant Aryan culture, lost their communal ownership of land, and have become objects of oppression in a stratified caste-ridden society.[41] Second, whereas the exodus experience created a people out of a no-people, the tribals are being forced to become a no-people (from being a people) with no rights and no dignity. Minz also finds a parallel between the introduction of monarchy in Israel and the stressful conditions in the history of the tribals, especially how the Brahmins (priestly group) used the creation myths to justify the hierarchy.[42] Finally, Minz points out that none of these covenants in the Old Testament, except the Noahite covenant, really offers any solutions to the tribal problem. But it should be pointed out that the opportunity to analyze their reality through biblical passages is its own reward. The Bible does not offer solutions. It invites us to be drawn into the process of struggle to which it bears testimony.

C. Feminist

Males dominate the Indian biblical guild, as most others. Few women occupy teaching positions in seminaries. Among those, the number in the biblical field is very small. However, in recent years some voices on the Indian theological scene have given expression to women's issues and concerns.[43] Aruna Gnanadason points out that feminist theology provides a "paradigmatic shift in biblical interpretation."[44] For her, the starting point is the women's struggle for liberation. This calls for a re-examination of the question of biblical authority and interpretation from the perspective of women. Gnanadason recognizes the dilemma of Indian women who cannot simply and whole-heartedly embrace the androcentric biblical traditions nor summarily reject them. A viable option is to reclaim the Bible as a source. She calls for a feminist hermeneutic that will enable women, and the whole Church, to become a new community in Christ.[45] Elsewhere, drawing on the rich symbolism of the common watering well/tap in rural India, Gnanadason offers helpful insights into the story of the encounter between Jesus and the Samaritan woman in John 4:5–30.[46] The source of empowerment in this story, according to Gnanadason, lies in Jesus not only dialoguing with an outcast but also transforming her into a missionary.[47] Also full of meaning is the action of the Samaritan woman who leaves behind the pot, symbolizing the break from her "life of oppression and sinfulness so as to internalize the liberating power of the living water."[48]

The dalit theology movement has been sensitive to include women's voices to speak on behalf of dalit women. As in the case of many other oppressed groups, the dalit women suffer not only as dalits but also as women because of the caste structure and the patriarchal nature of the society in India. Violence against these women, lack of education, and adequate health care have been the focus of some of the writings included in the volumes on dalits mentioned above.[49]

D. SOCIOECONOMIC

Any rereading of the biblical traditions will have to emerge out of and in response to the stark socioeconomic reality of the Indian society. Samuel Rayan focuses on the context of the gospel of John in an attempt to highlight a socioeconomic and political message for India.[50] This is an extraordinary approach because many Indian biblical scholars have been attracted to the mystical or spiritual aspect of this gospel. Rayan shows that John's mysticism entails a deep concern for the plight of the poor.

G. Soares-Prabhu interprets the task of theologizing on the model of Old Testament prophecy. Hebrew prophecy emphasized that theology must be rooted in concrete historical situations, the alternative vision of the exodus, and an appropriate effective language.[51] Elsewhere, Soares-Prabhu offers important insights into the biblical understanding of the poor. Integral to his analysis is the testing of the Marxian category of "class." On the basis of his analysis, he concludes that the poor in the Bible are (a) a sociological group; (b) a dialectical group whose position is determined by their opposites; and (c) a dynamic group through whom God shapes history.[52]

My own work on the eighth-century Hebrew prophets grew out of an awareness of its relevance to the socioeconomic aspects of the agrarian experience in India.[53]

E. POSTCOLONIAL

In the last five years postcolonialism has emerged as a distinct discourse. The longtime lack of interest or neglect of one of the most challenging and critical aspects of our time—namely the experience of colonialism—is surprising. Very few countries in the world remain untouched by some sort of colonial experience. Even more surprising is that despite the pervasive imperialistic and colonialist impact on Asia, Asian biblical interpretation has remained insulated from this discourse. But that may be changing. The works of R.S. Sugirtharajah have been pioneering contributions in this direction.[54] Sugirtharajah sees postcolonialism as a resistant discourse that tries to expose colonial assumptions, representations, and ideologies. One aspect of postcolonial discourse is a focus on how the West has been able to produce texts and portray the "Other" in the texts. By characterizing and defining the Other (Orient/East) in unfair and negative ways, the West has defined itself as a superior culture.[55]

Sugirtharajah exposes the stereotypical characterization of the Eastern peoples and customs in the works of Western biblical scholars. Even a great New Testament scholar such as Joachim Jeremias was not free from this. In his famous book *Parables of Jesus*,[56] he resorts to some stereotypical characterizations such as "the east is hot," "full of beggars," and "people go to bed early." In discussing the parable of the talents, when Matthew boosts the amount and Luke increases the number of servants, Jeremias attributes this to the oriental storyteller's tendency to embellish. Commenting on the parable of the laborers in the vineyard, he states that the excuse of the laborers for not being hired was their cover for their typical oriental behavior. In Luke 16 in the parable of the wicked servant, Jeremias attributes the steward's adjusting the accounts of the debtors to the lack of knowledge in bookkeeping on the part of the people in the East. In one strike he not only rules out the contribution of the Chinese, the Indians, and the Egyptians to the development of present-day mathematics but also elevates the European achievements.[57] Jeremias's characterizations resemble those of the colonial administrators and missionaries who resorted to mechanisms of stereotyping, distorting, and inferiorizing in an attempt to dominate the Other.

2. Ecological

Even though one could possibly see ecological concern as a liberation perspective, it is presented here separately because it is a unique issue. This is an area of increasing awareness among social action groups and individual activists in India. Jyoti Sahi sees the ecological task to be one of sharing in the act of creation. This stems from the biblical understanding of humans being made in the image of God.[58] Sahi interprets the curse on Eve (Gen. 3) with the pain of childbirth as a symbol of the pain of God in creation. God is continually involved in the process of creation by "communicating through life."[59] To this mystery of creation, Sahi also relates the whole idea of covenant. "What is being celebrated in the covenant is the affirmation of life and the constant program of renewing creation."[60] The Noahite covenant in Genesis 9 is not just with humans but also with nature.

Samuel Rayan has been a persistent voice in the ecological debate. He points out that the jubilant proclamation in Psalm 24–"The Earth is the Lord's"–is a summary statement of a recurrent confession in the Bible (Ps. 2:8; 8:6–9; 47:8; 65:6–14; 89:12; 95:4,5; Hos. 2:10–11; Lev. 25:23; Gen. 1:2; 8:21–22; 9:8–12).[61] The earth is God's creation and self-expression. But the earth is also ours since it is given to us. By celebrating the earth, we celebrate God. The earth is to be cherished because it is precious to us and to God.[62] The preciousness of the earth is a central witness in the Bible and of all tribal traditions. Rayan also rightly draws attention to tendencies that undermine the mystery of the earth, such as the commercialization of the earth, the imbalance in land/population at the global level, and the ecological crisis.[63]

R.J. Raja has studied the book of Revelation from the perspective of ecological concerns.[64] Raja points to a striking feature in the book: "the overabundant use of created realities, both good and bad." This combination of good and bad remind us that "creation-in-the beginning" must pass through "creation-in-history," which entails both good and evil, to "creation-at-end time."[65] The challenge of the book of Revelation for us, Raja argues, is that we become eco-spiritual, which entails being eucharistic (Rev. 4, praising and thanking God for the created realities) and prophetic (Rev. 8; 21, being justice-minded) in our relationship to all created realities.

3. Religiocultural

This section includes writings that specifically draw on the religious and cultural resources of India for biblical hermeneutics. With the attempt toward indigenization of Christianity also came a positive attitude to other religious traditions. In 1972 a seminar was held on the topic Bhagavad Gita and the Bible.[66] However, not much attempt was made to see the interface between the two. Individuals made presentations on their specialties without much cross-fertilization.

Another consultation in 1974 explored the relevance of the gospel of John for the Indian context.[67] The papers presented here illustrate the appeal and fascination that the gospel of John has had for the Eastern mind. The interiority of the Johannine material and its philosophical nature has drawn comparisons with phrases and thought forms from the Hindu religious traditions.

Another important work is the collection of essays focusing on sacred writings from various religions called *The Research Seminar on Non-Biblical Scriptures*.[68] These papers discuss the place and status of the Bible in relation to the scriptures of other religions. It dealt with crucial topics, such as revelation and inspiration as understood by Christians and other religious traditions. G. Soares-Prabhu examines how the New Testament views the question of inspiration of the Old Testament as a possible model to use in describing the Bible's relationship to other nonbiblical scriptures.[69] I. Vempeny's paper addresses the problem of inspiration in the nonbiblical scriptures.[70] Recognizing the predominantly Christian origin and connotations of the terms "revelation" and "inspiration," T.M. Manickam proposes equivalents—"insight" for inspiration and *anubhava* for revelation.[71] Sam Bhajjan discusses the Muslim understanding of scripture.[72] These and other essays in this collection raise crucial issues that are fundamental to biblical interpretation in a religiously pluralistic context.

Sr. Vandana's method of biblical interpretation often employs the *dhvani* (literally meaning "sound" or "resonance") method. Scholars trace the method back to a scholar/poet, Anandavardhana, who lived in eighth-century C.E. India. He first spoke of "dhvani" in relation to the soul of poetry. When a poet writes poetry he or she creates a *rasadhvani* (meaning literally a resonant field of emotions/moods/feelings) with evocative language. To enter into this field, the reader must also be on the same wavelength.[73] It demands the same sensitivity on the part of the reader. Vandana calls it the approach of the heart. *Water of Fire* illustrates this, where Vandana explores the many aspects of the all-pervasive symbolism of water in John's gospel using insights from Indian traditions.

Stanley Samartha's contribution to the discussion of interreligious dialogue issues has been widely recognized. He has addressed these issues in a sustained fashion in his works.[74] He brings a keen biblical interest to his discussions. One of the issues central to interreligious dialogue is the question of christology. The theocentric christology he puts forward has a strong biblical basis.[75] The argument for a theocentric christology is an attempt to move away from making normative exclusive claims for Christ. Very often these normative claims are made on the basis of the authority of the Bible. Biblical texts are hurled back and forth in justifying one's own position. The question that Samartha raises is: How can the claims of one group based on its scripture become normative for everybody else?[76] In another context, Samartha examines the task of hermeneutics in a multi-religious setting. He suggests that in a religiously pluralistic context, the primary task is to work out a broad framework of relationship between members of different faiths within which, then, insights from different scriptures can be brought together for mutual enrichment.[77] Samartha urges that a Christian quest for hermeneutics in Asia needs to pay special attention to two things:

1. the long tradition of study of texts in the original languages, the interpretation in particular contexts, and exposition of meaning in the life of the people and
2. that people of other religions have their own distinctive hermeneutics.[78]

One very fundamental insight that can be instructive from the study of the Hindu, Buddhist, Confucian, and Taoist approach to their scriptures is not so much "the rules of interpretation as the perception of truth or Sat or Reality or Dharma or the Tao itself."[79] How reality is perceived is the prime question. Rules of interpretation come later.

Ishanand Vempeny's dialogical textual study of the New Testament and the Bhagavad Gita, highlighting certain key concepts and themes, shows how insights found in Christianity and Hinduism can be complementary and useful for mutual enrichment.[80] He describes two different attitudes to life and reality using the symbols of the flute (used by Krsna, the playful deity in *Gita*) and the cross (of Christ). The flute represents playfulness, love, joy, charm, beauty, humor, romance, emotion, etc., while the cross represents love, sorrow, conflict, commitment, seriousness, challenge, etc.[81] In the process of mutual enrichment the dormant "flute-value" in Christianity and the "cross-value" in Hinduism can be brought out more and enriched.[82]

R.J. Raja provides another example of rereading the synoptic gospels from an Indian perspective.[83] His argument is that the characterization of Jesus in the synoptics corresponds to the three Indian *Margas* (ways) of attaining union with God. Mark, according to Raja, enables us to have a sense of the feelings and actions of Jesus, thus showing "the way" of *Karma* (action/service).[84] Matthew's emphasis is on Jesus' teachings. Matthew, the teacher of Christian faith, points to the Great Teacher as the way to divine knowledge and wisdom (*Jnana Marga*).[85] Luke highlights the kindness, tender love, and devotion of Jesus. This corresponds to the way of devotion (*Bhakti Marga*) to God and God's people.[86]

The treatment of the anti-idol polemic/satire in Second Isaiah (Isa. 40–55) by George Soares-Prabhu offers an example of an Indian reading.[87] With heightened sensibilities toward idol-worship as a result of being raised in a predominantly Hindu culture in India, Soares-Prabhu sees this passage as damaging because of its sinful representation of a people's culture and religion. He sees the same attitude reflected in the nineteenth century among the Christian missionaries toward Hinduism. The history of Christianity has been extremely destructive of peoples and cultures. This is due in part to the anti-Gentile attitude in the Hebrew Bible, paralleled by the anti-Semitic sentiment in the New Testament. Soares-Prabhu concludes with the thought that whether or not one agrees with the details of his arguments, a deeper purpose underlies his pluralist Indian reading–to discover the hidden roots of intolerance. Such readings, he feels, can take their place beside the Jewish critique of the anti-Semitism in the New Testament and the feminist critique of the biblical patriarchy, which can both defamiliarize and liberate the text.

4. Artistic

This is an area that has been long-neglected in academic disciplines. Art has been held in opposition to academic disciplines. The theological discipline is no exception to this. Yet, we do see a change in this perception. Theology is neither a statement of facts nor a matter of being engaged in mental gymnastics. As Samuel Rayan points out, it "is apprehended at levels deeper than reason" and expressed in appropriate language.[88] According to Rayan, that is what the Bible does. The beauty and appeal of the Bible is in its "imaginal quality, the rich variety, the concrete bodiliness and consequent directness of its theological expression."[89] Rayan identifies John's gospel for particular mention. Jesus and the woman at the well (Jn. 4), the clash between the blind man and Jews (Jn. 9), grieving over Lazarus (Jn. 11), and the workers' reunion over a breakfast (Jn. 21) are all examples of "dramatic writing."[90]

Art finds expression through many forms and media–poems, plays, music, paintings, etc. In India, as elsewhere, communication of the Bible has occurred through all of the above-mentioned forms–and probably through many more. Due to space constraints, only a brief discussion of suitable examples is possible here. I have already mentioned the literary accomplishment of Beschi, a Jesuit missionary in the seventeenth century. The poems and other works of H.A. Krishna Pillai (1827–1900), a Tamil Christian poet, are well known in Tamil Christian circles. Churches sing some of the lyrics composed by Krishna Pillai even today. His works are not particularly known for any revolutionary theologizing but nevertheless are artistically powerful expressions. The poems of Narayan Vaman Tilak (1862–1919), a Marathi Christian poet, have left their mark. Some of the poems have been translated into English and incorporated as hymns in the *Christian Conference of Asia Hymnal* (1974). Interestingly, Tilak was the first one to speak of Jesus Christ as "Mother-Guru."[91]

Abraham Mariaselvam's appreciation for Tamil *Akam* (love/devotion) poems led him to do a comparative study of the *Song of Songs* and Tamil *Akam* literature. Their common theme is the theme of love.[92]

Finally, we conclude this section with a reference to Indian Christian paintings, which have a long heritage going as far back as late eighteenth and early nineteenth centuries.[93] The most common themes in Indian Christian paintings have been the crucifixion, the Last Supper, the figure of Jesus, and scenes from the gospels. In the contemporary scene the works of some stand out not only for their artistic appeal but also for the creative theological inquiry they evoke. One such example is the work of Krishen Khanna.[94] Khanna is not a Christian but was profoundly influenced by the New Testament stories, particularly by the humanity of Jesus. He did not find this aspect adequately reflected in the Church.[95] That is why Khanna in his paintings makes Jesus look and act like an ordinary human being.

The work of Jyoti Sahi is important not only for the technique but also for theological content. Painting the picture of the nativity scene or Moses or the crucifixion does not make a painting Christian art. It has to do with the way the artist "looks at the world and human beings as bearers of the 'image of God.'"[96] The search and promotion of basic values such as *bhakti* (devotion to God) and *karuna* (compassion to creatures) set apart Christian art.[97] As an artist Sahi has been particularly drawn to the gospel of John. He has done two paintings, one on Nicodemus coming to Jesus by night (Jn. 3) and the other on the curing of the man born blind (Jn. 9). Sahi discusses the significance of these paintings in an essay.[98] Sahi also explores John's conception of the spatial structure of the universe that is akin to the Buddhist/Hindu idea of the Mandala as a way of illustrating why the gospel of John has held a fascination for the Eastern mind.[99]

Issues in Biblical Interpretation

This section identifies and highlights issues related to biblical interpretation in the Indian context. A full-length discussion of issues raised here is beyond the scope of this paper. My hope is that this will generate further discussion.

1. I begin with an issue over which there may not be a consensus: What constitutes an "Indian" interpretation? Does an interpretation become "Indian" if the interpreter is of Indian origin? In this paper I followed that assumption for the most part. I did not include scholars who were

not Indian or who did not have long-standing significant connections with India. I also used the guidelines of

a. the use of Indian religious and philosophical categories or concepts or methods; and

b. the incorporation of and response to concerns and issues in the Indian situation.

I don't believe this can be resolved by invoking any one single criterion. What is needed is a multi-criteria outlook. But the key, as Felix Wilfred has pointed out, is a "cross-cultural hermeneutics where the Christian faith and life is made to grow from the soil of a culture, which must first be fully respected and assumed."[100]

2. In continuation of the previous point, exegesis or hermeneutics in the Indian context cannot isolate itself away from the socioeconomic realities (the all-pervasive poverty, corruption, injustice, inequalities, and need for liberation and human dignity) or from the religiocultural plurality (the many religions and many cultures) of India. Both these aspects need to be addressed. Any interpretation that ignores them lacks credibility and quickly becomes an exercise in irrelevance.

3. The religious pluralism of the Indian context creates a unique situation for hermeneutics. The presence of scriptures in other religions presents challenges as well as exciting prospects. The challenge is to refrain from making absolutist claims from one's perspective. In a context with many religions and scriptures, the claims of one group cannot become normative for everybody else. Christians may have to face some tough questions regarding the understanding of revelation, inspiration, christology, etc. It is not a matter of giving up one's beliefs but rather redefining them. The prospects lie in our willingness and openness to learn from others. A comparative hermeneutic opens fruitful possibilities. Each of these religious traditions has had a long history and tradition of interpretation. A creative encounter with these traditions can bring about new insights. New challenges may lead to new learning. Further, the primacy of the oral/aural nature of scriptural traditions in Hinduism and Islam raises some key questions for an Indian Christian hermeneut:

a. It points up the preoccupation with the written text (a legacy from the West); the Western emphasis on reconstructing an "original" text may be an alien concept to the Hindu reality.

b. Therefore, a greater sensitivity is needed to such issues as the oral/aural nature of scripture and

c. This also brings up the need for developing a comparative hermeneutics appropriate to the context.[101]

4. Another issue pertains to the gap between piety and social awareness. Indian Christian reality is different from the Latin American phenomenon. The liberation theology movement has had a broad community

base. It has grown out of and has been a theology and exegetical reflection prompted by the life experiences of struggling communities. In India, theological enterprise has been more a matter of professionally trained clerics, exegetes, and theologians trying to reach across to an audience whose reading of the biblical traditions may be more individual- and piety-oriented. Is there an "Indian" reading? This may be an oversimplification, but it is an issue that needs a closer look.

5. Do the liturgical practices and theology of the Church reflect the vigor of the biblical renewal that has come about in the post-independence period? Also, do the art forms and other media of communication used by Christians exhibit the sort of vitality that has been seen in the biblical renewal?

6. As we take stock of the biblical hermeneutics scene, it is also important to take note of an emerging group of interpreters. Sugirtharajah calls them the "diasporic" interpreters. For a variety of reasons, some scholars find themselves moving across nations and cultures on a temporary or permanent basis. Many of the writers represented in this volume embody this experience. The state of being between two or even three worlds may not be a comfortable spot to be in, but certainly offers a unique horizon for interpretation.

2

Chinese Biblical Interpretation

History and Issues

JOHN YUEH-HAN YIEH
Virginia Theological Seminary
Alexandria, Virginia

Christianity first came to China in the early seventh century during the Tang Dynasty.[1] According to *Daqin jingjiao zhongguo liuxingbei* (The Nestorian Monument found in 1625),[2] a Nestorian missionary, Alopen, came to Changan (Xian) in 635 to preach the Christian faith. His church survived for about 200 years, but it did not spread outside the capital city. In the late thirteenth century during the Yuen Dynasty, not long after Marco Polo's visit to China, a Franciscan, John of Montecorvino, arrived in Beijing in 1294. His mission was successful among the Mongolian rulers without reaching the Han people, so the church declined when the Mongolian dynasty was overthrown. Then, in the late sixteenth century during the Ming Dynasty, a Jesuit, Matteo Ricci, came to Beijing in 1583 to reestablish the church with remarkable success.[3] Unfortunately, the infamous controversy over the rite of ancestor worship between the Jesuits and the Dominicans offended the Chinese Emperor Kangshi of the Qing Dynasty, so he banned missionary activities in 1720. It was not until the early nineteenth century that Robert Morrison, the first Protestant missionary from England, again landed in China in 1807. This was a time when China was fighting the Western colonial powers and trying to modernize its country. Missionaries faced strong resistance, but the seed of the gospel grew and the church survives today.[4] Different from the Nestorians and the Catholics, the Protestant missionaries began their work with the translation of the Bible and they emphasized the authority of the Bible. So a history of Chinese

17

biblical interpretation should properly begin with Robert Morrison, who translated the first Chinese Bible in 1823.

How can a history of biblical interpretation be constructed? In the West, it is often perceived as an intellectual evolution marked by paradigm shifts in research methods or scholarly interests. In *The New Testament: The History of the Investigation of Its Problems,* for instance, Werner Kümmel structures his discussion of the New Testament studies in Germany according to methodological changes from the so-called "consistently historical approach," to the "history-of-religion-school approach," and to the "historico-theological approach."[5] In *The Interpretation of the New Testament, 1861–1961,* Stephen Neill also divides the history of New Testament studies in the U.K. by tracking the shift of scholarly interest from the "challenge to orthodoxy," to "historical study of Jesus and the Greeks," and finally to the "re-entry of theology" in the pursuit of "the gospel behind the Gospels" and the "salvation of the Jews."[6]

The history of Chinese biblical interpretation is best seen, however, as a history of social revolution rather than intellectual evolution. It concerns ordinary Christians getting along with their neighbors more than biblical scholars writing in the libraries. This is not to say that biblical interpretation in the West has not interacted with its culture or society. Indeed, it has, especially with the intellectual challenges arising from the Renaissance, the Enlightenment, and existentialism. This is to say, however, that Chinese biblical interpretation has been so directly affected by the major social and cultural events that its genesis and development cannot be properly understood outside its social-cultural matrix. As a new group, the Chinese church has to defend its legitimacy as a worthy newcomer in a culture where Confucianism, Taoism, Buddhism, and folk religions have long existed and have taken deep root in the fabric of social life. Following a foreign religion, Chinese Christians are regarded as cultural traitors. As it is often said, "Missionaries invited themselves to China riding on the canon balls of the gunship," so Christians are frequently blamed for the upheavals caused by Western aggression. Under such circumstances, biblical interpretation is never a mere intellectual exercise formulated in the ivory tower or entertained in scholarly conferences. It is part and parcel of the life of Chinese people in conflict with Western imperialism.

In correlation to the major social changes of the nation, a history of Chinese biblical interpretation can be divided into four periods for discussion. In this brief survey, it is my intention to show (1) how Chinese Christians developed varied approaches to the Bible under each and all the social-cultural challenges, and (2) what specific issues stood out that deserve hermeneutical reflection. It is also my hope to identify some recurring motifs that might be characterized as "Chinese" in Chinese biblical interpretation.

"Difficult Infancy" (1807–1860)

The rebirth of the Chinese Church in the early nineteenth century was, figuratively speaking, an induced labor for a premature baby. It was a painful beginning. Since the Emperor Kangshi expelled Catholic priests over the "ritual controversy" in 1705, the succeeding emperors (Yongzhen, Chienlong, Jiaching) followed the same "closed door" policy banning foreigners from visiting Chinese cities, except for the employees of the East India Company, who were given special permission to land for a specific time for trading in the designated port city, Guangzhou. Chinese were also prohibited from teaching foreigners the Chinese language. It was not until 1842, when the British navy defeated the Chinese army in the "Opium War," that the Chinese government was forced to sign the "Nanjing Treaty," opening five port cities for trading and allowing Westerners to reside in those cities. This was the first of many humiliating treaties to follow—for example, the Wangshia Treaty with America (1844), the Huangpu Treaty with France (1844), the Tianjing Treaty with England and France (1858), and the Beijing Treaty with England, France, and Russia (1860). Having learned the Chinese language from overseas Chinese, some missionaries (e.g., G. Lay; DeLammarre) joined their naval envoys to negotiate the permission to preach Christianity under the judicial protection of their consuls. The door to China was thus cracked open, but the anger over humiliating treaties would give rise to countless *jiaoan* (religious riots) against missionaries and Christians. Christianity was considered foreign and anti-tradition, and the alliance between missionaries and colonial forces would later become a source of resentment haunting the Chinese Church for a very long time.[7]

The imperial ban made it impossible for Robert Morrison to conduct his mission in the territory of China, so he moved to Moluccas to preach the gospel to the Chinese in Southeast Asia. It took seven long years before he made the first Chinese convert, Tsai Gao, in 1814, and he made no more than ten converts in his entire career of twenty-five years. By focusing his energy on the translation and printing of the Bible, however, Morrison laid a solid foundation for the beginning of Chinese biblical interpretation.

During this infancy period, converting the Chinese people to Christianity was the missionaries' primary goal, but only a few people, those hired to do their housework or help translate the Bible, were converted. The only materials that could indicate some form of biblical interpretation were the "gospel sheets" or evangelizing pamphlets, produced by missionaries with the help of their first converts. The missionaries had limited knowledge of Chinese culture, and most of their converts were uneducated. These gospel sheets contained little more than the Christian basics, such as God's love, Christ's salvation, human sins, and the final judgment. It is interesting to note that they often borrow vocabularies and concepts indiscriminately from traditional Chinese religions, and they tend to highlight Jesus' ethical teaching, which is the message most accessible to ordinary people with little education. We do not know how effective these gospel sheets were, given that they contain short biblical quotes with a simplistic message in unpolished Chinese language. However, one pamphlet, entitled *Quenshi liangyien* ("Moral Exhortations to the World"), authored by Liang Fa, an assistant to Morrison and the first Chinese minister, reached the hand of Hong Xiuquan in 1836 and almost radically changed the history of China. Hong was converted by the pamphlet and joined *Shangdihui* (God-worshipers). When suppressed by the government, he started a peasant revolution that succeeded in occupying one third of China in the south and he founded the Taiping (Eternally Peaceful) Heavenly Kingdom that lasted for thirteen years (1851–1864).[8] With a simplistic but sincere belief in the authority of scripture, Hong ordered his army to hold morning prayers every day and recite scriptural passages in rhythmic verses. He ruled with a view to building the kingdom of heaven on earth.

"Traumatic Childhood" (1860–1911)

In the second half of the nineteenth century, Western countries enjoyed an economic prosperity brought forth by industrialization and exploitation of resources from their colonies in Africa and Asia. Meanwhile, great revival movements, such as those led by D.L. Moody and J. Edwards, were burning the hearts of the pious with passion. A great number of missionaries were thus sent out (e.g., the Student Volunteer Movement for Foreign Missions) to evangelize the world. Many came to China, as its door had now been opened. Numbers tell good stories: there were 81 missionaries in China in 1858, but the number reached 1,324 by 1893.[9] At this time, China's pride was deeply wounded by the invasion of the Western powers. Worried about his national defense, Emperor Guangshui sought to modernize the nation through Westernized education–the Wuxui Policy Change, led by Kang Yiu-wei and Liang Qi-chao, being one such attempt. Unfortunately, the powerful "old guard" defeated his effort, rallying around the Empress Cixi (or Tzu Hsi), who insisted on keeping the traditional policies. These anti-Western officials also endorsed the so-called Boxers to start an anti-Western uprising in 1900, which ended with the killing of 5 bishops, 48 priests, 18,000 Catholics, 188 ministers, and 5,000 Protestant Christians.[10] As the alliance of eight countries sent in their vengeful navies and took over Beijing, more than 100,000 additional people were killed. This horrific tragedy cut open a wound so deep that the Chinese people in later generations would continue to bleed and hurt.

Two decades before the uprising, a remarkable change in missionary strategy had already taken place. With the increasing financial support and human resources from their boards, missionaries began to replace "direct evangelism" (preaching on the streets or distributing gospel sheets) with "indirect evangelism" (opening schools, orphanages, and hospitals). As a result, the number of believers increased dramatically and churches were built in many places. Again, numbers tell good stories. In 1876 there were 744 ordained ministers and 290 teachers; by 1905 there were 7,121 ministers and 2,582 teachers; and by 1911 there were 12,054 ministers and 3,809 teachers.[11] After the uprising, in order to help rebuild China, missionaries founded universities to train Chinese leaders in business, law, and medicine. During this period, establishing churches and rebuilding the nation were the two most important tasks for the missionaries.

The influx of missionaries meant that many Western denominations were represented in China, all together more than 130.[12] They debated passionately about missionary strategies: for example, the "cultural approach" of Timothy Richard who sought to influence intellectual leaders and government officials, versus the "evangelical approach" of Hudson Taylor who wished to convert people from lower classes in inland provinces.[13] They also brought with them their historical feud and theological fight, which were perpetuated in theological education in the seminaries and were reflected in biblical interpretation. As a result, the young Church in China was bombarded with issues irrelevant to its life and mission. Since missionaries remained firmly in charge of the churches, schools, and charities, few Chinese leaders were raised.

During this period, Chinese biblical interpretation can be observed in two ways. First are the debates in Bible translation. Translation is interpretation. The translation of "God" into *shangdi* or *shen,* for instance, reflects two different views of God in the Chinese culture, the former being associated with the highest god in Taoist mythology and the latter with the deity in folk religions.[14] This debate discloses not only the levels of the missionary-translators' Chinese knowledge and theological judgment, but also the significant differences in the deep structure of the thought patterns of Western and Chinese cultures.[15] The translation of *logos* (Jn. 1.1) into "word" (spoken word) or *dao* (the unspeakable *dao* in Taoism or the moral principle in Confucianism) is another example of translation being an interpretation and cross-cultural communication. Second to be observed are the texts and lectures that the missionary-professors gave to their students in theological colleges. Comprehensive research in this area has yet to be done, but the results could reveal (1) the sources and impetus of Chinese biblical interpretation that was to blossom in the next generation, and (2) the roles and impact of Western theological debates and hermeneutical assumptions in shaping Chinese biblical interpretation. An example may be found in Jia Yu-ming, whose view of "perfect salvation" as the key to biblical interpretation may be traced back to that of B.B. Warfield of Princeton Theological Seminary, through the tutelage of his missionary-professors from the American Presbyterian Church in Wenhuiguan (Dengzhou College), Shangdong.[16] Even Watchman Nee, a self-taught preacher, was deeply influenced by John Nelson Darby, by way of the missionaries from the Exclusive Brethren.[17] For Chinese biblical interpretation, this was a time of incubation. Western missionaries still held the lecterns and pulpits, but a vital seed had been planted, ready to burst out of the soil at the first dawn of the spring.

"Challenging Adolescence" (1911–1949)

In 1911 Sun Yat-sen overthrew the Qing Dynasty to establish the first republic in Asia and abolished many unequal treaties with other countries. China regained some self-confidence. Before long, however, continuous fighting among warlords, such as Yuen Shi-kai, who wished to restore the imperial system, shattered the jubilation. Civil wars between the Communists and the Nationalists ensued. The aggression of Japan, a new imperial power in the East, led to eight years of Sino-Japanese War (1931–1939). In this period, the Chinese people suffered many devastating wars, so the survival of the nation preoccupied everybody's mind and nationalism rose to a new height.[18] This was dramatically demonstrated in the May Fourth Movement (1919) that began with a student demonstration against the handover of Germany's colony in Shangdong to Japan in the Paris Conference without any regard to Chinese sovereignty.[19] Nationalism was also expressed in the "Non-Christian Alliance" (1922–1924), a nationwide student protest against the World Student Christian Federation, which decided to hold its annual meeting at Qinghua University in Beijing on April 1, 1922.[20] Students in Shanghai University, soon followed by those in Beijing University and other schools, voiced their objection to allowing foreign and Christian students to meet at a Chinese University. They condemned Christianity as heralding the colonial policy of the imperialistic countries. Calling for the sovereignty of education, they wanted to take over church universities and eliminate religious education.[21] The President of Beijing University, Tsai Yuenpei, was a key supporter of the alliance and he advocated the study of aesthetics in place of religion.

Scientism was another serious challenge to the Chinese Church during this period. Since modernization was understood to be Westernization, the "new knowledge" in the West, such as Darwin's evolution theory, Marx's materialistic view of history, Russell's economic socialism, and Dewey's pragmatism were insatiably absorbed and indiscriminately transported to China by scholars trained in Europe and America. Most of these new ideologies or theories were critical of the Christian tradition, so their advocates condemned the Chinese Church as outdated, pre-scientific, anti-modern, and detrimental to the progress of a new China. Most notable was the "New Culture Movement" (1917) led by Hu Shih, a philosophy professor at Beijing University, who believed that only science could save China and denounced both the traditional culture and Christian religion as obstacles to the modernization of China.[22] Ironically, while the anti-Western riots of the nineteenth century led by local gentry accused Christianity of "anti-tradition," the anti-Christian movement in the early twentieth century instigated by university professors condemned it as "anti-scientific" and "anti-modern."[23]

In response to the challenges of nationalism and scientism, Christian scholars and preachers began to indigenize their gospel in Chinese cultural terms and to defend the usefulness of Christianity for the new China. This double-edged effort met a double jeopardy: indigenization may have befriended some traditionalists, but it offended modernists, while apologetics may have persuaded some modernists but it angered traditionalists. Despite and indeed because of these intellectual challenges, this period became the most exciting time in the history of the Chinese Church. The native leaders rose to the occasion to confront national crises and produced impressive quantity and quality of biblical interpretation in essays, monographs, and sermons. Suddenly, the Chinese Church grew into adolescence, claiming independence from Western missionaries and voicing distinctive views in biblical interpretation.

Among scholars, Wu Leichuan (1870–1944), a *hanlin* (scholar with the highest distinction) in the Royal Academy and professor and chancellor of Yenjing University, was a distinguished example. To show that Christianity, though from abroad, was not in conflict with traditional Chinese culture, he introduced Jesus as *sheng tien-tzu* (the holy son of heaven) who had the wisdom to serve as the perfect sage-king performing the functions of king, prophet, and priest.[24] He also compared the Holy Spirit to *ren*, the highest virtue of Confucianism in terms of functions.[25] By dressing Jesus in Confucius' robe, he meant to tell the nationalists that Jesus was not a foreign enemy to Chinese culture. To the anti-scientific charge, he once wrote, obviously with the New Culture Movement in mind, that "religious emotions are inspired by the recognition of reason."[26] Indeed, in appreciation of modern science, he adopted a historical-critical approach to the Bible, regarded prophetic claims, virgin birth, and miracle stories as literary expressions of faith experience,[27] and insisted that Jesus' moral virtue served as the perfect paradigm intended to reform human hearts and human society.[28] In Wu's view, religion's function is not simply to offer personal salvation but "to reform the society" (*gaizao shehui*), a frequent motif in his writings.[29] By transforming believers' moral character with the virtue of love and sacrifice, he believed, the whole society could be reformed, and this was the greatest contribution Christianity could make to China at a time when the government officials' cowardice and incompetence and the warlords' brutality and greed had caused so much national shame and widespread atrocity. Clearly, Wu's purpose was to show that Christianity was not anti-scientific and that it could play a crucial part in shaping the future of the new China.[30] It is noteworthy that his argument reveals a deeply held conviction in Confucianism, *nesheng waiwang* (to become a sage inside, and to govern the society outside), which regards the cultivation of moral character as the first step in the ordering of family, the ruling of the nation, and the peace of the world. The same assumption can be found in the works of many other Christian scholars of the time. As Tsai Yen-zen puts it, it may be called the "Zeitgeist" of that generation of Chinese scholars, when the deep-rooted traditional Confucianism and the strong desire to reform the society still resided in them.[31]

Another scholar, Chao Tzu-chen (1888–1979), professor at Suzhow University and Yenjing University, shared a similar view on the social function of Christianity.[32] To the Chinese people suffering from devastating wars and losing hope in their lives, he once wrote, "Religion concerns divine will and human life (*shangda tienxin, shiatong renxue*). It helps people adjust to physical and psychological circumstances. When the adjustment is perfect, they will acquire an abundant life."[33] In *Life of Jesus* (1935), Chao presented Jesus as a paramount moral example for emulation as Wu did, but he also emphasized Jesus' religious life as a model for a perfect communion with God.[34] Based on Jesus' religious experience, Chao criticized Wu's portrayal of Jesus as inadequate, as one in which he is merely a moral hero of "Confucianism that is bound up with human action."[35]

Different emphases notwithstanding, to counter the dominant ideology of *kexue jiuguo* (save the nation with science) advocated by the intellectual elites in the New Culture Movement, Christian scholars in unison proposed an alternative view, *renge jiuguo* (save the nation with character), attempting to address the national crisis at the moral and spiritual levels instead of material construction.[36] As such, the challenges of nationalism and scientism led Wu Lei-chuan and Chao Tzu-chen to find the Jesus of Nazareth in the gospel narratives a moral idealist and mystical sage whose mission was to reform the society, and whose moral and spiritual virtues deserved to be imitated. Solid education in Chinese classics may also have led them to see in Jesus a Confucian sage who bears the same optimistic mission of social reformation through character transformation, not unlike the vision of the social gospel movement in the United States in the 1930s.

On the other end of the theological spectrum were "fundamentalist" leaders such as Wang Ming-dao (1900–1991) and Watchman Nee (1903–1972), who were eloquent preachers and charismatic leaders of independent churches (in Beijing and Shanghai).[37] Both of them denounced the idea of the church as an institution, and were considered "sectarian" by some.[38] Like Wu and Chao, they were aware of the challenges of nationalism and scientism, but they did not think that liberalism or social gospel provided the right answer. With a dualistic view of the world, they did not believe that moral character (*renge*) could save anyone, let alone the nation. In fact, Wang Ming-dao insisted that it was not possible to build an ideal society, because humanity had become so depraved by sin that it could only wait for divine judgment.[39] Only through spiritual rebirth can a sinner be changed to live a new life. Thus, his ministry was to save souls, not to reform society.[40] Against the realized eschatology of Wu and Chao, they held a futuristic eschatology insisting that, when the new heaven and new earth come, the kingdom of God will be totally different than the society we know. At that time, the church will be raised into heaven and all the saved souls will be gathered together with God for eternal joy. Among New Testament writers, they favored Paul because his letters provided basic doctrines about personal salvation and specific guidance for the new life in Christ. They insisted that born-again Christians should live a life of holiness to serve as God's witness in this evil world, so they developed many "lessons" in their sermons, which could be placed in the tradition of psychagogy (*Seelsorge*) or spiritual direction.

One example may indicate how Wang Ming-dao's interpretive mind worked. In an exposition on Matthew 22:2–14 (the parable of the wedding banquet), Wang noticed a detail in the narrative, the guests in the wedding. If the groom is Christ and the implied bride represents the church, who are the guests? Noting that these guests are allowed to attend the feast but do not receive the highest glory or joy, Wang cited Paul's athletic imagery in 1 Corinthians 9:24 and Philippians 3:13 to urge his readers to strive to win the prize of the race in order to become Christ's bride, not just guests. Then, apparently referring to anti-Christian hostility, he encouraged them to endure suffering for their faith. If they could reject the way of the world, they would become Christ's brides with the highest glory and joy. Typically, he attended to the details, used the method of *linyi jiejing* (spiritual exegesis), cited Pauline passages for cross-references (*scriptura scripturum*), focused on the spiritual character of a faithful life, and set his reader's eyes on the reward or judgment in the future. He was very good at using psychagogy to help Christians face suffering and build up spiritual character.

The same hermeneutical features can be found in Watchman Nee's books, such as *Shulingren* (*The Spiritual Man*) and *Zhengchang de jidutu shenhuo* (*The Normal Christian Life*), in which he developed a tri-partite anthropology to show, step by step, how the spirit, soul, and body of a person can be justified, saved, and sanctified.[41] His detailed discussion of spiritual life and specific advice on spiritual discipline reflected a combination of Calvinist anthropology, mystical spirituality, and Chinese moral tradition of *chenxin, zhenyi,* and *xiushen* (train the heart to be sincere, keep the mind upright, and cultivate the character).

Wang and Nee liked to compare reading scripture to eating spiritual food, chewing on the word of God repeatedly, swallowing it joyfully, and digesting it internally until it nurtures the spiritual life. They provided meticulous analysis of every word in the text and used word association, often according to the Chinese translation rather than Hebrew or Greek, to come up with specific steps of spiritual development. This way of reading the text can be very persuasive, as the meaning thus constructed usually makes coherent sense, but oftentimes they also came up with idiosyncratic readings. They called their approach *lingyi jiejing* (spiritual exegesis), a method favored by fundamentalist Christians.[42] They believed in textual inerrancy, but even more so in theological inerrancy, so they took a metaphysical-deductive approach, using doctrines to interpret scripture. For them, Christ was the crown of orthodoxy. As the right understanding of Christ led Saint Paul to the right interpretation of scripture (OT), Nee insisted that orthodox faith should precede correct interpretation.[43] Their spiritual exegesis is similar to the allegorical interpretation of Origen, but, as Ka-lun Leung suggests, it may well be derived also from a hermeneutical tradition in the history of Chinese Confucianism that seeks to uncover the hidden meaning of the classical texts, especially the Gong-yang school that has produced commentaries to bring out the implications in the *Spring-Autumn Annuals*.[44]

The different approaches to biblical interpretation between the two camps, the liberal scholars and the fundamentalist preachers, seem to reflect a similar debate between the social gospel movement and the fundamentalist movement in the United States in the 1930s. Whereas Wu and Chao believed that the kingdom of God could be built in the Chinese society by transforming its ethos and culture, Wang and Nee believed in an apocalyptic view, seeing no possibility of social reformation until the day of divine judgment. Again, this may be a legacy of the theological debate among missionaries. Noteworthy is that, whether "moral character" or "spiritual character," the Confucian emphasis on the cultivation of personal "character" for a moral society remains the ultimate concern in both groups.

Between these two prominent groups were also numerous denominational pastors and traveling evangelists who helped shape the faith of the Chinese Church and whose influence continued beyond this period.[45] One good representative was Jia Yu-ming (1880–1964), a Presbyterian pastor from Shangdong, professor of Bible and Theology at the Union Theological College in Nanjing, and president of the College for Spiritual Formation in Sichuan during WWII. His commentaries on the Bible continue to be widely read today. In Jia's view, the salvation that God gives us through Jesus Christ does not simply concern personal salvation from divine wrath (Wang, Nee) but also the renewal of the world (Wu, Chao), including the whole creation as promised in Romans 8 and Revelation 21. Salvation in Christ demands a thankful response to God's grace with the offering of our moral (Wu, Chao) and spiritual (Wang, Nee) life. To read the Bible, Jia proposed a "hermeneutics of the Spirit," insisting that (1) the text of the Bible is inspired by the Holy Spirit, (2) the reading of the Bible should be guided by the Holy Spirit, and (3) the Holy Spirit should transform the reader of the Bible.[46] This last point about the transformed reader is particularly noteworthy. It distinguishes his view from the fundamentalist "spiritual exegesis" in emphasis if not in substance. Jia wrote, "A person whose reason (*lixing*) is spiritualized (*lingxinghua*) means that his reason is baptized by the Holy Spirit and undergoes a wonderful change. His reason becomes more alert, more powerful, and more useful. He acquires not only common sense but also spiritual wisdom. He can then understand the spiritual meaning of the Bible and comprehend the mystery of the spiritual world."[47] For him, human reason is to be utilized, but it needs to be spiritualized. He considered the spiritualization of the reader as a necessary prerequisite for a successful interpretation. Among recent hermeneutical theories, Sandra Schneider's "hermeneutics of transformation" may be comparable, because she urges the reader to accept scripture as a "revelatory text" and to surrender aesthetically and existentially to the text, so that the reader's life can be changed by the new vision constructed by the scripture.[48] As such, in the first half of the twentieth century, the first "spring" season of the Chinese Church, the garden of its biblical interpretation was filled with beautiful flowers of distinctive colors and fragrances.

"Growing Pains" (1949–2004)

The victory of the Communists in the civil war resulted in the establishment of the People's Republic of China and the withdrawal of the Nationalists to Taiwan in 1949. The Chinese people were divided into two worlds. The PRC practiced a totalitarian rule, and Taiwan was placed under martial law. The warring tension made the Taiwan Strait a hot spot throughout the Cold War, until today. In the name of national security, the Chinese people enjoyed no political freedom under either regime until recently. Meanwhile, Chinese living in Hong Kong, Singapore, Malaysia, and Indonesia faced colonial rule, racial discrimination, and religious oppression as they tried to survive and prosper among different ethnic groups.

In the second half of the twentieth century, Chinese Christians living in three areas faced different issues, but in reading the Bible they have all moved beyond the static model of indigenization and tried to contextualize their interpretations to meet the challenges at hand. In China, the Communist government wanted to clear away foreign influences and control its citizen groups, so it organized the Three-Self Patriotic Church, three-self meaning self-governing, self-supporting, and self-propagating. Christians were forced to sign the so-called "Christian Manifesto" and pledge their allegiance to support the Communist government.[49] Several preachers refused to do so and were imprisoned, the most well-known being Wang Ming-dao, who was jailed for twenty-four years, and their followers formed the house churches that met "illegally" and were often persecuted. In a totalitarian society and atheist ideology, the interest of the nation supersedes that of individual citizens. So, it is no surprise that the recurring themes in the sermons of Wu Yao-zong and Ting Kuang-hsun, leaders of the official church, are love, obedience, and service intended to turn Christians into loyal citizens of a socialist country.[50] Their contextualizing use of the Bible was unapologetically motivated by political purposes, which Ting justified as completing a hermeneutical circle to connect the two "C's," Christ and China.[51] The same tendency to read the Bible in service of the modern socialist China can be found in the decision by the Committee of the Three-Self Patriotic Movement and the Chinese Council of Churches to "de-emphasize" the doctrine of justification by faith in order to construct a new "Chinese indigenized theology."[52]

In Taiwan, the Nationalist regime discouraged the church from political and social involvement, though it allowed the church relative freedom of worship and organization. For C. S. Song, an influential theologian, justice for the poor and the suffering stands at the heart of the compassionate God and the center of the Bible. In contrast to Wu and Ting, Song places "people" above "nation," having the courage to challenge the earlier "police state" of Taiwan and the neocolonial exploitation of Asian peoples by capitalist countries in the name of global economy. The right of self-determination, both political and ecclesial, is the hallmark of his theology, as movingly expressed in *The Tears of Lady Ming* (1981), a theological interpretation of the legendary story about a powerless young woman looking for the body of her husband and bringing down the Great Wall with her tears.[53] Using story as a theological method, Song insists that, like the Jewish people's stories in the Bible, the Asian peoples' stories, in history and in contemporary life, can also reveal God's will. Hermeneutical process begins with the suffering people.

In Hong Kong, Singapore, Malaysia, and Indonesia, Chinese Christians live in multi-racial and multi-religious societies. The return of Hong Kong to China in 1997, in particular, marks the change of times between colonialism and postcolonialism, though the exploitation of neocolonialism continues. All Chinese sojourning in these areas and countries have recent experiences of a multicultural life under colonial rule and many of their scholars are trained in the West, so their approaches to scripture exhibit a hybrid tendency. The hybrid nature of their personal identity and interpretation provides an interesting locus for hermeneutical reflection on the social location of the reader, the multicultural contexts of interpretation, and postcolonial experience. Some scholars from those areas have displayed a strong interest in Chinese traditions, such as the cross-textual approach of Archie Lee and the cross-cultural study of K.K. Yeo,[54] while others have focused on gender equality and religious dialogue, such as the postcolonial criticism of Kwok Pui-lan.[55] In the garden of Chinese biblical interpretation, beautiful flowers in every corner are beginning to bear tasteful fruits.

Conclusion

In its short history, the modern Chinese Church has gone through rejections, persecutions, confrontations, and challenges by the emperors, gentry, mobs, and scholars. Missionaries were courageous and ingenious, but Christianity was rebuked as a foreign religion and a cultural invasion from Western imperial powers. Throughout the first two periods in the nineteenth century, therefore, conditions compelled the church to explain its gospel to the Chinese people in understandable language and to justify its legitimacy in a country whose pride was hurt. The missionaries had two main tasks–conversion and church building–and they faced two key issues–the hostility of traditionalism as expressed in the imperial bans and the local riots, and the need for self-definition as indicated in the gospel sheets and in theological education. In the beginning of the twentieth century when China began to modernize itself through Westernized education, the church entered the third period and was confronted by two new challenges: the anti-foreign nationalism among university students and the anti-Christian scientism advocated by leaders of the New Cultural Movement. They were also confused by the theological debates of the West imported by missionary-professors. Remarkably, though, these intellectual challenges did not destroy the budding church. Rather, they stimulated the growth of Chinese biblical interpretation. As a result, interpreters ranging from liberal scholars to fundamentalist preachers and conservative writers burgeoned to defend the usefulness of Christianity to the new China and solidify the development of the church. Indigenization of the gospel and psychagogy of Christian character were the main concerns in biblical hermeneutics, as can be abundantly seen in monographs, journals, and sermons. Chinese biblical interpretation quickly grew into adolescence. Then, in the second half of the twentieth century when the Communists acquired the power, the Chinese Church began to develop separately in three areas. During this fourth period, different political and ideological conditions created diverse challenges such as national interest, self-determination, and cultural identity, and encouraged new hermeneutical responses such as the patriotic emphasis, the concern for the suffering people, and the postcolonial criticism. Love, justice, and identity were the main themes of concern, and the churches became confident enough to contextualize the gospel to meet the political, social, and cultural challenges in respective locations. Well-educated in the West, Chinese theologians and biblical scholars also began to claim independence in their cultural approaches to biblical hermeneutics.

In this brief survey, we have seen Chinese Christians learning to use the Bible to defend Christianity as a friendly and useful religion to China in times of crises; to present Jesus as a Confucian sage, personal savior and social reformer; and to nurture moral and spiritual character to help Christians testify to the gospel and command respect from their neighbors. To tackle such issues as the relation between church and state, christology, and spiritual direction, scholars and preachers have developed the hermeneutics of character, the spiritual exegesis, the hermeneutics of the Spirit, the hermeneutics of stories, and the postcolonial criticism as ways of reading the Bible. With these approaches, they have done well to "indige-nize" and "contextualize" biblical messages to relate Christian faith to the Chinese people. The pressing need of the reader is obviously considered more important than the objective exposition of the text, and the present condition is more significant than the historical contexts.

In this survey, three recurring hermeneutical assumptions may also be noted, which seem to be distinctively, if not uniquely, Chinese: (1) The purpose of interpretation may be different (to save souls, to reform the society, or to save the nation), but the relevance of scripture to the life of the reader is always treated with urgency. For Chinese Christians, scripture is believed to be a revelatory text, so biblical study is always existential, not simply academic. (2) The cultivation of personal character, moral and spiritual, is assumed to be the ultimate concern of biblical interpretation. Orthopraxis is valued much more than orthodoxy, and practical application more than theoretical construction. (3) The perfection of personal character, it is further assumed, will eventually transform the entire society and strengthen the nation. It may seem naïve, but this assumption reflects a Chinese cultural tradition that places the honor of the entire community above the interest of individual members. Whether pragmatism, moralism, and communitarianism truly stand at the core of the "Chinese" biblical interpretation remains a debatable question. It is certain, however, that the precedents and insights learned in the history and issues of Chinese biblical interpretation can be instructive for a hermeneutical reflection on the cross-cultural studies and postcolonial criticism in which biblical scholarship everywhere is taking a serious interest.

3

Biblical Interpretation in Korea

History and Issues

SAMUEL CHEON
Hannam University
Daejon, South Korea

The intent of this study is to survey issues of biblical interpretation in Korea historically and critically. However, because of the extensive amount of material in biblical studies that has been produced, as well as the differences and diversity also in scholarly interpretation arising out of the rapid social changes in Korea, such review is not simple.[1] This survey attempts a systematic study of how the Christian Bible has been read and interpreted in Korea. Issues of biblical interpretation are dealt with historically in the social and ecclesiastical contexts of Korea and are accompanied by a review of the writings of biblical scholars and their related major events.

Koreans and East Asian Sacred Texts

Before the advent of Christianity, there were three major religions in Korea: Shamanism, Buddhism, and Confucianism. Besides these, Taoism, which was introduced into Korea from China in the mid-seventh century, was strong for a time, but disappeared as a result of its incorporation into the other religions.

Shamanism is the oldest among them. It has been most commonly transmitted as a native religion. Though its activity as a religion has been rapidly declining as the society has become modernized, its influence among the general populace and on the society and other religions, including Christianity, is still strong. However, shamanism has no written sacred text.

Buddhism came to Korea through China in 372 and became the state religion during the Koryo Dynasty (936–1392). Though its adherents were persecuted under the succeeding dynasty, the Chosun Dynasty (1392–1910), it has played a role as a major religion until the present time in Korea. Confucianism entered the Korean Peninsula from China in the third century B.C.E. and became the state religion during the Chosun Dynasty. It is still influential in the social order and moral attitude in Korea, though its role as a religion has declined. Buddhism and Confucianism, with Taoism, have their own sacred texts, which include their teachings for faith and morality. Thus, for generations the Korean people have read, taught, and interpreted their sacred texts, which were written in the Chinese characters, and applied their understanding of the texts onto their way of life.

Koreans have used the East Asian sacred texts as teaching materials for their youth at home, school, and temple. In particular, Confucianism's sacred texts were very important in ancient time. In order to become a royal official, one would have to pass a state examination, for which one would need to be well schooled in the Confucian sacred texts. Nowadays, the lessons from these sacred texts are still important for education at home and in school, no matter what religious beliefs one possesses.

Ancient scholars studied and interpreted these texts in order to inscribe social norms and philosophical concepts for ethical behavior and daily life. As in other Asian countries, when powerful social renewal movements emerged, they often relied on profound reinterpretations of the sacred texts.[2] To do so, they developed hermeneutic methods to interpret them, using traditions by which they thought they were supported. What this all means is that Koreans have considered traditional East Asian sacred texts as important sources for their education, politics, ethics, philosophy, faith, and daily life. Likewise, for Korean Christians, the Christian Bible has served a similar function; that is, Korean Christians have accepted this religious book as the most authoritative one for their faith and daily life.

The Early Period (1780s–1920s)

The Protestant mission to Korea began in 1885, when two missionaries arrived in Korea via Japan from the United States of America. One was Presbyterian, the other a Methodist. However, some Koreans had already become Protestant Christians, establishing a church in the Korean peninsula in 1884. Moreover, Catholic mission in Korea had started about a hundred years before the Protestant mission. Catholicism in Korea produced more than two thousand martyrs in the fierce wave of anti-foreign hysteria, among whom over one hundred were canonized as saints by the Vatican in the late twentieth century. However, for a long time Korean Catholics did not have a Korean Bible, but used a Chinese Bible instead. It was not until 1882 that several books of the New Testament were translated for the first time into Korean and published by Protestants.

Protestant missionaries increased the number of churches in this early period, when Korea began gradually reopening its doors to the outside world. They introduced their education and medical system as well as their beliefs. A few Koreans accepted the Western culture and felt their nation needed the modernization of the Euro-American model. Introducing the Western culture, missionaries completed and published the translation of the entire New Testament with the help of Korean Christians in 1900. They also finished the translation of the Old Testament in 1910, and published the entire Bible in the following year (1911). Since then Koreans have been able to read the Bible in their own language.

In the meantime, Japanese imperialism extended its power over the Korean Peninsula, beginning in the 1890s, and annexed Korea as a colony in 1910, a situation which continued until the end of World War II (1945). Consequently, Koreans, including Christians, engaged in the struggle for national independence. Many Christians were involved in that struggle both inside and outside the peninsula and provided significant leadership to the independence movement of Korea. Though it is hard to find scholarly biblical interpretations reflecting this situation, it should be noted that Koreans read and interpreted the Bible beyond the academic arena, reflecting their own crises.

Christian preachers, Bible teachers and laypersons in Korea read their scripture in relation to their own contexts. For example, when they read the exodus story, they thought of their own liberation that would be accomplished in the future. When they read about the Israelite slavery under Pharaoh, the wilderness, or the exile, they associated Israel's adversities with their own. When they read Jesus' proclamation to the powerless and the poor, they identified themselves with the deprived. They would read and understand the biblical stories as they engaged in imagination for their lives in the hearing of old stories or legends from their parents or grandparents. Such a reading and studying of the Bible led to a natural contextualization of Christianity. This was also a good way to live out their faith, expressing their patriotism under the Japanese imperialist oppression. They considered the Bible as the only scripture that included the message of salvation for their people and country. This means that Korean biblical interpretation began in a nonacademic context.

It is not surprising that academic or systematic biblical interpretation can hardly be found in the early period of the Korean church history. This was because the church did not produced well-educated Korean pastors or theologians according to the so-called Nevius Mission Policy, which was established in 1892 and applied to the Korean mission by the Presbyterian missionaries.[3] Early missionaries thought that intelligent Korean Christians would disrupt the increase of the number of evangelists. Thus, they had no intention to provide a high caliber theological education for Korean Christian leaders.[4] Nevertheless, in this period we can still find some reflections on the biblical text, which are mentioned in articles and books, albeit sketchily.

To begin with, we mention Byung-hun Choi (1858–1927), who may be considered the first Korean theologian.[5] Choi was originally a Confucian scholar but converted to Christianity and later worked as a translator of the Bible. As a Methodist minister and a seminary professor, he attempted to understand the Bible in the same way that he had studied the Confucian sacred texts. His major theological concern was how to understand Christianity within the religious pluralistic context of Korea. In an article published in 1901, the first theological writing produced by a Korean, Choi regarded the Bible in the same way as he had viewed the Confucian sacred texts.[6] However, he summarized the Bible in the perspective of traditional salvation history that was taught by Methodist missionaries. In other articles, distinguishing the gospel of Jesus in the Bible from the doctrinal teaching of Christianity as a religion, he argued that only the truth of Jesus witnessed in the Bible was right and absolute.[7] He considered Jesus both as the one who fulfilled God's salvation and as the one who brought to completion the truth of all great East Asian teachers and the teachings of all religions.

A second scholar from this period was Joo-sam Yang (1879–?). After converting from Confucianism and training at Vanderbilt and Yale (B.D.), he became a Methodist minister and the first Korean professor at Hyupsung Methodist Theological Seminary (1915).[8] In his article on the outline of the content of the Bible (*Shinhaksekye*, 1916–17), he introduced Euro-American biblical studies and argued that we had to know the history of the Bible and its historical and literary contexts in order to understand and interpret the Bible. Yang recognized that the Bible not only included God's instruction but also human free will. His view of the Pentateuch also showed evidence of the contemporary Euro-American biblical scholarship. Introducing the issue of Moses' authorship of the Pentateuch, Yang concluded that the important thing was not who wrote it, but what teaching was included in it. That is, he did not make a decision about the authorship of the Pentateuch, and he urged his readers to learn the holy instructions in it.

A third scholar was Hyuk Namgung (1882–?), who graduated from Princeton Theological Seminary and later received his Th.D. degree in 1927 from Union Theological Seminary in Richmond, Virginia.[9] He became a professor at Pyongyang Presbyterian Theological Seminary, teaching the New Testament (1925). He was the first Korean professor in the seminary and the first Korean with a doctoral degree in theology. He summarized his view of the New Testament in an article on the outline of New Testament theology (*Shinhakginam*, 1938). There he criticized the contemporary scholarly view that Jesus taught an ethical lesson but Paul created a theology. Following scholars such as A. Schweitzer and G. Machen, he argued that the theologies of both Jesus and Paul were not different. He constructed this argument through a comparative study of Jesus' teaching and Paul's letters.

A final scholar for this period was Chang-geun Song (1898–1950). He received his Ph.D. degree from Iliff School of Theology after having studied at Princeton Theological Seminary and Western (presently, Pittsburgh) Theological Seminary.[10] Working in a Presbyterian church, he agonized over social problems in Korea, especially the issue of the poor under the oppression of Japanese imperialism. In an article written in 1923 (*Shinsaengmyung*), he described Jesus as an ordinary person, a laborer like his father Joseph, a proletarian, one who was forced to die on the enemy's cross, one who was willing to find a place in the wilderness to pray, and so on. He portrayed Jesus not only as a social revolutionist, but also a leader of a spiritual salvation for everyone. He thought that for Jesus the latter was more important.

In summary, in this early period, though Korean theologians attempted to present their writings on the Bible, rarely did they produce biblical interpretation from a Korean perspective. Rather, most of their writings introduced academic trends in the Euro-American biblical scholarship. Nonetheless, one may think of Byung-hun Choi as a forerunner of the Korean indigenous theology, and of Chang-geun Song as a precursor of minjung theology.

The Decades of Debates (1930s–1950s)

As the number of Korean theologians trained in the United States multiplied, the debate on theological issues ensued. One of the hottest issues in biblical interpretation during this period was whether or not higher criticism of the Bible should be accepted.[11] This was a matter of dispute between conservatives and liberals. The former wanted to maintain the missionaries' fundamentalist perspective of the Bible, whereas the latter tended to accept the contemporary Euro-American biblical scholarship, especially in relation to neoorthodox theology.

One serious issue pertained to a biblical commentary from the United States. In 1935, fifty-two Koreans translated the *Abingdon Bible Commentary*.[12] This translated work was the first one-volume Bible commentary in Korean. Although the Methodists had control over this work, Presbyterians were also involved in its translation and publication. Nevertheless, Presbyterians, of whom most were fundamentalists, rejected the commentary because it reflected the influence of higher criticism.

1. The Conservative Tradition

There were two significant proponents among conservatives. The first was Hong-gyu Byun (1899–1976), who graduated from Drew University with his Th.D. degree in 1931, and became an Old Testament professor at the Methodist Theological Seminary in 1933. His dissertation was on a study of the holiness theme, which he summarized in Korean for a journal *Shinhaksegye* (1933). According to Byun, "holiness" is a key to understanding the Bible. Although "love" or *agape* is a major concept in the New Testament, it is rooted in God's holiness represented in the Old Testament. The Bible includes four kinds of holiness—ritual holiness in the Pentateuch, moral holiness in the Prophets, individual holiness in the Writings, and spiritual holiness in the New Testament. Following the tradition of John Wesley, he argued that the Christian faith ought to experience all these kinds of holiness. He excluded higher criticism of the Bible and subscribed to Moses' authorship of the Pentateuch, criticizing the documentary hypothesis. Supporting the conservative view of the Bible, he insisted that God spoke directly to human beings, who wrote down God's words.

A second proponent was Hyung-ryong Park (1897–1978), a systematic theologian who studied at Princeton Theological Seminary and Southern Baptist Theological Seminary and taught at Pyongyang Presbyterian Theological Seminary. Fundamentalists such as G. Machen, L. Berkhof, C. Hodge and B.B. Warfield strongly influenced him. He sought to maintain the Calvinistic Protestant doctrine taught by American missionaries, rejecting modern theologies and higher criticism. He insisted on Moses' authorship of the Pentateuch, literal inspiration and absolute inerrancy of the Bible, bodily resurrection of Jesus, and the historical reliability of the biblical miracles. He believed the entire Bible as the word of God, following in the Westminster Confession of Faith that was completed in 1647. His view of the Bible is still influential among Presbyterian fundamentalists.

2. The Liberal Tradition

Two proponents among the liberals are worth mentioning. The first was Gyung-ok Jung (1903–1945), who studied at Garrett Theological Seminary and became a systematic theology professor at the Methodist Theological Seminary. He introduced form criticism in the mode of M. Dibelius and R. Bultmann through a theological journal (*Shinhaksegye*, 1934). The Bible played a most prominent role in his theology. Even though he was a systematic theologian, he placed the First Letter of John at the center of his theological thinking (*Shinhaksegye*, 1933–1939).

A second proponent was Jae-joon Kim (1901–1987). A Presbyterian Old Testament theologian, he studied at Aoyama Theological School in Japan before attending Princeton Theological Seminary and Western (presently, Pittsburgh) Theological Seminary in the United States.[13] Through his articles, he introduced historical criticism of the Bible from an academic perspective. Kim also criticized the theological teaching method and content of the missionaries, arguing that they did not encourage seminarians to engage in creative theological thinking, but rather crammed conservative thoughts into them. In fact, even at that time the educational goal was still focused not on producing theologically oriented ministers and theologians, but elementary evangelists for the ordinary people according to the so-called Nevius Mission Policy. He also refuted Hyung-ryong Park, who faithfully followed the doctrinal teaching of the missionaries.

Kim went on to found a liberal Presbyterian Seminary (presently, Hanshin University), at which he taught higher criticism and modern theologies, criticizing the literal inspiration of the Bible. Studying the Prophets, he emphasized Christian participation in society and in history. What Kim meant was that Christian theology should not overlook social problems, but engage them in the perspective of God's salvation history and present a way toward that salvation.

Conservatives labeled Kim a liberal, even a heretic. Conversely, later in the 1970s to the 1980s, many of his students and colleagues were involved in constructing and articulating minjung theology. Some were integrally involved in the Korean democratic movement, whereas the conservatives supported the dictatorship and concentrated on increasing church membership.

Korea was politically liberated from Japanese imperialism in 1945. However, it was soon divided into two countries: North Korea and South Korea. This led to the Korean War, which began in 1950. During the war, many theologians and pastors in the South died or disappeared, many churches were destroyed, and society was in chaos. When the war ended in 1953, the crisis in the church did not abate but continued with a heightened debate between conservatives and liberals. They continued to struggle with existing problems, whether they should participate in the World Council of Churches, and whether higher criticism of the Bible should be accepted in the church. This resulted in a serious and painful division of the Korean Church.

The Era of Social Response (1960s–1990s)

After the Korean War, society gradually became stable in spite of poverty and the struggle over ideology. As the church matured, most missionaries returned to their homelands. Korean theologians began to respond to their social and cultural issues. Three responses related to biblical interpretation will be dealt with: Korean indigenous theology, minjung theology, and reunification theology.

1. Korean Indigenous Theology

A debate over the theology of indigenization in Korea began to appear beginning in the 1960s, and was particularly lively in the 1970s. The social trend that Koreans should be mindful of their own traditional culture caused it. Such trend began in the 1960s and generated theologians of indigenization who attempted to reevaluate Korean traditional culture and religions through a dialogue with Christian doctrines. Pong-nang Park notes the following:

> There was a growing sense of autonomous "I" consciousness, as Korean existence in the Christian proclamation, since the heritage of the missionary church in the past was too orthodox, heteronomous, and exclusive to meet the Korea of today, changed culturally and economically. The church of Korea found it responsible and even inevitable to re-evaluate the Korean cultural traditions (including religion and culture), if she wished to be the religion for this people today.[14]

Korean indigenous theology, therefore, contributed a religiocultural interpretation of the Christian gospel in the religiously pluralistic society of Korea.

A primary contributor to Korean indigenous theology was Tong-shik Ryu, a former professor of Yonsei University. He studied at Boston University and taught religions and the New Testament. Even though he was more inclined toward becoming a scholar of religion, he also considered the New Testament as a very important subject for his study. He distinguished Christianity from the Christian gospel. According to him, the essence of the latter is that God's Word became incarnate in the Christ event (Jn. 1:14). This event was accomplished by God's self-denial (Phil. 2:7) or by the union between the Divine and the human. For Ryu, a Christian would become a new being through reconciliation with God and neighbors through self-denial.

Ryu attempted to find a parallel to the self-denial event of God in Korean culture, that is, how such revelatory structure of God was reflected in the Korean mind. He argued that religions in Korea—Shamanism, Confucianism, Buddhism, and Donghak—included such structure of self-denial.[15] However, he considered that such Eastern religions did not provide salvation for human beings. He believed that salvation existed only in the gospel of Christ.

Ryu pointed out that Euro-American theology was an interpretation of the Christian gospel from the Greco-Roman perspective. Korean spirituality, however, is different from Jewish or Euro-American spirituality. Thus, it means that Koreans must seek to understand the gospel in their own context and from their own perspective.[16]

Ryu made an important contribution to the development of cultural biblical interpretation in Korea. Taking into consideration both Korean traditional religions and Christian thought, he took a significant step toward interpreting the Bible within the cultural context of Korea. However, some criticized him for trying to understand the Korean culture from the perspective of Christian doctrine and for attempting to reshape Korean religious thoughts within a Christian spiritual scheme.

2. Minjung Theology

In the 1970s, Koreans experienced rapid economic and social changes. Under the military regime, they also experienced political oppressions and all kinds of injustices. The government required that the people make sacrifices for economic development. The rich and the ruling class continued to enjoy their wealth and power, while the poor and the laborers suffered and were exploited. However, the latter could not stand up against such unfairness and no one was allowed to criticize the government and the sociopolitical injustice.

Minjung theology soon emerged as the voice of the voiceless in this context of the mid-1970s.[17] It was a Christian response to the sociopolitical situation in Korea. It was a reaction to the injustice and the dehumanization brought about by the political authoritarianism and industrialization. It was a sociopolitical interpretation of the Bible from the experiences of Korean Christians involved in the political struggle for social justice and democracy.

Minjung theology originated with the reading of the Bible by Namdong Suh (1918–1984), a former professor of systematic theology at Yonsei University.[18] Although he was a systematic theologian, he regarded the Bible as an important source for his theology, along with the traditions and histories of the *minjung*. He wanted to read the Bible in the perspective of the suffering of the oppressed, the *minjung*, whom he identified with the *ochlos* in Mark.[19] He was inclined to interpret the Bible in the context of the human struggle for historical and political liberation today. Suh notes:

> [T]heological activities do not end with the exposition of biblical texts on the salvation or liberation of man by God. In the Bible, the Exodus, the activities of the prophets, and the event of the Cross offer new insights, but these texts ought to be rediscovered and reinterpreted in the context of the human struggle for historical and political liberation today.[20]

Thus, according to Suh, the total witness of the Bible may be clarified and understood in terms of two nuclear historical events: the exodus event in the Old Testament and the crucifixion-resurrection event in the New Testament. He considered them as the liberation events of humanity.[21] He argued that, though the Christian church viewed the events out of the context of the religious ideas of two thousand years, they were political events that occurred in socioeconomic history. It meant for Suh that God's intervention in history could be repeated and revitalized in the dimension of socioeconomic history at the present time in order to bring about the symbolic "millennium" presented in the book of Revelation or the Messianic Kingdom in Korea, in which the salvation of the whole social reality of humankind could be secured. For him, the "millennium" was a historical, earthly, and semi-ultimate symbol to be actualized in the future.[22] He considered the *minjung* as a messiah to bring about the "millennium."

Another student of minjung theology is Byung-mu Ahn, a former professor of New Testament at Hanguk Theological Seminary. Ahn studied the gospel of Mark from a sociological point of view to provide a biblical grounding for minjung theology.[23] He suggests that the words and deeds of Jesus have been de-socialized, because little attention has been paid to the social character of his audience. He argues that in Mark's gospel the term *ochlos* indicates a class marginalized and abandoned–the so-called sinners, tax collectors, and the sick, that is to say, the *minjung*. This class is different from the *laos*, who were the religious and chosen Jews. Ahn remarks: "The term ochlos is not consolidated into a concept but is defined in a relational way, and is therefore a fluid notion...The ochlos are feared by the unjust and powerful, but they are not organized into a power group... They are minjung...simply because they are alienated, dispossessed, and powerless."[24]

Ahn insists that, for Mark, Jesus did not separate himself from his audience, the *ochlos,* and that he accepted them completely and unconditionally to usher in the advent of God's kingdom, a new way and a new hope (Mk. 1:15). According to him, Jesus was the Messiah in the sense that he struggled together with the suffering *minjung* on the frontline of the advent of God's kingdom. This means that we cannot understand Jesus without the *ochlos* and vice versa.

A third advocate of minjung theology is Cyris Hee-suk Moon, a former professor of Old Testament at the Presbyterian College and Theological Seminary in Seoul. Minjung theology informs his study on prophetic literature, especially Micah, from a sociological perspective.[25] He argues that suffering and oppression in modern-day Korea are similar to those in Israel during the eighth century B.C.E. Moon suggests:

> While we cannot find a historical situation in the Bible which is identical to the one which exists in Korea today, a great similarity can be seen between the suffering and oppression experienced by minjung and that experienced by the oppressed class in Israel during the eighth century B.C., i.e., during the time of Amos and Micah. Although the Israelites were in a situation of oppression during the time of Moses, the liberation theology of the Exodus should be differentiated from that of minjung theology in Korea. Today Korea is no longer under foreign dominion, as it was under imperial Japan a few decades ago. Today, the minjung in Korea are oppressed by their own rulers.[26]

According to Moon, "my people" and "this people" should be differentiated in the book of Micah, because, while the former can be identified with the *minjung,* the latter are their enemies. He holds that the central issue for Micah was the suffering of "my people," who were oppressed and robbed of their property by "this people," the ruling class in the same nation. He points out that, like Moses and Amos, Micah as a commoner stood on the side of the oppressed people as their advocate, and lived and identified with the *minjung.* It meant also that Micah's suffering (Mic. 1:8) prefigured that of Christ's and that God's liberating act for the *minjung* through the true prophet should be continued in Korea.

A final proponent that deserves mention is Yong-bock Kim, who received his Ph.D. degree from Princeton Theological Seminary. Kim argues that, though the *minjung* could not be defined by a concept, their historical experience might be presented in their social biography. His aim is to read the stories of the slaves, the poor, the oppressed, the captive, and leading biblical figures—such as Abraham, Moses, Ruth, the prophets, and so on—in the perspective of the *minjung*'s social biography.[27] He also suggests that Jesus could be understood in the context of the social biography of the people of God. Thus, Kim writes:

> It is my contention that the social biography of the People of God is essentially intertwined with the story of Jesus in the New Testament. Jesus the Suffering Servant, Jesus the Pascal Lamb, and Jesus the Crucified are intrinsically intertwined with the stories of the ochlos, the poor, the sick, imprisoned and so on. Therefore, just as we cannot fully understand the story of the people of God, so we cannot fully understand the story of Jesus outside the context of the social biography of the people of God.[28]

For this period too, we need to take note of an important event in 1977, when both Catholics and Protestants jointly translated and published the Bible with the Apocrypha into Korean.[29] However, most Protestants rejected this ecumenical version, whereas Catholics accepted it as the official Bible for their liturgy. Fortunately, this translation was the basis for the North Korean Church's translation of the Bible, which was completed in 1984.[30]

3. Reunification Theology

Reunification has been the most important issue for Koreans since 1945, when World War II ended and the peninsula was divided into the North and the South. The division of the Korean peninsula caused the separation of over ten million families as well as leading to the Korean War in the early period of the 1950s. The Korean Church has been concerned about how it can contribute to the reunification of the Korean peninsula. However, an intense confrontation between the North and the South impeded their communication.

While North and the South had made an agreement for their peaceful reunification in 1972, it was not honored. Instead, both governments continued to sustain their military powers against each other. However, the intellectual community has taken the issue of reunification seriously in their discussions since 1980. The overthrow of the regime of President Chung-hee Park in 1979, a regime that controlled the South for eighteen years and monopolized the debate on reunification, made this possible. Although another military regime was created in 1980, the debate on reunification continued together with that of democratization in Korea. This led the National Council of Churches in Korea to proclaim "The Declaration of the Korean Church upon the Reunification and Peace of the Korean People" in 1988. In this declaration, the KNCC proclaimed the year 1995 as "the Jubilee Year of the Reunification and Peace in Korea." This meant that the present pain and suffering of the Korean people, brought about by their division, would end by the Jubilee Year–the fiftieth year since their separation in 1945. In this environment, biblical scholars produced many articles that sought to provide a biblical basis for the discussion of a peaceful reunification.

A number of biblical scholars have made significant contributions to this theological conversation. The first is Chan-kook Kim, a former Old Testament professor of Yonsei University, who studied Israelite unification in the Old Testament.[31] Surveying the ancient history of Israel, he argues that the political unification of the Israelites was accomplished for a while, but it could not be sustained for a longer time because of the tension and struggle among the powerful countries in the ancient Near East. However, biblical historians regarded highly the political unification and religious reform accomplished by David as well as Josiah's strategy for the political and religious reunification of the Israelites. In addition, biblical writers attempted to communicate to the later generations the message that they should try to accomplish their reunification in the future. Such a message developed into the belief of the expected messiah. Kim argues that Koreans should learn this lesson of the unification in the Old Testament.

Tae-soo Im, an Old Testament professor at Hosu University, also attempted to find messages for the peaceful reunification of Korea in the Old Testament.[32] Im notes that the ancient Israelites suffered separation at two different times–during the reigns of David and Rehoboam. It was the rulers' desire for power that brought about these separations and sufferings, as was the case in Korea. After the division between northern Israel and southern Judah, the rulers of both nations sought to accomplish reunification through military means but failed. However, the idea of peaceful unification was a hope in the Chronicler's history as well as in some prophetic books. According to Im, the Chronicler emphasized the idea of a unified Israel, including the North and the South, even in the post-exilic period. The historian pictured David as an ideal king of the reunited nation in the future. Im argues that the Chronicler's idea was similar to that of some prophets, who expected their people's reunification through God's power and the idealized king David in the future. It meant that the Chronicler reinterpreted Israelite history from the perspective of Israel's unification theology based on faith in Yahweh.

Hoping that the peaceful reunification of Korea would take place in the year of the Jubilee since their liberation from Japan in 1945, biblical scholars suggested modern meanings of the law of the Jubilee year in Leviticus 25. The reunification theology movement of the KNCC that began in the early 1980s strongly encouraged such studies of the Jubilee law. Such studies in turn provided biblical support for the Korean churches in North and South Korea in 1986, when they had a meeting in Switzerland, sponsored by the WCC, to proclaim the year 1995 as the Jubilee for the reunification of Korea.

Yong-jin Min, a former Old Testament professor of the Methodist Theological Seminary and the vice-director of the Korean Bible Society, first presented the meaning of the Jubilee in 1982.[33] Min argues that the Jubilee law meant that all property—including land, house, and servant—ultimately belong to God. He suggests that, though God proclaimed this law to protect the poor people, Israel did not observe it, and that the Israelite prophets, inspired by the Jubilee law, urged their people to practice social justice. Relating to the New Testament, he argues that early Christianity regarded the Jubilee as the year of grace and expected its fulfillment through the coming of Jesus. The Jubilee law should be practiced for all people waiting for freedom and liberation.

Ee-kon Kim, an Old Testament professor at Hanshin University, endeavors to understand the Jubilee law in the context of an industrialized society.[34] He argues that the law requires not only the absolute protection of the basic personal property, but also a religious resolve on the part of an ideal egalitarian society to work against the indefinite expansion of one's individual property. Accordingly, Kim suggests that the basic personal property include three things—the land, the house, and the human body—that God has given as gifts by God's grace. In any case, one should not be deprived of these forever, and they should be returned in the Jubilee year. He insists that, corresponding to the theology of exodus and settlement, this law of liberation and salvation should still be good news for the suffering people, even though most biblical scholars consider it as just a utopian illusion.

Sa-moon Kang, an Old Testament professor at the Presbyterian College and Theological Seminary, presented a paper on the Jubilee law in the annual meeting of the Korean Society of the Old Testament Studies in 1995, in which he synthesized all the discussions.[35] According to him, the spirit of the law urges us to pursue a just community in which God's justice is alive. However, the division of Korea has prevented Koreans from following in such a spirit. He argues that, to overcome this separation, Koreans need a movement of repentance and reconciliation in accordance with the spirit of the law.

Conclusion

As we have seen above, issues of biblical interpretation in Korea are tied to historical events and realities. Besides the issues surveyed, there are other issues in relation to feminism, ecology, and spirituality. However, scholarship on these issues is still in its nascent stage and thus they are not dealt with here. Academic studies on them need to move beyond simply introducing Euro-American biblical scholarship and reflect more seriously the Korean context in order to create a theological trend in Korea.

This study indicates that there are two trajectories in Korean biblical interpretation, though they overlap in the writings of some scholars such as Tong-shik Ryu, a scholar of indigenous theology, and Nam-dong Suh, a Minjung theologian. The first looks to culture and tradition, while the second moves in the direction of responses to the sociopolitical situations. Thus, their interpretive questions can be summarized as follows: "How can biblical interpretation relate to the tradition and culture in the context of Korea?" "How can it respond to the sociopolitical situations in Korea?" The first question seeks support for the indigenization of Christianity in Korea, whereas the second strives at strengthening the sociopolitical response of Christianity.

These two questions are still dominant and should remain the focus for future biblical interpretation in Korea. Such biblical interpretation will not only help in the construction of the contemporary identity of Christianity in the society of Korea, but also make a significant contribution to the field of biblical studies.

4

Differences and Difficulties

Biblical Interpretation in the Southeast Asian Context

PHILIP P. CHIA
The Chinese University of Hong Kong

Introduction

Let me begin with a word of clarification. I have no intention of resisting the "differences" between and ignoring the "identities" of the various nationalities and races that inhabit the region the British Empire called the "Southeast Asia Command" during the Second World War. To this very day, there are still disputes among scholars of various fields on the definition of the term "Southeast Asia." Neither have I any intention of falling into the usual trap of the colonizer who ignores the heterogeneity and hybridity of the Southeast Asian peoples with regard to their cultures, languages, races, and religions. Thus, dealing with them as if they are one homogeneous community is by no means my intention, for to do so would definitely be a grievous mistake.

A word of apology must also be expressed at this point. As much as I had wished for this essay to be comprehensive in its inclusiveness and representation of the Southeast Asian context, as suggested by the subtitle, I must admit that the task is simply too difficult. Already in 1973, the sociologist Hans-Dieter Evers wrote:

> One of the most difficult tasks faced by South-East Asian states-men and scholars alike is to assess, understand and predict the major trends of social and political developments in the area. The task would be formidable in any society; in an area as complex as

South-East Asia, it appears to be doomed to failure right from the beginning.[1]

Thus, attempting to assess and understand how the Bible is being read in this part of the world is equally formidable. I find the task particularly difficult not only because of the fluidity of the context at hand, but even more so because of the inaccessibility and unavailability of materials, if they exist at all. The problem is further complicated by my own limited exposure to those communities that read the Bible, particularly those who do so in contexts that are rather different from my own. I am nevertheless compelled, however, to take up the task, largely due to my own identity as a fifth-generation Christian who was born and brought up in Southeast Asia, in a place the British once called Borneo (North Borneo to be precise) but is now known as Sabah, one of the states of Malaysia.

Perhaps a brief personal note might help in understanding the way by which I have come to perceive and persevere in the subject matter. I was educated in Malaysia, Singapore, Canada, the United States, and Great Britain, and I have taught biblical studies and interpretation in Malaysia, the Philippines, Hong Kong, Taiwan, and China both at the graduate level and to the laity for the last twenty years. I constantly struggle to strike a chord of harmonic mind in reading and teaching the Bible, especially when attempting to apply with sensibility and sensitivity to the East the knowledge, particularly in biblical studies, that I acquired from the West. I am forced to make instant executive decisions regarding the interpretation of certain passages that a group of Bible readers find difficult to comprehend, not because they live in a proverbial birdcage, but because their experience of reality is specific and contextual. Sometimes I find my context-insensitive readings, which may be regarded as authoritative interpretations, filled not only with fear, but with primal fear; I am the legitimate voice of the biblical authors, at times representing even God, the One with whom the West is familiar, yet who remains alien to those in the East. Colonizing "them," whoever they are, with knowledge proven by an advanced degree earned in the West, I have enjoyed very much the fruit of power. That "knowledge is power" has long been recognized, acknowledged by the philosopher Francis Bacon and elaborated more recently by Michel Foucault with sophistication. The will to power and the power to dominate has been instilled in my soul as the basis for practicing biblical interpretation in Southeast Asia.

Having located myself, let me proceed to provide, first, a brief sketch of the context, that is, a historical background of Southeast Asia, giving special attention to the expansion of Christianity in the region. This will allow us then to focus on the use of the Bible or modes of biblical interpretation in the region in an attempt to discuss issues and problems pertinent to interpreters in Southeast Asia.

The Context: A Historical Development
Geography and Demography

As noted earlier, the term "Southeast Asia" is relatively recent. Although there have been variant understandings concerning the region it represents, most scholars presently use the term Southeast Asia to include the geographical areas bounded by the states of Myanmar, Thailand, Malaysia, Singapore, Brunei, Indonesia, Laos, Cambodia, Vietnam, and the Philippines.[2] As such, Southeast Asia consists of the "mainland" and the "insular." The mainland consists of Myanmar, Thailand, Laos, Cambodia, and Vietnam. It is noted for its diverse mountain ranges and rivers running north-south, most of them originating in Tibet. The "insular" is made up of Malaysia, Singapore, Brunei, Indonesia, and the Philippines.

According to D.R. SarDesai, the dominant ethnic group in Southeast Asia today is the "brown-skinned" Malays who live mainly in Indonesia, Malaysia, Brunei, and the Philippines, and whose origin can be traced back to southern China.[3] With migrations from other regions, particularly India and China, the demographic composition in Southeast Asia has become even more diverse and complicated.

The population of Southeast Asia is 540.2 million (the U.S. population is 286.2 million),[4] and the region covers a combined area of 4,464,748 square kilometers. When comparing Southeast Asia with other Asian regions, Ashok K. Dutt notes:

> Southeast Asia stands out as distinctly different from other realms in Asia because of (1) a proliferation of individual country units with no single dominating nation, (2) two politically different systems—communist and capitalistic—in different parts of the realm, (3) a tropical humid land mass with relatively insignificant dry land, (4) archipelagos forming the major physical element, (5) a situation between two great historic cultures of China and India, which have remained regularly connected with each other over the last 2000 years using the realm as a mid-way halt.
>
> The South Asian and Siberian realms lack all the above elements, whereas East Asia has only one similarity with the Southeast Asia, i.e., existence of two politically different systems.
>
> Similarly the Middle East like Southeast Asia has a proliferation of individual country units without a single country dominating the realm. Southeast Asia possesses enough physical, economic and cultural oneness to be called a realm with unique characteristics of its own yet it is, at the same time, a realm full of contrasts.[5]

After identifying such distinct characteristics, differing from those of other Asian countries, we proceed to explore further the political, economic, sociocultural, and religious dimensions of the Southeast Asians.

The Political and Economic Contexts

Politically, Southeast Asia today represents four different systems: (1) democracy (Malaysia, Singapore, Philippines, Thailand, Indonesia), (2) military dictatorship (Myanmar), (3) communism (Vietnam, Laos, Cambodia), and (4) monarchy (Brunei). The modern history of Southeast Asia may be characterized by three distinctive periods: (1) the period of colonialism, before WWII; (2) the period of nationalism, after WWII; (3) the period of cooperation, in the post-Cold War era.

1. The Period of Colonialism

Except for Thailand, which managed to remain free from colonial domination, five non-Asian colonial powers controlled the region of Southeast Asia: the Netherlands in Indonesia; France in Laos, Cambodia, and Vietnam; Great Britain in Myanmar, Malaysia, and Singapore; United States in the Philippines (which had been colonized by Spain); and Portugal in Timor (and earlier also in Malaysia). SarDesai notes that such colonial rule was not received passively but was met with resistance movements, especially in Myanmar, Vietnam, and Indonesia. Addressing the situation in the Philippines, SarDesai goes on to note that the Philippines, as "a pioneer in the nationalist movements in Asia," was essentially cheated by the United States in the process of accepting their help in driving out the Spaniards, thereby ushering in a neocolonial era that lasted until recently.[6]

2. The Period of Nationalism

The route to independence for the Southeast Asian countries varies. For some, particularly Myanmar, Indonesia, and Vietnam, nationalism was "partly a reaction to colonial policies of discrimination and political and economic exploitation but also a result of Western education."[7] SarDesai suggests that these nationalist movements were influenced by momentous events in Japan (its victory over Russia), China (the revolution under Sun Yat-sen), and India (the Gandhi-Nehru nationalist movements). On the other hand, independence movements in Cambodia, Laos, Malaysia, and Singapore did not begin until after WWII due either to the lack of economic exploitation (as in Cambodia and Laos) or to benevolent foreign rule (as in Malaysia and Singapore).[8]

It must be noted, however, that former colonizers are not without opportunities to exert their influence on national leaders. Colonization has been replaced with a form of neocolonization: national elites who were colonized by the former colonizers through education and trade have continued to dominate and colonize their own people.

The period of nationalism eventually gave rise to efforts of communication and cooperation with one another in order to maintain a relatively peaceful region. As a consequence, ASEAN (the Association of Southeast Asian Nations) was established in August 1967 and is defined by its five founding members: Indonesia, Malaysia, Philippines, Singapore, and Thailand. For its first eight years, ASEAN seemed to achieve little more than its own survival, and observers assessing the organization in 1974 and 1975 predicted only a low-key and modest future for it. The impact of the communist victories in Indochina in 1975, however, induced the ASEAN members to revitalize their association in order to promote both their economic interests and the security of their political and strategic environment.[9] Over the years, ASEAN grew to include five additional members (Brunei, Vietnam, Laos, Myanmar, and Cambodia), and thus, by 1999, the entire region has become a part of the association. The region, called Southeast Asia, named not by its inhabitants but by the British, continues to struggle for its own identity and sovereignty, which is also the context of our study.

3. The Period of Cooperation in the Post-Cold War Era

Improved cooperation and communication between the Southeast Asian nations began in the period of nationalism and took on greater significance in the post-Cold War era. Nonetheless, policies of non-alliance and a nuclear free zone, yet dependent on foreign power to secure the region, exposed the fragility of the peoples and politics of this region. Southeast Asia has twice been invaded by outside forces. In the sixteenth century, the West was drawn to the region by the lure of trading profits; then, Japan during WWII sought to build a new Pacific empire based in substantial measure on the natural wealth of the lands to her south. Both intrusions generated rivalry and fostered greed.

Since then, the presence of foreign powers in the region has been an issue of concern to Southeast Asians. Foreign interference was prompted by the conviction that the end of colonial control had created instability and vulnerability that would inevitably be exploited as a matter of course by one or more of the great powers. Therefore, elaborate arguments were devised to justify foreign intervention. The foreign powers that have had great interest in Southeast Asia are the United States, Russia (and the former Soviet Union), China, and Japan.

Despite the good intention of the Asian peoples to maintain peaceful relations between fellow nations in the region, Southeast Asia is not without hidden dangers of its own. With the increasing global demand for oil, the Straits of Malacca (between Indonesia, Malaysia, and Singapore)–as one of the major sea passages for crude carriers between the Middle East and Southeast Asia–and the oil rich cluster of islands in the South China Sea–namely, the Xisha (Paracels) and the Nansha (Spratlys)–are two explosive land and sea issues that will determine the future of the ASEAN and the region's security.[10] Thus, the future of the region lies with the willingness of the ASEAN to negotiate their interests in peace rather than settling the dispute through the use of force.

The economies of the Southeast Asian countries reflect the political systems by which they operate. They range from planned economies (Vietnam, Laos, Cambodia) to market economies. Capitalism has been the dominant economic ideology in most of the countries, especially in the post-Cold War era.

In a paper first presented at the end of 1986, Hans Rieger notes that "the countries of the region have very different trade regimes and industrial structures." He goes on to point out that "if any progress is to be made in regional economic co-operation, then these differences must be taken into account."[11]

Regarding the socioeconomies of Southeast Asia, Milton Osborne has pointed out, "various countries have achieved independence through differing ways. Economic developments have shown that Southeast Asia was increasingly drawn into the international economic transformation in the domestic economies of each country. And some attention—perhaps too little—has been given to the social changes that have taken place in association with political and economic change."[12]

Social, Cultural, and Religious Contexts

Although multilingualism characterizes the identities of Southeast Asians, it also hampers communication between and among them. For some reason, perhaps because of their colonial experience, English has become the common language of communication. It is not only that relations to their former colonizers became a way of defining their identity, it is that the choice of a national language is a powerful means of uniting or dividing the many peoples of Southeast Asia, both internally and externally, as nations and as a region. In some countries, it is a common phenomenon that the language of the elites is that of their colonizers' and not of the common people. Language becomes an indicator of social status. Education utilizing the colonizers' language as the medium of instruction conveys superior status. Language is also linked to various domestic and national policies. Take Singapore, for instance. In order to develop into a competitive, industrial nation, Western technologies and advanced scientific knowledge had to be acquired. To do so, the international language and the language of science and technology had to be mastered by the nation. Thus, English became the crucial element for national advancement within the international arena.

Economic development was the driving force that dominated national and foreign policies. This brought about great changes in social structure and culture. Only elements in their social activities and cultural tradition that were clearly related to economic activities received welcome emphasis and propagation in governmental policies. In due time, it not only threatened the value and spirit of the traditional culture that constituted the society, but it also nurtured a new generation of persons with hybrid social and cultural identities.

Multi-racialism, multiculturalism, and religious pluralism are the distinctive characteristics of the peoples of Southeast Asia. In many nations, coexistence among the different racial-ethnic groups is often a hard lesson to learn. Southeast Asian cultures are essentially hybrid, "reflected in the psychological make-up of the peoples, influenced by religion, language, customs, heritage, environment, material well-being, and a stable political system."[13] Religions and racial problems have often been linked together, forming an explosive device that endangers social stability. For instance, the Javanese Moslem culture is different from the Balinese Hindu tradition; the north and central Philippines's Catholic culture contrasts and conflicts with its southern Muslim society; the Malay world, which is mainly Islamic in culture, is often felt as a threat to the millions of non-Muslims in the region who are Buddhists. Culturally, the hegemonic practices of the Protestant and Catholic missionaries have not only brought with them the Bible to the region, but also cultural domination.

With regard to the pluralistic nature of their societies, as demonstrated by the region's cultures and religions, Dutt points out, "A clash of cultures has been taking place in Southeast Asia since the beginning of historic times. It is not only that the different cultures within the realm have clashed with each other, but that these cultures have invaded from abroad."[14] In addition, the fluidity of the cultures and religions of the peoples of Southeast Asia also gave rise to various forms of Christian communities when the West met the East in the exchange of religious experience.

Christianity in Southeast Asia

The spread of Christianity in Southeast Asia cannot be separated from the presence of colonialism and imperialism from the West. All Southeast Asian countries except Thailand have experienced colonization in their national history. As noted earlier, five colonial powers colonized the region. These colonizers are also represented by their respective ecclesiastical institutions (for instance, Dutch–Reform, French and Spain–Catholic, American–Evangelical) which exported their missionaries, who in turn created an impact on the colonized peoples. The modes of reading the Bible within different communities are therefore characterized by the respective ecclesiastical orders and dogmatic theologies. Different emphases on the use of the Bible within different faith communities resulted in a vastly diversified Christian community that represented only a small fraction of the greater population of Southeast Asia.

This table, based on *Operation World*, 21st Century Edition, shows the percentage of the Christian population in various locales, the availability of the Bible in the preferred language, and the number of denominations

in each country. Together these factors suggest that the modes of reading
and interpreting the Bible may vary greatly even within a country.[15]

Country	Population	GNP (US$)~	% Christ.	Denom.	# Bible Trans.*	#Christians
Brunei	328,080	25,160	11.25%	19	8B/1NT	36,909
Indonesia	212,991,926	450	16%	264	20B/38NT/77P	34,078,708
Malaysia	22,244,062	4,530	9.21%	71	15B/9NT/16P	2,048,678
Philippines	75,966,500	1,200	93.19%	499	8B/52NT/37P	70,793,181
Singapore	3,566,614	32,810	14.60%	64		520,726
Thailand	61,399,249	2,740	1.62%	81	15B/9NT/11P	994,668
Myanmar	45,611,177	2,610	8.7%	69	2B/10NT/16P	3,970,000
Cambodia	11,167,719	300	1.19%	22	2B/1NT/1P	132,896
Laos	5,433,036	400	1.85%	8	10B/8NT/11P	100,511
Vietnam	79,831,650	310	8.16%	43	4B/11NT/8P	6,514,263
Total	518,540,013		22.98%			119,190,540

~Figure given is per capita.
* B = full version of the Bible; NT = only the New Testament; P = portion of the Bible/Books; Denom.= Denominations.
Population figures are provided by 1996 Asia Week journal.

With the exception of the Philippines, which claim a Christian
population of more than 90 percent, only two countries are above 10
percent, and three are below 2 percent. Only a small percentage of the
population in Southeast Asia who have access to a Bible in their preferred
language. Most of their history of biblical interpretation is, therefore,
relatively recent and dependent on missionaries from the West. Denominational characteristics are definitive elements that shaped ways of reading
the Bible. Furthermore, as throughout the world, most of those who read
and use the Bible are ordinary people rather than trained biblical scholars.
However, the social status of most of these ordinary people who read the
Bible is uncertain. It is not surprising to learn that Christianity has often
been associated with the middle-class or upper-middle-class people of this
region, perhaps because Christianity came with the colonizers. With this
complex picture of the socioeconomic, political, religious, and cultural
contexts of the peoples of Southeast Asia in mind, we shall now turn to
consider biblical interpretation in Southeast Asia.

The Reading: Issues and Problems
General Remarks

Unlike the South African context or the Latin American world, biblical
faith is a relatively recent religious phenomenon shared by a relatively
small percentage of the population of Southeast Asia.[16] Christianity is not
a native-grown religion of the culturally rich, yet highly pluralistic and
vastly diversified peoples of Southeast Asia. The role of biblical teaching
in shaping moral culture, if it does at all, is a recent development in Southeast

Asia. Western missionary efforts (inseparable from colonialism) especially contributed to the formulation of biblical interpretive principles and modes of reading among Southeast Asians. A cursory survey would reveal the domination of Western biblical interpretation in the former colonies. Viewed from a broad macro perspective, a theoretical analysis of the contemporary situation that constituted, and contributed to, the differences and difficulties in biblical interpretation within the Southeast Asian context is long overdue. We study seven areas grouped into three categories constituting the differences and difficulties in biblical interpretation in the context of Southeast Asia: (1) language and identity; (2) culture and religion; (3) socioeconomics, politics, and global relations. These are key areas that contributed to the development and destitution of biblical interpretation in Southeast Asia.

Language and Identity

David Clines has perceptively surmised, "the identity of researchers is being in some way negated if they are not free to write in their native language."[17] Speaking of identity, he recognizes that his own set of "distinctive beliefs—cultural, ethnic and religious commitments and inheritances—are what make me an individual. Call them my prejudices and presuppositions if you must, though I would rather call them the components from which I construct my identity."[18] The language and identity of most Southeast Asian peoples are highly hybridized due to the nature of their pluralistic environments. Loan words and foreign concepts are all too common in local languages. Class, racial, and political struggles are hidden within such hybridity. The postmodern self of the peoples of Southeast Asia is both fragmented and fragile, and, as such, vulnerable to any foreign influence, particularly one that comes with economic power. That such hybridized identity informs the prejudices of one's reading of the Bible only demonstrates the dynamism and fluidity of one's understanding of the Bible.

Such attitude is extremely vulnerable to the presence of colonizing power. Because the Christian population is a relatively small percentage of the national population, and those who read the Bible come from the middle or upper-middle class of the society and are closely linked to their former colonizers, it is not surprising to observe that biblical interpretation has seldom, if ever, been a local endeavor. Not until after the identity of the subject has awakened and gained a consciousness of its own will biblical interpretation cease to be a foreign game on local land. Passivity characterizes the mood of most biblical interpreters in Southeast Asia. Biblical interpretation is never a game of their own, rules of the game are set not by them but by foreigners who speak a different language and come from a different living experience. Furthermore, it is those with whom they are not familiar who blow the whistle and decide what counts as a correct or legitimate interpretation. To change the situation, the Bible must first be read by the peoples of Southeast Asia in their own languages and used in their own living experience. How can the Bible be discovered in a nonbiblical world when the peoples do not even have access to the Bible in their own language? Otherwise, being Christian or reading and using the Bible in Southeast Asia would mean abandoning one's own identity and cultural context.

Culture and Religion

Given that the realities of Southeast Asia are those of multicultural-ism, multi-racialism, and religious pluralism, one wonders how biblical interpretation as an enterprise of the Western biblical world can communi-cate with a world that is not only nonbiblical, but culturally, religiously, and traditionally somewhat "anti-biblical." More precisely, the question at hand is, What has the interpreter's cultural context to do with biblical interpretation?

In his attempt to clarify the questions for "cultural exegesis," Daniel Smith-Christopher argues one should ask whether any cultural reading can "give all of us new ideas about what the text *historically meant* [emphasis his]."[19] The question he has for the liberation theologian is "whether the poor Brazilian peasants who read the Bible can give any insights into what the text means *for others besides themselves*, let alone whether their observations can actually guide a process of rethinking historical-critical reconstructions of the past events [emphasis his]."[20] Perhaps Smith-Christopher is too concerned with the correct universal *historical meaning* of biblical passages and overly conscious of the universal "correctness" of the historical-critical method. But what Clines points out is also worth our consideration, that "it would be equally unfortunate if the distinctive ethos of biblical study in any country were to be subjected to some universal standard."[21] Smith-Christopher is concerned with establishing what he called "a basis for discussion" in clarifying the purpose of "cultural exegesis," but he seems to be promoting another form of domination. In that, he legitimizes the search for a historical meaning of the text as the basis for a universal standard in biblical interpretation. He seems to ignore the cultural and religious identity of the reader and the purpose of reading the Bible in the context of the reader. In recognizing that interpretation of data cannot escape cultural and experiential bias, Smith-Christopher admits, "The future of biblical analysis must include the encouragement and training of as many different cultural representatives as possible, and the encouragement of these new students and scholars to work within the context of their cultural identity, and not outside of it in the name of a misguided 'objectivity.'"[22] He con-cludes, "multiculturalist approaches to textual interpretation, by intentionally seeking and encouraging readings that are consciously influenced by the cultural identities and experiences of the persons involved in the exegetical process, will result in improved readings."[23] But even with such a conclusion, he is still consciously bounded by the "universal (gold) standard" concept, because his goal still is reaching "improved readings." The strong objection to "any move to reduce the diversity of human distinctiveness," as voiced by Clines, is a positive acknowledgment of the potential danger of the presence of (Western) domination and colonization tendency in biblical scholarship. The need to recognize the cultural differences of the interpreters of the Bible is no longer a dispute in biblical studies in our postmodern era.

The religious experiences of the peoples of Southeast Asia are pluralistic and multifaceted. They contribute toward the formation of their cosmic view and understanding of spirituality and reality. This phenomenon is in some way different from the Western living experience and it is therefore difficult for Westerners to comprehend and appreciate. In biblical studies, the issues related to the "risen from the dead," "casting demons," or "performance of miracles" do not need to be argued and persuaded by scientific or scholarly methods to be convincing for the peoples of Southeast Asia. It is part of their living experience and cosmic view. The importation of biblical issues from the Western biblical scholarship helps only to suppress their own burning issues in the Southeast Asia context and to subsume legitimate issues under the agenda of Western domination, especially when one considers that the Western agenda is preoccupied with problems out of its own context. For instance, agendas of biblical studies that arose from the liberal-evangelical or fundamentalist-evangelical battles have long been the dominating mentality or consciousness of biblical interpreters in Southeast Asia. This helps to evade and ignore problems of their own, and, at times, even nurture an irresponsible attitude on the part of the Southeast Asian biblical interpreters toward their communities and contexts. Biblical studies become an irrelevant activity for the religious community.

Socioeconomics, Politics, and Global Relations

The socioeconomies of Southeast Asia, as described in the first part of this study, are closely linked to their political practice. Recently, the focus of Southeast Asian countries has been financial gain and improved living standards for the nations as the ultimate concern for both domestic and foreign policies. With this common goal, Southeast Asians are also open to the influence and domination of those who are in control and economically powerful, particularly in the financial and scientific technological world. But the worst influence come from those who decide the rules of the game in a reality that endorses capitalism as the only way of survival and higher living standards. However, deciding not to be pampered by Western values and standards, Asians have sparked a series of reactions to Western domination of cultural values. The crux of Asian hermeneutics is "To Cane Or Not to Cane," with reference to the issue several years ago on the decision to punish the wrongdoing of an American in Singapore. The social values that characterize Southeast Asian societies have finally found a way to say no to foreign or alien domination. Such awakening in its subjectivity is largely because the per capita Gross National Product (GNP) of Singaporeans is now equal to that of the four largest West European countries, and because, politically and financially, the nation is less dependent on the United States of America. The rediscovery of Southeast Asian subjectivity is an awareness that biblical interpreters who claim to represent the Southeast Asian peoples must take into serious consideration in their practice of biblical interpretation. The danger of false representation, as pointed out in Edward Said's *Orientalism,* is a warning to those who are being colonized academically.

Asia, being one of the largest continents, has received some attention in recent years, thanks to its huge market and economic potential. Its economic growth and cultural certainty are closely related to each other. With its growth in economic strength and political independence, together with the recognition and reorientation of perceptions of the West toward the rest of the world, Asia (and Southeast Asia), as a legitimate subject who used to be colonized, de-colonized and re-colonized, has gained the acknowledgment of its existence. The shift from colonialism to neocolonialism and postcolonialism that dominated the production of knowledge has yielded a highly transparent consciousness of hegemonic behavior in real life, be it academic, political, or any socioeconomic environment. The rise of cultural materialism in Britain and new historicism in the United States as a challenge to poststructuralism and deconstructionism testifies not only to the power of market and consumer-oriented economy on the academic production of knowledge, but also to the creation of a neocultural imperialism within the interpretive communities. The legitimation of the presence of multiculturalism and multi-racialism threatens the dominant culture and power on the one hand, and relativizes sociocultural value on the other, which makes the world an absolute pluralistic environment. The Southeast Asian context has the potential to challenge the interpretive communities on the validity and vitality of biblical interpretation.

The shifts of interest within the interpretive communities in the West since the turn of the century have produced a variety of new methods. The subject of literary study has shifted from focusing on the author's intention to the text and onto the reader, as well as the effect of reading the text on the reader. In the process, the subject/text is either re-presented or deconstructed. All these phenomena of textual-reading are present, in one form or the other, within the Bible reading communities in Southeast Asia. This is due partly to the influence of Western ideology in the East, and partly to the economic dependence of the East on the West. The following are some suggestions for biblical interpreters in the Southeast Asian context in particular, and for other cultures in general.

Some Suggestions for Practitioners of Biblical Interpretation in Southeast Asia

1. Be aware of and be sensitive to various foreign theological or ecclesiastical alliances

Since the spread of Christianity means the introduction of Bible readings to the peoples of the region, the characteristics and distinctiveness of their ecclesiastical communities, be it foreign or home-grown denominations or sects, constitute the primary context where modes of reading the Bible are being nurtured, learned, adopted, practiced, and transmitted. As time progresses, the interaction between Bible readings and life experience creates and transforms traditions of biblical interpretation. The numerous denominations and sects, foreign and home-grown, that characterize the religious situation of this region only testify to the power of adaptation of Bible reading. The openness in sincerity to dialogue with local realities on the part of the ecclesiastical communities and biblical interpreters is an important element in their interpretive process, if relevancy is the concern.

2. Be sensitive to the sociocultural and religious experiences of the indigenous peoples

At least one geographical factor is common to most of Southeast Asia. The monsoons—southwest and northeast—dictate a way of life in many ways common to most of the region's inhabitants. Precipitation averaging 100 inches annually comes with the southwest monsoon winds that hit the leeward side of the various mountain ranges between late May and middle September, and the northeast monsoons that bring the much-needed rains between December and February. The accompanying gusty winds, developing at times into devastating hurricanes and typhoons, are the common experience of the peoples of Southeast Asia. As observed by SarDesai,

> The monsoon's vagaries have contributed to the peasants' belief in the supernatural, which leads to their propitiation of the appropriate spirits to ensure timely arrival of the monsoons and adequate sunshine during planting, weeding, and harvesting seasons. The location of their homes and temples preferably on elevated ground, the tapering design of the roofs of their homes, and the drainage and irrigation systems are all dictated by the often merciless monsoons flooding the dwelling areas and causing untold miseries to the population. The monsoons have thus governed the way of life, religious beliefs, commercial activity, and communications in the Southeast Asian world for ages.[24]

Though much has changed as science and technology conquered some problems brought by natural phenomena, tradition remains part of the living experience of the peoples.

Supernatural or magic in the sense of witchcraft is the common experience of the native peoples of Southeast Asia. Biblical interpretation in such context will be of no help if Western rationalism, historical-critical, or scientific criticism is the key mode of reading the text. Centuries of Western biblical scholarship, particularly since the Enlightenment, might need to be applied with care and constraint to the experience of the peoples of Southeast Asia. The days of the miracles as represented in the gospels and the Old Testament will have to be read in a different light, with greater sensitivity and sensibility toward the peoples of the region.

3. Minimize the superiority of Western imperialism in biblical scholarships

The experiences of the peoples of Southeast Asia during the colonial period cannot be undermined as part of the grown-up experience of the Church, and, therefore, must constitute the "pre-understanding" of the reader when approaching the text, the Bible. The normative mode of reading stories such as the conquest of the promised land will remind indigenous listeners of their experience with Western conquest. As Jonathan Rigg points out, the experience of being colonized is still a relatively newly recovered wound in the living experience of the peoples of Southeast Asia.[25] Thus, the reading of the legitimation of Yahweh's call for conquest needs to be dealt with care.

4. Avoid promoting biblical interpretations that are alien to indigenous living experience

The establishment of a single, monotheistic nation-state after the exodus is going to pose a problem for the peoples of Southeast Asia whose societies are characterized by multiculturalism, multi-racialism, multiple religions, and a highly pluralistic environment that demands a high degree of sensitivity to the "Other." Interfaith dialogue seems unavoidable, and Yahweh as the conqueror and warrior, as well as stories of land disputes, are issues pertinent to the interpreters in Southeast Asia. Since colonization is their common experience, except in Thailand, I would suggest that postcolonial discourse may very well be one of the most demanding modes of interpretation, and postcolonialism the hermeneutical ideology of the readers of the Bible.

5. Be sensitive to biblical interpretations that challenge cultural tradition

Filial piety is a highly respected virtue in most of the societies of the Southeast Asian peoples; obedience to the elderly and the respect of tradition is observed in most communities. The challenges of Jesus and Paul to the Jewish traditions will be questioned by the peoples of Southeast Asia if contextualizing the gospel is to be put into practice. Modes of Bible reading, if not done with sensitivity to the traditional culture of the peoples of Southeast Asia, will be resisted as an unwelcome faith.

6. Promote biblical interpretations that enhance indigenous theological education

The Asia Theological Association (ATA) and the Association of Theological Education in South East Asia (ATESEA) are the two major players in institutionalizing the theological education enterprise. "Train Asians in Asia" is one of the slogans of the ATA. Some form of dialogue between biblical scholars of the East and the West of different races, cultures, and faiths is an added advantage in promoting a better understanding of biblical interpretation within a global relationship.

Conclusion

Biblical interpretation in the Southeast Asian context has a long way to go in fulfilling its task and purpose. The differences instituted within the identities and cultures of people in the region will continue to pose a threat and challenge to biblical interpreters who are conscious of their postmodern self and subjectivity. The difficulties that are inherited within the highly diversified region and the scarcity of the Christian communities within the population, as well as the relatively small percentage of Bible readers–trained and untrained–in the Southeast Asian contexts, will continue to haunt and hamper serious biblical scholars in the region and abroad. Differences and difficulties existed not only as external phenomena–that is, East and West, Asian and non-Asian–they were also revealed from within as an internal factor that would determine or deconstruct the present course of interpretive direction, though it remains with the biblical interpreters to chart their own course at their own cost.

5

Reading the Bible as an Asian American

Issues in Asian American Biblical Interpretation

ANDREW YUEKING LEE

Oversea Chinese Mission

New York, New York

In addressing the question of what constitutes Asian American interpretation of the Bible,[1] one needs to acknowledge that Asian Americans live in at least a bicultural state and operate within a dynamic cultural continuum. On one end are those who live as though they are culturally still in their homeland clinging to their native languages, customs, and mores. On the other extreme are those who live thoroughly Americanized lives by embracing Western values totally while just as thoroughly rejecting explicit expressions of their ethnic heritage. Most Asian Americans can be located somewhere between these two poles in a dynamic continuum.[2] Thus to speak of Asian American biblical interpretation suggests a hermeneutic rooted in an ethnic theology that is neither purely Western nor purely Asian in orientation, but a synthesis of these two modes of thinking.

Yoshinobu Kumazawa has proposed that Asian American theology is a type of liberation theology. Of the three types of liberation theology, one stresses freedom from sociopolitical and colonial oppression; a second, freedom from ethnic and racist enslavement; the third, freedom from gender-based male dominance. An Asian American theology would identify closely with the second type of liberation, arising from those living in the

United States who are ethnically Asian in origin but culturally American via the process of acculturation.[3] The question of Asian American interpretation, then, focuses our attention on the issue of culture and its role in the formulation of theology. Thus, this essay addresses some of the primary issues that impinge on Asian American interpretation of the Bible.

Issues in Asian American Biblical Interpretation

1. Marginality and Liminality

Foremost is the concept of marginality[4] and how that has influenced the Asian American psyche. Because Asian Americans have experienced, at times bitterly, what it means to be marginal, their theology must incorporate this element to be true to themselves. This would mean identifying not with those at the center but with those on the margins of society.

An Asian American culturally lives between the worlds of Asia and America, fully belonging to neither. Clearly a common component of the ethnic experience is that of liminality.[5] They are caught between two worlds while finding nonacceptance by the dominant group.[6] Such experiences provide raw material from which theology is constructed.

For Asian Americans, liminal experiences normally begin at an early age. While the native language is spoken at home, the immigrant child is under pressure from home and school to learn English, the language of his or her new homeland (designated as L_2 in contradistinction from primary language L_1). One study concludes that it takes at least five years for a child to reach what is considered grade norm. Until this level of proficiency is reached, the child experiences feelings of self-consciousness and inferiority.[7]

In the process of language acquisition, however, L_2 takes the place of L_1 as the dominant language. It is especially difficult in the case of an East Asian language (with its unique orthography and literary tradition) for an immigrant child to retain the same level of fluency while becoming bilingual. L_1 becomes weakened or even lost.[8]

Where there is English proficiency, adeptness in American culture usually follows. Language acquisition opens the doors for increased assimilation and acculturation. Exposure to the media is facilitated; television, movies, radio, books, and magazines expose the immigrant child to Western customs and thinking.

Despite their best efforts to become integrated, however, there will always be reminders that they are not Western. While accommodation to lifestyles and values is pursued, total assimilation does not come about due to persistent racism.[9] For the more the marginal people attempt to move to the center, the more they will feel marginalized by the dominant group.[10]

But rather than viewing liminality as a negative factor, it can become the doorway to new approaches in theological thinking, for it is this in-betweenness within two or more worlds that creates the possibility for something new. Instead of regarding liminality as a situation in which a marginal person belongs to no world, marginality can be seen as being between worlds and in both these worlds! As marginality is defined as not being at the center of particular worlds, it simultaneously conveys that the marginalized person is yet part of those worlds, even if only at their edges. This in-betweenness leads to the creation of something new that can be complementary to the dominant groups.[11]

Experience in dealing with multiple worlds and cultures would seem to place Asian Americans and other bicultural Americans in a unique position to "read against the grain" when it comes to biblical interpretation.[12] Instead of embracing completely the theological presuppositions dominant in Western thought, an Asian American may address the same problems and arrive at a different reading.

When the apostles are confronted with the problem between the Hebrews and the Hellenists over the care of the widows in Acts 6, they arrive at a unique solution to ensure equity for both sides. One may read this passage as a struggle between the centrists and the marginal, the former as represented by the Hebrews, the latter by the Hellenists. It is *because* the twelve are marginal people themselves that they readily identify with the plight of the overlooked Hellenists and come to their rescue. Had they been firmly entrenched as centrists, they might not have so quickly recognized the cause of the Hellenistic Hebrews or granted them much attention at all.

Furthermore, the decision of the twelve served to empower the Greek-speaking elements of the church. The next step was to open the door to the Gentiles, and the last was to facilitate the passage of the gospel to the world. The mission of the Spirit "is not so much to create the structures and procedures by which the church must live forever, but rather to break open structures so that the church may be obedient as it faces each new challenge."[13] This same Spirit is present for each generation as it seeks to hear the Spirit's voice in a new way. The marginal reader finds affirmation in identifying with the underclass in biblical narratives and teachings. This approach may also yield new insights into the dynamics of these situations when viewed from a marginal perspective rather than from a centrist position.

2. Inclusiveness

The duality of Asian American life is another component that needs to be taken into account. The ambiguity of living in two worlds and making sense out of each of them means that life is filled with tension. At times it becomes a balancing act as two different worldviews are juggled to form a coherent whole. These diverse perspectives are juxtaposed into a complementary pattern. Similarly, an Asian American theology can find meaning in seemingly contrary positions.

A precedent for this practice can be found in the concept of yin-yang, which is prevalent in all schools of philosophy in China and is indigenous to East Asian civilization.[14] In yin-yang, the basic forces of life are bound together in tension, yet in the unity of the Tao.[15] Yin is fulfilled by yang and yang by yin. It is not a conflict between two sources but a complementary dualism within relationships.[16]

Yin-yang thinks in categories of "both/and" as opposed to the Western model of "either/or." The former is inclusive in nature while the latter is exclusive.[17] By thinking in either/or terms, a person may make absolute distinctions where none exist, leading to alienation.[18]

The apostle Paul is an example of biculturalism in action. On the one hand, his directives in 1 Corinthians make it clear that he considers circumcision to be nothing (7:19). He allows freedom to eat idol meat that has been sold in the marketplace (10:25). Both of these positions are scandalous to the orthodox Hebrew.

On the other hand, he upholds traditional Jewish teaching by forbidding idolatry (10:14), by condemning sexually immoral practices (5:1-7), and by insisting that women's heads be neither uncovered nor shaven (11:5-6). He sums up his position succinctly as one who is both under the law *and* outside the law because he is under Christ's law (9:20-21); he has become all things to all people (v. 22). Therefore, in the same breath he can permit women to pray and to prophesy in joint worship with men, yet insist that they do so with heads covered (11:5).

Living and moving about within several cultures, he displays the ability to reconcile theologically and ethically conflicting stances. Paul's biculturalism accords him a new freedom in which to minister to both worlds rather than having to make a rigid choice of one over the other.

3. Suffering and Sacrifice

Life lived on the marginal edges of society as part of the underclass necessarily entails rejection and distress. As mentioned above, part of the heritage of the Asian American includes a common sense of suffering and pain as a result of racism in the United States. This experience, which at times can be bitter, unites and creates a new community in its place among Asian Americans.[19]

This problem is not relegated to the lower or middle class, but may even appear in a modified form among the well-to-do. Taiwanese children from upper-class families may live with either the mother alone or with surrogate families in the United States while one or both parents return to Asia to seek their fortune. The children may be reunited with their parents during summer vacation, but long absences are not uncommon, leading to emotional separation and pain.

The more common immigrant experience is financial and material deprivation to a degree not experienced by the typical middle-class American family. The consequent economic suffering and sacrifice required for the family to survive enables the Asian American (especially the first generation, less so in the second generation) to understand what sacrifice means.

Such common experiences of racial and economic suffering while growing up in the United States should sensitize the Asian American to identify with the Suffering Servant of Isaiah and the paschal lamb of God. Other passages that call the true disciple to lay down one's life and take up one's cross daily for a higher cause (Lk. 9:23–25) or to look beyond one's own interests to the interests of others (Phil. 2:4) should resonate with those who have undergone affliction themselves.

4. Pilgrimage Versus Materialism

According to the theologian Sang Hyun Lee, one of the symbols that will help Asian American churches to cope with the suffering caused by marginality is that of pilgrimage. Pilgrimage refers to the state of change whereby one leaves the familiar to sojourn to a place that is not one's true homeland. As Asian Americans will never be able to enter fully into American society the way that a European immigrant can, this should help them to comprehend the transient nature of their time on earth. The concept of biblical pilgrimage should call them to a heavenly home and to the church as "the home for the homeless."[20] This was true for the marginalized Christians of Asia Minor in the setting of 1 Peter, and it is true today.[21]

In reality, once Asian Americans have "made it" in society, they are inclined to forget their roots. For the most part, they flee to their middle-class neighborhoods and become preoccupied with raising their middle-class families. Second- and third-generation Asian Americans in particular have tended to forget that they are pilgrims and have made this country their homeland in more ways than one. In the process of setting down their stakes in the United States, it seems that they have acquired the desires and dreams of middle-class America. That, in turn, has shaped their values and theology. Rather than empathizing with the plight of other Asian Americans who are still struggling, some undergoing the same sets of problems they themselves encountered growing up, many have neglected the task of being role models, encouragers, and helpers in the pilgrimage of faith.

Asian Americans on the whole ignore the social ills around them. Preoccupied with economic success and upward social mobility, they seemingly forget that the presence of Christ is found among the poor (Mt. 25:40).[22] As reported by the *Chronicle of Higher Education,* an unusually high concentration of Asian Americans can be found in health care, the physical sciences, and computers. Relatively few can be found in the humanities, arts, and social sciences.[23] In his examination of the Asian American presence in evangelical organizations on college campuses, Rudy Busto presents this opinion: "My suspicion is that campus Christian organizations, besides offering a supportive and familial structure for Asian

American students, reinforces an upwardly mobile middle-class ethic consonant with the model minority image."[24] These students feel pressured to conform to the image of success.

5. Corporate Versus Individual Thinking

Whereas Descartes' well-known statement, "I think, therefore I am," reflects Western anthropology, Asian cosmology focuses on the individual as a part of the universe, "therefore I think and feel who I am."[25] Whereas in Eastern philosophy the self merges with nature, the empirical ego objectively standing in an "I-Thou" relationship dominates Western thought. In the West, one cannot conceive of consciousness without an ego.[26]

To the Asian mind, staying together and working together constitutes harmonious living. In the Korean language "I" and "we" (*Oori*) are synonymous. To speak of "I" is to speak of "we." "My" car is "our" car, "my" home is "our" home.[27]

The Chinese view things as relative. Thus, one is part of a group built upon mutual interdependence versus the rugged individualism that has been a foundation of American history. The individualistic competitive and creative fires of America that have pushed and shaped this country are not emphasized in Asian culture because of its self-interest. It is more important that there be harmonious relationships among all. Duty and obligation are more valued than self-gratification.[28]

Within the United States, there is clearly a faith that is expressed by the pronoun "I" rather than "we." Personal meetings, personal needs, personal preferences in the selection of small groups dominate the spiritual landscape. Social and political concerns are pushed into the background.[29] This type of thinking has certainly infiltrated Asian American interpretation where the needs of an individual or a specific interest group are a matter of deep concern.

Despite this, Asian Americans are still more inclined to develop an identity that has communal versus individual roots according to Fumitaka Matsuoka.[30] They can lead the way in the areas of community, engagement, and dependence within a western setting, as opposed to the American emphasis on competitiveness, uninvolvement, and rugged individualism.[31]

Biblical passages that address the element of life together, especially in regard to the family, would be in harmony with traditional Asian teaching. The immigrant parents of the second generation Asian Americans have sacrificed much for their children. Educated parents have left positions of standing in their homeland to journey to the United States for the sake of their children's future. For some this has meant much added hardship for them to relocate and labor in lesser occupations for the sake of the family. The better life the second-generation children have is a direct result of the efforts of their parents. The parents take pride in the accomplishments of their children whether they verbalize it to them or not.

Thus, the Asian American appreciates how families are interdependent even if language and cultural differences impose some barriers. The stoning of Achan's family (Josh. 7) is a negative example of the principle of corporate personality in operation, yet comprehensible to the Asian American mind. More appealing would be exhortations about family relationships (Prov. 4:1–4; Eph. 5:21–6:4). The peculiar bilingual and bicultural situation of many Asian American churches readily lends itself as an embodiment of the principles Paul enunciates regarding unity in the midst of diversity (1 Cor. 12). Harmony is espoused as all segments work together for the corporate good. Whether these principles are understood and applied in the multicultural church is another story, however.

6. Law Versus Grace

According to one sociological study, Korean American youth have very high expectations. They desire a happy family life; they want to make their parents proud of them; they wish for important accomplishments in life that will make them feel good about themselves; they aspire to respected schools so that they can go on to prestigious careers; and they are concerned for the larger society and world.

The perception is that these findings are true not only for Korean Americans but also for Japanese Americans and Chinese Americans as well. Most significantly, the study determines that these aspirations may have much to do with parental influence, for the expectations expressed are identical with the desires of the parents for their children. These same youth also verbalized the belief that their parents place unreasonably high expectations on them to fulfill.[32]

The high expectations placed on Asian American children to prosper and to become the "model minority" have been a significant force in pushing them toward their success. Undoubtedly these immigrant parents (some high achievers in their own right) have sacrificed much and expect results for their efforts. In addition, the traditional Asian expectations placed on children to be dutiful to country, family, and society may be present in the immigrant family though not reinforced to the same degree as in the home country.

The concept of *face,* of representing self and family well to the outside world, means that there are certain values to be cherished and a code of moral conduct to be followed. The second generation is expected to conform to norms so that family is not shamed by their behavior. There are accomplishments to be earned so that the family name is honored.[33]

It is to be expected that the scarcity of objective societal values in the postmodern world has eroded the sense of obligation in the present generation when compared to previous ones. Nevertheless, Young Pai's study cited above confirms the continuing influence of parental expectations on the behavior of Asian American children.

Is the implication, then, that Asian Americans have a better comprehension of obligation and obedience to duty? Are they able to relate better to codes of conduct such as the *Haustafeln* (Col. 3:18–4:1; Eph. 5:21–6:9) than the typical American because they are more comfortable with norms of conduct? And if they are driven by a demand for accomplishments, might not they also *need* a word of grace? If immigrant children feel that their parents place on them unreasonable expectations to achieve, the requirements of the "law" must be balanced by the grace of the God who forgives and unconditionally loves. The appeal of the gospel lies in a God who accepts us, irrespective of a person's accomplishments.[34]

Current Practice in Asian American Biblical Interpretation

In recent years the world of academia has discovered Asian American interpretation to be fertile ground.[35] However, this is not the case in the realm of contemporary church practice. When Asian American Christian leaders were asked to define what an Asian American theology meant to them, many were unable to do so with much clarity, having given little thought to this matter. Others expressed the view that an Asian American reading was unnecessary; what was important was interpreting the scriptures "biblically." In their minds, there was a normative approach to scriptures that was over and above culture.[36]

One factor that has been suggested for the lack of interest in an Asian American interpretation is that the passiveness and submissiveness to authority characteristic of Asian culture, coupled with American racism, hastened an easy transition to obey the dominant institutions in this country.[37] In confronting injustice, for example, Japanese Americans have at times resorted to the tactic of accommodation, which is similar to the actions of a small stream. When faced with obstacles in its path, the stream goes around them and follows their contours, avoiding direct confrontation. When confronted with hurdles, Japanese Americans sometimes follow the path of least resistance.[38] With some Japanese Americans submitting and adapting to the political, social, and cultural forces ruling over them, it has been said that if you scratch a Japanese American you will find a white Anglo-Saxon Protestant underneath.[39] Such a stereotype has led to the perception of Japanese Americans as among the most Americanized Asian groups.[40]

Many Asian Americans can be depicted as being Americanized. As the model minority they mirror the aspirations, lifestyles, and habits–as well as the income–of the middle class. Theologically, they identify so closely with middle-class evangelical Christianity that their ethnicity becomes secondary.[41]

The perception is that Asian Americans are overrepresented among evangelical parachurch organizations on college campuses. Sixty-five percent of the 300-student-member InterVarsity College Fellowship chapter at the University of California, Berkeley, in 1991 were Asian Americans. At the InterVarsity missions conference Urbana '93 demographic analysis revealed that Asian Americans constituted 25 percent of the attendees.[42] Moreover, various Asian American evangelical Web sites on the Internet emphasize an evangelical identity that is devoid of race.[43]

Thus, Asian Americans seem to have found a home in evangelical Christianity while neglecting their distinctive history and outlook on life. This approach, as typified by writer Ada Lum, is that "God is far more interested in what is happening to us inside. Are we becoming more like Jesus Christ his Son? That is what counts in the end (Rom. 8:29)."[44] Lum's statement conveys the belief that reflection on the distinctiveness of an Asian American perspective is unnecessary and that culture is both secondary and constitutive of a fallen and sinful world. Those who share this perspective have assimilated the particular cultural interpretations of scripture promoted in certain evangelical churches, seminaries, and books–views that are traditionally Western in orientation.[45]

Even those who attend an Asian church are unlikely to perceive scripture from an Asian American perspective. Christian missionaries have had a long history of outreach in Asia. For the most part, these missionaries brought with them a conservative brand of Christianity: "Modern evangelicalism, in fact, arises out of the muscular Victorian Protestantism that accompanied American imperialism to Asia at the turn of the century."[46]

The appeal of evangelical theology to Asian Americans may be a result of shared values such as family, work, and education.[47] Even as traditional Asian culture emphasizes obedience to the family, diligent work, and advancement through education, conservative theology likewise stresses these values. It would seem that culture has played a significant role in the appeal of evangelical theology to the Asian American Christian, so that for the most part, S.H. Lee's concept of pilgrimage has not struck a responsive chord. The question of an Asian American identity is still being defined.

Even as Asian American churches struggle to find their rightful place, the challenge Dennis Loo issued thirty years ago still holds true today:

> Asian Americans need to begin the process of developing an interpretation of the Christian faith which encourages self-affirmation and indigenous self-development in Asian churches and communities. It must encourage a critical analysis of ideas, values, customs and structures in America which oppress not only Asians but others as well. It must encourage collective action for changing that oppression. It must also encourage the development of an Asian American frame of reference which can make its own unique contribution to the developing Third World theological dialogue, to the global theological task, and to liberation movements in the United States and in the world.[48]

Unquestionably, progress has been made in recent years in the areas delineated by Loo, with Asian American scholars spearheading these developments. However, if history provides any clue about the future, the prognosis is that it will take many more years before these academic endeavors bear fruit in Asian American church life.

6

Neither Here nor There

Boundary and Identity in the Hagar Story

LAI LING ELIZABETH NGAN

George W. Truett Theological Seminary

Baylor University, Waco, Texas

The term "Asian American" is used to classify an extremely ethnically diverse group of people. It signifies persons of Asian heritage who identify themselves as Americans. Whether they are of the first or fourth generation in the United States, they have settled and negotiated their way into the dominant American culture. They are at home with American English and the American way of life. Even though the continent of Asia includes the Middle East, the countries of Central Asia and a large part of Russia, the term "Asian American" is mostly applied to persons whose ethnic origins are from South Asia, East Asia, and Southeast Asia. They are thus identified based on outward markers such as skin color, facial features, and physical stature. Asian Americans share many of the physical features of their forebears, but Asian American culture and values have more in common with the West than the East. The ideal that many Asian Americans aspire to is an ability to realize the best of both cultures and forge a wider path that incorporates both worlds.

Our Asian forebears have been doing Asian hermeneutics for many decades, but much of the printed resources and results have been unavailable and unnoticed due to language barriers and the failure of American theological libraries to acquire journals from Asia. Asian journals and hermeneutical methods are still deemed as inferior by many scholars in the West. Furthermore, the geographical and cultural distance has posed a formidable challenge to creating and maintaining dialogue between Asian and Asian American biblical interpreters. Despite such distance, the availability of resources has been improving steadily and the field has witnessed the increase of intentional conversation between the various groups. The number of international congresses that biblical scholars have convened in Asia in the last few years evidences the hope of more dialogue and cooperation.[1]

Both Asian and Asian American biblical hermeneutics are highly contextual. Asian Americans interpretation is largely shaped by the social, historical, political, and economic realities in which Asian Americans live in the United States. What may be most notable in Asian American hermeneutics is the centrality of the Bible. Asian American Christians tend to hold a very high view of the Bible, regarding it as the word of God that guides Christian faith and practice. Christians represent a higher percentage of Asian Americans than of Asians; exceptions include Korea, which has a very high percentage of Christians. Perhaps the high ratio of Asian American Christians is because the dominant religion in the United States is Christianity. Another possible explanation may be rooted in the church's role as a haven for the cultivation and survival of ethnic identity, especially in circumstances in which ethnic minority communities fear the erosion of such identity. For Asian American Christians, the Bible is both a resource for learning how to live and a source of identity and self-understanding.[2]

Most Asian American biblical scholars have been trained in European and North American institutions of higher education and in historical-critical methodologies. Like many Western-trained interpreters, they have put an eclectic group of methods in service to Asian American hermeneutics. The goal of interpretation has been not only to understand the text in its cultural and historical contexts, but to derive from it its meaning for the present. Since there is no purely objective reading of a text, such readings begin with the presumption that the interpreter's social location and experience will affect the questions and issues that she or he chooses to explore. An unavoidable hermeneutical lens through which one reads the scriptures is one's racial and ethnic identity.

For an Americanized Asian woman living in a predominantly white section of the United States where my ethnic difference is obvious, the questions I ask reflect my concern for ethnic identity, power, and voice. Will my difference cast me as a "foreigner" forever? Do I have the same access to power structures afforded others in the dominant society? Will I be encouraged or allowed to have my own voice? Since the Bible is so vital in informing my self-understanding, with whom can I identify in scripture? Which characters does the narrator cast as "others"? How does their difference affect their access to power and their ability to have a voice? Does the text allow only negative assessment of their presence in the stories or can it be read differently and in a positive light? Which characters and their encounters with God give hope and direction to ethnic/racial minority persons, such as an Asian American woman in my present social location? These are questions that are at the forefront of my hermeneutic approach.

Marking Differences

For much of the twentieth century, persons who were not white, black, or Hispanic were classified as "others" in U.S. demographic data. The civil rights movement called attention to the equal rights of all races, which are now recognized by law. The addition of the category of "Asian" or "Asian American" in the past few U.S. censuses represents an improved awareness of the existence of large groups of persons whose ethnic origins can be traced to parts of East and South Asia. Whether the application of these labels is an advantage or a liability depends on their usage and the persons using them. The labels can conjure up stereotypes that lump all Asians together, stereotypes that are neither characteristic of nor applicable to all Asians/Asian Americans.

To take notice of someone's ethnic identity is to distinguish a person from others, identify a person by her or his features, or prejudge a person's abilities or worth. Human beings draw lines and set boundaries continuously, but the lines that are drawn and the meanings that are given to them are socially formed and informed. They are social-mental constructs that we share in common with others who belong to our cognitive communities. Eviator Zerubavel reminds us that "the way most of us happen to process the world in our minds is neither naturally nor logically inevitable."[3] As social beings we learn where to draw lines and set boundaries through the process of cognitive socialization.[4] Lines and boundaries divide insiders from outsiders and make some things visible and others invisible. Drawing lines, however, is not a value free exercise in classification; every choice has social, political, economic, material, and ethical/moral ramifications. Visibility as an Asian American in a predominately white community can be an advantage or a disadvantage. The social dynamics may not afford equity in all things, but for those who are marked as different and as "others," their response to the social reality plays a significant role in determining their direction and well-being.

Marking differences is not limited to the dominant group that labels minority groups; such labeling also takes place within Asian and Asian American communities. Newly arrived Asian immigrants are called, often with a hint of disrespect, FOBs, or "Fresh-off-the-boat," while Asian Americans who have fully acculturated are called, with equal disdain, "bananas," that is, yellow on the outside, white on the inside. It is not uncommon for Chinese elders to call younger Chinese Americans, "bamboo sticks," to taunt them as incapable of communicating effectively either in Chinese or American English, or of understanding either culture. Asian

Americans are still negotiating their place in their respective communities and in the wider society at large. Since the marking of boundaries and ethnicity is socially constructed, Asian Americans must ask if these boundary markers are valid and whether lines should be drawn differently.

Asian American women have little difficulty identifying with Hagar in the book of Genesis. She is a woman relegated to an inferior social status with an ethnicity that is different from the dominant characters in the story. She is an Egyptian in a story world focused on Israelite ancestry. The narrator has marked her as "other." Because of the issues of ethnic identity, power imbalance, self-understanding, and empowerment that are embedded in the text, the story of Hagar is a good text for practicing Asian American hermeneutics.

Reading Hagar's Story

And Sarai, wife of Abram, she bore no children to him. To her, (she has) an Egyptian maid and her name is Hagar. And Sarai said to Abram, "Look, please, YHWH has restrained me from bearing children. Go in, please, to my maid. Perhaps I will be built up from her." And Abram heard the voice of Sarai. And Sarai, wife of Abram, took Hagar the Egyptian, her maid, at the end of ten years; Abram lived in the land of Canaan. And she gave her to Abram her husband, to him as a wife. (Gen. 16:1–3)[5]

Over the past three decades, literary critics such as Robert Alter, Adele Berlin, and Meir Sternberg have heightened our appreciation for the narrative artistry of the Hebrew Bible.[6] We have learned to read the text closely, acknowledge the brevity and high degree of selectivity in the storytelling, note the many gaps in the text and the ambiguities that such gaps produce, as well as attend to the signification that repetitions, actions, and dialogues may imply. A reading of the three brief verses of Genesis 16:1–3, therefore, can raise a plethora of questions as to what that text tells/says, what it may mean, and what may be inferred about the three human characters and their relationship with one another and with God.

The Sarah-Hagar cycle in Genesis 16 and 21 is, no doubt, about the struggle of these two women for their social standing in Abraham's household. Their story is about a domestic quarrel between women and struggle between persons with unequal access to power. But other issues are also embedded in this story. Out of their historical and cultural experiences, African American scholars have examined the Sarah-Hagar cycle from the perspective of slavery, while African scholars have noted the underlying issue of polygamy. From an ethnic minority perspective, what is also hidden in plain sight is the issue of race and ethnicity. By highlighting Hagar's ethnicity and keeping silent on that of Sarah and Abraham, the storyteller has set the masters' ethnicity as the norm.

Sarah and Hagar do not merely represent themselves; they also represent their respective people groups. This representation is especially significant for Hagar, since she is noted repeatedly as an Egyptian. Such notice is more than a reference to her place of birth or ethnicity. F.V. Greifenhagen states that the name Egypt "functions more as a multivalent metaphor or symbol in which the geographic or ethnographic referent is overdetermined by the values or ideology of the producers of the document."[7]

As the conspicuous outsider in the story, her Egyptian identity marks her as belonging to a people who oppressed the Israelites in the land of bondage and slavery. The Israelites' suffering in and deliverance from Egypt are commemorated at the Passover Seder so that they will not forget the repeated call to be a people separated unto YHWH. They are not to be like the people around them; this injunction certainly included the Egyptians. The historical review in the Pentateuch warns against the temptation of longing for the comfort and security of Egypt. Yearning for Egypt brings judgment and death (Num. 11:4–6, 18–20). Can anything good come out of Egypt? Hagar's ethnic identity has become for her a liability.

Like all stories, the Hagar-Sarah cycle was told from a particular perspective and heard or read in particular social locations. How would an ancient audience have heard the Sarah-Hagar story? This is the first question that this essay seeks to address. Traditional biblical interpretation, following the story's narrative point of view, has usually cast a negative light on Hagar. When readers take the text of Genesis 16 at face value, Hagar is often criticized for her unbecoming attitude toward Sarah when she becomes pregnant. Not only is Hagar's son a threat to the future legitimate heir of the promise, she oversteps the acceptable bounds of her social position as Sarah's maid. Sarah is cast as the heroine and Hagar the villainess. With "Egypt" serving as a multivalent metaphor, how might Hagar's ethnicity as an Egyptian be perceived by competing groups in the postexilic Judahite community from which much of the Pentateuch was produced?

Another concern of this paper is how to read Hagar's story today from the social location of an Americanized Asian woman. Just as Hagar does not get to identify herself as an Egyptian but is thus identified from the dominant perspective of the storyteller whose own ethnicity serves as the norm in the story, Asian Americans, whether females or males, are often identified as the "other" by the dominant society of America. Some consider us as forever "foreigners." The label of "other" is used to lump together diverse ethnic groups who are neither white, African American, nor Latino. Even the labels of African American, Latino, and Asian are problematic because the diversity within each grouping is wide beyond description. Not all blacks are descendants of slaves, not all Latinos are Mexicans, and not all Asians are Chinese. These labels too often carry with them negative connotations that are used callously and prejudicially. Ethnic minorities are just as guilty of misusing these descriptive labels as whites. Ethnic descriptions are exactly that, descriptions of ethnic origins. They ought not to serve as the basis for judging a person's dignity or worth.

Since every human being is created in the image of God and should be deemed a person of worth, Hagar is also a person of dignity and worth. Her story should be told with this in mind. It seems appropriate, therefore, to read her story *with* her, while resisting the negative framing of the storyteller. The intention of this paper is not to create Hagar *ex nihilo*, but to recover her story from the text. Using literary critical and social scientific approaches such as cognitive sociology, this paper will seek to reclaim the dignity and worth of Hagar, who is castigated as an "other."

Telling Hagar's Story *in situ*

The story of Hagar is recounted primarily in Genesis 16 and 21, which source critics have identified as Yahwistic and Elohistic, respectively. These designations placed the formation of both accounts of the Hagar story in the first half of the Israelite monarchy. Recent studies which emphasize the social function of the final form of the Hebrew Bible, however, tend to place the formation of the various corpora of the Hebrew Bible at a much later period in Israel's history. The proposals focus on the Babylonian Exile and the Achaemenid period as the most probable time frame for the production of the final form of Deuteronomy/Deuteronomistic History and the Pentateuch.[8]

The Babylonian Exile was certainly a period of crisis and ferment. John Bright considered this the watershed event in the history of ancient Israel.[9] The trauma of destruction and displacement affected every level of life, from the national to the provincial to the individual. The monarchy, the temple, and family units were destroyed, along with individual hopes and aspirations. The humiliation and devastation of national defeat struck deep in every life.

The crisis of the exile, nevertheless, proffered both death and life. It disturbed long-established social norms and structures, and allowed space for the evaluation and reshaping of Jewish life. New leadership occupied former power domains, new behavioral patterns replaced established ones, and new customs and values were adopted and created for new situations. The power of Babylon, however, was not the only locus of contention as the exiled Israelites found themselves as one group among many displaced peoples gathered from across the empire, trying to reconstitute life in the shadow of Babylon. They faced simultaneous contestation from groups competing for a place in the new world order from without and within. Their identity and survival as a distinctive people were at stake. Resistance to admixture and redefinition of membership were paramount to group survival. The need for clarifying group boundaries was a major impetus in the production of portions of the Hebrew Bible, the texts that informed the Israelites of their ethnic history and religious tradition.

The Achaemenid period provided similar conditions for the production and preservation of sacred and "historical" texts. The Jews from the exilic period, who, by and large, survived the assault of absorption and resisted assimilation into the Babylonian Empire, continued on as a distinct ethnic group under Persian rule.[10] Those who had assimilated quiescently lost their Jewish identity; they had, in effect, become Babylonians, and perhaps with further assimilation during the Achaemenid reign, they would become Persians. The Achaemenid rulers, however, did not pursue a homogenizing policy, but encouraged the coexistence of multiethnic groups in the empire. With imperial blessing, the Jews, as with other ethnic groups who were settled in Babylon by their former overlord, were permitted to go back to their homeland. The Edict of Cyrus encouraged the exiled peoples to relocate, resettle, and rebuild temples and shrines with the cooperation and assistance of the local residents (Ezra 1:2–4).

Whatever the imperial intentions may have been, the Jewish returnees found themselves facing similar issues as exiled Jews of a previous generation. They were one group among many in a new land, albeit, in the province of Judah. Although the fame of Judah may have been made legendary through prophetic proclamation and traditional tales, it was, nevertheless, an unfamiliar land. It was not the garden of Eden that the prophets had promised (Ezek. 36:35; Isa. 55:12–13), but a land requiring much toil and struggles for its yield (Hag. 1:2–11). To make matters worse, the returnees could only "reclaim" occupied land by displacing others who made similar land claims as they did. Different groups were competing for the same limited resources. The resultant conflicts over land claim went hand in hand with insistence on ethnic distinctiveness. This insistence bolstered one's right to repatriation. It was not merely nurtured by religious or ideological ideals, but infused with strong political and economic overtones.

In an environment in which ethnic identity determines not only group membership and the right to land and livelihood, but also community solidarity and mutual support, to identify someone as belonging to a different ethnic group has significant implications. Not only does it label that person as "not one of us," but her or his "otherness" invokes fear and suspicion. The response to the interjection of the "other" varies, depending on the individual and the group, and can lie anywhere along a continuum of welcoming inclusion or uncompromising exclusion.

The books of Ezra and Nehemiah give clear examples of an exclusionary policy. In spite of a royal decree calling for the cooperation of returnees and settled residents in their rebuilding efforts (Ezra 1:2–4), the Judahite returnees under the leadership of Zerubbabel, Ezra, and Nehemiah blocked local participation by people identified as ethnic "others." The exclusion of alien groups may have been justifiable, but it engendered hostile feelings among the local folk (Ezra 4:1–23). Furthermore, since Jewish ethnic boundary in fifth-century B.C.E. Judah was defined primarily along supposedly pure bloodline, marriage with women of other ethnic descent was perceived as polluting the "holy seed" of the reconstituted Judahite community (Ezra 9:2). The solution proposed by the leadership was the separation from anything and anyone deemed "foreign," including the "sending away" of "foreign" wives and children contaminated by such marriages (Ezra 10:3, 11; Neh. 13:3, 23–30).

The call for separation from other ethnic groups, especially women among alien groups, finds full support in the book of Deuteronomy. The obedience to the law extends to the annihilation of the indigenous Canaanite population in order to avoid any cultural and religious contamination by them (Deut. 7:1–6, 16); this is exemplified in the book of Joshua by the *herem* declared on Jericho and Hazor.

If Deuteronomy sets up the ideal prototype for defining Israel's boundaries as the people of YHWH, and the Deuteronomistic History serves as its supporting document, the latter corpus can nevertheless be read as a text of resistance. The book of Joshua shows that full obedience to the *torah* is not so simply and easily observed.[11] The call in Deuteronomy 7:16 to "devour all the peoples" is breached as early as Joshua 2 with the sparing of Rahab and her entire family. This is followed immediately with the escape of the Gibeonites from the ban in Joshua 7–8 and the troubling notices that there are Canaanites living among them (Josh. 13:13; 15:63; 16:10; 17:11–13). And although there are plenty of unsavory characters among Israel's resident aliens, such as Doeg the Edomite (1 Sam. 21), there are also plenty of noble foreigners living among them, such as Uriah the Hittite. The line for deciding whom to include and whom to exclude is not so easily drawn.

Nevertheless, the books of Ezra and Nehemiah legislate against admixture with other ethnic groups. Yet, the necessity of such legislation only demonstrates the tenuousness of the exclusion policy in the fifth-century B.C.E. Judahite community. The long list of men who had married "foreign" wives in Ezra 10:18–44 includes families of priests and Levites; these obey Ezra's injunction to "send away" their wives and children. However, two men, Jonathan son of Asahel and Jahzeiah son of Tikvah, are cited as openly opposing Ezra's coercive ruling (Ezra 10:15). The postexilic Judahite community as shown in the books of Ezra and Nehemiah, then, is not a monolithic community in regard to ethnic identity and relations. Some have no trouble incorporating members of other ethnic groups into their own. Still others oppose inclusivity vehemently. It is in just such a multivalent society that the Pentateuch was formed.

The telling of Hagar's story in postexilic Judah would have elicited varied responses. For those who insisted on clear separation from other ethnic groups, Hagar's story would have produced no sympathy for the

Egyptian woman. She is an ominous counterpart to Israel's foremother, Sarah, and her son is a direct threat to the legitimate heir, Isaac, and those of subsequent Israelite descent. For those who welcomed inclusion as a possible social reality, the hearing of Hagar's story would have produced the opposite sentiments. It is with this latter group that I propose to read Hagar's story.

Reading Hagar's Story *with* Hagar

Hagar's story is the story of the "other." She is a person thrice marginalized because of her gender, social status, and ethnicity. As a woman in a patriarchal society, she is automatically deemed inferior in comparison to men. In this regard, Hagar and Sarah share a common predicament. Hagar, however, fares far worse. She is the maid and Sarah is her mistress; she is an Egyptian and Sarah is the foremother of the Israelites.

The text of Genesis 16 does not specify how Hagar came to be Sarah's maid (*shiphchah*) or how long she has been in her mistress' service. As E.A. Speiser notes in his commentary on Genesis, *'ishshah*, which may be traced to its Akkadian root, *ashshatum*, may refer to either "wife" or "concubine."[12] Sarah and Hagar quite clearly occupy contrasting positions and possess unequal status in Abraham's household. Genesis 16:1 and 3 state that Sarah, the *'ishshah*, cannot give children to Abraham, but she can give what belongs to her, her *shiphchah*, Hagar. By giving her maid to Abraham as an *'ishshah*, Sarah has inadvertently raised Hagar's status to nearly her equal.

Perhaps Hagar is one of the maidservants acquired after the fateful encounter with Pharaoh in Genesis 12, for Abraham is said to have been given many *shĕphachoth* on account of Sarah. Genesis 16:3 places the phrase "at the end of ten years" between the notice of Hagar the Egyptian as Sarah's maid and Abraham's residence in the land of Canaan. Does this phrase apply only to Abraham's period of sojourn, as is commonly translated in English versions, or does its placement in the Hebrew Bible imply a dual reference to both Abraham and Hagar? If Hagar has been in Sarah's service for ten years, does the phrase "at the end of ten years" indicate temporally when she was given to Abraham, or does it signify the end of her service as Sarah's maid?

The word *shiphchah* is also used to refer to Bilhah and Zilpah, Rachel and Leah's maids, whom they gave to Jacob as wives (Gen. 30:4, 9). The ethnicity of these maids, however, is not specified in the text. Is this because they are from the same ethnic group as Rachel and Leah? Apparently, their ethnicity is a nonissue in the Jacob-Leah-Rachel story. Why, then, is Hagar's Egyptian ancestry repeatedly noted in Genesis 16 and 21? If Hagar is not the only foreigner in Abraham's household, and probably not the only Egyptian among them, then the reference to her ethnicity is noticeable, as if the narrator wishes to highlight her otherness.

Cain Hope Felder points out that in the Hebrew Bible distinctions between people groups are based not on race, but on national identity and ethnic tribal association: "All who do not meet the criteria for salvation as defined by the ethnic or national 'in-groups' are relegated to an inferior status."[13] Outsiders, including Cushite, Midianite, and Moabite women, Ethiopian eunuchs and Hittite warriors, are always viewed in relation to Israel's God. The Canaanites are considered the ultimate "others" deserving annihilation, but do Egyptians present a particular problem for Israel? What images does "Egypt/Egyptian" conjure up in Israel's historical memory?

No doubt, the proximity of Egypt and Israel/Canaan means that contact and mutual influence are unavoidable. Although Egypt's role as the "Empire that ruled the East"[14] ebbed during the period of the Israelite monarchy, it continued as a major power broker in the region into the Persian period and beyond. As the significant "other" in Israel's historical memory, Egypt is a site of hate and envy. Egypt is the land of their affliction and slavery. Egypt is a land of abhorrent idolatry, of excessive arrogance, of ruthless oppression. Egypt is the land from which YHWH redeemed his people. Egypt is a land of dreaded diseases, diseases that YHWH afflicts only on those who hate Israel (Deut. 7:15). The implied message is that Egypt is not only the "Other," it is *the* cursed enemy.

But Egypt is also Israel's object of envy. Egypt is known for its ease and pleasure of life. It is a land fed by canals directing water from the Nile, a land where weather is predictable, food is plentiful, and savory herbs grow abundantly (Ex. 16:3; Num. 11:5). Egypt is also technologically and militarily superior in many ways. Their horses and chariots are renowned (Isa. 31:1), and their military support is desirable (Isa. 30:1–2). Anthony D. Smith notes that when an ethnic group comes into contact with a culturally and materially superior ethnic group, the significant "outsiders" might become a reference group or a model for the former.[15] Egypt would have been a significant outsider in Israel's historical memory, an object of both envy and of hate.

As an Egyptian, Hagar represents not only herself, but also her people. As a representative of the significant Other, she is the focus of envy and hate in the story. The narrator in Genesis 16 places the blame squarely on Hagar for her misfortunes. When she sees that she is pregnant, her mistress becomes "slight" in her eyes (v. 4). Sarah intends to benefit from Hagar's service, a circumstance to which she is no doubt accustomed, but she is taken aback by her maid's infuriating reaction. It is Hagar's contempt that drives Sarah to extreme measures. It is her arrogance and unbecoming attitude toward her mistress that caused her affliction (v. 6). Sarah is only putting her in her place. Even YHWH's speech justifies Hagar's affliction. He continues to recognize her as Sarah's maid and instructs her to return to suffer under Sarah's maltreatment (Gen. 16:8–9).

The narrator has certainly placed the blame on Hagar, but the question of her contempt deserves further pondering. Has Hagar raised her own status because she has what Sarah wants, a conception? Can her loathing be a result of the betrayal she felt after serving Sarah for ten years as her confidant and companion, then to be cast off so casually as a means of self-gain? Sharon Jeansonne points out that "the word for 'became contemptible' or 'became lightly esteemed' (*kalal*) expresses disdain for human beings when they do something significantly wrong."[16] The text, therefore, may explain why Hagar felt what she felt without stating specifically Sarah's offense.

Neither does the narrator reveal how Hagar's interior perception of her situation is represented in action; but, apparently, she recognizes that as the carrier of Abraham's child she is in a new position. Redefinition of self and redrawing of boundaries are now available to her in the familial and social structures. This new status is not lost on Sarah, who perceives, also correctly, that she is no longer on the same rung of the former power hierarchy. To reassert her own position as the sole wife of Abraham and reclaim her place as Hagar's mistress, Sarah acts to stem the tide; she complains bitterly to Abraham and is granted free rein in dealing with the presumptuous woman. Hagar's first misstep is to desire betterment for herself. Her greatest offense is in disturbing the status quo. Sarah subsequently treats Hagar so harshly that she flees into the wilderness. The reader may wonder if this was the first mistreatment that Sarah has meted out to her maid in her time of service. The harsh treatment is so unbearable that Hagar chooses to risk her life to escape from Sarah. Her flight from Sarah may be a gamble for life, but it could just as well have resulted in death. How ironic that Hagar's first true act of volition is only an act of self-defense. The narrator in Genesis 16 affords her no offensive or other power actions.

The Hagar of Genesis 16 is the subject of only three verbs: Hagar conceives (v. 4), she sees (v. 4), and she flees (v. 6). In each case, she acts and reacts from the underside of the power hierarchy while Sarah acts from above: Sarah takes (v. 3), she gives (v. 3), and she afflicts (v. 6). It is ironic that Hagar's expression of self-will and agency as the subject of verbs is turned so quickly against her. Her greatest sin may have been to take on an active voice. Even reading with the narrator that Sarah has become slight in Hagar's eyes, Hagar's new attitude toward Sarah may be read as a sign of defiance, a character trait that speaks of personal strength, a trait necessary for surviving difficult circumstances. Hagar has come into her own. She will give birth to a son who will also live in defiance and will stand up to all his kin (Gen. 16:12). As John Van Seters points out, the destiny of Ishmael "…will be anything but submissive and his defiance will be her ultimate vindication."[17]

The Hagar of Genesis 21 appears initially as a passive, silent victim who endures Sarah's berating. "Cast out *this* woman and her son, for the son of *this* woman will not inherit with my son, with Isaac" (Gen. 21:10, author's emphasis). Sarah's demand to cast out the mother and son is made in the hearing of Hagar, but not a word of protest is heard from Hagar. In this episode, Abraham's action parallels Sarah's in Genesis 16: Abraham takes, he gives, and he sends away (Gen. 21:14). This time, Hagar has not fled into the wilderness on her own accord. She and Ishmael have been forced out with a small provision of food and water. Her aimless walking and wandering illustrate her lostness and desperation (Gen. 21:14). When the water is gone and their hope of survival likewise dissipates, Hagar set herself resolutely to refuse to watch her son die, "I will not see the death of the child."[18] It is in the face of death that Hagar's strength and resolve are most evident. The Hagar who emerges at the end of the story acts with self-determination: She sees; she walks; she fills and she gives drink; she is the only mother in the Bible who is said to have taken a wife for her son. The turning point in her character in Genesis 21 is her double encounter with death and with YHWH.

The way Sarah and Abraham relate to Hagar is in stark contrast to the way YHWH relates to her. The human masters never speak directly to Hagar or address her by name. She has no voice; she has no name. She is an object that is taken and given without consultation or consent. Her station in life may mean that her destiny is in the hand of others, but in the complex story of Genesis 16 and 21, the lack of signs of compassion and sensitivity on the human level is striking. As the narrator reports, Abraham washes his hands of the entire affair and places Hagar back into Sarah's hands, and Hagar suffers such harsh affliction that she flees into the wilderness. What is a pregnant woman to do to survive in the wilderness? Her escape from Sarah is a step toward death. Yet, although YHWH recognizes Hagar's continued role as Sarah's maid and instructs her to return to her mistress, YHWH's word may be read not as an indictment against Hagar but as a directive for her to choose life over death. Hagar recognizes that she will continue to be Sarah's maid; it is not yet time for her independence. Her return will mean continued hardship under Sarah, but it will also mean survival for her and her son.

The encounter between the messenger of YHWH and Hagar is also striking in other ways. The first reference in the Hebrew Bible to the "messenger of YHWH" occurs in this encounter between God and Hagar (Gen. 16:7). She is the first woman to receive a theophany, and, a foreign woman at that. Genesis 16:7 states that the messenger "found" Hagar, implying an active seeking on YHWH's part. In addition, the first word out of the messenger's mouth is the name "Hagar." Whereas Sarah and Abraham always refer to Hagar as "my maid," "your maid," and in Genesis

21:10, she is referred to as "this slave-woman," YHWH always addresses her by her name, "Hagar."

The instruction to return and submit to Sarah is followed by YHWH's promise to Hagar, a promise similarly made to Abraham, a promise of uncountable offspring (Gen. 16:10). The messenger of YHWH, furthermore, made the first annunciation in the Bible of the birth of a child, Ishmael (Gen. 16:11). He will be a constant reminder that God heard Hagar and understood her affliction. Hagar is so awestruck by this experience that she names YHWH, El-roi, "the God who sees me," and the site of the theophany, Beer-lahai-roi, "the Well of the Living One who sees me" (Gen. 16:13–14). Hagar is the only person in the Hebrew Bible to name God! Not only has God heard her cry, she herself saw God and received promises from God for a hopeful posterity.

An Asian American Christian Reflection on Hagar's Story

In the story world of Genesis 16 and 21, Hagar is an outsider whose social status disallows her equal access to power or recognition under normal circumstances. She is noted as an Egyptian. Her ethnicity is a given that cannot be changed. Even though she had served Sarah for many years and is probably not the only Egyptian in this household, the storyteller highlights her difference. For much of the narrative, she is a passive, voiceless object that is given and taken by those who have power over her. Her life as Sarah's maid is difficult at best. If it were not for the need for Abraham to acquire an heir, her lot in life may have remained the same.

Things do not always remain the same, however. By a twist of fate, or perhaps the providence of God, Hagar finds herself as the mother of Abraham's child. Though this new role has been forced on her, the pregnancy presents an opportunity to elevate her status. More importantly, Hagar recognizes the change that has occurred and asserts herself as Sarah's equal, an assertion that will bring her much hardship and affliction.

How should Hagar have responded to her new realization? Sarah expected her to remain as before, a passive and voiceless object, a role that Hagar will no longer accept. The reality of the pregnancy awakens in Hagar her sense of personhood and dignity. She will no longer be satisfied with just being Sarah's maid. She has come alive to herself and becomes an important part of Abraham's family. She refuses the boundaries others have drawn to delimit her and redefines her own boundaries and identity.

As Asian Americans, we sometimes find ourselves in similar situations as Hagar. Our physical features will mark us as different from the predominantly white society, but it is neither possible nor desirable to blend in as if there is no difference. Our differences should be celebrated, not hidden away. Our superficial differences, however, should not be cause to prejudge another person's worth or dignity, nor should it be used to privilege some and castigate others. As Asian American Christians, we must uphold every person's dignity because every person is created by God and made in the image of God. Likewise, we must resist and reject attempts to denigrate who we are and our rightful place in society. Everyone must be allotted a place under the sun regardless of outward appearance, mental capacity, or physical ability.

What is also noteworthy in Hagar's story is the way God relates to her. God does not despise her because she is an Egyptian or because she is a maid. God's providential care is for her and seeks her out in times of distress. God not only knows her, but always calls her by her name, Hagar. She is a person of worth in God's eyes, and, like Hagar, we are also persons of worth in God's eyes. God knows our names.

Hagar Will No Longer Accept

The story of Hagar provides a lens through which Asian Americans can see themselves and their place in the world. It is like a mirror that can be held up to catch a glimpse of one's reflection. We have much to learn from Hagar. Whether intended by the storyteller or not, the story of Hagar can be read in a positive light. It tells of a woman who redefines the boundaries that others have inscribed for her. Her encounters with God altered her life. She takes what she has and forges a new identity for herself as the mother of a strong, defiant people, and as the ancestress of an offspring that is too numerous to count. Her survival and her countless descendants are her ultimate vindication. From a social perspective that champions inclusion over exclusion and a theological perspective that sees God as caring for the afflicted ones, Hagar stands as a symbol of strength and hope.

7

The *Realpolitik* of Liminality in Josiah's Kingdom and Asian America

URIAH YONG-HWAN KIM
Hartford Seminary
Hartford, Connecticut

The Politics of Interpretation and Identity

The account of Josiah, king of Judah from 640 to 609 B.C.E., in 2 Kings 22–23 in the Hebrew Bible has played an extremely important role in the development of modern biblical scholarship. The discovery of the "book of the law" and the subsequent "reform" in the narrative of Josiah have captured the imagination of several generations of biblical scholars, thereby helping to construct, among many, a discourse on the history of ancient Israel. Since Martin Noth suggested in mid-twentieth century what is known now as the "Deuteronomistic History Hypothesis" to describe the corpus of works from Deuteronomy to 2 Kings as a self-contained history,[1] it has become standard to read the story of Josiah as part of the Deuteronomistic History (henceforth DH). Subsequent to Noth, the only real problem in the scholarship on DH was the choice between following F.M. Cross, who argued for an original pre-exilic edition of DH during the reign of Josiah,[2] and Rudolf Smend, who maintained Noth's position of an original exilic edition but argued for additional editors.[3] These two schools, even with differences, have collaborated in shaping and dictating the discourse on DH as merely a choice between original pre-exilic edition(s) or the exilic edition(s). Their bipartisan rhetoric has dominated the politics of interpretation of DH.

What goes unnoticed in their politics of interpretation is that they have been engaged in politics of identity. One of the more enduring legacies of Noth is the idea that the Deuteronomist (the hypothetical writer of DH) was a historian in the likeness of modern historians, and, thus, DH is understood as history in the likeness of Western history. Although Noth and Cross differ significantly in their views of the function of Josiah in DH, they both collaborate in placing the discussion of Josiah within the discourse of history. But the fact that modern history is a Western project that emerged within the context of the Western imperialism and colonialism that produced two enduring metanarratives–Orientalism and nationalism–is seldom noted in biblical studies.

Modern history, as it developed in Germany in the nineteenth century, and was then exported to the world, served as an instrument of European nationalism. History is no more than an identity discourse of the West. It legitimates the West and not others. In narrating the West's identity through history, it sees the West as the subject of history and other peoples' histories as no more than footnotes in its narrative. Thus, while DH is understood as a historical account of ancient Israel's past (which is problematic in its own right), a prevailing tendency also construes it as the wellspring and touchstone of Western civilization. Such a view imagines DH as a narration of the original model of the nation. The West imitated and fulfilled the model. This tendency, thereby, puts the West as the subject of DH. DH is thus viewed as the first and archetypical Western history. It describes the creation of an all-Israel state in Palestine, as the bringer of proper civilization to the region. This establishes a rightful hegemonic culture before which all must yield as being other, or less than, or, as Homi Bhabha puts it, "unhomely"–not at home in one's own land. An understanding of Josiah and his kingdom that is framed within DH as a history that narrates the identity of Western civilization is still affected by the legacy of Orientalism. Such an understanding is complicit in the politics of identity that legitimates the experience, history, destiny, and aspirations of the West but not that of others. Such politics of identity in interpreting Josiah needs to be recognized and put to critique.

The Discourse of Nationalism

We must recognize the persistent tendency among biblical scholars to appeal to the metanarrative of nationalism in their interpretation of Josiah. Nationalism narrates the identity of the West more directly than Orientalism, which was also about the identity of the West through the (mis)representation of the East. Orientalism and nationalism are two sides of Western imperialism. The rise of nationalism and nations is a historical event that had no precedent before the West imagined and experienced it. It is hard to believe that concepts such as "nations" and "nationalism" were rather recent inventions when they seem so firmly fixed in the contemporary imagination and seem so self-evident and timeless. Benedict Anderson comments that "nation" is "the most universally legitimate value in the political life of our time."[4] Ernest Gellner comments, "A man must have a nationality as he must have a nose and two ears...Having a nation is not an inherent attribute of humanity, but it has now come to appear as such."[5]

The modern understanding of the term "nation" is based on the principle that a particular culture/people and a particular polity/state belong to each other from primordial time. This represents a congruence of state and people. The state has a centralized government and defined borders within which it has a monopoly of legitimate force. Identity markers such as race, ethnicity, history, and culture define the people. The people have the legitimacy to occupy and to exercise ownership of the state.

The correspondence between a political state and a particular group of people is historically contingent. That is to say, people and nation emerged independently, not destined for each other. Benedict Anderson's now classic essay about the origin and spread of nationalism argues that the nation is "an imagined political community" that emerged by means of "print-language capitalism"–the wide-ranging effects of the printing press and the replacement of language used in printing as an "official" language of the people–which provided the technical means for re-presenting the kind of imagined community that is the nation.[6]

The nation as an imagined community takes the place of kinship and religious communities that provided a sense of belonging and comradeship prior to modernity. Anderson argues that a nation imagined in terms of kinship, deeply rooted in primordial time, "makes it possible, over the past two centuries, for so many millions of people, not so much to kill, as willingly to die for such limited imaginings."[7] Gellner agrees with Anderson that the emergence of nations was a recent historical phenomenon that became possible only during the industrial society.[8] Gellner argues that the congruence of culture and polity, the most important feature of nationalism, was nearly impossible in agrarian society, becoming possible only during the industrial society when the relationship between culture and polity changed radically: "What happens when a social order is accidentally brought about in which the clerisy does become, at long last, universal, when literacy is not a specialism but a precondition of all other specialisms, and when virtually all occupations cease to be hereditary?...In an age of universalized clerisy...a high culture pervades the whole of society, defines it, and needs to be sustained by the polity. *That* is the secret of nationalism."[9]

The people of Josiah's kingdom were unfamiliar with the modern understanding of the term *nation,* and Josiah's kingdom never developed into one. One needs to be careful about using and appealing to the discourse of nationalism when discussing Josiah's kingdom even if there seem to be similarities between that kingdom and modern nations. We need to keep in mind that Josiah's kingdom was a typical state in agrarian society maintained through religion (the temple, the law, and Yahweh) and dynasty (the house of David seated in Jerusalem). Josiah's kingdom featured nothing extraordinary. Its features were common to the agrarian society. Gellner lists some general features of agrarian society: "The majority of the population is made up of agricultural producers, peasants. Only a minority of the society's population are specialists, whether military, political, religious or economic. Most agrarian populations are also affected by the two other great innovations of the agrarian age: centralized government and the discovery of writing."[10] The fact that Josiah's kingdom was a form of centralized government, namely a state, and that it had a clerisy, does not make Josiah's kingdom closer to being a nation than other agrarian states. Josiah's kingdom, even if Josiah had a program to form a nation, could not have been a nation. This is true since, as Gellner claims, "in the agrarian order, to try to impose on all levels of society a universalized clerisy and a homogenized culture with centrally imposed norms, fortified by writing, would be an idle dream. Even if such a programme is contained in some theological doctrines, it cannot be, and is not, implemented. It simply cannot be done. The resources are lacking."[11]

This is not to deny that the origins of the nations, based primarily on ethnicity and religion, can be traced prior to modernity. Some scholars argue that nation-formation and nationalism have nothing to do with modernity, that the nations were natural outcome from some ethnic communities.[12] I believe the confusion in the debate over when the nation was born is related to the use of the word *nation*. It is used to designate the people as well as the state. Obviously, the "nation" as a people, united primarily through ethnicity and religion, existed prior to modernity, as argued by Adrian Hastings.[13] However, the "nation" as a nation-state (the congruence of the people or "nation" and the state) did not exist prior to modernity according to the modernist view exemplified by Hobsbawm, Gellner, and Anderson. The point is not to find the exact moment in time when the nation was born. The point is that the nation was born in history, in the writing of the history of the West.

To use the models and elements of nationalism to understand Josiah's kingdom is to put ourselves in the danger of appealing to the identity discourse of the West. I am not saying that we can somehow completely avoid using or appealing to the discourse of nationalism since it is inherent in the conditions of our time; however, we need to be wary of what we are doing and acknowledge the danger of framing one's discussion within the identity discourse of the West.

For example, when scholars use cultural artifacts to draw the boundaries of Josiah's kingdom, they are following the nationalist logic. David's conquest of Palestine represents the moment of "primary acquisition," conquering once and for all the land that would forever belong to David's progeny. Once the territory had been demarcated as Israel, cultural artifacts discovered within the geographical limits of Israel are deemed ethnically Israelite. Geary describes the practice of ethnoarchaeology: Once the physical location of a "people" is determined, "then it was up to archaeologists to find the physical evidence of the cultural specificities of that people. Surely if language corresponded to a specific people who shared common customs and values, these same cultural differences would manifest in the physical artifacts recoverable by archaeologists."[14]

To complete this circular logic, biblical scholars use Judean "ethnic" artifacts to draw the territorial limits of Josiah's kingdom, three hundred years after the house of David had ceased to be a power over greater Palestine. Not surprisingly, many scholars envision Josiah's kingdom to be similar in size and influence as that of David's kingdom. Thus, Josiah's supposed conquest of the Northern Kingdom is justified not as a *conquest* but as a *reunification*. This is a modern nationalist reading that needs to be questioned.

The Space of Liminality

Then how can we imagine communities, groups of people, outside of the discourse of nationalism when it is so fixed in our imagination? How do we talk about non-Western peoples without going through the narration of nation, when any discourse or narrative of nation and nationalism is susceptible to being framed within the identity narrative of the West? How can we talk about the "other" without always referring to the West?

Homi Bhabha suggests that we need to move away from seeing the Western nations as the center of history and explore new places from which to write histories of peoples.[15] Homi Bhabha suggests a new site of narration: the space of liminality. The nation is not a fixed social formation. Its instability to unite the people/culture and the state/land shows up as self-evident in "a process of hybridity" and in the space of in-betweenness where people and culture do not simply comply with the script of the national discourse. Somehow the people have survived the homogenization of the nation.

Bhabha argues that when we look at the nation from liminality, when we acknowledge that "the nation is no longer the sign of modernity under which cultural differences are homogenized" and that the nation is an ambivalent and vacillating representation of the people, it "opens up the possibility of other narratives of the people and their difference."[16] Bhabha's purpose is to break away from the dualistic thinking that lies behind nationalism and Orientalism. This dualistic thinking is an "us and them" thinking that sees the people and culture within the borders of the nation as "us" and any people or culture outside of the imagined community as others. Bhabha argues that reality does not work according to such a scheme. Hybridity in culture and people is reality at the local level. Thus, Bhabha argues that once it is acknowledged that the nation is the space of liminality, then "its 'difference' is turned from the boundary 'outside' to its finitude 'within,' and the threat of cultural difference is no longer a problem of 'other' people. It becomes a question of the otherness of the people-as-one."[17] In the space of liminality different voices of the people emerge.

Then how is it possible, given the all-encompassing sway of the colonialist reading of DH, to understand Josiah in other than colonialist terms? How does one draw attention to the connection between Western imperialism and the production of Western knowledge? How does one overcome the outrageous insularity of biblical studies–the separation of the world of biblical studies from the world at large, and particularly the failure of biblical studies to come to terms with its colonialist legacy?

One must read Josiah from the space of liminality. That reading must apply the historical imagination and make undiminished use of the tools of the critical historian. This reading must be informed by the experience, expressed with acute honesty and in all its complexity, of those who have lived as the other, as the colonized, as not at home in their own land, as interstitial beings. Asian Americans know much about being "unhomely" in the racialized landscape of North America. Perhaps examining the *realpolitik* of liminality in Asian America–Asian Americans' experience of living as interstitial beings and their struggle to recover and to reconstruct their history and identity in North America–may inform us of an alternate reading of Josiah.

The *Realpolitik* of Liminality in Asian America

Asian Americans know all too well about living as interstitial beings in the racialized landscape of North America. We all know the common experience of being asked by other Americans, "Where are you from?" It is not about our hometowns that the inquirers are searching to know. If we respond by naming our hometowns in North America, they are not satisfied until they find out where we are from "originally." The inquirers may or may not be aware that their investigation is based on the premise that Asians or people of Asian descent are aliens in this nation. Their investigation follows the logic of identity politics and the contour of the racialized landscape of North America. Their investigation follows the script formulated by American Orientalism and nationalism that view people from Asia, no matter what their ethnicity may be, through racial categories–white, black, Hispanic, and Asian.

I, too, have my own stories of what it is to live as an interstitial being in North America. The experience of "unhomely" in the land I call my home may be seen as no more than the problem or the whining of an ill-adjusted minority living within the white majority society, as no more than an existential crisis on the individual level. But my experience is, as Henry Yu puts it, "also the result of journeying through a certain kind of landscape."[18] American Orientalism shapes this landscape. Henry Yu traces how American sociologists have studied Asian Americans in the framework of the "Oriental Problem"–the question as to why Asians failed to assimilate into the mainstream and what to do with them in light of that fact–in the first half of the twentieth century. Yu shows how this legacy still shapes much of how Asian Americans are studied and viewed today. Asian Americans as "Orientals" are studied as objects.

The problem is related to identity and race politics in North America. Orientals are viewed as a problematic object that needs to be managed and controlled. They are advantageous and desirable if they would just stay in their place and play the subordinate role they are assigned in America. They are undesirable and dangerous if they refuse to stay in their place and play the role assigned to them, that is, if they demand to be accepted as full Americans. The descendants of white Europeans are the rightful inhabitants of the land, but Asian Americans are lumped together as aliens in this land. Asian Americans are viewed as permanent strangers, foreigners, aliens in the United States due, in part, to the politics of race and identity in the United States based on the nationalist principle of the congruence of the nation and the people.

How Asian Americans are viewed is related to the question of who are "real" Americans–those who have the legitimate claim to the land in which they live. Robert Lee examines six representations of Asian Americans in American history that illustrate this point: the pollutant, the coolie, the deviant, the yellow peril, the model minority, and the gook. These representations portray Asian Americans as "an alien body and a threat to the American national family."[19] Lee argues that these faces of the Oriental are not arbitrary but are connected to economic changes, particularly during the periods of transformations of the structure of accumulation, and social crises, particularly during identity crises among white Americans, in American history. A particular representation of the Oriental arises during times of change and crisis in America to help define who real Americans are. Lee concludes, "what produces these stereotypes is not just individual acts of representation, but a historical discourse of race that is embedded in the history of American social crises."[20]

Asian Americans are caught in the middle of identity politics in North America. In the racialized landscape of America shaped by American Orientalism and nationalism, Asian Americans are racialized as yellow. The racial politics in America defines yellow in opposition to white but also as different from black. This sets up a peculiar problem for Asian Americans: is yellow white or black? Okihiro notes that this question is multilayered: "Is yellow black or white? is a question of Asian American identity. Is yellow black or white? is a question of Third World identity, or the relationships among people of color. Is yellow black or white? is a question of American identity, or the nature of America's racial formation."[21]

Okihiro argues in his book that the position of Asian Americans caught in-between two racial poles (black and white) has caused unique disabilities as well as special opportunities. Whites often used Asian Americans to punish blacks and other minorities. Asian Americans received opportunities to work because they were not black. Being yellow, being in the middle, produces a state of liminality. At times this is desirable, but it can also be dangerous as well. Okihiro summarizes this problem of being colored as yellow: "Asians have been marginalized to the periphery of race relations in America because of its conceptualization as a black and white issue—with Asians, Latinos, and American Indians falling between the cracks of that divide. Thus, to many, Asians are either 'just like blacks' or 'almost whites.'"[22]

Even the model minority stereotype, which credits the common elements between Asian culture and Anglo American culture with having enabled Asian Americans, like all of America's white immigrants, to move from the margins to the mainstream, illustrates the ambivalent position of Asian Americans. The model minority stereotype, "instead of deconstructing the European identity...reifies and attests to its original."[23] At the same time, it reflects the "ambivalence" that the dominant group feels toward Asian Americans. It refers to a simultaneous attraction and repulsion from what the dominant group sees as Asian Americans' mimicry of the American identity. The model minority stereotype is used to uphold Asian Americans as "near-whites" or "whiter than whites" (as fully assimilated Americans) in bipolar racial politics, but it ignores the white racism that Asian Americans continue to face. The stereotype is used to discipline African Americans and other minority groups, thereby drawing suspicion and hatred.

Asian Americans are familiar with identity politics in which they are viewed as interstitial beings. They have experienced the *realpolitik* of liminality, the danger of being in a political, ideological landscape not of one's own making, throughout their history in North America. They have been victims of violation and exploitation, collectively as well as individually, in their own home/land. Asians, understood as a race of aliens in opposition to whites, were victimized by the institutionalized racial immigration policies. The well-known Chinese Exclusion Act of 1882 prohibited the Chinese from immigrating to the United States and prevented foreign-born Chinese already living in the United States from citizenship for ten years (renewed indefinitely in 1902 by the Congress). The Chinese were the only group of people singled out on a racial basis from entering the United States. They were excluded because of identity politics in America that defined the Chinese as undesirable pollutants to white America.

Another tragic moment in American history was when President Franklin D. Roosevelt set aside the Constitution of the United States and issued Executive Order 9066, which resulted in the incarceration of Japanese Americans in internment camps by the federal government. Although two thirds of the 120,000 internees were American citizens by birth, their rights and liberties guaranteed by the Constitution were not protected. Their own government betrayed them.

These moments in American history are reminders that Asian Americans are only a step away from experiencing the *realpolitik* of liminality, from being viewed as aliens within their own land. This could well result in discriminations and violence against them. One of the latest events to remind Asian Americans of the danger in being in a state of liminality were the Los Angeles riots that occurred between April 29 and May 2, 1992. Robert Lee states what many Asian Americans believe–the predominantly "colored" neighborhoods of Los Angeles became free-fire zones after the verdict in the Rodney King case: "The LAPD sealed off the 'colored' zones of the city from White LA and let them burn. The LAPD's strategy of containment was effective in protecting White LA; it brought massive destruction and death to LA's 'Third World.'"[24] The damage done to ethnic neighborhoods was mere collateral damage in the attempt to protect "real" Americans. In particular, Korean Americans suffered about half the estimated $850 million in material losses. The Los Angeles Police Department did not protect Korean Americans because they were not quite white, but other ethnic groups attacked them because they were not blacks.

Lee comments that the people who were targeting Koreans were following the "mere gook rule"–the rule that any dead Vietnamese could be counted as a dead enemy during the Vietnam War–"Koreans were the closest and most vulnerable Asian Americans in sight."[25] Many individual victims of injustice remind us again of the positionality of Asian Americans in North America. Lee lists many individual victims who experienced the danger of looking like an Asian:

> In several of these cases and in many others, it did not matter that the victim was Chinese, or Korean, or Vietnamese; the mere gook rule overrode ethnicity. Vincent Chin, a Chinese American, was taken to be Japanese and killed by two white, furloughed auto-workers in Detroit. Jim Loo, also a Chinese American, was killed by two white men who thought he was Vietnamese. In 1990, Tuan Ana Cao, a Vietnamese American, was beaten and severely injured by a group of black men who though he was Korean. In January of 1996, Thien Minh Ly, a Vietnamese American, was killed by two White drifters who called him a Jap. In these cases it didn't matter what ethnicity or nationality the victims really were; the only significant issue was that they were the gook.[26]

These are reminders that Asian Americans are still viewed as aliens. This often results in violence against them because they are viewed as the Other in the discourse of identity and race in America. Indeed, Asian Americans have experienced the *realpolitik* of liminality throughout their history.

Asian Americans have been writing a history of their own:

- in spite of being viewed as others, as a race of aliens, as permanent strangers;
- in spite of being represented as the pollutant, the coolie, the deviant, the yellow peril, the model minority, and the gook;
- in spite of experiencing the *realpolitik* of liminality–discrimination, betrayal, and violence by being placed in the space of liminality in the racialized landscape shaped and maintained by the politics of race and identity grounded in the nationalist discourse in America.

Yes, Asian Americans are writing a history of their own by refusing to view their history as an insignificant footnote in the national history of the United States:

- they are writing a history of their own by rejecting the assimilationist model that requires relinquishing their own unique identity and history;
- they are writing a history of their own by rejecting the model minority thesis that requires Asian Americans to imitate the dominant group;
- they are writing a history of their own by seeing themselves as agents of their own history and destiny;
- they are writing a history of their own by recovering their past and imagining an alternate view of America.

Asian Americans have turned Orientalism on its head. They have rejected the connotation of the term "Oriental"–an objectification of Asians in America–and began to use the term "Asian American" in the 1960s. "Orientals are rugs, not people. Asian Americans are people." This often-used statement illustrates the difference between "Oriental" and "Asian American." Okihiro explains that the term "Asia" was "a European invention that named the Orient as spaces east of Europe." Europeans and Americans used it to lump together various Asian groups as an undifferentiated group in the United States from 1850 to World War II. "But that essentializing name was also made in America by Asians during the late 1960s, when they sought a pan-Asian identity premised on a common past in the United States and on a racialized politics that they would enable and lead to mobilization and empowerment."[27]

Ronald Takaki's *Strangers from a Different Shore* was the first comprehensive Asian American history that treated Asian Americans not as objects for study but as agents of their own histories.[28] Asian American historians have rejected the assimilationist approach of writing history of Asian Americans that requires Asian Americans to be a mere footnote in the national American history and to relinquish their unique identity and experience. Gary Okihiro states the goal of Asian American historiography:

It started with the idea that American society consisted not only of Europeans but also of American Indians, Africans, Latinos, and

Asians. It went on to propose that the histories of all of America's people were so intertwined that to leave out any group would result in sizable silences within the overall narrative. It noted a global dimension to the American experience, both in the imperial expansion of European peoples and in the incorporation of America's ethnic minorities.[29]

This does not mean that Asian American communities are to create exact replicas of those in Asia, as if that were possible. At the same time, they are not "carbon copies of other communities in mainstream American society."[30] Chan suggests that Asian American communities "are components of an increasingly multiethnic American landscape and can best be understood and appreciated as such."[31] Asian Americans need to form more than a synthesis of Asia and America; they need to form an interstitial community, refusing to disconnect with any community, but not assimilating into a community to the extent that they lose their own unique identity and history.

Asian Americans are writing "a history of their own" that helps to resist cultural imperialism in North America. They are doing this by writing without always referencing to the national history of the United States. It is a history that helps to form an Asian American identity that is separate from the national identity and to inscribe their subjectivity. The homogenization of Asian Americans definitely provides an advantage. By consolidating various Asian groups as a distinct group with its own shared history and destiny, it helps to resist cultural imperialism. However, the homogenization of Asian Americans also hides a danger. It can alienate some Asian groups, especially the most recent immigrant groups from southeast Asia, that are not included in the standard Asian American history. Alienation will force these groups to feel "unhomely" in the land. We must begin to ask: Who are being left out of Asian American history and identity?

The *Realpolitik* of Liminality in Josiah's Kingdom

Josiah's kingdom was located in the shadow of the Assyrian Empire, in the ideological landscape of Assyrian imperialism, where it experienced the *realpolitik* of liminality. Judah was no more than a petty state caught in the political, commercial matrix shaped by the Assyrian Empire, driven by its ideology of expansion. Hayim Tadmor comments that the political-ideological factor that shaped the Neo-Assyrian Empire's territorial expansion was the view that the primary duty of every Assyrian king was to expand the borders of his land.[32] The command, "With your just scepter, extend your land!" attested first by Tulkuti-Ninurta I, is again attested six hundred years later in Ashurbanipal's reign: "Extend your land at your feet!"[33]

The presence of the Assyrian arms left no doubt as to whose political landscape Judah was located in. The Neo-Assyrian hegemony over the west was maintained and expanded throughout the Sargonid dynasty:

Sargon II, Sennacherib, Esarhaddon, and Ashurbanipal. Judah was one of several states in Syria-Palestine caught between Assyria and Egypt, in a bi-polar system dominated by Assyria for the duration of the reign of the four kings. After the death of Ashurbanipal in conjunction with the rise of the Neo-Babylonians and the Medes, the power shifted from the Egypt-Assyria alliance to the Babylonia-Medea alliance. However, the status of Judah remained the same. It was a small state located in a political landscape shaped first by the Neo-Assyrians and maintained as a unified whole by subsequent empires.

As is well known, the Assyrian kings used terror to maintain their control over their subjects. Carlos Zaccagnini suggests that the royal inscriptions' purpose was very specific: "They were an optimal instrument for conveying (ideological) messages to serve a practical purpose: e.g. terror to be inspired upon inner or outer 'subject.'"[34] If we accept at face value the royal inscriptions' descriptions of what the Assyrians did to their enemies, it is truly terrifying: flaying alive, impalement, cutting or excising, burning alive, smashing, heaping up of corpses or of heads, etc. K. Lawson Younger states that the king would conduct exemplary punishments on those enemies "who have shown a stiffer resistance" and "the more specific punishment of flaying alive seems to have been reserved for Assyrian traitors and usurpers."[35] These punishments were used as psychological warfare to instill fear in their enemies and subjects to deter them from rebellion and to give the Assyrians a psychological edge over their subjects.

But the most telling indication that Judah was located in a state of liminality during Josiah's reign is not the witness of Assyrian inscriptions or the political situation at the time of Josiah's reign. The *realpolitik* of liminality is illustrated more powerfully in the way Josiah's story is framed within two deaths: the account of Amon's death in 2 Kings 21:19–26 and the account of Josiah's own death in 2 Kings 23:28–30. On one side of Josiah's story, Amon's death attests to the danger of maintaining the *status quo.* On the other side of Josiah's story, Josiah's death attests to the danger of disturbing the *status quo.* Amon followed his father's ways—"He did what was evil in the sight of the Lord, as his father Manasseh had done. He walked in all the way in which his father walked, served the idols that his father served, and worshiped them" (2 Kings 21:20–21)–including his father's pro–Assyrian policy. But his decision to maintain the *status quo* cost him his life.

Some argue that Amon's assassination had a religious origin. This theory asserts that a religious party assassinated Amon because it wanted to remove Assyrian influence on religious practices in Judah. However, "the people of the land," fearing the retaliation by the Assyrians, restored the *status quo* by eliminating the assassins. Cho suggests that Amon's death was a result of factional infighting among Judaean elites.[36] He suggests that there were severe factional struggles among elites within the court of Judah. Anti- and pro-Assyrian factions coexisted during the time of Amon and Josiah due to the Judaean kings' vacillating foreign policies in relation to the Assyrian hegemony. Cho notes that this factional infighting that resulted in Amon's assassination and the subsequent killing of the assassins is an attestation that "Assyria influenced the shape and dynamics of Judahite policy."[37] Judah's location within the Assyrian hegemony resulted in the assassination of Amon and the subsequent killing of the assassins. It was a reminder of the *realpolitik* of liminality.

At the time of Josiah's death, the political situation had changed from the beginning of his reign. Assyria became only a shadow of its dominating self. The army encamped at Carchemish was only a weak remnant of what had been the Near East's most powerful empire for over a hundred years. Egypt, under the leadership of Necho II, was on its way through Palestine to help its ally, Assyria, against the Babylonians. At Megiddo, Necho II met Josiah (2 Kings 23:29–30). What happened at Megiddo is unclear. Many believe that Josiah died in a battle against Necho II, following the account in 2 Chronicles 35:20–27. A minority voice questions this view and suggests that Josiah did not die in a battle but was a victim of *realpolitik*.

According to some, what happened at Megiddo was not so much a battle between rivals but a court-martial based on sovereign-vassal relations. Therefore, the version of Josiah's death in 2 Kings 23:29–30 may not tell much about how or why Josiah died, but it is more historically reliable because it, at least, does not embellish his death with a fictitious war. The account in 2 Kings is a dispassionate account that leaves a lot of questions unanswered, but it seems to express the sentiment of shock and disbelief at the sudden death of a righteous king. Josiah's death in 2 Kings 23:29–30, although it is outside of the Josianic edition of DH, tells much about the *realpolitik* of liminality. Josiah was a victim of being located in-between the confrontation of the two powers (Egypt-Assyria and Babylonia-Medes) competing to control the Near East. Josiah's death was a reminder of Judah's position in the political and ideological landscape shaped by imperialism.

Josiah and his people also experienced the *realpolitik* of liminality. They had experienced firsthand the might of Assyria. Their fate was connected to the whim of larger political forces. Their experience of the danger of being located in a political, ideological landscape not of their own making is best illustrated by the way the story of Josiah is framed within two accounts of death. On the one side, the account of Amon's death illustrates what could happen if a *status quo* is maintained, and, on the other side, the account of Josiah's death illustrates what could happen if a *status quo* is disturbed. There is no safe ground for the interstitial beings. They can be victims of the *realpolitik* of liminality whether they follow the script of the empire or choose not to.

Josiah and his people were located in a political, ideological landscape not of the Judaeans' own making. During this time their history and culture were "overwritten" by the Assyrians, and although they experienced the *realpolitik* of liminality throughout the reign of the Sargonid dynasty, they refused to allow their history to be framed within the narrative of the empire. Even though Assyria's power had reached its apogee during the reigns of Manasseh, Amon, and the first half of Josiah's reign, Josiah and his court ignored Assyria after the siege against Jerusalem during Hezekiah's reign (2 Kings 18) and attempted, in part, to write "a history of their own." It was a subversive strategy to give agency to the colonized (to imagine one's own history and destiny apart from the empire, an alternate view of the world).

By omitting the presence of Assyria, the Josianic editor(s) attributed agency to the people of Judah, rather than to the empire. They wrote a history of their own in which the empire plays no part. They wrote a history of their own in which they were the subject of history, where Yahweh–not the power of Assyria–is the divine agent controlling their history, destiny, and aspirations. They wrote a history of their own by recovering the "over-written" or forgotten "inscriptions" of their past. Josiah instituted a pilgrimage festival to Jerusalem through reinvention of the Passover festival to consolidate the various groups living in Judah and perhaps to stop the Israelite Judaeans (descendants of former immigrants or refugees from the North) from going back to Samaria. He was perhaps in competition with the politically organized people of Samaria for the allegiance of the Israelite Judaeans. Josiah was trying to consolidate the native Judaeans and the Israelite Judaeans into one people, united under one God, one cult, one dynasty, etc. It was an attempt, not necessarily to resist the empire, but to promote their own identity and destiny apart from the empire.

However, by homogenizing various factions in his kingdom as one people united under one God (Yahweh), one temple (in Jerusalem), and one dynasty (the house of David), Josiah alienated several groups in this process. Josiah alienated those who did not worship Yahweh exclusively and the rural population who were negatively affected by the centralization of the cult. But, mostly, the people of Samerina (the Assyrian name for Samaria), who were made up of various groups from the Assyrian empire, did not fit the definition of who the true Israelites were and so were not included in DH. Indeed, the people of Samerina were the subaltern of Josiah's story.[38] The rhetoric of DH made the diverse population of Samaria, who continued to worship Yahweh next to other gods, feel "unhomely" in their own land. We must begin to ask who are being left out in the identity discourse of DH.

Conclusion

In my effort to decolonize Josiah, I have read the story of Josiah intercontextually with the story of Asian Americans from the place of liminality. I have read the story of Josiah in conversation with the experience, aspirations, and history of Asian Americans so that Asian Americans can see themselves in the story of Josiah. However, it is not my intention to make the story of Josiah a "safe" text for Asian Americans. The story of Josiah has been "unsafe" for, among others, the people of Samerina who must have felt "unhomely" in their own land due to the politics of identity in Josiah's kingdom. The story of Josiah as an illustration of an attempt to write "a history of their own" may be used to affirm the effort of Asian Americans to construct their own subjectivity by writing "a history of their own," but it can also be "unsafe" when it is used to homogenize various groups into one community, thereby making those who are left out in the standard Asian American history and identity feel "unhomely" in their own land. We must keep in mind that politics of interpretation goes hand in hand with politics of identity.

8

Empowerment or Enslavement?

Reading John 4 Intertextually with Ezra-Nehemiah

JEAN K. KIM
Moravian Theological Seminary
Bethlehem, Pennsylvania

Miss Saigon Meets the Samaritan Woman

Although the musical play *Miss Saigon* and the opera *Madam Butterfly* may be different in terms of genre, they tell the same story: an American military man forms a liaison with a young Asian woman before returning to the United States. Over time, the Asian woman comes to regard herself as the wife of the American and bears a son in his absence; when he returns three years later with an American wife, she sends her son to his father and kills herself.[1] With the Asian woman's death thus dramatically romanticized as an act of loyalty, the colonial histories of Vietnam/Japan/Asia and the real-life situation of a military bride, unfortunately, remain largely unexamined by Western audiences.

Such romanticizations of military brides recall romantic interpretations of the Samaritan woman in John 4:7–42. In ancient Jewish society, women could divorce three times at most.[2] Nevertheless, the Samaritan woman is presented as one who had divorced five times and was living with a sixth man. With regard to the puzzling marital status of the Samaritan woman, Craig R. Koester suggests that the woman's former five husbands might stand for the five countries which had invaded Samaria and intermarried with the Samaritans, and the sixth man might stand for the Roman Empire, which ruled over Samaria in the first century, but whose citizens did not settle in Samaria or intermarry with the local inhabitants.[3]

Western feminist biblical scholars, moreover, similarly have not suggested any possible explanations for the woman's puzzling marital status, nor have they considered the impact that the various colonial powers might have had on her life. Rather, they have romanticized the Samaritan woman's story by regarding her as a female disciple who converts from a sinful life to follow Jesus, or as a missionary who brought her people to Jesus after she recognized him as a prophet.[4] In so doing, they have been accomplices to the charge that the Samaritan woman was a sexually immoral woman (just as contemporary military brides are disregarded as sexually immoral military prostitutes). The Samaritan woman's story has been a driving force in Christian feminist biblical interpretations which have co-opted Christian missiological ideology by simply emphasizing Jesus' inclusion of the Samaritan woman and her people into his inner circle. However, a critical reading reveals that there is nothing in John that indicates Jesus' approval of the woman as a disciple or that her ministry continued after their encounter; rather, a close reading of the Samaritan woman's story shows us that her role is gradually diminished by her townsmen (4:41–42). Furthermore, an intertextual examination of John 4 with Ezra-Nehemiah (which concerns itself with the issue of intermarriage) supports the contention that the tension between the Jews and Samaritans (4:7–8) proceeds not simply from a religious issue but from a sociopolitical one. A thorough reading thus shows that the story does not support the woman's role as a missionary or as an exemplar of faith.

In contrast to Western interpretations, postcolonial biblical critics have insisted that the gospel of John should be read critically in light of its imperialist ideologies.[5] It cannot be denied that in most of the countries colonized by the West, Jesus became an imperial figure that legitimized Christian domination over native religions and cultures. Yet this kind of religious imperial domination became possible only after Christianity had been established as the official religion of the Roman Empire under the patronage of Constantine. Richard A. Horsley has pointed this out: "Christianity was a product of empire. In one of the great ironies of history, what became the established religion of empire started as an anti-imperial movement."[6] Just as Western biblical scholars have anachronistically interpreted the Samaritan woman's story from a Christian point of view, postcolonial biblical scholars have also conducted anachronistic interpretations that do not take into account that John was written under the Roman Empire.[7] In so doing, they muffle or distort the voice of the Samaritan woman, who may well have been a victimized woman in a colonizing context, like the contemporary military brides who have been ostracized from their community because of their sexual engagement with U.S. soldiers.[8]

Growing up in the postcolonial context of Korea and living in the United States, I became aware of my outsider-insider status in a Korean American church I was attending. The membership of this church included many military brides; I was welcomed by them because I was married to an American just like them, but at the same time I was alienated from them not only because my husband is not a soldier, but also because of my privileged social status. I became increasingly aware of their status as "only outsiders" both to Koreans, who consider their intermarriage unacceptable, and to American-in-laws, who demand that their daughter-in-laws fulfill American cultural expectations.[9] The difficult situation of military brides in the United States has compelled me to lift the veil from the romantic interpretations of the Samaritan woman's story.

Most of the military brides were born and raised in poor families in the (de)colonizing context of a Korea that went from being a Japanese colony to being a neo-colony of America, and they have managed their lives by going through multiple marriages. The unhappy marital status of these military brides resembles the Samaritan woman's multiple marital status.[10]

By utilizing the basic plot of *Miss Saigon* as a postcolonial lens through which we can reveal unobserved features of the Samaritan woman's story, I first argue that the Samaritan woman can represent a sexually victimized product of the various colonial occupations of Samaria.[11] Second, through an intertextual reading of Ezra-Nehemiah as a backdrop to John 4, I emphasize that unequal relationships between autonomous men and dependent women can put women—especially women who are intermarried to other ethnic men—in no-win situations according to varying sociohistorical and econopolitical contexts. Third, I argue that John utilizes the Samaritan woman as an object of exchange between the Jews and the Samaritans for the sake of a coalition between these two groups in their struggle against the Roman Empire. Lastly, I suggest that the military bride's disturbing identity in the Asian American Diaspora can be seen as site of empowerment rather than enslavement, as is currently being demonstrated by emerging communities which exemplify the concept of a "Third Place."[12]

The Samaritan Woman's Unsavory Marital Status

Jesus initiates his dialogue with the Samaritan woman by requesting water from the well (4:7). Yet he abruptly changes the topic of their conversation from the living water (4:7–15) to the woman's marital status by commanding her to bring her husband (4:16–18). By reading John 4 in relation only to 2 Kings 17, some biblical critics have suggested allegorical interpretations that equate the Samaritan woman's five husbands (4:18a) with the foreign deities that the Samaritans were believed to have worshiped after the fall of the Northern Kingdom (2 Kings 17:24, 29–31).[13] However, these allegorical interpretations falter in part because of the following reasons.[14] First, 2 Kings 17:13–34 suggests that the five foreign nations brought seven not five deities into Samaria: Babylon/Succoth-Benoth; Cuthah/Nergal; Avva/Nibhaz and Tartak; Hamath/Ashima; and Sepharvaim/ Adrammelech and Anammelech.[15] Also, whereas these deities were worshiped concurrently, the Samaritan woman could not have been married to all five husbands simultaneously.[16] Second, as a product of the Deuteronomistic circles that were responsible for editing the books of Kings, 2 Kings 17 criticizes the syncretistic cults of northern Israel even before the newcomers had totally assimilated with Israelite cultic norms.[17] As long as we depend on 2 Kings 17:13–34 as a backdrop of John 4:18, it is thus difficult to accept the allegorical interpretations that the woman's previous five husbands represent the idolatrous status of the Samaritans.

In his insightful analysis of John 4, Koester argues that the issue at hand need not have been religious idolatry at all. He employs John's tendency to utilize an individual as a spokesperson for a large group (1:23; 3:7, 11–12; 4:12, 19–22, 25; 9:4a, 22; 16:2) to claim that the Samaritan woman's personal history parallels the colonial history of Samaria, which had been under colonial domination since the Assyrian occupation brought five foreign nations into Samaria.[18] By analyzing the sociopolitical context– that the Samaritans practiced intermarriage with the five groups of colonists but did not engage in Roman intermarriage during the reign of Herod the Great–Koester suggests that the Samaritan woman's previous five husbands and sixth man allude to the five former groups of colonists and the Roman imperial power respectively.[19]

In order to identify the sixth man with whom the Samaritan woman was living, we need to consider the sociohistorical context of the Roman Empire in the first century, especially Augustus's legislation concerning Roman marriage. For the sake of the survival of the governing class, Augustus promoted legislation regulating extramarital relationships between consenting men and women. This legislation regulated the order of the household by setting up strict norms that controlled the choosing of an appropriate wife: Roman marriage usually took place along class lines, and cross-cultural or cross-racial marriages were forbidden.[20] According to this legislation, while both men and women were liable to charges for *stuprum*, only women were subject to being charged for adultery.[21] Yet the legislation ironically created a safe zone for certain women, such as prostitutes or female pimps, who could still conduct their trade without worrying about being caught as criminals.[22] The masculine orientation of this legislation is further expressed in the legislation regarding a soldier's marriage. For the sake of the efficiency and good order of the army, soldiers' marriages were banned for the duration of their service, and soldiers' wives (if they were already married) were forbidden to follow their husbands. The average Roman army recruit was eighteen or nineteen years old. At the age of eighteen, only a few were already married, and the recruitment period of the Roman army was longer than twenty-five years. In a context where the prohibition of soldiers' marriage undoubtedly must have run counter to the sexual inclinations of the soldiers, there would have been many illegal relationships with concubines or prostitutes.[23] From this sociohistorical point of view, Koester's suggestion that the sixth man with whom the Samaritan woman was living might stand for the Roman Empire sounds very persuasive.

From a feminist point of view, however, we may further consider the possibility that the woman, to survive in a colonizing context, might have adopted the strategy of "voluntary rape." As Marlene Epp states, a woman "favored voluntary rape in order to avoid ongoing brutal attacks from numerous soldiers and to obtain assistance in crossing tightly guarded borders."[24] Voluntary rape is a radical way in which women can achieve an active will in a context that threatens to dehumanize them completely and almost destroy them. In his Korean postcolonial novel, *Silver Stallion,* Ahn Junghyo depicts a period during which voluntary rape was not uncommon. Ahn's female character, Ollye, became a *Yang-gong-ju* (Yankee princess) who began to receive U.N. soldiers to avoid being raped continuously after she was first raped by two U.N. soldiers.[25] Regardless of whether women are raped or submit voluntarily, however, they are ridiculed and eventually ostracized from their own community and wind up drifting in male areas, just like the Samaritan woman who came to a public place in the daytime (a time reserved for men's affairs) without the company of other women, and who returned not to her private women's community, but to the townsmen.[26] Considering this intercontextual possibility that she, as a wanderer among men, might not have had her own community to return to, we may plausibly imagine that the sixth man with whom the Samaritan woman was represented as cohabiting—whether her portrayal reflected a simple cohabitation or a case of voluntary rape—might well have stood for the Roman colonizer/soldier.[27]

From this postcolonial perspective, allusions to the Samaritan woman's marital status might well extend beyond questions of morality. In a patriarchal society, women without husbands found themselves in quite powerless positions. The decision to divorce was mainly a male choice, and therefore the Samaritan woman may have simply been abandoned or expelled from her other marriages. Yet Jesus does not seem to show any concern for her presumably painful past, nor does he seem to care how her five previous marriages might have ended. There is no indication that Jesus defended her position in society by challenging male privilege, or that he invited her into his inner group. Koester also does not develop further the relationship between the Samaritan woman's personal life and Samaritan history. Yet his suggestion that the woman's marital status signifies Samaritan history leads us to believe that the Samaritan woman's complicated marital status might point to the condition of sexually exploited or marginalized women throughout the various colonial periods. In other words, her marital status reflects that she was the product of a patriarchal power game between a masculine colonizer and a feminized colonized.[28]

Ezra-Nehemiah's Prohibition of Intermarriage

When Jesus asks the Samaritan woman for a drink, she says to him: "How is it that you, a Jew, ask a drink of me, a woman of Samaria?" (4:7–8). This dialogue hints that there is a conflict between the Jews and Samaritans. In the previous section, I have shown that the uneasy relationship between Jews and Samaritans might not be due to the Samaritans' religiously idolatrous behaviors. An intertextual consideration of John 4 with Ezra-Nehemiah, which reflects significant tension between Jews and Samaritans, not only strengthens the claim that their uneasy relationship is not simply a religious matter but also suggests that their relationship varied according to the sociohistorical context.

According to Ezra-Nehemiah, the returned Judeans do not seem to dispute the Samaritan declaration that they also worshiped the God of Israel. Though the reason for Zerubbabel's rejection of the Samaritan's offer to help rebuild the temple (Ezra 4:1–3) is not clearly expressed, Mordechai Cogan suggests that idolatrous practices of Samaritans do not appear to be at issue.[29] The Samaritans were contemptuously regarded as being of doubtful stock. Because of this, they were often described as *shetuki,* which means anyone who knows his or her mother but does not know his or her father, or as *asufi,* which means anyone picked up from the street without knowing his or her parents (*t. Kiddushin* 4:16; *m. Yevamot* 7:5).[30] In this regard, it is likely that the Golah-community, by its own admission, opposed contact with all foreigners who were potential sources of hybridity, such contact being perceived as a danger to the purity of the "holy seed" (Ezra 2:62; 4:1; 6:21; Neh. 10:31; 13:23–28). In other words, the tension between Jews and Samaritans reflected in Ezra-Nehemiah might thus have been conditioned by the particular form of exclusivism based on ethnicity (Ezra 10; Neh. 10) rather than on suspicion of religious idolatry, an exclusivism developed during the exilic and post-exilic periods.[31]

Yet whether Ezra-Nehemiah prohibited intermarriage as a means to secure the "holy seed" is still open to debate. According to Gary N. Knoppers's observation, the social and ethnic diversity the Chronicler imputes to Judah contrasts with the exclusivism promoted by Ezra-Nehemiah in the context of the Persian and early Hellenistic periods, and intermarriage among different ethnic groups played a "strategic" role in creating and consolidating links between peoples in ancient Jewish society.[32] Indeed, the prohibition against Jewish marriage with all Gentiles is not Torah Law, since Torah prohibitions of intermarriages refer only to the seven Canaanite nations (Deut. 7:3–4; Ex. 34:15). As Shaye J.D. Cohen observes: "Moses did not think it necessary to forbid marriage with all foreigners, but later Jews did. During the period of the second temple, with the loss of national sovereignty and the increased interaction with gentiles, the Jews sensed that their survival depended on their ideological and social separation from the outside world."[33] So the Mosaic tradition was changed during the period of the Restoration by Ezra-Nehemiah, who endorsed a very restricted notion of what constituted Israel not only by reserving the term "Israel" for the returned exiles but also speaking of the "people of the land" (Ezra 3:3; 9:1–2, 11, 14; 10:2, 11; Neh. 9:30; 10:29, 31–32; cf. Esth. 8:17; 1 Chr. 5:25).[34]

With regard to Ezra-Nehemiah's prohibition of intermarriage, Daniel L. Smith-Christopher insists that the language of purity ("holy seed") can be interpreted as Ezra-Nehemiah's means of emphasizing their "social identity and nonconformity to the world" since the preservation of the "holy seed" is deemed necessary to secure the future of Israel (Ezra 9:2; 2:43–55; Neh. 7:46–57).[35] According to Ezra 10:18–44, however, the number of those who had married foreign women and divorced them is no more than 110. Also, when the Babylonians deported the Israelites, they did not deport the entire Judean population, but only an urban minority; most of the Judean population was still there when the exiles returned to Jerusalem. Yet Ezra-Nehemiah implicitly includes Judeans among "the peoples of the lands with their abominations" (Ezra 9:1, 11; Neh. 10:28; cf. Ezra 4:4; 10:2, 11; Neh. 9:24; 10:30–31) by ignoring that the land is populated with Judeans when the exiles return.[36] It is then hardly believable that such few foreign women could seriously threaten the Ezra-Nehemiah community's ethnically pure identity. Rather, it seems more plausible that Ezra-Nehemiah's prohibition against intermarriage based on their "holy seed" strategy might have econopolitical implications, especially when we consider the aggressive actions against exogamy, mandating divorce and exclusion from the community of the exiles, eventually leading to the confiscation of property (Ezra 10:8).[37]

To understand better Ezra-Nehemiah's prohibition of intermarriage, Kenneth G. Hoglund suggests that we need to put their reform policy within the compass of Persian imperial decentralizing strategy, since Ezra and Nehemiah were acting within the community as imperial officials of the Persian government, which not only structured groups of displaced ethnic nationalities into collective units, but also strove to keep these units ethnically separate by employing a colonial atomizing policy.[38] Nehemiah was asked to rebuild Jerusalem's wall as an "inland defensive center," and his mission was combined with a socioeconomic reform strategy conforming to the pattern of transformation of the relationship between an imperial center and an outlying territory.[39]

Nehemiah, however, suspected that the local power structure (e.g., the Jews, the priests, the nobles, the officials, and the rest of those who were to do the work) would oppose his mission, given that these groups were competing for political power and authority in the Persian Empire. Since wealth accompanied the power and influence of the members of nobility in the empire, the aristocratic families of Nehemiah's adversaries inter-married among themselves or with other members of the nobility (Neh. 6:18; 13:4, 28; *Antiquities of the Jews [Ant.]* 11.2; 12.4, 16). In other words, the intermarriages among these families meant that the land possessions of the families of Nehemiah's adversaries were spread throughout the satrapy.[40] Ezra also focused his mission on legal reform by emphasizing the need for the "assembly" to refrain from intermarriage for the purpose of clarifying the membership of the community for the empire. According to Lisbeth S. Fried, it could not have been local leaders but royally appointed governors–the Persian judges or magistrates who informed Ezra of the Jews' marriages to the people of the lands (Ezra 9:1)–who had the power to order the destruction of property (Ezra 10:7, 8), and who had the authority to impose sanctions for failure to divorce (Ezra 10:14, 16). Ezra, the Persian imperial agent, appointed these judges and magistrates.[41] From this sociopolitical perspective, we can assume that Ezra-Nehemiah's missions, as part of the imperial decentralizing policy to create a web of economic and political relationships that would tie the community more completely into the imperial system, enhanced the empire's ability to determine who was part of a new collectivity that enjoyed privileges from the hand of the empire and also served to prevent any "diminution of collective privileges or property" enjoyed by their ethnically circumscribed community.[42]

Having identified Israel with the Diaspora group, Ezra and Nehemiah used "the idea of defilement as their political weapon." Their mandate of the divorce of the foreign wives was coercive dictatorship.[43] Yet nothing is said of females within the diasporic group who may have taken foreign husbands (cf. Deut. 7:3–4), or of the divorced wives and their children who were forced into no-win situations. In this silence, both Ezra-Nehemiah's prohibition of intermarriage and John's presentation of the Samaritan woman are blithely immune to any qualms about the complete autonomy of the men and the utter dependency of the women.

Woman as an Object of Transaction

In a colonizing context, native uprisings caused by political discontent as well as by economic pressure on the ordinary people were common.[44] Josephus informs us about widespread popular movements in Galilee, Judea, and Perea, which took place as the distinctively Israelite social form of popular messianic movements (*Ant.* 17.271–85; *Jewish War [J.W.]* 2.56–65). Also, Josephus describes a Samaritan leader (*Ant.* 18.85–87) who was leading a large crowd and who was ruthlessly suppressed by Pontius Pilate as a political revolutionary, since he was believed to have a messianic potential somewhat similar to that of John the Baptist (*Ant.* 18.116–119).[45] Colonial strategic logic of political control is based on a practice of fragmenting and isolating political activity of the colonized within the confines of local administrative subdivision and thereby inhibiting the spread of opposition and resistance to the colonizing power,[46] as we have seen in Ezra-Nehemiah's utilization of the prohibition of intermarriage as a part of the imperial decentralizing policy (cf. Jn. 4:1–2). It is thus probable that tension among Jews/Judeans, Galileans, and Samaritans was continually present, especially when the Roman imperial power was making use of decentralizing strategy. Yet the tension among these groups might have lessened when they shared the common purpose of opposing the Roman authority.[47] Indeed, Josephus' report on the Galileans' involvement in the protest alongside the Judeans and others (*Ant.* 17.204–218, 254–58) confirms Gary B. Miles's observation that an anti-colonial resistance movement against colonial power has a tendency to forge a new sociopolitical group in the name of the common identity by uniting within the colonial territory groups and peoples who previously regarded themselves as essentially separate and distinct.[48] When we consider that Jesus' mission took place in the Roman imperial context, and also when we look at a recent evidence (fragments of scrolls from Masada) suggesting that the Samaritans were among the revolutionaries who participated in the defense of Masada,[49] it seems plausible that Jesus' journey to Samaria represents a journey seeking to assimilate Samaritans into his group for the sake of solidarity against the Romans.[50]

The assimilation of Samaritans into Jewish groups was not unusual. According to the Chronicler's view, not only are the residents of the north mostly Israelite, but aliens residing in the land are fully members of the people of Israel (cf. 2 Chr. 30:25; 34:33). Throughout Chronicles, the presence of displaced foreigners is not acknowledged in the territory of the former kingdom of Israel. In other words, it is likely that the land was occupied throughout by native Israelites, who were fully acceptable within the community of Israel (2 Chr. 30:17–19; 23–27). Cogan suggests that the text's negligence about the question of foreign elements in Samaria was intentional, since the Chronicler and his audience had already been prepared to assimilate non-Israelites into the community of the worshipers of the God of Israel.[51] From this historical perspective, Jesus' intention to assimilate Samaritans into his groups seems to mirror the Chronicler's openness to the make-up of the population in Samaria.

This is well reflected in Jesus' dialogue with his disciples. Jesus and his disciples conduct their dialogue based on the theme of "food," through which John develops the metaphor of the harvest (4:31–38): the woman is compared to a field or land where a man (Jesus) sows the seed while his disciples go to the harvest (cf. Jer. 2:2–3; 3:1; Hos. 2:2–3, 14–23).[52] A symbolic interpretation of Jesus' description of fields being ready for the harvest (4:35) might suggest that the harvest connotes the offspring that the Samaritan woman produced after Jesus had provided her with living water.[53] Yet the woman remains as a merely passive recipient of the seed, whereas the seed-sowing male is active in this imagery. One may raise a question regarding her passive role because the woman's role has been understood as a very active one in that she contributed to bringing her people to Jesus' circle. This seemingly active role, however, does not last long. With Jesus' disciples returning to him, the Samaritan woman went to her people. In her witness to her townsmen, she refers to Jesus, who told her everything that she had ever done (4:29). Yet her witness was not based on the Messiah's proclaiming everything to her people but on Jesus' telling her about her marital status. In other words, it is not clear whether she is proclaiming Jesus as Messiah or as some kind of prophetic crystal ball gazer. The questionable character of her witness is further developed by her people's response: the townsmen from that city believed in him "because of the woman's testimony [word]" (4:39); many more believed "because of his word" (4:41); they said to the woman, "It is no longer because of what you said that we believe, for we have heard for ourselves..." (4:42). Ironically, the Samaritans who had not been welcomed by Ezra-Nehemiah's community, possibly because of their frequent intermarriage, also renounce the Samaritan woman's contributive role in bringing Jesus to their community, possibly for the same reason that Ezra-Nehemiah had rejected their own forebears (Jn. 4:39–42; cf. 4:16–18).[54]

Through the contrast between the Samaritan woman's words in verse 42 (Greek, *lalian*–which was often used as the equivalent to "gossip") and Jesus' words in verse 41 (Greek, *logon*), John seems intent on taking away the woman's contribution to the advancement of her townsmen's confession of Jesus as the Savior of the world (cf. Jn. 17:20).[55] This narrative context thus supports the idea that the Samaritan townsmen, as well as Jesus, did not allow the woman to have a real place of honor in the familial relationship that Jesus tries to build between his group and the Samaritan people. Although the Samaritan woman is temporally portrayed as an active woman responding to Jesus and producing a great harvest, she disappears from the story without being appreciated, since she, as an object of exchange between groups of men (Jesus and his disciples/Jesus and the Samaritans), remains no more than a necessary literary device who functions to establish a relationship between men.[56]

Discomfort Women as a Site of Empowerment for Asian Americans

As implied in Ezra-Nehemiah and in the Samaritan woman's story, when women are objects of transaction in a patriarchal society, they become conduits of a relationship between the men, who are the subjective agents of the exchange. According to Gayle Rubin, women, especially in a (de)colonizing context, are merely objects of exchange between men, which is well reflected in the stories of the lives of military brides.[57] During the

Chinese and Japanese invasions of Korea, Korean women were sent as tributes to *Qing* China and recruited or kidnapped as "comfort women" for the Japanese Imperial Army. When U.S. forces occupied Okinawa after World War II, the Japanese military offered them the former Korean comfort women. The U.S. forces in Korea thus began to take over the bodies of Korean women that the Japanese had occupied before them: the business did not close, but merely changed hands.[58] However, it was not only U.S. militarism but also the Korean government that contributed to the expansion and perpetuation of the "Recreation & Rest" business in the U.S. military base areas. The Korean government, as the client country of the United States, has paid the expenses for this lucrative business, and supports the U.S. military's strategies in order to keep the soldiers content.[59] Whenever the subject of domination is changed, women are thus tossed between men. Once such cooperation between a patron and its client countries has been established, the sacrifice of those women is enforced for the sake of national security as well as national economic development. Yet for the sake of the honor of family and nation, the sexually marginalized women are silenced– in the text as well as in history.[60] In other words, once independence or cooperation between groups of men is achieved, people return to their so-called normal lives, where the male double standard operates effortlessly regardless of how much their women contributed or were victimized during the colonial period, as we have also observed in the Samaritan woman's story. In this postcolonial context, the issue of comfort women or military brides has become a discomforting issue, and as a result of this, the male double standard has rewarded these women with "triple jeopardy," as Trinh Minh-ha states: they are accused of betraying men, their country, and themselves, in that some of them respond to their victimization by becoming man-haters, while the others are forced to turn their backs on their country, and still others "betray" their sexual identity.[61]

In contrast, in the United States, as Leslie Bow points out, popular imagination and mainstream histories have represented the military bride as a "determiner of inclusion" into the mainstream sociocultural and legal-political milieu of the U.S. nation state.[62] Indeed, Asian American military brides' new lives as Americans have been structured by racial, cultural, and gender ideologies privileging white male authority, as Ji-Yeon Yuh epitomizes through her sharp analysis of the 1957 movie, *Japanese War Bride*: "The heroines' troubles are linked to her friendship with Japanese American neighbors. She achieves happiness only by rejecting Japanese Americans and ensconcing herself within a nuclear family household headed by her white American husband."[63] From the American point of view, military brides are outsiders "whom red-blooded American" soldiers had inexplicably married, whereas for their own ethnic group they are impure women because they married foreigners.[64] In this no-win situation, becoming American means discarding one's culture and forsaking relationships with ethnic kin in order to cleave to the culture of a husband. According to Yuh's observation of the lives of Korean military brides, the gaze of both other Koreans and Americans has been a strenuous pressure on their lives. As a desperate response to the lack of respect by other Koreans as well as Americans, the military brides have begun to demand their right to enjoy companionship and mutual respect by organizing their own imagined community.[65] After experiencing one Korean military bride's suicide, Korean military brides founded a military bride organization in 1979, and they began to find solidarity among themselves through networks, churches, and informal groupings.[66] Yet the community that they have built has a twofold aspect: on the one hand, it is deliberately Korean as a response to the forced Americanization and deprivations of their culture; on the other hand, as a response to the other Koreans who consider them lesser Koreans, they want to show the world who they are and against what prejudice they fight. As military brides, the women acknowledge their difference from both mainstream ethnic immigrants and Americans, while simultaneously asserting that their difference does not make them inferior. The outsiders' gaze has thus motivated the women to portray themselves positively to both Koreans and Americans.[67] The socially organized community of military brides serves as a challenge to both Korean and American definitions of self, and thereby challenges both Korean and American nationalism. Their identity, which has been forcefully given to them based on gender, class, and race in the Korean postcolonial context, challenges the validity of a monolithic Korean identity, and their identity as mothers of biracial Amerasian children opens up spaces for difference within Korean communities. At the same time, their insistence on their own culture challenges the valorization of American multiculturalism, the language of which is used to prove America's superiority and exceptionalism with regard to subordinate cultures.[68]

Among many socialized communities, the Korean immigrant church lies at the heart of their community, including Korean American churches located near military bases. Although the military brides as church members are actively involved in churches, the churches are under the formal control of denominational organizations. The ministers are usually Korean men who often have little knowledge or understanding of military brides before they are assigned to a "military bride" church. To be successful in these churches, they often disrespect the military brides by attaching themselves to the mainstream Korean American community that habitually considers military brides less Korean. In so doing, the male ministers often use the Samaritan woman's story as a means to force military brides to accept Jesus' gracious forgiveness, just as he forgave the sinful Samaritan woman with whom they are forced to identify.[69] Unlike the Samaritan woman, however, who did not have her own identity or her sisterhood community, these military brides have created a hybrid space where they can share their sisterhood and where they can be freely themselves by resisting both American and Korean prejudices toward a transformation of both their Korean and American identities, away from the narrow and exclusive and toward the broad and inclusive.[70]

Postcolonialism grounds investigation of the past's significance in the present, especially for Asian Americans who are living as hyphenated Americans with an instability of both power and powerlessness in the American diaspora, which reveals the irretrievable hybridities conditioned by both Japanese and American imperialism. In this regard, the claiming of military brides as an Asian American issue can contribute to shape Asian American inquiry as it translates into the advancement of a critique of the racialized and sexualized practices of the intersecting modernities of Japan, Korea, the other Asian countries, and the United States, because it speaks to the operation of the inequalities of gender, sexuality, class, race, empire, and nation. The presence of military brides in the United States, especially their building their own community as a site of empowerment rather than enslavement, invites us to envision a transnational and postcolonial horizon that radically disrupts singular narratives of subject formation. By sharing their view, therefore, we need to find a way of confronting the discomforting issue of military brides in our Asian American (church) community in order to provide a site where the military brides can insert their voices into history and where they can move from a state of selflessness to selfhood. I believe that this goal can be furthered through Asian American readings of the Bible, such as I have conducted through my reading, hoping to lay a bridge between the Samaritan woman and the military brides who have lived as sexually marginalized women in a (de)colonizing context.

9

A Light to the Nations

The Sociological Approach in Korean American Interpretation

JOHN AHN
Hartford Seminary
Hartford, Connecticut

In the 2003 SBL Annual Meeting in Atlanta, Benny Liew presented an interesting paper in the Asian and Asian American Hermeneutics Group. The theme of the session was entitled "Exploring the Contours and Seams of Asian American Biblical Interpretation: Current Work, Standing Questions, and New Directions." Liew expounded on the means for constructing a new postmodern Asian American hermeneutic. However, there was an issue at stake. Liew seemed to have gone beyond Asian American hermeneutics by being too inclusive and expansive in his approach. His approach seemed no longer about biblical interpretation or even biblical studies, but, following in the shadows of Derrida and Foucault, more generally about philosophical epistemology. I addressed this question during the open question and answer session moderated by Mary Foskett. His answer did not satiate my inquiry. My concern, which I share with others in this discipline, is with biblical interpretation and methodology. After years of reflecting on this issue under the tutelage of C.L. Seow, then B. Childs, and most recently with R. Wilson, I wish to join and contribute to this cutting-edge discussion from a (second-generation) Korean American perspective.

Thus, four sections comprise this piece. First, I introduce the context in which the discipline of Asian and Asian American hermeneutics has unfolded. Second, I review for the nonspecialist reader recent examples of Asian and Asian American hermeneutics. This assists us in demarcating the third section, the Korean American approach that I am proposing. Lastly, the cadre of the essay highlights and resolves the problem in Isaiah 42:6b "a light to the nations" as reflected in Kenton Sparks's *Ethnicity and Identity in Ancient Israel*.[1]

Definitions

According to Jeffrey Kuan, Asian biblical interpretation has been practiced within the following methodological approaches: *Wissenschaft,* cultural hermeneutics, liberation perspectives, feminist hermeneutics, and postcolonial interpretation.[2] Chan Hee Kim notes that Asian Americans read the Bible as Holy Scripture. He points out that there is no monolithic group called "Asian Americans," but specific subgroups such as Chinese Americans, Japanese Americans, Filipino Americans, Vietnamese Americans, and Korean Americans, among others. The hermeneutical principle that Asian Americans employ in reading the Bible stems from the context of immigration. These immigrants regularly encounter issues of assimilation, bifurcated culture, and dual or several languages in the midst of racial discrimination and inequality in a predominately Euro-American setting. The drive to succeed economically is also a common experience.[3]

The staccato of Asian American biblical studies in this context is audible in Tat-siong Benny Liew's edited volume of *Semeia* 90/91.[4] This is a collection of eighteen essays employing the Bible (loosely) for definitions, comparison, and application. Although it is not without problems, the volume is the first work to bring Asian American biblical studies to the foreground. One problem was its attempt to bridge biblical studies with the academic discipline of Asian American Studies without precursor, training, or even referring to works established by Don Nakanishi (UCLA) or Gary Okihiro (Columbia), among other Asian American specialists.

Korean biblical interpretation, represented by Cyris Heesuk Moon, stems from *minjung* theology (liberation for the poor with past and current socioeconomic and political overtones).[5] Moon reads the *apiru* or *habiru* (a term that is associated with the Hebrews of the HB/OT) of the ancient Near East as *minjung* who brought about their own liberation out of Egypt through God's help.[6] He reads the Old Testament through the lenses of Korean history.[7] Lastly, Korean American biblical approaches have remained largely unexamined to date, and no methodological approach has been offered in print. This essay is an attempt to envision in broad strokes what a Korean American approach may look like. I see a Korean American approach being distinctive in comparison to Asian, Korean, or even Asian American hermeneutics. My fundamental questions are: "What's in it for the biblical text? What critical problem(s) is our method attempting to resolve? What is our controlling methodology?"

Asian and Asian American Hermeneutics

Asian Biblical Interpretation[8]

George Koonthanam's essay, "Yahweh the Defender of the Dalits: A Reflection of Isaiah 3:12–15," is an example of contextual hermeneutics.[9] Koonthanam begins the essay with a brief overview of prophets in ancient Israel. He then relates the abuse of power by the upper crust of society against the poor and marginalized (e.g., Jer. 22:3–19; Mic. 3:1, 9–12; Am. 5:12; Hos. 4:4–10). Koonthanam carefully examines Isaiah 3:12–15 in its proper social and textual setting. The Malayalam proverb, "The fence itself devours the crops," functions to transit the historical critical into the realm of the contextual. After an intertextual word study of First Isaiah's notion of the "poor"–the widow (one without husband), the orphan (one without parents), and, although a bit redundant, the poor (one without money)–a major shift is heard with the following words: "The message of the prophets has its relevance today. Of all the various and varied oracles the prophets left us, their diatribes against those who oppress the weak are perhaps the most frighteningly relevant ones to our Indian situation. In the place of the widows, orphans, and the needy, we must put the dalits."[10] The oppressors are on two levels–international and national. Koonthanam views the G-7 (G-8), IMF, and other powerful corporate economic colonizers who, as international oppressors, strip nations such as India of their dignity while–on the national level–corruption of the judicial system, the local police, and other internal institutions that take advantage of and mistreat and abuse the dalits are the other oppressor.

Koonthanam speaks of crimes and atrocities committed against the Harijan (a term Gandhi coined to refer to the untouchables or dalits in positive affirmation as "children of God"), women, the flesh trade, the overly demanding heavy loads of work involving physical labor, unjust work quotas, rape, discrimination in wages, bride-burning, wife-beating, and the widespread employment of child labor in factories, estates, and hotels.[11] Levels of bribes and corruption cannot be over-emphasized. Even when natural disaster relief funds arrive, those funds wind up in the pockets of local administrators. So Koonthanam asks, "Where are the Prophets in and for modern India?" For Koonthanam, the church, with its Old and New Testament, functions as a voice for the untouchables in modern India.[12]

Asian American Biblical Interpretation[13]

Mary Foskett begins her essay "The Accidents of Being and the Politics of Identity" with the cutting edge issue of the "accidental Asian," which in this case pertains to Asian American adoptees, that is, children who were born in Asia by Asian mothers and then adopted by families in the United States. Although there is newfound joy and hope for these children, the punctuated separation from the original culture, surrounding, and identity into a new context without foresight, understanding, and transition is troubling. Foskett provides the latest figures from the U.S. State Department in which, among the 16,000 immigrant visas issued for adoption in 1999, more than 7,000 were for children coming from Pacific Asia.[14] Foskett explains that certain ethnic agencies attempt to ameliorate the challenges of cultural variances–two examples are the Korean American Adoptive Family (KAAN) and Mam Nan, a Vietnamese organization.

After introducing Eric Liu's memoir *The Accidental Asian,* Foskett moves into two biblical pericopes–Exodus 1–2 and Romans 8–9. Moses' adoption by an Egyptian princess is discussed in light of ethnic and social norms. The process of discovering one's true identity, that is, no longer being an Egyptian, but an Israelite, is vividly described. She ends the section by relating that "[f]or Asian-American adoptees who yearn to claim both their American lives and identities as well as gain at least some access to their families of origin and heritage in Asia, the identity issues it raises are particularly pertinent and potentially painful."[15] After briefly examining spiritual adoption in Romans 8–9 and further developing the imagery of believers being conjoined in the adoptive process as exemplified in Christ and God, Foskett seeks biblical grounds for adopted children–a "recovery of lost origins," while reading for a certain telos.

In short, the message of the biblical text is central for both Koonthanam (Asian) and Foskett (Asian American). A modern situation is healed or brought to awareness or even buttressed by selected pericopes via the application of the biblical text. However, what's in it for the biblical text? How are these interpretations or approaches helping us to better understand that text? It should be noted that cultural, contextual, postmodern/colonial– be it liberation, political, or theological–approaches are a breath of fresh air and genuinely needed in a rapidly expanding milieu of biblical studies. However, the aforementioned inquiries persist.

At the outset of this essay, I referenced the work of Jeffrey Kuan who noted that Asian biblical interpretation falls into the methodological frameworks of *Wissenschaft,* cultural hermeneutics, liberation, feminist, and post-colonial approaches. The fundamental positioning of the *Wissenschaftlich* approach should not be dismissed or ignored. Moreover, Chan Hee Kim remarked that "contextual eisegesis" (reading into the text) should be placed alongside the historical critical "exegesis." What stands out in Kim's remark is that "eisegesis" is taking precedence over the historical critical "exegesis." For Kim, the cultural immigrant's personal or collective experience is brought into the text as those agendas or ideologies are then used to form common ground for appropriation and application in the contemporary setting. The text with its message becomes the guiding principal for parallel contemporary circumstances. Where I differ with Kim is in the use of sociological and contemporary social scientific theories rather than the subjective orientation of the reader (or communities). Moreover, in place of appropriation or application, my objective is to resolve critical problems of the text for the text. Lastly, rather than eisegesis being placed beside the exegesis, I choose to remain in the grounds of the latter, refining the sociological approach to illuminate the products of the sixth century B.C.E.

Both Kuan and Kim have noted key fundamental methodological approaches. These two voices must resonate in the future of Asian American hermeneutics. Hence, to refine my running motif, "What's in it for the biblical text or studies?" it is not enough that the historical-critical approach takes precedence while cultural, liberation, feminist, postcolonial (poststructuralist/ postmodern) approaches are then worked into reinterpreting or applying the text in the modern setting. If Asian American biblical approach or hermeneutics is to impact and contribute to biblical scholarship at large, it *must resolve critical problems.* The objective of the Korean American approach that I am advocating for is to focus on the sociological settings of first- and second-generation Korean Americans to help resolve critical problems of literature and theology of the forced migrations period of the sixth century B.C.E. (otherwise known to biblical scholars as "the exile").[16] Without discussing all scholarly contributions on the "exilic" or forced migrations period, suffice it to say that as important and fundamental as the sixth century B.C.E. is, we know little about this period.[17] Hence, the Korean American approach I am proposing, one girded in sociology, is limited to the time frame of the Babylonian forced migrations (597/587/ 582 B.C.E.) until the time of returned migrations period (Ezra-Nehemiah), and will function to highlight and tackle issues of the biblical texts and theology of the sixth century B.C.E. An example of such is provided below.

A Korean American Approach

In *Sociological Approaches to the Old Testament,* Robert Wilson relates that even prior to the formalization of the sociological approaches, medieval commentators, such as Rashi's disciples Samuel ben Meir and Joseph Behor Shor, were employing their own contemporary society to explain certain pericopes in the Bible.[18] Upon relaying the pitfalls of subjective reading, Wilson says:

> The worldview of the biblical writers was shaped by a society very different from the modern industrialized societies with which we are familiar. The Old Testament is filled with references to various aspects of this society and to the cultural phenomena which it contained. Some of these references may be unintelligible to us if we have no additional information from ancient sources or from archeological excavations and if we know of no comparable phenomena in our own society. In such cases we may be able to supplement our regular sources of information by drawing on social scientific research conducted in modern societies having a social

structure similar to that of ancient Israel. To be sure, each society is in a sense unique, and it would be misleading to assume that ancient Israelite society can be reconstructed solely on the basis of modern analogues. Still, if the sociological information is used judiciously so that the unique features of Israelite society are not obscured, a social scientific approach can bring us closer to the world of the biblical writers than would be possible if we relied on our own cultural experiences.[19]

Two points are central in presenting a Korean American biblical approach: first, as Wilson observes, we must "[draw] on social scientific research conducted in modern societies having a social structure similar to that of ancient Israel"; and second, the "social scientific approach can bring us closer to the world of the biblical writers than would be possible if we relied on our own cultural experiences." Such an approach bridges the variance of time and space via the social structure, while preventing our own personal reading to holistically affect the outcome of the reading. These points are reviewed and employed by Stephen Cook in *Prophecy and Apocalypticism*.[20] Central to our task is to recognize the parallel social structures of the first- and second-generation Korean American immigrant community to that of the first- and second-generation Judeo-Babylonian immigrant community.[21]

Anthony Giddens, in *Modernity and Self Identity,* says,

But what exactly is the self-identity? Since the self is a somewhat amorphous phenomenon, self-identity cannot refer merely to its persistence over time in the way philosophers might speak of the "identity" of the objects or things. The "identity of the self," in contrast to the self as a generic phenomenon, presumes reflexive awareness. It is what the individual is conscious "of" in the term "self-consciousness." Self-identity, in other words, is not something that is just given, as a result of the continuities of the individual's action-system, but something that has to be routinely created and sustained in the reflexive activities of the individual.[22]

This reflexivity and reality is created and sustained by the individual in interaction with others.

Berger and Luckmann note that the reality of everyday life generates the theoretical through phenomenological analysis. The *realissimum* of consciousness is present in the "here and now" of everyday experience: "I experience everyday life in the state of being wide-awake."[23] In addition, "The reality of everyday life further presents itself to me as an *intersubjective* world, a world that I share with others...Indeed, I cannot exist in everyday life without continually interacting and communicating with others [emphasis mine]."[24] According to both Giddens and Berger and Luckmann, the

First- and Second-Generation Korean Americans*	First- and Second-Generation Judeo-Babylonians
Minorities in United States—new environment more cosmopolitan	Minorities in Babylon—new environment more pluralistic
Superpower in 20th and 21st century c.e.	Superpower in 6th century b.c.e.
Room for economic, intellectual, sociopolitical upward mobility	Room for economic, intellectual, sociopolitical upward mobility
Downward loss of ethnicity & culture	Downward loss of ethnicity & culture
Notion of home in Korea differs between generations in the United States	Notion of home in Judah differs between generations in Babylon
Interaction with others in a hegemonic society	Interaction with others in a hegemonic society
Issues of assimilation and isolation, acceptance or rejection of imposing culture as seen in retrospective	Issues of assimilation and isolation, acceptance or rejection of imposing culture as seen in biblical narrative set in Babylonian era—Daniel and his three friends
Religion—Christianity is the nexus that keeps the scattered Korean American immigrants unified	Religion—Judaism is at the cadre of those in forced migration
Preserve traditional theology or revamp, emend, or abolish	Preserve traditional theology or revamp, emend, or abolish
Preserve language (Korean) while acquiring English and Spanish for opportunities	Preserve Hebrew while acquiring Akkadian and Aramaic for opportunities
Defining role of Korean American women	Postexilic—books of Ruth & Esther (combat exclusivity)
Metropolis is where large numbers of immigrants still reside	Communities by the waters of Babylon (Ps. 137; Ezek. 1:1)
Issue of intermarriage as negative in first generation	Issue of intermarriage (Ezra-Nehemiah; Malachi)
Role of religious leaders, elders, for sociopolitical and economic status	Role of priests, Levites, elders, priestly class in general, rise of synagogues
Politically divided nation into North Korea and South Korea	Politically divided nation (north/south), loss of Israel in 721 and Judah in 597/587 b.c.e.
Upper level of educated persons reduced to menial occupations—grocery store worker/ owners, cab drivers, etc.	First wave of skilled and upper level of society reduced to work on irrigation canals

This list may reflect other Asian or Asian Americans. However, I am not in a position to relay with confidence the social structures of the Chinese Americans or other ethnic groups. I wish to acknowledge the affinities that Seung Ai Yang and Lai Ling Ngan noted in the 2004 Annual SBL Meeting. The emphasis, however, lies in the entire set, not on eclectic selection of one or two issues that may resonate.

construction of identity and reality are based on the individual or the collective group's association and interaction with other individuals or groups. This is central in Second Isaiah's overall message of individual and collective redemption, a message of inclusivity. However, what kind of inclusive message is Second Isaiah referring to? Is this inclusivity focused and narrow, or overwhelming and overarching? This is the task at hand in Isaiah 42:6b.

Problem in Second Isaiah 42:6–7: A Light to the Nations

In *Ethnicity and Identity in Ancient Israel*, Kenton Sparks's section on Deutero-Isaiah's message of inclusivity ("a light to the nations" motif in Isa. 42:6–7; 45:5; 49:16) is overly inclusive (cf. Isa. 43:3–4).[25] In the early stages of identity formation, exclusivity–which builds on a narrow and limited group of issues and familiarity–may be more central and warranted. Specifically, the problem of "the nations" in Isaiah 42:6b will be central to the present discussion.

At the outset, we should note the centrality of both the diachronic and synchronic approaches in Isaianic scholarship. Moreover, understanding the multilayering editorial work in Second Isaiah is paramount. The works of M.A. Sweeney, R.F. Melugin, R. Rendtorff, H.C. Spykerboer, R.E. Clements, C. Seitz, B. Childs, and most recently, R. Albertz, are worth noting in Isaianic redaction and expansion.[26] The problem of the four suffering servant passages, however, will fall outside the scope of our discussion. We are interested in solving the problem of who Second Isaiah or the redactor is referring to in "a covenant to the people, a light to the nations" (Isa. 42:6b).[27]

Sparks contends that the phrase "light to the nations to open the eyes that are blind" (42:6–7) is a message of universal salvation; inclusive of not only Israel/Judah, but also foreigners. Continuing the thought of S.R. Driver of the late nineteenth century, Sparks takes this message to refer to the spiritual welfare of foreigners. He reads 42:6–7 and 49:6, "to reach the ends of the earth" as spiritual blindness rather that the political removal of Babylon. Sparks indicates that he is going against the works of Whybray, North, and Westermann.[28]

In addition, employing the work of John Van Seters, Sparks connects the Abrahamic promise in Genesis 12:1–9–the blessing through association of "a great nation"–with Second Isaiah. The third reference of Isaiah 44:5 is argued in favor of ethnic foreigners assimilating and rejoining Yahweh as God. These inclusive notions are essential in Sparks's overall work of demarcating Second Isaiah's inclusive theology in contrast to the exclusivity found in Ezekiel and the "Holiness Code." The message in Second Isaiah and Third Isaiah 56:3–7 is understood by Sparks as the assimilation of foreigners not as separated aliens but as one in Jacob (Isa. 44:5).

Sparks is wide off the mark.[29] Moreover, every major commentator (except John L. McKenize), including Oswalt, Blenkinsopp, and Baltzar, has freely inserted the definite article into their translation when there is no marker of the definite article in the Hebrew text of Isaiah 42:6b. For example, Oswalt translates it as, "I will make you a covenant of the people, and a light to the nations,"[30] while Blenkinsopp translates, "I preserve you and present you as a covenant for the people, a light for the nations,"[31] and K. Baltzer translates, "And I <took> your hand and <formed> you and <made> you to be a covenant to the people and light to the nations."[32]

The Masoretic Text of Isaiah 42:6b reads:

וְאֶצָּרְךָ וְאֶתֶּנְךָ לִבְרִית עָם לְאוֹר גּוֹיִם.

Keeping poetic parallelism of ABA¹B¹ and the Qal imperfect commentary (vv. 5–9) on verses 1–4 and the succeeding verse 7, I prefer a more context-pericope-based rendering–"I will preserve (in the sense of guarding from danger) you (2ms pronominal suffix; cf. Isa. 49:9; 26:3), I will make you (2ms pronominal suffix) into[33] covenant of people,[34] into 'light (of instruction'[35]) of nations (Judah and Israel)." A more wooden apposition-oriented literal translation would be "I will preserve you, I will make you into covenant-people, into light-nations."

There is a major difference between "the nations" (הַגּוֹיִם) or more specifically "to the nations" (לְגּוֹיִם) in Second Isaiah (cf. Isa. 42:1) and "nations" (גּוֹיִם), which refers to Judah (42:6b and 49:6) or Judah and Israel. The purpose clause, "[So] that my salvation may reach the ends of the earth" (Isa. 49:6) has been rendered and read as a message of universal salvation reflecting "light to the nations" (NRSV). However, in light of the context of verse 6 of chapter 49, this message cannot reflect universal salvation–"For He [Yahweh] has said 'It is too little that you should be my servant, in that I raise up the tribes of Jacob and restore the survivors of Israel: I will also make you a light of nations, that my salvation may reach the ends of the earth." The purpose clause reflects the tribes of Israel and Judah, who are now understood as nations–without the definite article. The detriment is the careless insertion of the definite article (cf. the NRSV, RSV, NIV).

This essential marker or lack of the definite article is central in correctly transmitting the message of Isaiah 42:6–7. The definite article differentiates a universal reading from the more narrow and closed notion of nations in an Abrahamaic sense, i.e., nations or peoples descending from Abraham as the BDB suggests.[36] Second Isaiah is extremely careful in employing "nations" without the definite article, in contrast to "the nations" with the definite article. The school of Second Isaiah or his disciples were cognizant of this essential variance. This point is primarily evident in First Isaiah's usage of "the nations" (הַגּוֹיִם) and "nations" (גּוֹיִם).[37] In Second Isaiah, the lexeme "the nations" is employed in five instances to relate to all known nations (Isa. 40:17; 42:1; 43:9; 45:20; 52:10) whereas "nations" demarcating Israel and Judah occurs in 40:15; 42:6; 49:6, 22; 54:3.[38] Another point of departure is the difference between how the lexemes "nation" and "nations" are employed in the final form of the book of Isaiah.[39]

There is nothing wrong with a message of salvation (light[40]) to only Judeans and Israel in Second Isaiah.[41] This does not go against the theology of hope and renewal, new creation and new exodus. Second Isaiah's self-reflexivity as well as the *realissimum* of everyday life was for his immigrant community. This immigrant context was not a message about universal and overly inclusive salvation as Sparks contends. Rather, the web of social setting that *routinely created and sustained the reflexive activities of the Judeo-Babylonians was that they were the descendents of Abraham as Judah and Israel in forced migration.* They were the recipients of this light and this covenant. Israel and Judah were the ones who needed to have their eyes opened from blindness, to be released from the shackles of the prison in darkness (Isa. 42:7). I wish to substantiate this point by drawing a further social structural parallel in terms of "nations."

Within the contemporary first-generation Korean American context, North and South Koreans (Israel and Judah) are considered to be different groups/nations, distinctive in culture and tradition, with dialect difference in language. However, in North America, though different, they are one people. This is evident in social, political, and religious gatherings. The nomenclature "nations" may be further extended to include the variances in rural and urban, the educated and laborers,[42] and even the first and second generations.[43] In our poetic parallelism, "people" (עַם) and "nations" (גּוֹיִם) are understood as parallels.

In the Korean American immigrant community, these noted points are especially visible among the people in the approximately 870 Korean American churches from Boston to Washington, D.C.[44] Each congregation is a compilation of various sub-geographical groups from provinces in Korea (Cholla, Kwang Won, Choong Chung, Jae Ju, etc.). The lexeme גּוֹיִם in the plural as reflected in the poetry of Second Isaiah represents the various groups within Israel and Judah. Hence, there is no need for an overly inclusive message at this rudimentary setting as Sparks and others argue. Duality or bicultural integration of being a Judeo-Babylonian with particularities from one's own subculture is the nascent stage of ethnic formation for an immigrant community.[45] This exclusive inclusivity is a celebration of commonality, uniformity, and salvation in the midst of the diverse plurality in Babylon. This in itself is internally inclusive, though the definition may be exclusive from an outsider's point of view.[46]

For Second Isaiah's community in forced migration, it is the transformation "into" the product of Abrahamic blessing; "I will make you 'into' a great nation" is that which is being appropriated in a grander and more luminary means through the words as "a light of nations." Here, the reference is to Judah, or Israel and Judah. This is carefully demarcated over against the phrase "to the nations," as seen in verse 1 of the same chapter. This same import is also found in 49:6, 22. The fault, however, lies on translators who have freely inserted the definite article where the

Masoretic Text has none. This observation, along with the parallel social Korean American matrix, has assisted us in resolving a literary and theological problem of the sixth century B.C.E. context as seen in Isaiah 42:6b.

In closing, the insertion of the definite article "the" before nations into a translation when the original Masoretic Text text does not have the definite article has generated an incorrect view of Second Isaiah's message of salvation. Rather, "light of nations" refers to Judah, or Israel and Judah. We began this essay with current definitions followed by demarcations of Asian and Asian American hermeneutics. Central inquires were: What's in it for the biblical text? What critical problems is our method attempting to resolve? And what is our controlling methodology? A Korean American approach has shown the importance of עַם and גּוֹיִם in Second Isaiah. The sociological approach is the controlling methodology, as a Korean American approach is limited to the literary and theological problems of sixth century B.C.E.

10

Lot's Wife, Ruth, and Tô Thị

Gender and Racial Representation in a Theological Feast of Stories

MAI-ANH LE TRAN
Pacific School of Religion
Berkeley, California

Introduction

In the beginning were stories, so the theologian C.S. Song convinces us in his book *The Believing Heart: An Invitation to Story Theology*: "The Bible is a world of stories in the world of stories, the world in which God is involved from beginning to end."[1] Increasingly, however, it is acknowledged that the "Christian" world is not the only world in which God is active, nor is the "Christian Story" revealed in the canonical scriptures the only grand narrative that tells of the activity of God within creation. From an Asian perspective, for instance, Song asserts that theologians are regaining a "theological taste" for their own "living space." Song's eloquent exhortation to fellow theologians reads:

> We must whet our appetite for the songs and hymns that our poets, ancient and modern, sing in praise of nature and in despair of life. We must develop an eye for works of our artists who paint the hopes and frustrations of life with primitive forcefulness. We must read records of suffering and joy, mistakes and glories of our people, with our hearts beating fast and with our blood throbbing in our veins. Then we can do our theology.[2]

Thus, we are invited to engage in God-talk and human-talk amidst a wider world rich with stories, such that our individual stories become intricately connected to one another, just as God's story became intricately connected with human stories when "the Word became flesh and lived among us" (Jn. 1:14).[3] What results from this "interchange" of stories is "a theological feast of stories–the story of Jesus, stories from Asia, stories from Hebrew Scripture, stories from the Christian community, and stories from the rest of the world, told as stories of God's dealing with humanity."[4]

The celebration of such enlivening possibilities, however, is not without serious consideration of a darker reality: through stories, we not only liberate, but also dominate. Power and control can be exercised through the telling of certain narratives or the reinforcing of particular interpretations and ideologies. Thus, while the invitation to "a theological feast of stories" is itself a refreshing challenge to Christian theology, the theological enterprise must also engage in a critical examination of the stories that are being told and exchanged among different traditions. Such critical engagement follows the conviction that narratives, which are articulations of everyday reality, are as socially conditioned as are our lives. Attention to the contextual, situational, and political nature of narrative practices enables us to take seriously what biblical scholars such as Fernando Segovia call the "flesh-and-blood reader," one who is "historically and culturally conditioned, with a field of vision fundamentally informed and circum-scribed by such a social location."[5] Hermeneutical approaches that begin from the standpoint of the "flesh-and-blood reader" call for our particular attention to the contextuality of meaning and the political ramifications of the production and reception of meaning through language–more specifically, through narrative practices. That is, the invitation here is for readers to examine how the texts serve as normative and normalizing narratives by which ancient and contemporary audiences are to "script" their lives. This exercise is particularly meaningful for the feminist and postcolonial subject, who narrates, reads, and interprets from within the interstices of society (whether or not by choice) and under the weight of intersecting forms of biases, prejudices, and oppression.[6]

Here, I respond to Song's invitation to the theological feast by initiating an "interchange" of stories from two worlds–namely, that of the Hebrew Scripture and of the Vietnamese folk traditions. Exhilarated by the promising vision of a theological feast, I eagerly looked toward a cultural-religious repertoire heretofore relatively unfamiliar to me as a Vietnamese American, the repertoire of mythic stories and legends, of folk traditions and songs that have been transported and transmuted with diasporic imagination from the land of Vietnam. The task presented a daunting question: Can anything good come out of Vietnam–a "Nazareth" of contemporary global and theological communities? Where should one begin banging one's theological stick into a space filled with over two thousand years of history embellished with legends of dragons and kings, poetry and proverbs, religious practices and rituals? How are we to discover the strokes of God's saving love in a people who pride themselves as *con rồng cháu tiên*–children of dragons, descendants of immortal fairies? Obviously, the questions posed betray the conviction that much can come out of this land that was once referred to as the Pearl of Asia. With the images of two biblical "pillars" in mind, I looked and discovered a tale of the "pillar of longing" and realized that this culture's story–with all of its liberative and hegemonic manifestations–can be brought into what Kwok Pui-lan calls "dialogic imagination" with the other two familiar biblical narratives.

Thus, what I have at hand for the theological feast are three female characters from two cultural-religious narrative repertoires: Lot's wife, Ruth, and Tô Thị. Two are silent, frozen pillars–one of salt (Lot's wife), the other of stone (Tô Thị)–and the third heralded as a pillar of redemption (Ruth). In juxtaposing these three different narratives, I ask what has been said about them. Not only that, I wonder how they have been used to sustain certain normative scripts by which ancient and contemporary listeners and readers of the tales are to interpret gender and racial roles and identities. This examination of such narrative encoding of ideologies of subordination and domination through gender and racial representation follows a postcolonial feminist attentiveness to the intersection of gender and race, especially as we identify questions that have been raised about misogynous interpretations of the three female characters. A postcolonial feminist consciousness sharpens our investigation of how these stories and such interpretations may serve to perpetuate certain modes of gender or racial representation that sustain ideologies of subordination and domination that service male-dominant and/or Western-imperialist systems. With such heightened consciousness, we can then freely imagine possibilities for rereadings or reinterpretations that liberate rather than dominate.

Introducing the "Pillars": Lot's Wife, Ruth, and Tô Thị

Lot's Wife: The Pillar of Salt

Within the image-filled Genesis narrative of the destruction of Sodom and Gomorrah is a single mysterious sentence: "But Lot's wife, behind him, looked back, and she became a pillar of salt" (Gen. 19:26).[7] Of all the spaces available in the biblical text, Lot's wife gets one sentence. No history, no story line, no beginnings–only one terse statement narrating the ill-fated and untimely ending of her life. Although this single sentence may have the power to personalize the destruction that took place at Sodom and Gomorrah, it is not enough. Not only was Lot's wife's story glossed over by ancient biblical narrators, it also was generally overlooked by older biblical commentaries. Many spend but a few sentences on her. And if there were any interest in interpreting this character, the one sentence allotted to her in the biblical text would likely be referenced as the piece of incriminating evidence against this woman, resulting in the commonly accepted justification of her death.

Perhaps G.J. Wenham's comments best represent the established interpretation that has for so long influenced popular understanding and perception of Lot's wife:

> By looking back, Lot's wife contravened the instruction not to look back in verse 17 (Gen. 19). By disobeying a God-given instruction, she forfeited her God-offered salvation. In looking back, she identified herself with the damned town...Finally, it creates sympathy for Lot...It is not so much his bereavement that evokes sympathy but the fact that he was a husband who did not enjoy whole-hearted support from his wife...Like their mother, they [Lot's daughters] too had imbibed a love of Sodom and its attitudes.[8]

J.B. Coffman draws from the same hermeneutics certain "lessons" that one must learn–"lessons" that no doubt have frequently been taught in Sunday school classes to the young and old, "lessons" that Jesus himself may have referred to in Luke 17:32 when he said, "Remember Lot's wife." We are to learn these things from Lot's wife, according to Coffman:[9]

1. She is a warning to all who are tempted to sacrifice their safety in order to win or keep more of this world's goods.
2. If we strive to possess the best of both worlds, we are likely to lose both.
3. She is a reminder that being "near safety" is not enough.
4. She is a warning that, having begun to follow the Lord's Word, one may still turn back from the way and be lost.

Coffman goes on to explain that the command to "not look back" really referred to "a purposeful 'returning back' to the doomed city."[10] Thus, she was not "changed" into a pillar of salt as though it were a divine "vengeful retribution." Instead, according to Coffman, God had every intention of saving her. Unfortunately, "Lot's wife entered the disaster zone contrary to the will of God and against his [*sic*] specific commandments," and for that she lost her life.

Ruth: The Pillar of Redemption

But Ruth said,
"Do not press me to leave you
  or to turn back from following you!
Where you go, I will go;
  Where you lodge, I will lodge;

your people shall be my people,
   and your God my God.
Where you die, I will die—
   there will I be buried.
May the LORD do thus and so to me,
   and more as well,
if even death parts me from you!" (Ruth 1:16–17)

Surely these beautiful words attributed to a widowed Moabite woman have been cited and recited to extol the timeless virtues of love, loyalty, faith, and self-sacrifice. Traditional commentaries one way or another lead us to this conclusion about her life:

> For this one pleasing instance of fine instinct and motive in the life of a peasant home is made to suggest the truth that...the constant sanctities of the cottage and the family altar were the saving of the nation...[It is] as if God would...assure us that the quiet power of woman and the patience of home-keeping lives and the care of the cradle and the hearth mean as much in His [*sic*] eyes as the work of the statesman and the warrior. There are both struggle and victory here, but they are those of virtue—the virtue of all gentle and gracious womanhood.[11]

Some call the story a Hebrew idyll,[12] others a Hebrew historical "nouvelle."[13] However one may categorize this narrative, its female protagonist Ruth is "beloved by all who read her story."[14] According to E.F. Campbell, Ruth is "'the gleaner-maid, meek ancestress' of David the psalmist for Dante, model for Christiana's youthful companion Mercy for Bunyan, chooser of the better part, and thus, like Mary, the paradigm for Milton's virtuous young lady."[15]

The words attributed to Ruth in 1:16–17 seem to build up one of the central themes of the short story—that of common people engaging in the covenantal practice of *hesed,* or loyalty, integrity, responsibility, and kindness, through ordinary activities within human relationships.[16] Commentaries that praise Ruth for her extraordinary embodiment of *hesed* would probably agree with Campbell's observation: "What makes Ruth a true Israelite is that she, like others in the story who are generically Israelites, behaves like one."[17] That is, while there is no outright proselytizing depicted in the story, it makes for a good argument that the way of Yahweh, as lived by Yahweh's people when at their best, is the model for being in human relationship regardless of racial lineage.[18] Thus, as the story unfolds, Ruth the Moabite woman makes it into Israel's history as the foremother of David the king, and is adopted by Christians as a redemptive figure, the foremother to Jesus the Messiah. After all, "Ruth the Moabite woman is the one who shows Israel the way of faithfulness that leads to redemption"![19]

The interpretation of Ruth's loyalty, faithfulness, self-sacrifice, and resourcefulness takes various forms across the hermeneutical gamut. For instance, Gillian Rowell reasons in *The IVP Women's Bible Commentary* that by committing herself to Naomi, "Ruth unknowingly secures for herself the role of redeemer, for her covenantal confession reveals a loyalty and commitment that will be borne out in the rest of the text and that results in God's blessing."[20] Through "loyalty" and "self-sacrifice," Ruth "pledges allegiance" to Naomi, to Naomi's people, and Naomi's God, and in doing so God redeems her through the wealthy Boaz.[21] Meanwhile, Julie Chu extols the ability of Ruth and Naomi to "dedifferentiate" their culturally ascribed gender roles–that is, "to redefine the restrictions for gender and to liberate the traditional patriarchal value of women"–which enables them to affirm their own value as women despite all odds.[22] Ultimately, "Ruth [breaks] the rule for her sex and [finds] a new future in a strange land."[23]

Tô Thị: The Pillar of Longing

It is said that on the mountains near the Vietnamese-Chinese border stands a rock formation that resembles the figure of a woman standing with a child in her arms. According to traditional Vietnamese folklore, a young wife–named Tô Thị in many versions–there stood fixedly in quiet longing for her long-lost husband. A contemporary storyteller writes: "She was changed into stone, and it is in this form that one can still see her, upright against the sky, motionless in her eternal waiting."[24] Popular imagination suggests that the husband had been called to war.[25] Numerous poems and folksongs have been written about this story, which itself has been told in multiple versions, all to herald the virtues of women who, like Tô Thị, remain selflessly devoted to their husbands and children regardless of circumstances, and particularly through the trials and tribulations of war and poverty. The pillar is named *Hòn Vọng Phu*. *Hòn* can be translated as "pillar," *Vọng* interpreted as "waiting" or "longing," and *Phu* means "husband."

It could be said that the character Tô Thị remains peripheral to formal Western academic discourses. The story itself is well recognized within the Vietnamese folk tradition, popularized by means of cultural songs and poetry. Chinese scholars also confirm the existence of a similar storyline in their cultural repertoire. It would not be a stretch to argue that the implicit cultural understanding of this story is that it speaks of the very same virtue of "gentle and gracious womanhood" that has easily been attributed to the biblical character of Ruth.[26] With patience and resignation, Tô Thị stands on the hills, fixated in eternal waiting for her husband. The idea that this pillar may be holding a male child in her arms suggests that she fittingly embodies the three traditional Confucian virtues of obedience for women: acquiescence to (1) fathers when young, (2) husbands when married, and (3) sons when old or widowed.[27] Most popular versions of the tale simply suggest that the husband has been called to war. Regardless of the plot, however, the role of Tô Thị is to remain the same—patient, resigned, faithful, loyal, selfless, steadfastly committed to her husband and his seed.

Re-imaging/Re-imagining the "Pillars"

Ancient Israel, in its attempt to explain a peculiar salt deposit, told an etiological tale of Lot's wife. Similarly, ancient Vietnam created its own imaginative story to explain the existence of a strange rock formation within its land. Interestingly, whereas the biblical story has largely been read in ways that evoke unsympathetic reactions to an ill-fated woman and has been used as a solemn warning against various social and religious taboos, the Vietnamese folk tradition has inspired its hearers and readers to admire the presumably time-honored virtues of women. One woman stands lifeless, forever looking forward into the horizon; the other frozen in a backward glance. Then there is Ruth, a timeless "pillar of redemption"—with all of the virtues exemplified by Tô Thị and none of the vices characterized by Lot's wife—a figure upheld for women to emulate. From all that has been said of the three pillars, we are presented an opportunity within this discursive space to re-image/re-imagine these characters, specifically as we contemplate the ways in which gender and racial ideologies encoded in these narratives intimate particular theologies of "sin" and "redemption." In doing so, we expose ambiguities, complexities, and paradoxes that may be more reflective of and meaningful for everyday living.

"Sin" and Gender Representation: "Fallen from Grace" or Ridden with "Han"?

Of the three female characters highlighted here, Lot's wife is the one most readily condemned for the "sin" of identifying with the cursed city of Sodom. Her story echoes the ancient narrative motif of the "taboo on looking back."[28] How fitting that this narrative would have a woman character representing the violation of such taboo: her "looking back" is conveniently interpreted as a sign of excessive love for the alleged immoral city of Sodom and its attitudes. We look at this indictment and ponder: If Lot's wife was punished for having "identified herself with the damned town,"[29] then how are we to really interpret the difference between her identification with the "damned town" and Abraham's own identification with it in his pleading with God earlier in the narrative, especially as his action is admired rather than condemned? What is it about Sodom and its attitudes that make them so undeserving of love? And if the backward glance of Lot's wife signifies her lack of "support" for her husband, as some claim, then what in his actions showed his support for her? If Lot were a second slower, would he have shared her fate? How ironic that "it is the single backward glance of Lot's nameless wife rather than the petty protests of Lot that meets with instant retribution."[30]

A freed imagination takes us to some Midrashic traditions to discover a story of Irit–or Mrs. Lot–who had four daughters altogether, two of whom chose not to flee the city with their parents but stayed behind with their Sodomite husbands instead. Out of her "motherly instinct," Irit could not help but look back to see if their daughters were following behind them.[31] It is said that from heaven rained "sulfur and salt,"[32] hence the city was incinerated into sulfur and the people turned into pillars of salt. In this sense, Irit shared the fate of the people of her city:

> Irit looked back to see if her two first-born daughters were follow-
> ing, and she saw that they weren't and what had become of them.
>   In such a moment of grief one knows only one desire: to follow
> after one's child, to experience what she's experienced, to be one
> with her in every aspect of suffering. Only to be one with her.
>   And it was for this desire that Irit was turned into a pillar of
> salt. She was turned into salt either because God couldn't forgive
> her this desire...or because He could.[33]

The image of a lonesome, abandoned pillar looking over the hills toward a site of destruction calls to mind many other lonely "pillars" in our history and in our midst–women who for one reason or another are unwilling to turn their backs against what was behind, so they "look back" against all odds and in spite of warnings, and become forever changed–for better or for worse. One cannot help but see the parallel between the striking image of the pillar of Lot's wife and that of weary and desolate Vietnamese mothers–such as the young woman Tô Thị–frozen as they look back at what is left of their war-torn country. How easily many Vietnamese mothers can identify with Lot's wife in this regard, for they, too, have turned their back against freedom and deliverance to run back into unforgiving infernos...only to be with the children they were unwilling to leave behind. What some consider to be the pit of hell, the cauldron of iniquities, the seat of immorality, the heart of darkness, the axis of evil, others may think of as *home.* Danna Fewell and David Gunn offer this poignant insight:

> So where are the *women*? Where are the young, not the young
> men but the *children*–the daughters and sons. Where are the *babies*?
> Where are all these in this facile talk of the righteous and the
> wicked? This language is inappropriate, even more so in tradi-
> tional translation: choose "righteous" instead of "innocent" for
> *tsaddiq* and the translator has semantically excluded the
> children...Why look back? Because Sodom has been *home*–Lot's
> wife's belonging.[34]

Was it simply for the sake of rhetorical convenience that in the text Lot's wife became a pillar of *salt*–the "preservative" of life? Fewell and Gunn write: "Salt preserves Lot's wife as a monument which cries out in distress to heaven. For salt is tears, anguish for the women and children of Sodom."[35] The salty tears that fell from her face–they may very well be the same tears that Lady Meng shed for her ill-fated husband in the fable mentioned by C.S. Song in *The Tears of Lady Meng*,[36] the same tears that Vietnamese mothers shed holding burnt picture albums, rocking empty hammocks, sipping lonely cups of tea, or lighting sticks of incense in mourning for their dead. "O God, save us from turning into statues of tearless-ness!" is the prayer that should echo in our hearts.[37] For when there are no tears, there is no salty taste, no stories, no feelings. And without stories, without feeling, without salt...there is no life.

Lot's wife, Tô Thị, women trapped in ill-fated situations, innocent children caught in the midst of evil, members of a diaspora who carry memories of pain and joy, of despair and hope: these are *han*-ridden pillars. The now-familiar concept of "han" has been defined as "frustrated hope," "the collapsed feeling of pain," a release or loss of self-center and self-control, resentful bitterness, a "wounded heart"; "Han is the division of the tissue of the heart caused by abuse, exploitation, and violence. It is the wound to feelings and self-dignity."[38] It is "a sense of impasse," an "unexpressed anger and resentment stemming from social powerlessness [which] forms a 'lump' in [one's] spirit."[39] In this light, Lot's wife and Tô Thị are figures of han-ridden women being caught in the interstices of social-cultural worlds governed by ideologies of domination and submission. A popular Vietnamese song, loosely translated below, expresses the "lump" in a Vietnamese mother's han-laden spirit:

Ca Dao Me[40]
(The People's Song about Mother)

She sits rocking her child in that sorrowful hammock
She sits rocking her child...clouds pass by the treetops...may
  rain fall from heaven
May rain fall from heaven that the soil may soften and the field
  may blossom
She sits rocking her child, with tears of travail, in anguish over a
  sorrowful fate.

She sits rocking her child in that sorrowful hammock
She gazes at her homeland...
hearing the sadness of her children, shedding a tear of remorse
A tear of remorse and repentance, of self-pity and shame,
as she sends her child back into the earth
A river flows whirling up into the sky, takes with it the fate of a
  human being.

She sits rocking her child, her song adrift
She sits rocking her child, mesmerizing a soul

> She teaches her child the language of the homeland
> She sees her child gone...stunned, dazed, stupefied.
>
> She sits rocking her child in that sorrowful hammock, lulling her own fate
> She sits rocking her child, and hears the call of the earth...a wandering fate
> She sits for a hundred years like a sad pillar, leaving behind her homeland
> A forsaken, desolate age, a world of hatred and bitterness, of war and imprisonment.

The stirring lyrics (more poignant in the original Vietnamese) seem to conjure up for us a ghostly figure, a sad pillar beside a swaying hammock, eyes fixed in a deadened gaze at a forsaken, desolate age, a world of hate and bitterness, of war and imprisonment. The heartrending image strikingly parallels those of Lot's wife and of Tô Thị—the frozen "pillars" looking out to the horizons of their homelands. Perhaps if they could, these two pillars would tell us that to "look back" is to simply be human.[41] All that talk about "righteousness" versus "wickedness," "right" versus "wrong"—perhaps it is the rhetoric of conquest, of domination and subjugation. When might we speak of love—particularly a mother's love? And if we speak of love, might we also ask, *At what cost?*

In the end, we look at Lot's wife and Tô Thị and wonder: Where lies their redemption? Traditional interpretations would afford none to Lot's wife, and to Tô Thị, only a patronizing celebration of her "gentle and gracious womanhood." In contesting the ways in which these female characters are represented in their respective narratives, we see them not as symbols of "sinfulness," or worldliness, or even exemplars of quiet submission. If anything, they are han-ridden women who stand looking back or staring forward, perhaps in defiance, perhaps out of solidarity, or perhaps simply rendered lifeless due to an overwhelming "lump" in their spirit. Above all else, their stories demand a different understanding of divine and human justice.

"Redemption," Race, and Gender Representation: Saved from What and for What?

If Lot's wife is traditionally condemned for being reluctant to let go of what is behind, the character Ruth has no apparent attachment to her own past. As the story is told, Ruth secures her own salvation when she selflessly identifies with Naomi and professes a commitment to the god, people, and place of her mother-in-law. Not only that, but, through her own resourcefulness as a "model minority" within a foreign land, Ruth is bestowed the distinctive role of "redeemer" in Israel's salvation history.

Fewell and Gunn provide an example of imaginative readings that challenge simple character or thematic development in their literary critical midrashic analysis of Ruth. Opting for a "leaner, tougher" read, they question why "the story's ultimate endorsement of the women seems to be that they serve the interests of men."⁴² That is, whether she is in her father's house, her first husband's house, her mother-in-law's house, or her second husband's house, Ruth is in the service of men. Moreover, her "assimilation" as an "other woman" is subjected to the terms of inclusion and exclusion of her new host society. In exploring the characters as "complex" and "multi-faceted" figures,⁴³ Fewell and Gunn expose ambiguities, ironies, and negotiations in the story, thus challenging flat characterization or simplistic thematic development. The following excerpt of their retelling illustrates their approach to imaginative reading of the biblical text:

Damn it, life could go on without husbands and sons...[Ruth] had made up her mind. And when Naomi made some remark about how she should go back with her sister-in-law to her own people and her own gods Ruth smiled to herself: it's always religion, isn't it, Naomi–religion and country. Difference really does bother you, doesn't it. But now she knew exactly how to make her rejoinder: "Stop telling me to leave you and quit following you. I'm going where you go. I'm going to stay where you stay. Your people can be my people. Your god can be my god." (That ought to get her goat, she thought.) "And I'll be damned if I let even death separate us." Death has separated you from all your men–everyone who counts–and you think that death is all that's left for you. If you go it alone, she thought, death will surely beat you.⁴⁴

As evidenced by Fewell and Gunn, despite various readings affirming Ruth's agentic character or subversive role, and despite the apparent "happy ending" that many commentaries embrace, there are still questions to be answered, gaps to fill, and new readings to imagine. Examining the social markers ascribed to Ruth within the dominant Israelite social milieu, we see a widowed, immigrant, "foreign" woman. We could employ a postcolonial feminist interpretive lens to explore the following questions: Why does Ruth choose to leave her homeland to follow her mother-in-law? What does Ruth forfeit in identifying with the people who speak ill of her Moabite ancestry? What are the terms of "inclusion" imposed on Ruth by her new host society? Is there true liberation from nationality, class, and gender in the end, as some would have us believe?⁴⁵ Is the "other" to forfeit their identity so that they may overcome boundaries of race, gender, and class? And, if Ruth is to be praised for her "faith," then we must ask, what exactly is "faith" in this narrative? Faith in what? What is "redemption"?⁴⁶ What is Ruth saved from? And for what?

Juxtaposing Ruth and Lot's wife for comparison and contrast, we see that in addition to a name, Ruth has something that the hapless "Mrs. Lot" does not: a so-called "happy ending" to her life story. Unlike Lot's wife, Ruth is "redeemed" in the end. However, whether she is interpreted as a passive willing "vessel" of God or an agentic woman crafting her own plans for a better future, we wonder how costly "salvation" is for this foreign woman. In a sense, the story would have us believe that Ruth makes a decision which Lot's wife is unable to make—that is, leaving behind her past, her home, her identity to adopt a new future, new home, and new identity. It is an either/or decision: return to her own people and forfeit "salvation," or adopt a new identity according to the way of Yahweh's people and be "saved." Commenting on the possible intention of the biblical narrator for having constructed the story of Lot's wife, Gerhard von Rad writes: "Where God intervenes in a direct act on earth man [*sic*] cannot adopt the stance of a spectator; and before divine judgment there is only the possibility of being smitten or of escaping, but *no third alternative* [emphasis mine]."[47] Ironically, just a chapter before the destruction of Sodom (Gen. 18), the patriarch Abraham thought that a "third alternative" was possible as he initiated a plea bargain with God. And then a few verses before the death of his wife, Lot successfully begged for a "third alternative": he was granted permission to flee to Zoar. Why for some and not for others—and, incidentally, why for men and not for a woman? Perhaps Ruth saw no "third alternative" in her plight either: return to her "mother's house" as an "Israelite-lover" to be arranged for another marriage, or sever ties from her native kin, neighbors, and land and venture to foreign soil?[48] Neither seems to be a promising choice.

How an "alien woman" stands out as the heroine in Israel's story of salvation history invites an exploration of its gender and racial politics. From a theoretical framework of the symbolic politics of immigration, Bonnie Honig begins her discussion of Ruth by suggesting that the parallel dynamics of inclusion and exclusion in the story are contingent on the *foreignness* of the model immigrant.[49] Responding to the writings of Cynthia Ozick and Julia Kristeva on Ruth, Honig notes their reference to two dominant modes of responses to immigrants in a society: either "welcoming" or "wary"; that is, "either immigrants are valued for what 'they' bring to 'us'…or they are feared for what 'they' will do to 'us.'"[50] More often, it is the combination of the two responses, so that on the one hand immigrants provide a morality boost to the ethnocentric or nationalistic pride of their host society by assimilating to it, while on the other hand they pose a threat to its established order or its sense of cultural and political identity. Honig makes the following observation of a "deep and abiding ambivalence" about foreigners that pervades the story of Ruth:

> After all, it is Ruth's *foreignness* that enables her to choose the Israelites in a meaningful way. Indeed, the more radical her

foreignness, the more meaningful the sense of chosenness that results from her choosing. The more deep the enmity between Moab and Israel, the more profound the friendship that is declared in its midst. The more radically particular the convert, the more obviously universal the divinity that compels her to join up. The Israelites' own insistence that *their* god is (uniquely) universal is what puts them in need of periodic new testimony to his charms. Even as they eschew converts, they rely on them in this deep way. The most powerful testimony to Judaic monotheism's attractions is the testimony provided by the *most* unlikely person, the one coming from the most radically particular and hostile culture. It is because Ruth is a Moabite that her conversion, if a conversion it was, is fabulous. Indeed, were it somehow possible to cleanse Ruth of her foreign Moabite identity, the price of such a cleansing would be the very gift she has to offer.

And yet, that same foreignness makes Ruth deeply threatening to the order she might otherwise simply reinvigorate. There is no way around it: a *Moabite* has come to live in Bethlehem![51]

In the end, "redemption" as inscribed by the story leaves us wondering from what Ruth is saved and to what (or for what) she is saved. If it is any consolation, she finds security in a husband and a new home—better that than petrify like Lot's wife and Tô Thị? How liberating is this redeemed and redemptive figure for the postcolonial subject, for those whose lives must be scripted by virtues encoded in these seemingly timeless narratives?

Looking at the "pillar of salt," the "pillar of longing," and the "pillar of redemption," we insist that they not categorically personify so-called sinful worldliness or so-called redemptive virtues of "gentle and gracious womanhood." The genderized and racialized ways in which "sin" and "redemption" are insinuated in these narratives reveal interstructured forms of submission and subordination that sustain ancient as well as contemporary patriarchal/kyriarchal and ethnocentric/imperialistic ideologies, resulting in multilayered han for the "pillars" and for the many "other" women they represent. As argued here, narratives that seemingly celebrate or liberate may very well be used to denigrate or dominate depending on how they are interpreted within the socio-politico-cultural-religious matrices of the "flesh-and-blood reader."

Conclusion

In this discursive space, we have picked up on what has already begun: to raise questions, to discover what has been left out of the stories, to "fill in the blanks," and to bring to life the lost "pillars" by engaging in imaginative conversations about them. Not only that, a freed imagination convinces us that there exists many "pillars" in various colors, shapes, and sizes. They, too, are the figures that have been or are continuing to be left frozen, forgotten, lost, ignored, silenced, misunderstood, misused…When we attempt to listen to the "voice" of one "pillar," all of a sudden we can hear voices of the others as well.

As it is in our reality, stories *about* "pillars" are usually created and told by "non-pillars." As such, they potentially encode ideologies that keep "pillars" silent and sustain "non-pillars." What new truths might be revealed if we were to let the "pillars" speak for themselves and tell their own stories? That being impossible here, we work with what is available and begin the hermeneutical task by bringing together the three narratives from different cultural-religious repertoires. We scrutinize what has been said about the pillars found in the narratives; we expose how they may have been misunderstood, misused, and misinterpreted by the communities that created them as well as the communities that have read about them. Ultimately, gleaning from the insights of fellow interpreters of cultural and religious stories, we uplift the various challenges to interpretations that perpetuate hegemonic modes of gender or racial representation, interpretations that inscribe certain virtues and vices that the three pillars supposedly represent. The hope is that new understandings will emerge out of this imaginative endeavor, resulting in new liberating possibilities for the general readers of these tales, for the descendants of dragons and immortals, and particularly for women reading the Bible from the interstices of their society.

The legend of the "pillar of waiting" (*Hòn Vọng Phu*) also gives evidence that much can come out of the elusive and controversial land of Vietnam, a "Nazareth" of the global, religious, and theological communities. It is hoped that the juxtaposition of the three "pillar" figures here will contribute to the "theological feast of stories" for the reading and interpreting of biblical texts as well as cultural texts. Theologians find that once the fear of their own cultural space has been overcome, a world of stories opens up, yielding glimpses of God's revelation. If we are to discover how God meets people at the base level of human existence, and if we are convinced that it is where the hermeneutical task should begin and end, then perhaps we would do well sitting alongside of rocking hammocks, or taking risky steps into disaster zones, or standing by frozen "pillars," looking in the direction of their gazes as they stare into the face of pain, suffering, and desolation. Only then might we find the courage to believe and assert that descendants of dragons and immortals can be and have been theological *subjects* in their own right, having already been touched by God's saving love.

11

Betwixt and Between

Toward a Hermeneutics of Hyphenation

SZE-KAR WAN
Andover Newton Theological School
Newton Centre, Massachusetts

Some time after I had decided on the title of this essay, I came upon the remarkable work of Peter Phan bearing a similar title.[1] I considered using something other than "betwixt and between" to introduce my topic, the hermeneutical task of Asian-American biblical scholars. But I resisted the temptation. It is said, imitation is the sincerest form of compliment. In that case, this essay is a tribute to Phan and others like him for having charted *terra incognita* and mapped the experiences of Asian-American theologians. Fruits of their labor have been instrumental in creating a conversation, indeed a community of conversation for Asian-American theological scholars, in the land of betwixt and between, the newfound territory where I now know I have always resided and where I always will, the wild earth where only those who seek out and recognize each other will survive.

For our conversation to forge ahead, Phan calls for a renewed appreciation of our Asian-American identity in terms of an "anthropology of time." By that he means the task of holding our past and future with equal tenacity, the paradox of critically appropriating our ancestral history in order to shape our vision ahead. He characterizes the task a "fusion" of our past memories with future imagination, as preconditions to address our theological task at hand in the here and now. While we are between cultures and political centers, we also live in the in-between time. The past insistently insinuates itself into our present, even as the future holds out promise for us with tantalizing expectancy. Our in-between-ness is therefore not an ineluctable trap but a hopeful starting point. According to Phan:

> We who live in time do not experience the past as something irretrievably lost and gone but as truly present, effectively shaping our identity and our destiny. Similarly, we do not experience the future merely as something empty and unreal; rather, we experience it as a lure and a challenge, inviting us to move forward to actualize our potentials. In this human time, the past is gathered up and preserved in our *memory,* and the future is anticipated and made real in our *imagination* [emphasis his].[2]

If the nexus where past and future meet and where memory and imagination conspire to form an organic whole conditions our theological task, then it is even more true for biblical hermeneutics. This is a field in which battles continually wage between historical critics and ideological readers, between those who favor doing nothing more than excavating the brute fact of historical datum and those who fix their suspicious gaze on the use and abuse of the Bible in the world of ideology. For Asian-American biblical scholars, then, betwixt and between describes not only the temporal tension between past and future but even more keenly the tension between two hermeneutical camps in the guild. While the different methodological proposals are themselves built on different valuations of the past and present, it is the political blocs of competing allegiances in the academy that make our job daunting.

For Asian-American biblical scholars, the task of remembering and imagining must fulfill at least two prerequisites before we can set out on our task with inventive faithfulness. First of all, we must become aware that we live in the in-between world, caught not only between our double cultures but also between political factions. This lays the critical foundation of conscientization. Second, we must learn to negotiate the thickets and trenches of the battleground, that we be knowledgeable and wise in it as much as we are competent and skilled in our technical craft. Only then can we examine the biblical text through our unique cultural eyes. It is hoped that this essay, modest in conception and scope, can provide a bird's-eye view of the land's layout, so that our future travels together might be as creative as safe.

The Politics of Hyphenation

In the last half century, American biblical studies have finally matured as a discipline. I use "mature" in the sense used in developmental psychology of a child becoming stable and independent. More than a century ago, ever since Moses Stuart introduced continental biblical criticism to the United States, American scholarship had in the main followed the European lead. From historical criticism to biblical theology, from the classical quest for the historical Jesus to the so-called "second quest," from form criticism to redaction criticism, American scholars seemed content simply to transplant continental approaches with little translation, either reluctant or unable to venture beyond the boundaries and delimiters set by their contemporaries across the Atlantic.

The sixties and seventies witnessed a fundamental change in the direction of American biblical scholarship. The emerging civil rights and feminist movements impacted every facet of American society and directly challenged the intellectual citadels of the academy. Every field in the humanities, especially biblical studies, had little choice but to respond to the social challenges mounted in society. This was the decisive moment when American biblical studies gained independence from Europe and began to mature. For a time in the seventies, structuralism and literary criticism, both imports from Europe, enjoyed brief, sporadic popularity among biblical scholars, but soon it became clear that only through engaging the most potent and most provocative questions in American society could a hermeneutical movement stand the test of time. The rise of African-American hermeneutics, feminist and womanist reading of the Bible, liberation hermeneutics, even the Jewish-Christian dialogue, which have dominated biblical studies the last quarter century, are all examples of the abiding influence of cultural upheavals in the field. For better or for worse, perspectival readings such as these are here to stay, even as traditionalists resist and resent their steady advances in the academy. The investment of these readings in the American culture is simply too extensive and too deep, and their contributions to the continual vitality of the discipline too great and too important, to be ignored even by their opponents.

Historical Criticism Versus Ideological Reading

The current debate is at heart a hermeneutical one. On the one side are the old guards of historical criticism, who in spite of decades of attacks by their opponents still hold sway in the most powerful institutions in the academy. The premise of this group is a familiar one: the meaning of a text is delimited if not determined by the authorial intention. Consequently, the aim of biblical interpretation is to excavate the historical meaning the original author vested with the text, and tools appropriate for such an interpretive enterprise must be able to bracket the interpreter's subjective assumptions and prejudices out of the equation, lest they taint the supposedly unsullied, pristine meaning of the author. Then and only then, so goes the argument, could the scientific, objective meaning of the text be obtained.

On the other side, in contradistinction to historical critics stand (at the risk of gross simplification) the "ideological readers," so called because they emphasize the modern situatedness of the interpreters. They criticize historical critics for giving legitimacy to an illusory task: since an objective reading of a text without the presuppositions of the interpreters is impossible, historical criticism is nothing more than a mode of meaning production by the modern readers. If that is the case, the ideological critics propose, it is far more honest, not to mention methodologically more consistent, to take the interpreters' sociopolitical situation as the context within which to seek solutions to the problems they face. This reading strategy privileges the modern readers and their sociopolitical, cultural, linguistic location, and it sets as its final goal a subjective reading of the text.

Even though these two opposing camps may seem poles apart, in one respect they are identical: namely, their tendency to separate the subjective from the objective, with the result that the interpreter is isolated from the text. The distinction between the investigator and the subject matter is, of course, a fundamental axiom of the modernist epistemology, the very definition of positivistic objectivity. The subject matter must be removed from history and from the experience of the investigator before its contents can manifest itself. When applied to the humanities and especially biblical interpretation, this means isolating the interpreter's starting point, assumptions, prejudices, commitments, questions, tastes, faith, and the like from the act of interpretation so as to arrive at a supposedly pure interpretation untainted by the interpreter's involvement. The result is "a mode of inquiry that tries to deny its own hermeneutic character and mask its own historicity so that it might claim a historical certainty."[3]

But on closer examination the problem of severing the text from the interpreter burdens not just the historical critics. In rejecting the failed objectivity of positivism and in privileging the readers' position in their own location, ideological readers are always in danger of denying the independence of the text or, worse, creating a text after their own image. While historical critics replace the text with an imputed original meaning behind it, ideological readers might also be guilty of bypassing the text to reconstruct a symbolic universe based on their own perspectives. As a result, the text vanishes from view, the dialogue between reader and text weakens to a monologue by the interpreter, and the rupture between interpreter and text becomes unbridgeable. While both camps tend to regard understanding as a conception out there that must be captured and formulated, Hans-Georg Gadamer, following Martin Heidegger's phenomenology of being, regards understanding as an event that unites the interpreter to the text, because both participate in a tradition that is centered in and defined by language. In the final analysis, true understanding is a creative encounter between the interpreter and the text, with the result that neither is left by the wayside.[4]

Elisabeth Schüssler Fiorenza offers a solution to the current impasse between historical critics and ideological readers. In her 1987 Society of Biblical Literature presidential address, she advances an ethical proposal to biblical scholars that balances a concern for their ethical responsibilities with a stress on the historical task of biblical scholarship. She begins with a rejection of the positivistic view of the biblical text and proceeds to define the nature of the biblical studies as one of reconstructing the sociopolitical discourse embedded in and embodied by the text:

> A rhetorical hermeneutic does not assume that the text is a window to historical reality, nor does it operate with a correspondence theory of truth. It does not understand historical sources as data and evidence but sees them as perspectival discourse constructing their worlds and symbolic universes. Since alternative symbolic universes engender competing definitions of the world, they cannot be reduced to one meaning. Therefore, competing interpretations of texts are not simply either right or wrong, but they constitute different ways of reading and constructing historical meaning. Not detached value-neutrality but an explicit articulation of one's rhetorical strategies, interested perspectives, ethical criteria, theoretical frameworks, religious presuppositions, and sociopolitical locations for critical public discussion are appropriate in such a rhetorical paradigm of biblical scholarship.[5]

While Schüssler Fiorenza's "rhetorical hermeneutic" places her squarely in the corner of the ideological readers, she also advocates that biblical scholars must first follow an "ethics of historical reading." Such a historical reading gives the text its due "by asserting its original meanings over against later dogmatic usurpations," and it gives the text the freshness of an "other" that can confront, even irritate, our self-interests.[6] In so doing, Schüssler Fiorenza is following Gadamer's and especially Paul Ricoeur's notion of "distanciation," which gives space for the text to stand in judgment of the readers without being co-opted by them.[7]

According to Gadamer, and before him Rudolf Bultmann, the text does not yield an infinite number of possible interpretations, as if the text had a life of its own and could reveal meaning at will. This is so even if the interpreter's only goal is to uncover the original meaning of the text. The reason for this is that any historian must approach the text not with a *tabula rasa* but with a prior set of questions, questions that stem from the reader's own socio-political and cultural contexts.[8] Schüssler Fiorenza takes to her hermeneutical task with a similar hermeneutical assumption. By "historical," she means finding out not "what the text meant," as if that were a value-neutral question, but "what kind of readings can do justice to the text in its historical contexts."[9] It is the readers ultimately who have final say in determining what questions are legitimate and what are not. While there may be a multiplicity of interpretations available for every text, she maintains that there can only be a limited number of interpretations "that can *legitimately* be given to a text [emphasis mine]."[10]

If so, one could draw the inescapable corollary: Since all questions are posed by enquiring subjects firmly situated in their own sociopolitical context, what makes this historical reading "ethical" ultimately depends on whether the exegetical results of a text could legitimately address *that specific* context. This is precisely the underlying assumption of Schüssler Fiorenza's second principle of interpretation, the "ethics of accountability," by which she means:

> ...the responsibility not only to interpret biblical texts in their historical contexts but also to evaluate the construction of their historical worlds and symbolic universes in terms of a religious *scale of values*...[Biblical interpretation must] include the elucidation of the *ethical consequences and political functions* of biblical texts in their historical as well as in their contemporary sociopolitical contexts [emphasis mine].[11]

If I understand this correctly, Schüssler Fiorenza is suggesting that any historical interpretation of the biblical text and the construction of the historical world behind the text must correspond to a certain "scale of values" and that the reconstructed historical world somehow must correspond to our contemporary social and political contexts in "ethical consequences and political functions."

It would be a caricature of hermeneutical theories to say that one's starting point already determines the destination and one's question predetermines the answer. As Gadamer makes clear and Schüssler Fiorenza further reinforces, the starting question determines only *what kind* of answers we would receive in return, not the specific answers. Interpretation, according to Gadamer, is an event, an encounter between the interpreter and the text, in his language a "fusion" of the horizon disclosed by the text and the horizon that circumscribes the interpreter's own visions and assumptions. It is precisely the interpreter's own location or horizon and the questions posed proper to it that form the start of a hermeneutical event. While what type of encounter it is to be is predetermined by the interpreter's pre-understanding, what the encounter finally looks like and what synthesis the encounter would produce remain indeterminate and open-ended. In this regard, it is perfectly legitimate for us to pose certain types of questions but not others. For Schüssler Fiorenza, the ethical questions biblical scholars ought to pose are social and political ones, ones that effectively challenge and transform society.[12]

Betwixt and Between

But is Schüssler Fiorenza's rhetorical hermeneutic a satisfactory solution to the Asian-American dilemma? Despite its balance between historical reconstruction and social and political concerns, does it help Asian-American biblical scholars to achieve the same balance? Almost two decades after her call, it has yet to make a difference in how Asian-American biblical scholars encounter and are accepted by the academy. It is a reality that the vast majority of the training centers for biblical scholars remain in the hands of historical critics. While scholars today pay lip service to the need for contextual biblical scholarship, and while neither Gadamer nor Schüssler Fiorenza denies the importance of historical reconstruction in biblical studies, it remains true that almost all graduate programs in biblical studies today still place heavy emphasis on historical criticism in their curriculum, with the aim of producing more historical critics. What is true in graduate education is even truer in job searches after graduation.

Faced with this dilemma, Asian-American scholars are forced to make a choice between two equally undesirable alternatives. Either become a full-fledged historical critic–to play the academic game as it were–and buy into the claims of universality, thereby reinscribing the dominant discourse that marginalizes all who do not share its assumptions and perspectives; or retool to become an ideological reader who must now join other ideological readers who have already staked out their claims at the by-now crowded margins. If we were to remain historical critics, we would have to bracket our ethnicity and allegiance to our constituencies in order to subscribe to the fiction that the fruit of such scholarship represents the objective, the universal, the true. There would be no room for suspicion of or inquiry into the foundational claims that are tacitly assumed in the academic halls of power. Such a move would imply a capitulation to a discourse structured and maintained by the dominant culture, and subsequently lead to assimilation and loss of identity.

It is, however, equally perilous for Asian-American scholars to become ideological readers. For one, it means leaving behind traditional structures that have nourished their maturation and through which they have attained a modicum of status within the academy. In the conflict between the universal and the particular, Daniel Boyarin and Fernando Segovia pro-posed that we must adopt a "diaspora identity," an identity that critically engages texts of antiquity from a particular vantage point.[13] Boyarin seeks to construct an idealized diaspora in which there are only slaves and no masters, while Segovia proposes an ideological and polyglot hermeneutics based on the concrete experience of the readers. Since both proposals begin with their own cultural and social locations, they are both autobiographical.[14] But, as I have written elsewhere, it would be the height of irony, not to mention injustice, that just as we are invited to the table for the first time, we are told we ought to abandon it for another table elsewhere, away from the center, at the margins:

Now..., after we have learned the language, we are all of a sudden told that it is the wrong language after all–this is a catch-22 situation postmodernism has created for us. Now that we have learned to speak and write like our white teachers, we are told we should develop and construct our own narratives, or in Boyarin's terms divest our power and basis for that power of which we have never taken hold—even now. Well, not so fast. Give us a chance to consolidate our community, give us a chance to create a place for ourselves in the academy, let us have some power, if you will.[15] Once that is established, then and only then, can we fully embrace Boyarin's suggestion that a diasporized identity can in fact be the key to communication with all other diasporized groups.[16]

In other words, will an adoption of an ideological reading strategy doom Asian-American scholars to self-ghettoization? Do we risk creating a self-exoticizing enclave within the academy that uses our own specialized idioms, with little communication with, and even less recognition by, those on the outside? As Timothy Tseng notes, Asian-American religious studies has yet to become a legitimate part of the academy: While mainstream theological scholarship treats it as an exotic form of ethnic studies, which means it can be safely ignored, within Asian-American study programs across the land, religious studies are simply ignored or, worse, vilified. Are Asian-American biblical scholars working themselves into further marginalization by being too enamored with the margins?

But our difficulties with an ideological reading go beyond the political culture of the American academy; they are also deeply embedded in the Gadamerian phenomenological hermeneutics. For Gadamer, it is possible for the interpreter to come to an understanding of the text, because both text and interpreter are located in an "effective history" (*Wirkungsgeschichte*) that embraces both text and interpreter. Neither is found in a vacuum; both participate in a "life-world" that is grounded in language. In short, it is the supposedly unbroken stream of tradition from text to interpreter that makes interpretation possible and acceptable. Because the interpreter experiences the text already in tradition, he or she comes to it with certain assumptions and prejudices. This initial pre-understanding is itself made available to the interpreter through tradition, even if in the course of further encounter with the subject matter of the text it is revised or discarded. However, this would happen within tradition and consequently the new and adopted understanding comes also through tradition. It is in the give-and-take between interpreter and the subject matter in and through tradition that one gradually distinguishes between truth and error. So, far from being objective in the modernist sense, the interpreter is deeply involved and actively participates in tradition. Tradition is for Gadamerian hermeneutics the *sine-qua-non* condition for understanding to take place at all.

If that is the case, this raises the question about the nature and shape of this "tradition." As Michel Foucault would put it, who gets to define this tradition and who determines what is considered a legitimate part of it and what is not? Georgia Warnke and others have criticized the Gadamerian tradition for being "conservative." She asks:

What guarantees that the views we explicitly adopt from the tradition are any less arbitrary than the prejudices that we previously held in an unreflective way? If the learning that occurs through the anticipation of completeness reflects simply the acceptance "with agreement" of an aspect or interpretation of the tradition other than that to which we previously held, why assume that it involves learning at all? We seem to be able to revise the prejudices we have inherited from the tradition only by assuming the validity of other prejudices the tradition contains.[17]

To the charge that this is simply substituting one's own prejudices with those available in the tradition, Gadamer replies: just like practical reason (*phronesis*), truth becomes real understanding only when its general claims can be concretized in particular situations and circumstances. Truth has no independent, dogmatic application apart from its application to specific contexts. Tradition can only supply the general shape and parameters for any truth-value, but there is no hermeneutical understanding unless it is tailored to the different needs of different people under different circumstances. Understanding in this respect is always situated and contextual. Hence, Gadamer's oft-repeated conclusion: "We understand differently if we understand at all."[18]

Quite aside from the possible charge that such an understanding could be seen as arbitrary and opportunistic,[19] such a view assumes the existence of a relatively uncomplicated tradition that transmits the values and truth claims of a text in straightforward, linear fashion. For Asian-Americans, however, this is far from being the case. The nature of our hyphenation bespeaks not a single tradition but a multiplicity of traditions, all of which impose varying, at times contradictory, values on the biblical text. In some traditions, the Bible might have been experienced as a foreigner's book in the context of an imperialistic or colonial discourse; in others it might be a religious text that speaks of piety or personal devotion. In some, it may be used as an oppressive text used in the service of subjugating minorities and women; in others it is found in a tradition of freedom and liberation that affirms the fundamental worth of human beings. Since the Bible is received through the refraction of a multiplicity of circumstances and contexts in the Asian-American experience, all these "traditions" play equally constitutive roles in how we receive the Bible, and it is from within the totality of these variegated traditions that we approach the Bible. While Gadamerian hermeneutics would see the truth of a text revealed in the dialogue between interpreter and text and in its application to different contexts, tradition as a hermeneutical category is an inherently unstable and ambiguous concept for Asian-American biblical scholars.

Boyarin and Segovia could find comfort in their positions, partly because their particular, self-limiting definition of tradition affirms, and is in turn confirmed by, their membership in their respective ethnic groups. The general shape and parameters of either the Jewish-American or Hispanic-American communities in the United States are stable and recognizable, as is the place of the biblical text in both traditions. While this does not deny the diversity within either of the communities, the stability of these communities relative to Asian-Americans enables them to opt for a reading strategy that is confidently and particularly Jewish or Hispanic. For both Boyarin and Segovia, the hyphen signals a bridge that brings their own particularistic tradition to bear on American culture. For Asian-Americans, by contrast, the hyphen marks an interstitial space, betwixt and between two dominant traditions but belonging to neither.[20]

Toward a Hermeneutics of Hyphenation

To be betwixt and between is to be neither here nor there, to be neither this thing nor that. Spatially, it is to dwell at the periphery or at the boundaries. Politically, it means not residing at the centers of power of the two intersecting worlds but occupying the precarious and narrow margins where the two dominant groups meet and clash, and denied the opportunity to wield power in matters of public interest. Socially, to be betwixt and between is to be part of a minority, a member of a marginal(ized) group. Culturally, it means not being fully integrated into and accepted by either cultural system, being a *mestizo,* a person of mixed race. Linguistically, the betwixt-and-between person is bilingual but may not achieve a mastery of both languages and often speaks them with a distinct accent. Psychologically and spiritually, the person does not possess a well-defined and secure self-identity and is often marked with excessive impressionableness, rootlessness, and an inordinate desire for belonging.[21]

While describing the negative aspects of the hyphenated existence, Phan, a Vietnamese-American theologian, also points out the creative and productive side of being between two worlds. "Being neither this nor that," he says, "allows one to be *both* this and that. Belonging to both worlds and cultures, marginal[ized] persons have the opportunity to fuse them together and, out of their respective resources, fashion a new, different world, so that persons at the margins stand not only between these two worlds and cultures but also *beyond* them."[22] Gadamer made a similar observation, albeit in the context of hermeneutical understanding: the gap between the interpreter and the text is the impetus for understanding. It is the closing of that gap, the in-between space that separates us from the text, that constitutes our hermeneutical effort. Speaking to the same hermeneutical moment in different language, Phan proposes a way of doing theology betwixt and between by honoring the memories we bring with us into our hyphenated identity and, at the same time, plan for the future with creative imagination.[23] The old world, our ancestral culture that we leave behind, forms the bedrock of our foundation, but it is a foundation that, Phan cautions, must be reappropriated and recreated on the basis of the future that we anticipate. The future is an imaginative "extrapolation" (Karl Rahner's *Aussage*) into the future. It is therefore the creative layering of past, present, and future to form the substratum of a hyphenated identity.[24]

Phan's optimism is in part influenced by Jung Young Lee's notion of marginality. The classic definition of marginality by Robert Park and Everett Stonequist describes marginality as a social and psychological disorder characterized by conflicted personality, psychological uncertainty between social worlds, schizophrenic maladjustment—all negative traits that discursively brand the marginalized as diseased and inferior.[25] Lee prefers rather to speak of not in-between but in-both:

> I have been taught that I am in-between, between two antagonistic worlds without belonging to either. I don't deny it, but what I want to stress is my positive perspective of myself as a marginal person. I am in-both, in both the world of my ancestors and the world of my residence. In other words, I am both an Asian and an American. The contemporary self-affirming definition of marginality emphasizes the idea of in-both rather than in-between. "In-both" complements and balances "in-between."[26]

To be in-both becomes a positive affirmation of our identity when we take our both-and-ness with seriousness and realism, Lee suggests. So, an Asian-American is more than Asian because he or she is also American, and more than American because he or she is Asian.[27] In fact, because there is no third independent space between the two dominant groups, Lee contends that one could make the best of the situation by combining the in-between and in-both qualities of marginality, a condition he calls "in-beyond."[28] Indeed, this positive valuation of the hyphenated identity of the Asian-American echoes what Wesley Woo articulated almost thirty years ago: "Lest you think by 'hyphenated' being I mean schizoid being— I don't. The hyphen I find symbolic of an enriching and multifaceted dimension of being in spite of the negative feelings bred by racism in this country."[29]

Double Identity, Double Rejection

The hopefulness of Jung Young Lee, however, is not totally embraced by all his Korean-American colleagues. While acknowledging Victor Turner's view that marginality could have positive potentials, Sang Hyun Lee argues that what Asian-Americans experience is a "coerced liminality," a status the dominant culture out of oppression and downright racism forces on a minority group. While anthropologists wax optimistic that "liminality is society's subjunctive mood where suppositions, desires, hypotheses, possibilities...all become legitimate" or that "the marginal space is the gap in which hermeneutics begins and ends–forms and reforms," Lee points to the existence of ideology in society that creates a specific form of liminality for Asian-Americans.[30] In the experience of the Asian-American minority group in the United States, "[liminality] is not just an in-between experience but also an experience of being dominated and dehumanized by...the racist hegemony of a society's controlling center."[31] If there are creative potentials in liminality, they coexist in tension with a destructive oppression that frustrates and debilitates Asian-American potentials–an oppression made all the more destructive by legitimating racist domination with naturalistic and scientific theories.[32]

The feeling of rejection is registered in Julia Ching as well, except that this rejection comes not only from the Western side of her identity but also from her Chinese side. She makes explicit something to which a few others have also hinted: the experience of double rejection. A Chinese Catholic Sinologist, born and bred in China but educated in the West, Ching speaks of her being caught between the East and the West but belonging to neither. In her numerous trips to China, she finds that she is no longer at home in her birthplace; at home in the West, she does not feel entirely at home either–all this in spite of thorough familiarity with both cultures. For the Chinese she is too Western; for Westerners she is too Asian. Instead of looking for community in the two cultures, she now finds meaning and identity in the intimacy of her family and friends.[33]

Others have also experienced this double rejection. Phan notes that the Vietnamese government only considers a Vietnamese who has left his or her ancestral country a *viet kieu* or "a sojourner of Vietnamese descent."[34] Even in the midst of an otherwise hopeful celebration of his double identity, Jung Young Lee also admits that he is "in-between, between two antagonistic worlds without belonging to either."[35] Chinese-Americans have also recorded exasperating experiences of being branded as "second-class Chinese" by Mainlanders.[36]

If these experiences are any indication, the flip side of the Asian-American double identity is double rejection–rejection by the host culture for being foreign and rejection by the ancestral culture for being impure. However one views the reality of our hyphenation, be it seen as a bridge joining two cultures or as a chasm separating the two, the Asian-American identity is characterized by doubleness: a double vision directing our gaze forward and back, a double pull tugging us in opposite directions toward the centers, a double repulsion driving us to the margins, to that in-between nonspace that both centers share but neither wants, a double representation by both centers of us as not just an "other" but *the* "Other" in order to justify continual confrontation and conflict between the two. At the heart of our doubleness, then, stands the double exploitation of marginalization and confrontation, and in the heart of this confrontation we are the perpetual and persistent enemy from within.

The power of this representation is derived from a perverse act of mimesis, an act perpetrated by both centers. Wesley Woo speaks of the experience of Chinese-Americans' first being singled out as the enemies during the McCarthy era and then treated with more sympathy and respect after the Nixon visit to China, without any perceptible internal changes in the Asian-American community.[37] One need only mention the case of Vincent Chin who was brutally murdered because he was thought to be one of the "Japs" who took the auto manufacturing jobs from white Americans in Detroit. The fortune of Asian-Americans rises and falls with how Asia is constructed in this country at any particular moment. The opposite is no less true. Our visits to Asia these days are greeted at once by scorns and derision, for we are now mimetically constructed as representatives of the Evil Empire, the *jia yangguizi* ("pseudo-foreign devil") who abetted in world conquest and prisoner torture. However we stress our solidarity with those from our ancestral land, our native colors have been irrevocably and permanently bleached out of us. Inasmuch as we have been colorized by white America, we are also whitewashed by our own kin.

Hybridity in Betwixt and Between

Homi Bhabha has theorized a similar doubleness in the context of the colonial experience of India. Commenting on Frantz Fanon's *Black Skin, White Masks*,[38] Bhabha suggests that the divide between blacks and whites–social constructs both–or that between the colonizers and the colonized, is not as clear-cut as one might think. There is a continuum between the extreme poles of the "Colonialist Self" and the "Colonized Other," and it is this in-between, interstitial space where one could legitimately talk of hybridity. Hybridity, in Bhabha's eloquent words, is:

> a doubling, dissembling image of being in at least two places at once which makes it impossible for the devalued, insatiable evolué (an abandonment neurotic, Fanon claims) to accept the coloniser's invitation to identity: "You're a doctor, a writer, a student, you're *different*, you're one of *us*." It is precisely in that ambivalent use of "different"–to be different from those that are different makes you the same–that the Unconscious speaks of the form of Otherness, the tethered shadow of deferral and displacement. It is not the Colonialist Self or the Colonised Other, but the disturbing distance in between that constitutes the figure of colonial otherness–the White man's artifice inscribed on the Black man's body. It is in

relation to this impossible object that emerges the liminal problem of colonial identity and its vicissitudes.[39]

While Bhabha sees the colonized subject as represented as weak and dependent, Asian-Americans could well be represented as powerful and intelligent. The "whiz kid" phenomenon popularized by American mass media in the eighties and the "wealthy cousin from America" image in Asia conspire to have created for the Asian-American identity a powerful mystique, which is to say a powerful stereotype and misrepresentation. Rapid globalization and the rise of East Asia as an economic powerhouse and South Asia as a hi-tech haven do nothing to correct this image. We are still perceived to be the successful minorities who have managed to pull the wool over white America's eye. To my announcement of an upcoming junket through New Zealand sponsored by my relatives, my otherwise liberal white colleague ejaculated, with a note of protest, "That's why everybody hates you guys, because the Chinese have taken over the world!" Little did he realize that my relatives slaved over their fish-and-chips shop for over twenty years to earn themselves a small corner of the white men's world.

If that is the case, Bhabha's notion of hybridity would need to be revised. The relationship between the colonialist and the colonized is one of domination between master and slave, with the master inviting the slaves to become like him, which is to say to become *different* from other slaves, not in order to grant the slaves liberation, but, on the contrary, in order to confirm their status as slaves. It is in the ambivalent space of similar yet different that Bhabha locates the essence of hybridity. "The liminal problem of colonial identity," consequently, is the creation of a neither-nor identity that is, in Bhabha's terms, neither totally white nor totally black. The relationship between Asian-Americans and the center of power is also one of domination, but it is one based on confrontation between two centers that confront each other by proxy through a (mis)representation of the Asian-American identity. If so, the double rejection we experience as Asian-Americans paradoxically also gives us more independence and more self-determination than we might realize. We are therefore in a better position to play an active role in shaping our guild, our world, our future than we might think possible.

Robert Young helpfully distinguishes between two forms of hybridity. Drawing on Mikhail Bakhtin's discussion of linguistic hybridity, Young cautions against an *organic, unintentional hybridity* used in eighteenth- and nineteenth-century colonial Europe to justify the superiority of the "pure" race. In such unintentional hybridity, "the mixture remains mute and opaque, never making use of conscious contrasts and oppositions."[40] But *conscious and intentional hybridity* is political and contestatory, stressing division and separation, even as an internal dialogue continues.[41] Thus, "in organic hybridity, the mixture merges and is fused into a new language, world view or object; but intentional hybridity sets different points of view against each other in a conflictual structure, which retains 'a certain elemental, organic energy and open-endedness.'"[42] Hybridity is properly a "disruption of homogeneity,"[43] as Bakhtin and Bhabha argue, that relies on a "double logic, which goes against the convention of rational either/or choices."[44] In this double sense of hybridity, the term means making the same out of different entities and forcing sameness into difference.

Accordingly, hybridity in the Asian-American land of betwixt and between must be one of *conscious integration* of two cultures even as we are keenly aware that we occupy the margins of both cultures. A passive acquiescence to the social role the dominant culture assigns us is an acceptance of the constructed homogeneity of society and the fictitious normativity of the prevalent discourse. Only by challenging these assumptions and by constructing a culturally complex map of who we are as an alternative can we hope to challenge the discursive hegemony of the dominant culture.

Conclusion

After a discussion of Gadamer's understanding of art as mimesis, Georgia Warnke concludes that Gadamer's position can still be defended today, not because an artwork truly represents reality as it is, but rather because art represents truth only as it appears to us where we are. As hermeneutical understanding, artistic expression, if it is to be true to its nature, is contextual. "Artistic representation is a representation of truth in the sense that it releases its subject matter from its contingency."[45] In that case, what is the "subject matter"?

If the foregoing discussion is any indication, the doubleness of Asian-American biblical scholars colors everything we do, so that betwixt and between means also *both this and that.* Our tradition is double: we stand with one foot in our ancestral culture and the other in the West. Our text is double: we read the Bible as a sacred text that once lifted our communities from hopeless isolation, but we also read it as it is enfleshed in the experience of the Asian and Asian-American people. Our hermeneutics is double: we earn our entrance into the guild by perfecting our historical-critical task, but we verify its validity continually against the authenticity of our experience in the guild and in society.

Yin/Yang Is Not Me

An Exploration into an Asian American Biblical Hermeneutics

GALE A. YEE
Episcopal Divinity School
Cambridge, Massachusetts

I am grateful for this opportunity to explore the contours and seams of Asian American biblical interpretation, something that I have wanted to do since delving into the politics of national identity as an Asian American woman for an AAR Women and Religion session back in 1994.[1] Over ten years have elapsed since that presentation. In many ways what follows is a very personal account of my efforts to theorize and problematize Asian American biblical hermeneutics since then. All theories, whether consciously or (more often) not, arise from the diverse experiences and social locations of their theorizers. I will thus use two stories as springboards into a discussion of an Asian American biblical hermeneutics.

Anecdote One

When I had my first job interviews just after graduate school in the early 1980s, my (primarily male) interviewers wanted to know if there was a difference in my interpretation of the biblical text as a woman. The presumption was, of course, that their (male) way of interpreting the Bible was the "traditional" (read: real) way, and then there was the "woman's way." During job interviews in the 1990s, however, when feminism became more established in the guild, my interviewers would turn to my race/ethnicity and whether or not it made any difference in my biblical interpretations. This usually happened at the awkward moment when people could think of no other questions regarding my scholarship. They could always ask me something about my race/ethnicity. I do remember that I resented such questions more than those based on gender, because I at least knew that the white women in the group might know something of what I was talking about with respect to gender. I recall one occasion when I commented obliquely on the appropriateness of such questioning, that a white German male would never be asked in an interview, "What does a white German male interpretation of the biblical text look like?" I did not get that job.

I remember feeling pressed to conform to some nebulous ideal of an Asian American woman, to perform according to some preconceived script of what an Asian American woman should be. Whatever I said would not have been understood. Although I look Chinese, I do not have the usual markers of Asianness.[2] I cannot draw on immigrant experience, since I am a third-generation Chinese American. Unlike Maxine Hong Kingston's mother, mine never told me Chinese legends of ghosts and woman warriors,[3] probably because she didn't know about these herself as a second-generation Chinese American. Although I grew up in a Chinese-speaking household, my parents deliberately did not teach me to speak Chinese. So I do not have a Chinese accent. I did not live in Chicago's Chinatown, but in the gang-ridden Blackstone Ranger territory of Chicago's South Side. My cultural formation was not among other Chinese Americans, but among African American and Puerto Rican slum dwellers, like my family and me. My parents were zealous Roman Catholics, not practicing the traditional Asian religions: Buddhism, Taoism, and Confucianism. *So Yin/Yang is not me.* Except for my face and name, none of the usual ethnic markers of being Asian fit me, yet white society compels me, however well-intended, to explain how my Asian Americanness makes me different. And this particular volume asks me to discuss Asian American biblical hermeneutics as an Asian North American woman.

A book by Rey Chow helped me immensely in understanding my antipathy against racial/ethnic pigeonholing by white society. According to Chow, ethnic persons become like animals in the zoo, under the gaze of the present politics of ethnicity in capitalist liberalism.[4] Chow distinguishes three levels of mimeticism or imitation in postcolonial cultural politics. At the first level, the colonized *had* to imitate the white man, whose language, culture, and values were considered superior, while her own were regarded as inferior. At the second level of mimeticism, the colonized *wants* to imitate white society. In contrast to the *imperative* of being white (ontologically unattainable by a non-white) is now the *desire* to be white. What results is a more fluid, unstable form of mimeticism where the colonized subject simultaneously wishes to be like the colonizer, but hates him at the same time.[5]

By concentrating on whiteness as the original superior, Chow thinks that cultural theorists have neglected a third level of imitation, in which the ethnic person is expected by white culture to resemble what is recognizably ethnic. Instead of imitating white society, the ethnic person is now obliged to conform to a stereotypical construction of ethnicity. Chow calls this a "coercive mimeticism," in which racial/ethnic persons are expected to resemble and replicate certain socially endorsed preconceptions about them, and in doing so, authenticate the familiar descriptions of them as ethnics.[6] She describes the dilemma of the racial/ethnic scholar thusly:

> If an ethnic critic should simply ignore her own ethnic history and become immersed in white culture, she would, needless to say, be deemed a turncoat (one that forgets her origins). But if she should choose, instead, to mimic and perform her own ethnicity in her work–that is, to respond to the hailing, "Hey, you!" that is issued from various directions in the outside world–she would still be considered a turncoat, this time because she is too eagerly pandering to the orientalist tastes of Westerners. Her only viable option seems to be that of reproducing a specific version of herself–and her ethnicity–that has, somehow, already been endorsed and approved by the specialists of her culture. It is at this juncture that coercive mimeticism acquires additional significance as an institutionalized mechanism of knowledge production and dissemination.[7]

Chow helped me see that in those job interviews, I was like a caged animal, bred in captivity, under voyeuristic scrutiny, expected to respond and behave according to hidden parameters of an ostensibly recognizable Asian American female identity. On the one hand, my white interrogators, male and female, defined Orientalist boundaries. On the other hand, there is an added institutional script, one that I am still trying to decipher, that constructs ethnicity "that has, somehow, already been endorsed and approved by the specialists of [my] culture."[8] Negotiating the coercive mimeticism of these cultural "specialists" is another constraint that I labor under. For example, Chow describes the disciplinary conflicts within Asian Studies and between Asian Studies and Asian American Studies. In the former, certain Western sinologists (who may not be Asian themselves) privilege *ancient* Chinese literary works as more "authentically" Chinese than those of modern Chinese writers, whom, they feel, have become too "Westernized." By privileging knowledge of the ancient Chinese *language* as a marker of authenticity, many of these sinologists also regard Asian American studies disparagingly, because Chinese American writers in this discipline use English as their preferred mode of expression.[9]

In Henry Yu's provocative investigation of the Chicago school of white sociologists who devoted their efforts to the "Oriental Problem," he uncovers that race was a theatrical drama for their discipline to examine:

The job of the exotic, unknown ethnics was to play their roles on stage for the edification of the audience. Race was a performance, complete with masks and costumes and uniforms. What was most interesting to the audience was what was exotic. Elaborate costumes, funny accents, and fantastic tales of exotic origins were part of the proper role for Orientals in the playhouse of America. Who wanted to see a play about Orientals in which all the actors wore three-piece suits and acted exactly like white people?[10]

Yu will go on to say, however, that the white sociologists really did want to see the performance of ordinary Americans in Oriental drag: "As an audience, they still demanded the exotic costumes, but in the end they preferred to see the mundane acts of everyday life…What made such a performance racial was the necessity of acting like everyone else, except with the constant constraint of not being like everyone else."[11] Whether in a zoo or on stage, the metaphor of being on racial display puts in the foreground the power differential between the racial-ethnic individual and the Anglo-establishment. As my mind tries to navigate individual and institutional minefields to determine what it means to be an Asian American biblical scholar in a predominantly white guild, I recall the scene at the zoo in the film *Harry Potter and the Sorcerer's Stone.* The muggle Dursleys are banging on the cage window and yelling at the snake to move. When the snake refuses to respond, Dudley declares it to be "boring."

Anecdote Two

The problematics of an Asian American identity became quite evident for me during August 2003 when, as a visiting professor at the Chinese University of Hong Kong, I applied for my Hong Kong I.D. card. On the application form, I put down "Chinese American," for "Nationality," an identity I claim in the States. However, the immigration officer said that I could only be one or the other. I had to choose between being "Chinese" or being "American." I could not be both. Since I had been waiting two hours to see this officer, this was not the time or the place to enter into a discourse about dominant and minority cultures in the United States. I had to choose, and I chose "American." The few weeks I had spent in Hong Kong up to that point reinforced my choice. I may look Chinese, but in Hong Kong I am as American as the white tourists there. The major difference is that Hong Kongers do not speak Cantonese to these tourists, as they always do to me. These tourists also do not suffer the embarrassment that I feel when I must say that I do not speak the language.

Is my identity "Asian American" only in the U.S. context, and "American" in the Hong Kong context where I taught for the year? Am I simply an "American" when I am in Hong Kong, becoming an "Asian American" again when I return to the States? And how does this slippage of identity affect my interpretation of the biblical text? Is my interpretation of the Bible different in each context? *Time* magazine devoted a special Asian issue to Asian Americans journeying to their ethnic homelands. In the issue, Chinese American writer Gish Jen recalls a crisis of identity similar to mine, but in reverse. When her sister became ill during the family's first trip to China in 1979, the local officials refused to recognize her as a "real" American. Thus, she was not eligible for the best hospital in town, which was reserved for white foreigners. Jen and her family were considered Overseas Chinese and were put in a completely substandard hospital, filled with trash. The doctor there carried the sister on his back because the hospital had no elevator.

In a Chinese context, Jen and I experienced in different ways the struggle to claim a Chinese American identity as a "real" American identity. Although our Chinese officials would not accept a pluralistic notion of an American identity, definitions of identity among the Chinese themselves are clearly unstable. Jen relates: "A few years ago in Hong Kong, for example, I had heard Chinese intellectuals question whether anyone was really Chinese anymore. After all, they joked, the Chinese in Hong Kong were so British, the Chinese in Taiwan so Japanese, the Chinese on the mainland so communist."[12] Does it follow then that Chinese in America are no longer Chinese, but American, I ask myself? With shifting notions of Chinese identity, coupled with the plurality, heterogeneity, and hybridity of Asian American identity,[13] is it any wonder that I find an Asian American biblical hermeneutics elusive?

These anecdotes reveal that, in America and in Hong Kong, I am an ethnic foreigner. I remain an oddity in both contexts, and my identity and my biblical hermeneutics are shaped as such.[14] The mere fact of being a woman does not mean an individual is a feminist. In the same way, I know that my being a Chinese American woman does not automatically mean that my interpretations of the Bible are from an Asian American advocacy stance. So in what consists my Asian Americanness, and how does this identity affect my biblical interpretation? Does "Asian American" refer to my ethnicity as a biblical scholar or to the thematic content of my biblical interpretation?[15] If it refers primarily to content, can a non-Asian create an Asian American reading of the biblical text? Conversely, would all of my previous published work not be regarded as Asian American because it did not deal specifically with an Asian American subject matter?

Toward an Asian American Biblical Hermeneutics

In 1926 W.E.B. Du Bois sketched the following criteria to determine an authentic Black theater:

> The plays of a real Negro theater must be: 1. *About us.* That is they must have plots which reveal Negro life as it is. 2. *By us.* That is

they must be written by Negro authors who understand from birth and continual association just what it means to be a Negro today. 3. *For us.* That is, the theater must cater primarily to Negro audiences and be supported and sustained by their entertainment and approval. 4. *Near us.* The theater must be in a Negro neighborhood near the mass of ordinary Negro people.[16]

Can we apply these criteria in an analogous way to understand Asian American biblical interpretation?

The first criterion, that Asian American biblical interpretation should be *about* Asian Americans, might be difficult for the simple reason that the Bible is primarily *about* ancient Israel and the early Church. One could shift the emphasis from the biblical text to its cultural consumption in specific Asian American communities. This paradigm change is the guiding principle behind Vincent L. Wimbush's outstanding collection of essays dealing with the numerous and eclectic ways in which African American communities engage the Bible.[17] Asian American interaction with the biblical text is historically not as extensive or as rich as in African American communities. However, the *Semeia* volume on "The Bible in Asian America," edited by Benny Liew and myself (vol. 90/91 [2002]), provides an excellent beginning in discovering the importance of the Bible in various Asian American contexts and how Asian Americans read themselves into the text.[18]

By underscoring the racial/ethnic individual as the subject (*about us*), one of the values of this criterion is that it attempts to counteract racist biblical interpretations by white society, such as "slaves should be obedient to their masters," and the conversion of the "heathen Chinee"[19] with its attendant colonialism. In a similar vein, early feminists sought to discover or recover positive images of women to counterbalance sexist portrayals. Highlighting positive images to counter negative ones, however, is methodologically limited, because it is prompted largely by what the white male world thinks, believes, or constructs about Asian Americans. The danger here is allowing the primary focus to be the white male superior that Chow cautioned against for cultural studies.[20] Biblical interpretation *about* Asian Americans should be guided by the positive *and* negative engagement of these communities with the biblical text and not solely by the negative use of these texts by white male society against Americans of Asian descent.

The second criterion, that Asian American biblical hermeneutics should be *by us,* written by Asian American authors who "understand from birth and continual association" what it means to be Asian American today, is a problematic one. Who is the "us" who are deemed "Asian American"? The term Asian American emerged during the 1960s as a political category. On the one hand, it was meant to unify culturally different Asian groups with their varied U.S. histories of immigration and racial inequities. On the other hand, by claiming an authentic *American* identity, it tried to repudiate the collapsing of these numerous and diverse groups monolithically known as "Orientals" and "perpetual foreigners."[21] Earlier definitions of "Asian American" based on birth, ethnicity of descent, or cultural tradition have been criticized for being too essentialist, failing to account for historical, economic, and political structures and conditions that are fused with ethnic identities.[22] These circumstances are too varied to insist on a pan-Asian American identity based solely on ethnic or cultural origins. No one experience binds Asian Americans together. We have nothing in common that resembles the history of slavery that African Americans share. Moreover, African Americans do not understand their identities in terms of their African origins. They do not refer to themselves as Ghanan American, Senegalian American, Nigerian American, much less their tribal origins as Mandingo American, Ashanti American, or Yoruban American. Asian Americans, however, often highlight their ethnic identities as Chinese American, Japanese American, Korean American, and so forth, because of the unique histories of these groups and their interaction in the United States. During WWII, for example, Chinese Americans consciously differentiated themselves from Japanese Americans, so that they would not be interred with them or otherwise subjected to anti-Japanese racism.

In contrast to an identity rooted in some essentialized past or fixed cultural heritage, the tendency now among Asian American theorists is to characterize Asian American identity through the lenses of heterogeneity, hybridity, and multiplicity. In an important essay, Lisa Lowe describes heterogeneity as the differences among Asian American groups with respect to national origin, immigration histories, class backgrounds, generational and gender specific attitudes, and so forth. Hybridity results from the accommodation and negotiation of these groups in and among various relations of unequal power. Multiplicity specifies the various ways in which ethnic subjects are positioned across and within different axes of power.[23] Ethnic identity could thus be inherited and invented at the same time, involving both personal exchanges and social construction.[24] Such an understanding of identity underscores the continuous interplay of history, culture, and power in the mutable act of defining: "Identities are the names we give to the different ways we are positioned by, and position ourselves within, the narratives of the past."[25]

An Asian American biblical hermeneutics *by us* will therefore be created by ethnic Asian individuals who, at some point in their histories in the United States, have consciously adopted an Asian American advocacy stance. "Asian American" becomes the name one gives to his or her specific positioning by and within the narratives of the "past" in the United States. The question shifts here from "being" to "becoming," from "Who is an Asian American?" to "What are the different ways of becoming Asian American?"[26] What are the personal, interpersonal, cultural, and systemic influences that allow, trigger, or compel one of Asian descent in the United

States to become an Asian American and appropriate this nomenclature intentionally for herself? I will describe my own process of becoming one shortly.

If one follows Du Bois's reasoning, an Asian American biblical hermeneutics *for us* must cater primarily to Asian American audiences and be supported and sustained by their entertainment and approval. Du Bois's argument, however, relates to African American theater, in which "catering" to a particular "audience" for "entertainment and approval" would be appropriate. Such features do not fit the context of an Asian American biblical hermeneutics. A hermeneutics *for us* does not "cater" to Asian American communities, but rather interprets the biblical texts on their behalf. These communities are not like theatrical audiences who come to see a play, but places in which the Bible has a powerful prescriptive influence, for better or for worse, in the lives of its citizens. The purpose of an Asian American biblical hermeneutics is not to entertain or seek the approval of these communities. Such a hermeneutics may, in fact, critique the ways in which Asian Americans use the Bible to legitimate sexism, racism, or heterosexism in their congregations. Such a hermeneutics may edify, strengthen, and empower Asian American communities. It also may take an oppositional, prophetic role in condemning any biblically based histories or actualities of injustice or oppression within them.

According to Du Bois's fourth and final criterion, a "real Negro theater" must be *near us,* i.e., located in a Negro neighborhood near the ordinary Negro people. This criterion highlights the praxis face of an Asian American biblical hermeneutics. Contrary to the distancing and disinterested training of most biblical scholars in the ivory tower, an Asian American biblical hermeneutics demands that interpretation be *near us.* An Asian American biblical scholar combines theory and practice from a specific and *interested* position in studying the biblical text. We read our own history, experiences, and stories as Asian Americans into the biblical story, as well liberate ourselves from that story, when it becomes a source of injustice.

My Asian American Condition

I now examine my own process of becoming an Asian American by outlining, for the sake of argument, what is Asian about me and what is American, the two prongs of my hyphenated condition.[27] Let us begin with the Asian part. Aside from the fact that I look Asian (which Hong Kongers do recognize), how am I culturally Asian?

Essential to my own self-understanding is that, during my formative years, my grasp of what is Asian has been mediated, for the most part, by American Orientalism: the American representation of Asia, as a geographically remote, foreign land filled with exotic and suspicious cultural practices. This land is thought to be discovered, described, and dominated by the United States.[28] Since I have only recently gone to Hong Kong (which is itself markedly distinct from mainland China and Taiwan), my early contact with what is Chinese and Asian has been through Charlie Chan and Pearl Buck[29] movies, in which the main characters were played by white actors with scotch-taped eyes. Think John Wayne as Genghis Khan: "I feel this tartar woman is for me. My blood says take her!"

Every Saturday morning, I was enthralled by re-runs of *Flash Gordon*, with Ming the Merciless from the planet Mongo. Not knowing who she was or what she represented, I adopted the nickname Dragon Lady in college because of its Chinese connotations. I even named my used Ply-mouth Duster, Dusty Dragon, because of this nickname and that it was painted Earl Scheib green. Only many years later did I discover that Dragon Lady was a ruthless witch (with a capital B) with long fingernails.[30] I was captivated with the martial arts of Mrs. Peel in the TV series *The Avengers* until, after several rigorous years of karate and kung fu during graduate school, I realized that her flailing arms and legs were caricatures of real martial arts. As an avid reader of mysteries, I devoured all of the Judge Dee novels of Robert Van Gulik,[31] which, along with a Chinese detective, often featured his Orientalist etchings of half-naked Chinese females. I was fascinated by the pleasure pearls, one of the *harigata* (erotic toys) in the sexual arsenal of the Japanese geisha in James Clavell's *Shogun.*[32] And, I am ashamed to say, that I consumed arrogant, cheesy novels like Trevanian's *Shibumi,*[33] whose Western protagonist, steeped in the amatory arts of the Orient,[34] would punish a woman by giving her a sexual "high" that she would vainly try to replicate with ordinary men for the rest of her life.

I am one of those Asian Americans "who got their China and Japan from the radio, off the silver screen, from television, out of comic books, from the pushers of white American culture..."[35] Maxine Hong Kingston would interrogate me this way: "Chinese Americans, when you try to understand what things in you are Chinese, how do you separate what is peculiar to childhood, to poverty, insanities, one family, your mother who marked your growing with stories, from what is Chinese? What is Chinese tradition and what is the movies?"[36]

As I turn to the "American" prong of my hyphenated condition, things become even more complicated. Who I am as an American is directly affected by my Asian ethnicity. What remind me every day of my Asian identity are my name and my face: Something you hear, my name Yee, and something you see, my Chinese face. The historical responses of American white society to markers like my name and face has been *racism.* I have experienced this racism in its violent forms as a child growing up and in more subtle forms of American Orientalism, which I have consumed—a murky brew of both external and internalized oppression. What defines Asian Americanness, for me, is not essentialist categories marking what is authentically Asian and what is American. Rather, it is the historical and cultural experiences of personal and collective racism of the dominant white society in America, perpetrated against Americans of Asian descent. This racism runs the gamut—from the predacious Yellow Peril to the Model Minority success story. A number of studies have documented its history.[37]

Pyke and Johnson contributed extensive studies of the external racism of white society and its correlation with the internalized oppression of Asian American women.[38] Attempting to integrate gender with the study of race, Pyke and Johnson found that Asian American women used the term "American" as a code for "white" in describing their self-understanding as female. Many of these women claimed that they were not Asian at all, because they rejected the controlling images of Asian women as meek and submissive. Asian cultures were deemed bastions of patriarchy, from which they escaped by denying any affiliation with them. They regarded themselves as American, identifying with the hegemonic femininity of white American society. They constructed white femininity as monolithically self-confident, independent, and successful, traits that ironically replicated white hegemonic masculinity.[39]

One of the challenges in counteracting the external racism against and the internalized oppression of Asian Americans is making "whiteness" visible "as a culturally constructed ethnic identity, historically contingent on the disavowal and violent denial of difference."[40] Instead of admitting its own sociohistorical production, whiteness sets itself up as *the* universal norm, disparaging all others as pitiful aberrations. Those who are white often fail to see how their racial position (pre)determines the social realities of which they are a part. "When Americans with the privileges of being white deny the relevance of race in their own lives, it is functionally equal to preserving the historical inequities in American society that have been built on racial exclusion."[41]

If they do acknowledge their ethnicity, as the Irish on St. Patrick's Day or the Germans during Oktoberfest, they have the luxury of choice to claim this identity and select which parts of it to incorporate into their lives. For the rest of the year, they can be indifferent to their ethnic identity.[42] Asian and African Americans, however, do not have choice in the matter. They cannot escape the material indicators of race. Race for them is "skin-deep," and they must continue to live in a society that has historically and systemically marginalized them because of the color of their skin or the shape of their eyes.

Because whiteness is not named and remains hidden, white society places the burden of accounting for racial difference on the racial-ethnic individuals themselves.[43] The un-hyphenated American (read: white) is unconsciously assumed to have no race. It is those other Americans—Asian, African, Native, and Hispanic—who must defend their racial differences in this society. Because their own racial makeup was unacknowledged, my ostensibly "colorless" interviewers, to whom I referred at the beginning, asked that I expound on the ways my Asian American identity affects and influences my biblical interpretation. Because whiteness currently functions incognito, we can go only so far in developing an Asian American biblical hermeneutics. Because our hermeneutics does not develop in a vacuum, but is conducted within larger white institutional–and often racist–contexts, it is vital that we Asian American biblical scholars make whiteness transparent as a culturally constructed and racialized category. I related at the beginning of this essay about how white society compels me, however kind-heartedly, to tell them how my Asian Americanness makes *me* different. I think the time has come for white men and women to reflect critically and honestly on how their whiteness makes *them* different. How their whiteness accords them privilege and access to resources that they withhold from those who are "not their kind." How their whiteness has been made the unacknowledged norm of what it means to be human. How their whiteness has brought hardship and misery to millions. Critical "White Studies" is a field in its infancy,[44] but we Asian Americans, who live and work in the belly of the beast, should keep tabs on the developments in this field, as we create our own Asian American biblical hermeneutics.

An Asian American Reading of Judges 4–5

I now turn the discussion to how would I interrogate the biblical text from an Asian American perspective. I have chosen the story of Yael in Judges 4–5, as an experiment for such cross-examination. With an Asian American appraisal of Judges 4–5, I return full circle back to Yael. I had studied her text in a previous investigation of woman warriors in ancient Israel.[45] When I wrote this article over ten years ago, I remember entitling Yael as a woman warrior, because of Maxine Hong Kingston's memoir, *The Woman Warrior*. I had bought this book when it first came out in 1976, because I was attracted by the concept of a powerful Chinese woman, embodied in the woman warrior. Because of space constraints, I can only offer some of the questions I would ask of Judges 4–5 as an Asian American biblical scholar.

Yael (Jael in the NRSV) was outside the mainstream of Israelite society, as a woman and probably a foreigner, a Kenite.[46] As my surname Yee is a marker of my ethnicity, I inquire first into the etymology of Yael's name to see if it bears on her Kenite origins or her characterization. I inquire into the nature of her ethnicity: Was Yael a foreigner (non-Israelite) like her husband, Heber the Kenite? Was Yael a Kenite like her husband? What was the nature of Kenite/Hebrew ethnic, political and/or economic relations? Was Yael's ethnicity different from Deborah the prophet? What was Deborah's ethnicity? How does Yael's ethnicity influence her status as a woman warrior? What is the nature of her class status? Yael's story is a site of struggle for Israel's identity. In the book of Judges, foreigners are represented as a snare or trap. How then does Yael as an ethnic foreigner serve the ideological interests of the biblical author? Does the fact that Yael has her own tent have ethnic significance? Baruch Halpern argues that the Kenites were fifth columnists in ancient Canaan, working for the invading Israelites.[47] Are there intertextual connections between Judges 4–5 and alleged Japanese American fifth columnists during WWII, or are they both propaganda, serving political interests?[48] How does gender intersect with ethnicity and ethnic otherness in the woman warrior? For example, the Chinese woman warrior, Fa Mulan, used deception and *disguised her gender* to become a military hero for her country against *foreign* invaders. Yael also used deception, but *exploited her gender* as a *foreign* woman to become an Israelite military hero. What happened to Yael's ethnicity in the later retelling of her story? Are there any racist sentiments in these retellings? These are just some of the questions I would ask, as I consciously read Judges 4–5 from an Asian American perspective.

Conclusion

I have raised problems and questions in theorizing about an Asian American biblical hermeneutic more than I have laid out the parameters of one. I began my article with two personal anecdotes that have highlighted these difficulties. On the one hand, we face personal and institutional pressures to conform to some recognizable Asian American identity. On the other hand, mutable notions of both Asian and Asian American identities make an Asian American biblical hermeneutics a hard one to pin down. If we apply Du Bois's criteria, "about us," as a way to conceive our biblical hermeneutics, we shift our point of departure from the biblical text to Asian American communities absorbed in the text, both positively and negatively. An Asian American biblical hermeneutics "by us" also shifts the identity question from "Who is an Asian American?" to "What are the different ways of becoming an Asian American?" An Asian American biblical hermeneutics is fashioned by an American of Asian descent who has intentionally adopted a stance of Asian American advocacy. An Asian American biblical hermeneutics "for us" will interpret the biblical text on behalf of Asian American communities, motivating and enlightening them, as well as critiquing and admonishing them. An Asian American biblical hermeneutics "near us" reminds us of praxis: as Asian American biblical scholars we need to keep our fingers on the pulse of what is going on in Asian America, religiously and socially. In all of these endeavors, we must keep in mind that we do not interpret in a vacuum, but must negotiate a white hegemonic guild. Making whiteness visible is one of our challenges in creating our own biblical hermeneutics.

13

Constructing Hybridity
and Heterogeneity

Asian American Biblical Interpretation
from a Third-Generation Perspective

FRANK M. YAMADA
Seabury Theological Seminary
Evanston, Illinois

... *"It won't always be like this," he remembers his teacher in the camps
saying. "After the war you will be free again and back in American
society. But for your own sakes, try to be not one, but two hundred
percent American..."*

*I am American, he says to himself. I am glad we won. The light
through the leaves is bright, blinding. The heat immense, oppressive. The
sounds all over town joyous. He repeats his mantra over and over. He
learns to believe it.*

DAVID MURA[1]

In his memoirs, David Mura, a Sansei (third-generation Japanese
American), explores his racial identity, its complexities, and its incongruities.
In the passage cited above, he imagines what life was like for his father at
the close of World War II. The setting is Kalamazoo, Michigan, after his
father's release from the internment camps. It is late in the summer of
1945, just after the bombings of Nagasaki and Hiroshima. A national holiday
has been proclaimed to mark the end of the war. People are celebrating in

public, marking America's victory. Amid the cheering throngs and blaring loud speakers, Mura's father contemplates his shifting identity as a Japanese American. He resolves the painful dichotomy between Japanese and American by force. He will be two hundred percent American.

The story that Mura tells of his father is common among many in the Japanese American community, particularly among those Sansei who had parents, grandparents, or other relatives in the internment camps. More importantly, Mura's characterization of his father raises issues that are important for understanding Japanese American experience in that it points to the ways in which this cultural identity was constructed through a difficult negotiation between his father's sense of being Japanese and being American. In the case of many Nisei (second-generation) Japanese Americans there was little choice but to be more American than Americans. The camps had already taught them the lesson of what it would cost to be Japanese in this country.

Mura's memoirs, *Turning Japanese* and *Where the Body Meets Memory,* explore the conflicted cultural configuration of Japanese American identity from a Sansei's perspective. His work suggests that identity is more complicated than a simple assimilation of one culture (Japanese) into another (American). Contradictory silences from the camps, a hidden anger in his parent's generation, transform his sexuality into rage. Whiteness becomes an obsession. Thus, the object of his desire—the white woman—is simultaneously an addiction and a visible reminder of the shame that he feels about his own skin. From this series of contradictions and complexities one can posit that Asian American cultural identity from a third- or later-generational perspective is not tidy but messy. In this essay, I argue that later-generation Asian American culture and interpretation problematizes essentialized categories such as "Asian"/"Japanese" and "American," preferring more conflicted and hybridous notions of what it means to be and interpret as an Asian in America.

Conflicts in Culture and Interpretation

Culture is a double-edged sword within discussions of Asian American identity. It is both necessary and problematic. The label "Asian American" was a uniting force during the 1960s and 1970s within the context of civil rights. It allowed disparate groups of people to have a political voice. It also spoke then and continues to speak now of how peoples from different Asian countries have been racialized in the United States within a predictable and demeaning set of characterizations associated with Asianness. In spite of this problematic situation, the term "Asian American" has functioned as a strategic identification for social justice and political empowerment among people of Asian descent.[2]

The term, however, is also inherently problematic. It is limited in its descriptive value. To put all Americans of Asian background into one racial grouping does not do justice to the particularities among the different groups. The racial category of Asian American covers people from many different nationalities–Japanese, Chinese, Korean, Filipino, Vietnamese, Indian, etc. Thus, one can see that the category is not very useful in accounting for the variety of cultures and ethnic backgrounds that fall under this label. When one considers the racist history of race classifications, the term becomes all the more problematic. Hence, it should come as no surprise that Asian Americans find themselves resisting oversimplified generalizations of this racial category even when they recognize the political expediency of it.[3]

Therefore, when one proposes an Asian American hermeneutic, the problems and conflicts inherent in such a project should be immediately clear. Biblical scholarship has had a strong and persistent Eurocentric bias. Hence, voices from the racial and ethnic margins, following modes of empowerment modeled through the civil rights movement, have tended to collaborate with each other in order to speak from a space of empowerment. Perspectives from African Americans, Latino/a Americans, and Asian Americans have contributed important advancements in the field of biblical hermeneutics. By collecting their interpretative energies, these scholars have opened up new avenues for approaching the biblical texts. Within these movements, there has been an understandable idealism about culture.[4] The collective energies of Japanese Americans, Chinese Americans, Korean Americans, Filipino Americans, etc., have led to the establishment of Asian American biblical interpretation even as these scholars' differences and particularities threaten the implied unity within the term "Asian American."

I contend that Asian American interpretation must move beyond idealized and essentialist notions of culture. Hence, I contend that Asian American interpretation should emphasize particularity, contradiction, and complexity in order to counter oversimplified personifications of what constitutes Asian American. The theological discourse of Asian Americans has relied too often on images that assume the exotic or otherness of Asians in America. As I show, the context for this theological discourse is best situated within or near realities of an immigrant ethos. While this is an important context within which Asian American theology can emerge, it is not the only context. Some Asian American groups, for example Japanese and Chinese Americans, have had three or more generations in the United States.

Within an earlier generational context, themes such as marginality and liminality have become associated with Asian American experience and theological discourse. I will argue that these themes, while relevant to an immigrant context, become increasingly complicated and complex as succeeding generations work out what it means to be Asian American. The experience of later-generation Asian Americans suggests that simple dichotomies between insider/outsider, colonized/colonizer, and home country/host country become increasingly problematic and complex. Within this context, cultural identity is not viewed as pure, fixed, and stable, but hybridous, fluid, and conflicted.[5] Thus, Asian American biblical interpretation, when viewed from a later-generational perspective, seeks to expose conflicts, resists overly simplistic or pure evaluations of cultures or texts, and refuses traditionally held boundaries between texts, interpreters, and the social location of interpreters. Asian American theological discourse, similar to Asian American literature more generally, requires an ethics of reading that challenges identity politics, which tend to idealize the other. Such reading practices should seek to allow texts, readers, and the culture of readers to emerge in their full complexity. Rey Chow summarizes the needs for such a critique of cultural idealism:

> Granting such density and complexity would mean refusing to idealize the non-West—be it in the form of a culture, a class, or a gender group; a text, an author, or a character—and instead reading the non-West in such a manner as to draw out its unconscious, irrational, and violent nuances, so that, as an "other," it can no longer simply be left in a blank, frozen, and mythologized condition known perfunctorily as an "alternative" to the West. My implied object of criticism is, accordingly, also the controversial identity politics that has unavoidably shaped our readings of "other" cultures. Rather than attacking identity politics per se, however, my point is that we need to be more precise in our attack: we need to point more accurately at the idealism that is at the heart of identity politics.[6]

The reading practice and criticism for which Chow advocates moves biblical interpretation beyond Fernando Segovia's desire to introduce biblical criticism to the real "flesh-and-blood reader."[7] The notion of a "real reader," which is itself an idealized embodiment of a literary construct, has as its objective the desire to move interpretation out of the world of theory and into the realm of politics—to put that which is marginal at the center. What I am proposing, however, is not an idealized cultural other, but a complicated and constantly renegotiated web of conflicted significations that point to the construction of Asian American experience and culture.

Before I proceed to examine in more detail the trajectories of Asian American theological and biblical discourse, it is important for me to acknowledge my own situatedness. Many texts, experiences, and cultures collide in my reading of biblical material. The present interpretative musings have been shaped by my experience as a Sansei who grew up on the West Coast of the United States, one generation removed from the dislocations of World War II. I was trained in the traditional historical and literary critical modes of biblical criticism at a Protestant seminary, though my interpretative practices are heavily shaped by postmodern and postcolonial theory. My interests in Derrida, Foucault, and others, however, have led me back to critical evaluations of culture. I am less interested in deconstruction as a reading practice, deciding instead to focus on how readers have used poststructuralist thought both to perpetuate reading practices that create cultures of exclusion and to open space for minority voices to speak.[8]

The Context of Asian American Theological Discourse

Asian American theologies have proliferated within recent years. Theologies from Asians and Asian Americans are now standard within seminary and graduate school curriculums under the general heading of contextual or constructive theologies.[9] Among Asian American theologians themes such as marginality and liminality are prevalent. Asian American experience is described as being "in-between" two worlds, caught between the cultures of their Asian ancestry and the dominant American society. Matsuoka describes this double bind:

A liminal world is the "place of in-betweeness." It is at once the world of isolation and intimacy, desolation and creativity. A person in a liminal world is poised in uncertainty and ambiguity between two or more social constructs, reflecting in the soul the discords and harmonies, repulsions and attractions. One of the constructs is likely to be dominant, whether cultural or linguistic. Within such a dominant construct one strives to belong and yet finds oneself to be a peripheral member, forced to remain in the world of in-betweenness.[10]

Similarly, Sang Hyun Lee and Jung Young Lee have described Korean American experience as a negotiation between two or more cultures. Hence, ideas such as liminality and marginality seek to describe the position from which Asian Americans speak.[11] It also provides a simultaneously creative and dislocated context from which Asian American theological discourse can emerge.[12]

These Asian American theological trajectories helped to define Asian American theology as a discipline, and Asian American biblical interpretation is indebted to the themes and trajectories that were set forth by such theologies. This influence can be seen in recent attempts by scholars to characterize Asian American biblical interpretation.[13] I would argue, however, that the perspectives within these early movements of Asian American theology are representative of issues that relate to or reflect an immigrant ethos. Polarized notions of an American dominant society in conflict with a traditional Asian culture make the most sense within the experiences of first- and second-generation Asian Americans, where such navigations of culture are more pronounced and stark. Issues of language acquisition, the fear of assimilation, and dislocation from homeland mark such a generational context. This does not mean that theological metaphors such as liminality and marginality are meaningless to later-generation Asian Americans. Rather, such themes are taken up and embodied in different ways by succeeding generations of Asian Americans.

By stressing themes such as marginality and liminality, Asian American theologians have constructed a theological discourse of identity that locates itself "in-between" worlds and speaks from the "margins" of two different and yet overlapping cultures. Essentialized notions of culture undergird these theologies. Even if Asian American identity is a constant negotiation between cultural spaces, as it is in many of these models, the notion of a marginal or liminal space suggests a fairly stable definition of what it means to be Asian and what it means to be American. A problem arises, however, for later-generation Asian Americans, who are typically labeled as "assimilated." If the space between the two constructed cultural designations, Asian and American, breaks down or is complicated by structural, economic, or social factors, how does one properly speak of Asian American identity and theological discourse? It is to this problem that I now turn.

Rethinking Asian American Culture from a Later-Generational Perspective

Typically, later-generation Asian Americans like the Sansei are described as being the most assimilated of their particular ethnic group. Harry Kitano and Roger Daniels state:

> The Sansei and the Yonsei, or fourth generation, are the most "American" of any Japanese group; many of them have never faced overt discrimination, and some have never had close ethnic ties or ethnic friends. They flock to colleges and universities, eager for good jobs, especially in medicine, engineering, and law. Like many of their mainstream peers, they question the life-style and values of their parents but are the primary beneficiaries of the material success of the previous generation...Most of the old Japanese ways are also passing with the Issei; new input, new technology, and "modern American values" appear more comfortable for each new generation.[14]

They suggest further that these later-generation Japanese Americans are more likely to identify with the culture of their geographical locale than with their Japanese heritage. In other words, "A Japanese American growing up in St. Louis will be more Missourian than Japanese, just as a Sansei from Los Angeles, Honolulu, and New York will reflect the culture of these cities."[15]

The sentiments of Kitano and Daniels represent the popular belief that Japanese cultural values and beliefs begin to disappear as succeeding generations assimilate to the dominant American culture. Other studies have shown, however, that ethnicity-based assimilation theories do not adequately describe the later generations' sense of being Japanese or Asian American.[16] It is beyond the scope of this essay to rehearse the entire debate about cultural identity, or better the argued lack of Japanese cultural identity, of later-generation Japanese Americans. I want to emphasize, however, that the notion of cultural assimilation as it is described above, like Asian American theologies discussed earlier, assumes a certain essentialized notion of culture(s). According to such theories, as Japanese Americans become more integrated into American society, they simultaneously begin to lose elements of their Japanese traditions and culture and become more American. The problem with essentialized notions of Asian American culture is that they categorize various peoples of Asian descent, and in this case people of different generations, into a homogenous group, subsuming particularities and distinctions into characteristics that reinforce the otherness of Asian Americans. Such constructions of Asian American identity "remain bound to, and overdetermined by, the logic of the dominant culture."[17] Within this framework, Asian Americans who do not conform to traditional notions of being Asian are assumed to be more American.

I would argue, however, that the cultural identity of the Sanseis, like that of other later-generation Asian Americans, is more complicated than traditional assimilationist theories would have one believe. Following the lead of scholars like Lisa Lowe, I would argue that later-generation Asian Americans are constructing and renegotiating their cultural identity within the constantly shifting landscape of racial identity politics. I find the work of Michael Omi and Howard Winant to be useful in this regard. Omi and Winant argue for the importance of understanding racial formation in the maintenance and transformation of cultural meaning at both the social and individual levels.[18] They define racial formation as "the sociohistorical process by which racial categories are created, inhabited, transformed, and destroyed."[19]

There are two important ideas that emerge from Omi and Winant's discussion for this essay. First, they emphasize race as the category from which meaningful cultural construction emerges. Hence, even if later-generation Asian Americans do not share ethnicity traits with their generational predecessors, one can still properly conclude that they are Asian American based on certain social forces that racialize people of Asian descent in certain ways. Thus, for example, the Asian American political movement in the 1960s and 1970s, though comprised of people of different ethnicities and generations, was able to develop a unified cultural resistance to dominant perceptions of Asian Americans based on a shared experience of racial discrimination.

A second important idea from Omi and Winant is found in what they call "rearticulation." In their discussion of how the black movement was able to reformulate the idea of race in the civil rights era, the authors suggest:

Social movements create collective identity by offering their adherents a different view of themselves and their world; different, that is, from the worldview and self-concepts offered by the established social order. They do this by the process of *rearticulation*, which produces new subjectivity by making use of information and knowledge already present in the subject's mind. They take elements and themes of her/his culture and traditions and infuse them with new meaning [emphasis theirs].[20]

Though Omi and Winant suggest that intellectuals do the work of rearticulation, it is clear that they apply the concept to larger social groups. Within discussions of Asian American culture, the idea of rearticulation can be used to provide a better understanding of how later generations like the Sanseis reformulate cultural identity. Rather than losing their culture through assimilation to American ways, as some ethnicity theorists claim, these later generations can be understood as being in the continual process of reformulating new meanings of what it means to be Japanese American.[21]

Hence, I stress heterogeneity and hybridity when examining later-generation Asian American cultural identity and biblical interpretation. Following Homi Bhabha's notion of the hybrid, I would argue that Asian Americans, both in their bodies and in their construction of cultural identity, re-present imposed constructs of Asian-ness and American-ness in such a way that renders the authority of the dominant culture's perception problematic.[22] For example, the common myth of American assimilation, which is reinforced through metaphors like "the great melting pot," can be rearticulated within the context of the Japanese Americans' experience of the internment. Many, if not most, Nisei survivors came out of the camps vowing to be two hundred percent American. This problematic national loyalty, which is expressed as hyper-assimilation, was most certainly a strategy for survival—a way to protect the succeeding generations from the humiliation and degradation of the camps. Hence, the assimilation of Japanese Americans after World War II exposes the violence of American cultural assimilation, even as the Nisei's assimilated response reinforces "traditional" Japanese values of loyalty and the sacrifices of early generations *kodomo no tami ni,* "for the sake of the children."[23] Silence becomes resistance. Assimilation becomes survival. Being doubly American ironically becomes an expression of Japanese American virtue. Through rearticulation and the destabilizing force of the hybrid, Japanese American experience reshapes the ways that we think about "Japanese" and "American." The collision of the two terms creates a hybrid that complicates and calls into question the dichotomy between them, while simultaneously resisting the assimilation of one into the other or the dominance of one over the other.

Japanese American Experience and Asian American Biblical Interpretation

Though I am arguing for a destabilized or nonessential understanding of Asian American culture generally and Japanese American culture specifically, there are still themes and configurations of historical experience that are informed in particular ways by later-generation Japanese American identity. From the discussion above, I would propose an Asian American biblical interpretation that recognizes *generational difference,* is shaped by *the construction of cultural identity,* and stresses *hybridity* or *heterogeneity.* A Sansei approach informs these three trajectories for interpretation in a way that connects them to later-generation Japanese American culture and identity. The first of these, *generational difference,* is rooted in the experience of Japanese Americans, who identify and differentiate between the generations through the terms Issei, Nisei, Sansei, Yonsei, etc. Some scholars have sought to identify the different characteristic traits of each group.[24] I would suggest, however, that such definitions are often too confining to the particular experiences of Japanese Americans. What is important to point out is that Japanese Americans have used identifications of generational difference in their construction of cultural identity. In this way, different ways of being Japanese American are understood through the constructed lens of generational change. Hence, within these communities, Sanseis can refer to the "Issei and Nisei work ethic," and Niseis to "Sansei outspokenness." I am not suggesting that these labels are essential characteristics of each group. My point is that Japanese Americans use these meaningful structures to understand and construct generational difference.

Recognizing generational difference in biblical interpretation means that later generations of Asian Americans will surface different interpretative issues than their first- or second-generation forerunners–themes that reflect their experience of being Asian in America, e.g., hybridity instead of marginality, or tensions of being a citizen within empire rather than longings for homeland. Moreover, such interpreters will also reshape themes like marginality or liminality in ways that reflect the particularities of later-generational experience. In the broader hermeneutical discussion, recognition of generational difference contributes to the burgeoning field of culturally contextual biblical interpretation. Interpretative practices can rightly be situated not only within racial, cultural, gender, or sexual orientation markers, but also within generational differences.

Japanese American biblical interpretation from a later-generational perspective would also concur with recent trends in cultural studies that assume *the constructed nature of culture and cultural identity.* The implication for this assertion is that Asian American biblical interpretation, like Japanese American culture and identity, is not fixed within static categories. It will be determined and even created as Japanese Americans and Asian Americans *rearticulate* biblical texts in relation to their experiences of being Asians in America and Americans of Asian descent. Lowe, in her discussion about Asian American literature, concurs by suggesting that "the making of Asian American culture may be a much 'messier' process than unmediated vertical transmission from one generation to another, including practices that are partly inherited and partly modified, as well as partly invented."[25] Hence, themes and historical experiences such as the Japanese American internment, the problematic "model minority" label, Japanese notions of loyalty, *kodomo no tami ni,* cultural systems of shame, etc., will be shaped and reshaped from a later-generational perspective in conversation with the biblical material. The emerging and constructed interpretation will produce biblical readings that enhance and complicate both the biblical texts and Japanese American experience and culture. The resulting intertext will prove to be less stable and more complex.

Moreover, later-generation Japanese American biblical interpretation will stress *hybridity* and *heterogeneity* over essentialized ideas of culture, identity, and texts. The notion of hybridity questions strict boundaries between cultures and problematizes configurations that assume the binary opposition between the words *Asian* and *American.* The lives of later-generation Japanese Americans and Asian Americans have challenged scholars to think beyond simple polarizations. The literature on later generations points to a high percentage of mixed-race marriages.[26] In assimilationist models, scholars interpret this data to suggest an erasing of Japanese and/or Asian culture. However, recent studies suggest that a more complex configuration of Asian American-ness is emerging within such marriages.[27] This dynamic within Asian American communities represents a structural hybridity that reflects the cultural heterogeneity of later-generational experience.

The hybridous and heterogeneous character of the later generations has implications for Asian American biblical interpretation. Within culturally contextual biblical studies, a Sansei perspective would question essentialized notions of Japanese American or Asian American cultural identity, preferring instead heterogeneous and even conflicted character-izations. Reading for hybridity disrupts the "the dominant discursive construction and determination of Asian Americans as a homogenous group."[28] Thus, Asian American interpretation should stress particularities and complex cultural constructions over monolithic notions of Asian American otherness. The destabilizing force of the hybrid calls into question fixed boundaries and "pure" notions of culture, both in the culture of the reader and the world of the text. Similarly, Asian American biblical interpretation from a later-generational perspective refuses assumed boundaries between texts. In my own interpretation of biblical texts, I am interested in the collision of texts that have shaped and complicated my sense of being a Japanese American biblical scholar. What would the Japanese internment and Israel's exile look like through Derridian deconstruction? What would a conversation about culture look like between David Mura, Homi Bhabha, and the book of Jonah? What does Buddha have to say to Jesus and Jesus to Levinas? Such intertextual hybrids can point to a fruitful understanding of Asian American biblical interpretation—a form of hermeneutics that refuses the fixed boundaries between the biblical material, texts from Asian American culture, and contemporary theory.

Dealing with the Internment

One way that hybridity can be practiced in Asian American interpretation is through the mutual interposition of biblical material and Asian American historical experiences—"texts" that, upon initial reflection, do not display any immediate sense of connection to each other. I conclude this essay with a brief intertextual exploration between Genesis 2–3, the story of Adam and Eve in the garden of Eden, and the Japanese American experience of internment during World War II.[29]

The internment, discussed above, was the central and problematic event of Japanese American experience in the twentieth century. On February 19, 1942, Franklin D. Roosevelt signed Executive Order 9066, which ordered the internment of 120,000 Japanese and Japanese American people. The U.S. government's infamous act left an indelible mark on Japanese American community and identity. The already difficult negotiation between maintenance of cultural identity and the social pressure of acculturation was made increasingly problematic through the camps. Most Isseis and Niseis responded with silence. As stated above, many—though not all—of the Japanese American communities vowed to be super-Americans, a declaration that would result in the reconfiguration of Japanese American culture for future generations.

In identity literature from later-generation Japanese Americans, such as David Mura's *Where the Body Meets Memory,* the internment looms large.[30] Mura writes about how the silences of his interned Nisei parents, probably linked to the Japanese notion of *gaman,* the internalization of emotion, represented their attempts to cope with the humiliation of the camps. However, the Nisei's swallowing of their shame had pronounced effects upon the identity of the Sansei generation. Mura, in a painful and imaginatively woven autobiographical tale, recounts his struggles for identity that revolve around the intersection of race and sexuality. He suggests that the internment, which was an imprisonment based on the physical appearances of the Japanese, and the threat that such appearances represented, tied the Nisei shame directly to the body. Therefore, the Nisei's internalization of this shame was written on the bodies and identity of the third generation. In this way, Mura's sexuality becomes a complicated outworking of self-hatred and desire that are inextricably tied to his Asian body and face.[31]

Mura's story points to the significant way that the internment impacted Japanese Americans cross-generationally. It is the crucial event that profoundly affected Japanese American culture and identity. Thus, the internment functions as a historical filter, out of which many issues of cultural and identity construction emerge. For Japanese American biblical interpretation, I would argue that the internment as event and constructed historical text also looms large. Like the Babylonian exile and the Holocaust, the internment acts as a historical moment that shifts reality for a community, and hence, shapes future trajectories of discourse and theological reflection.[32] In my own reading of biblical texts, however, I would avoid oversimplified identifications between the exile and the internment, though some striking congruencies exist.[33] Rather, I would suggest that the internment, like the exile, functions as a gravitational center from which Japanese American theological reflection emerges. Hence, the internment, as historical text or interpretative lens, can function as a compelling intertext with the biblical material. What emerges is a rearticulation of the biblical themes, cast in the distinct tone of Japanese American historical experience, which complicates the boundaries between reader and text.

Having laid out the groundwork for understanding the internment as a theological intertext, I will proceed by positing some preliminary reflections on the intersections between the internment and Genesis 2–3, the story of Eden. A full exposition of Genesis 2–3 is not possible given the constraints of space. I will focus my interpretative thoughts on the theme that I believe emerges from the story of Eden when read in conversation with the Japanese American experience of the internment. That theme, human survival in the midst of a life of adversity, is one that I have failed to find in commentaries and articles on this text.

The narrative of the first human family in the garden is etiological in nature. That is, it is a story that explains why things are the way that they are: Why do people leave their families to build one with another partner? Why are we ashamed of being naked? Why do women experience pain in childbirth?, etc. The story, however, is more than a series of etiologies. It is framed in the context of a genealogy, in Hebrew a *toledot* formula. The first half of Genesis 2:4 reads, "These are the generations of the heavens and the earth when they were created."[34] From a narrative perspective, this phrase serves as a transition between the two creation stories in Genesis. The first, which is the Priestly account, describes in an almost liturgical way the creation of the heavens and the earth in six days, Elohim resting on the seventh day. The second, the Yahwist account, begins at 2:4b and recounts the mythical beginnings of the first humans. In this way, the genealogical formula in 2:4a both summarizes the creative activity in the first story and prepares the reader to understand the second. Hence, the story of Adam and Eve in the garden is a story of the first generations of humanity. It points the reader to the beginning of the earth and human life. It not only mythologizes from where human beings come, but also describes what human existence is like. Thus, Genesis 2–3 is a formative story that helps the people of God remember who they are–that their generations go back to the beginning of the world.

How does this text describe human existence? What are human beings like? I would suggest that reading Genesis 2–3 through the experience of the internment provides us with a story about untidy human survival in the midst of adversity. The internment was about more than survival, but the persistence of the Japanese Americans and their communities is certainly a strong theme that emerges from the experience. The survival strategies were conflicted and complex. Stories of the heroic efforts of the all-Japanese American 442nd Regiment and 100th Battalion, on the one hand, and the "No-No Boys," who refused to disavow loyalty to the Japanese government and serve in the U.S. military, on the other, are two contradictory examples of how the Japanese Americans sought to preserve their dignity within the camps. Moreover, the complicated declaration of many out of the camps was to be doubly American. As suggested above, the harsh realities of government sanctioned racism, combined with concern for the future generations, determined this conflicted patriotic response. Hence, survival within this context was far from uniform and represented the internal and external contradictions of being exiled within a country that the Japanese American community called home.

When one turns to the biblical material, a problematic detail arises for the reader in relation to Genesis 2:16. The LORD commands, "You may surely eat of every tree of the garden, but from the tree of knowledge of good and evil you shall not eat from it, for in the day that you eat from it you shall surely die." The surprising turn in this text is not that the human couple later eats what they are not supposed to eat. Nowhere in the text does it suggest that humans were created without the ability to do wrong, contrary to most traditional interpretations of this story. Nor is it surprising that humans experience shame and painful consequences from their acquisition of knowledge. The ending of this etiology, as with most etiologies, assumes the audience's knowledge of the conclusion. The surprise in this text is that the human beings eat but do not die. Though interpreters through the centuries have tried to see death in this text (e.g., spiritual death, death of naïveté, etc.), there is no death in the garden. In fact, one would expect, given the divine command, that the LORD, after cursing the snake to live a life in the dust, would sentence the humans to die. Instead, the LORD simply announces the consequences of what life will be like with true knowledge– a life filled with pain and frustration. Women will bear children in pain and men will work the ground, but the ground will fight back.

The human beings do not experience death; they survive. This Yahwist (J) story immediately follows the first Priestly creation text, in which Elohim commands things into existence, and everything happens just as God had commanded it. In Genesis 3, the divine command from the LORD does not come to pass. In fact, the garden narrative seems to suggest that even the LORD is not prepared for the human beings' actions. Genesis 3:22 reads, "Then the LORD God said, 'See, the human has become like one of us, knowing good and evil; and now what if he stretches out his hand and takes also from the tree of life, and eat, and live forever?'" This unexpected situation has the LORD concerned about other potential actions from the human beings. Hence, the LORD sends the humans forth from Eden. Cherubim and a flaming sword are placed at the garden boundary so that the humans cannot return. Adam and Eve are barred from immortality. In spite of the fact that God had decreed death as punishment upon the human couple, resulting in the humans being exiled from a land that was their home, in the end they do not die as had been proclaimed but continue to live their lives beyond the boundaries of Eden.

The story continues by showing that many generations come from this first human family. Chapter 4 begins, "Now Adam knew Eve his wife, and she conceived and bore Cain." Hence, though their death sentence had been announced through an arbitrary law from the Ruler of the garden, yet the human beings survived. Though they experience the knowledge of human life as painful, yet they continue to live and produce generations in a place of divinely sanctioned dislocation.

This genealogical story, which traces its roots to the beginning of creation, describes how the human family has an almost stubborn instinct for survival, even if this survival is messy, untidy, and painful. This theme continues to show up throughout the story of Israel. When the earth is filled with violence and the LORD judges the earth with a flood, one human family reflects its lineage to the Edenic parents by building an ark to survive the destruction of the earth. Extending into other Israelite traditions, the theme of human survival continues to surface–through the exodus, the wilderness, into a new land, all the way through the Babylonian exile. Survival is a part of what makes Israel, Israel. The name Israel, attributed to their ancestor Jacob, is remembered in a folk etymology to mean "one who strives with God." Israel wrestles with God and lives. As the story in Eden suggests, survival is what makes these humans, human. Like the Japanese Americans who were exiled within their own land but continued to survive, some would say even thrive, in an untidy world filled with the painful knowledge of life in North America, so too the Israelites persisted and continued to live even when death was proclaimed for them. Their survival in a land that was not their home becomes paradigmatic through the tracing of this characteristic back to its genesis, "in the beginning."

Obscured Beginnings

Lessons from the Study of Christian Origins

MARY F. FOSKETT
Wake Forest University
Winston-Salem, North Carolina

In the field of biblical studies, few areas of inquiry have received as much public notice or stimulated as much popular response as the so-called quest for the historical Jesus and the study of women in early Christianity. The overwhelming attention won recently by Mel Gibson's film *The Passion of the Christ* and Dan Brown's novel *The Da Vinci Code* attest to an ever-increasing public interest in Christian origins. The intensity of popular reaction to reconstructions of the life and death of Jesus and the role of women in nascent Christianity—measured in no small part by the many conferences, courses, essays, and Web blogs devoted to these issues that scholars and clergy have produced and to which many nonspecialists have attended—reveals a deep religious and cultural investment in the study of Christian origins. Though obviously historical, such interest is also deeply theological and self-referential, for what historians, filmmakers, and writers conclude about who Jesus was, and who women in the Jesus movement were, impacts how many people understand their faith and themselves. The study of Christian origins has much to do with how we envision what Christianity and its adherents should be. Origins, then, are as much about the present and future as they are about the past.

It is the question of origins and their examination that I consider further in this essay. As an adoptee, I have been interested in beginnings for as long as I can remember. Having been born to an ethnic Chinese woman residing in Japan in the early 1960s, placed in a baby home managed by Franciscan Missionaries of Mary, and then adopted as an infant by a Caucasian American family and raised in Japan and then the United States, I have neither memory nor direct knowledge of my family of origin. Neither do I possess anything but the barest of historical information about my birthmother. Thus, my beginnings are all but completely obscured. Over the course of engaging the study of earliest Christianity in seminary, graduate school and beyond, I have been struck by how such inquiry has helped me address my very personal interest in the notion and significance of origins. It is lessons learned along the way that I now address.

Pacific Asian Adoption and the Problem of Lost Origins

The adoption of children born in Pacific Asia has become so common in the United States that even a casual observer will recognize the phenomenon of a growing, multigenerational population of Pacific Asian–born Americans who, having been adopted as infants or children, have been or are being raised in the urban, suburban, and rural United States. As journalist and adoptive parent Adam Pertman observes in *Adoption Nation: How the Adoption Revolution Is Transforming America,* adoption is not only booming in the United States, it is increasingly public, no longer the taboo topic it once was. Pertman is surely not alone when he writes, "Suddenly, or at least it feels sudden, adoption is being transformed from a quiet, lonely trip along America's back roads to a bustling journey on a coast-to-coast superhighway. The infrastructure has become so extensive that it has made all of us–not just adoptees' birth parents, and adoptive parents–into fellow travelers."[1] Every year, tens of thousands of immigrant visas are issued to foreign-born orphans entering the United States. Of these, nearly half are extended to children coming to the United States from Pacific Asia. Reflecting in some ways the experience of first-generation Asian Americans and, in others, that of their American-born sons and daughters, adoptees represent a distinct subculture within Asian America.

I am one of the many thousands of Pacific Asian–born girls, boys, women, and men who have been adopted and raised in the United States. As such, I am also a member of a large, multi-ethnic cross-section of persons who identify ourselves as Pacific Asian North American. As Asian American hermeneutics has emerged in the field of biblical studies over the course of the past twenty years or so, it has increasingly given voice to the diversity of experience, history, and perspective that constitutes Asian North America. Thus, it is from the perspective of the adoptive experience that I speak as a Pacific Asian North American and co-chair the Asian and Asian American Biblical Hermeneutics Group of the Society of Biblical Literature.

North Americans, especially Caucasians, have adopted children from Pacific Asia for decades. The Korean American Adoptee Adoptive Family

Network (KAAN) estimates that well over 100,000 Korean children have been adopted into the United States.[2] In 2000, the American population of adoptees born in China was already nearly 30,000.[3] Multiple adoptee networks of Korean, Chinese, and Vietnamese Americans have committed themselves to encouraging critical reflection on the construction of Pacific Asian, Asian American, and American identities. They are particularly attentive to forging connections between Asian North American communities and adoptive families across the United States.

Despite the history of Asian adoption in North America, until recently, little attention and effort had been given to tracking and seeking to understand the collective experience of the first generation of adoptees, now well into adulthood. In the year 2000, the Evan B. Donaldson Adoption Institute published the results of a survey aimed at learning "adoptees' perceptions of international adoption."[4] The survey itself was part of a larger project—a meeting entitled, "The Gathering of the First Generation of Adult Korean Adoptees." The meeting "was the first of its kind. From September 9–12, 1999, nearly 400 adult Korean adoptees, adopted between 1955 and 1985 at the median age of 2 (76% of the girls before or at the age of 3 and 53% of the boys before or at the age of 3) gathered in Washington, D.C. They represented over 30 states in the United States and several European countries."[5] As part of the event, the Donaldson Institute, together with Holt International Children's Services, undertook a comprehensive survey of the Gathering participants to gain greater understanding of the experiences of Korean adoptees and to put such knowledge to work in the field of international adoption. The survey succeeded in setting before the adoption community the experiences, reflections, and insights of persons who had negotiated over the long-term issues pertaining not only to adoption, but to the complex constellation of issues concerning race and ethnic identity that accompanies international and interracial adoption in the United States. Not surprisingly, many of the issues raised and explored by adult Pacific Asian American adoptees resonate with those with which many Pacific Asian North Americans contend. But in contrast to most other Asian Americans, adoptees' questions about race/ethnicity and familial obligation are predicated on the dual realities of relinquishment and adoption, of lost origins and initiation into new familial histories.

The reflections of adult adoptees underscore how the negotiation of—sometimes expressed as the search for—one's origins is constitutive of the construction of identity. In this sense, access to one's past becomes access to oneself. Hence the question that many an adoptee has wrestled with—namely, whether or not one ought to begin "the search," that is, the search for one's birth family—is a matter that concerns the reconstruction of both the past and the present, and of one's identity and place in both. Respondents to the Gathering survey reported that whereas 29 percent were not interested in searching and 15 percent were uncertain of whether or not to embark on a search, 56 percent were either interested in, had searched for, or were in the process of searching for a birth relative or family. Furthermore, despite the range in individual response to the question, the weight of the question (whether or not to search) was underscored by facilitator's reports:

> Many of the participants who were mothers themselves grappled with their birth mothers' decisions to place them for adoption. Some were in awe of the difficulty their mothers faced in making such decisions, but most stated that they were unable to comprehend how their mothers could have made such decisions. Coming to terms with being relinquished or "abandoned" was one area in which participants were not able to comfort each other. One facilitator described how her group "was stuck and just sat there" when someone asked "how could a woman ever give up a child?"[6]

Though certainly not for all, for many adult adoptees, relinquishment gives rise to deeply placed ambivalence and self-doubt. Often the search for origins becomes as much a search for one's self as a query into one's past. This facet of the adoptive experience is rendered all the more poignant when one considers the thousands of infant Chinese girls who have been adopted by European and North American families and have been systematically denied by the Chinese authorities any access to their parents' identities and histories.

Moreover, as the findings of the Donaldson project imply, the question of origins is linked specifically to the construction of racial/ethnic identity. When asked about their identity, 14 percent of the respondents indicated that when they were children, they thought of themselves as Asian or Korean; 22 percent thought of themselves as American or European; 28 percent identified themselves as Korean American or Korean European; and 36 percent thought of themselves as Caucasian. By contrast, as adults, 14 percent of the respondents now identify themselves as Asian or Korean; 10 percent (down from 22 percent) think of themselves as American or European, 64 percent (up from 28 percent) identify themselves as Korean American or Korean European and 11 percent (down from 36 percent) think of themselves as Caucasian. Clearly the most striking shift occurred in the perception and self-identification of male adoptees. Whereas 45 percent of the men surveyed reported that they thought of themselves as "Caucasian" when they were children, not a single male respondent claimed Caucasian identity as an adult.

The results of the Donaldson survey resonate with anecdotal accounts reported in adoption literature and the numerous Web sites and online networks devoted to supporting all members of the adoption triad (birth family, adoptee, adoptive family). The question of origins lost and/or recovered and the pertinence of aborted histories and lives not lived reverberate throughout the adoptive experience. They bring into sometimes uncomfortable focus the problem of defining and constructing not only what "family" means, but what origins, biography, family history and ethnic identity also mean. Constructs that many others simply assume and take for granted are revealed by the adoptive experience to be simply that— social and cultural constructs.

Perhaps one way of opening these categories up to critical examination is to consider them in the context of specific discourses that lend shape to, and which themselves are shaped by, the ways in which we think of origins. Lessons learned from the study of Christian origins shed some needed light on some of the presuppositions, values, and aims that figure in adoptees' concerns for origins. A review of relevant aspects of the scholarly search for Jesus and the lessons learned from feminist studies of Christian origins, specifically, can help us reflect on the project of recovering lost origins in the context of international adoption.

Origins and the Search for Jesus

The search for the historical Jesus illustrates the ambivalence that permeates the quest for origins. Since its inception in the late nineteenth century, the search for Jesus has turned again and again to a consideration of the proper relationship between Christian faith and historical reconstruction of the life, ministry, and death of Jesus of Nazareth. Study of the historical Jesus has not only queried whether we can historically identify Jesus, it has also asked what difference it ought to make if we succeed.

A brief survey of some key figures and their respective positions in the study of the historical Jesus demonstrates the uneasy conversation about history that characterizes this area of New Testament scholarship. Part of the first wave of historical Jesus research, David Friedrich Strauss sought to clarify the mythical nature of the gospels to liberate the true religious message of Jesus of Nazareth. In *The Life of Jesus Critically Examined*, Strauss took on two camps in the historical Jesus debate: the supernaturalists who held to the tradition of trusting the historical veracity of the New Testament writings; and the naturalists who maintained skepticism toward the canonical accounts of Jesus' miracles and signs but not the historical accuracy of the gospels, in general.[7] But the most relevant issue for Strauss was neither the historicity of the gospels nor its lack thereof. What Strauss sought to unveil and promote was how early Christian proclamation was the product of a collective religious imagination that enabled religious truth to be communicated through narrative. The essential message, as he saw it, could be freed from its ancient context and recontextualized for every age.

Other interpreters drew the lines between religious truth, ancient context, and modern Christianity quite differently. Rather than focusing on "myth" as a vehicle for proclamation and "history" as "what really happened," Albert Schweitzer's work was representative of scholarship that understood "history" in terms of both event and context. Believing that the context of Jewish apocalypticism held the key to understanding the life, ministry, and person of Jesus of Nazareth, Schweitzer realized a Jesus who was both historically tenable and historically alien to liberal theologians. Aware of the theological challenge he had created by closing his classic *The Quest of the Historical Jesus* with reference to Jesus "as one *unknown and nameless*" (emphasis mine), Schweitzer revisited the theological implications of his historical Jesus research.[8] In his 1933 autobiography, Schweitzer argued that the responsibility of the interpreter was nothing less than to determine the "original meaning" of Jesus' sayings and "work his [*sic*] way up through the historical truth to the eternal."[9] In place of dogma (public enemy #1 to liberal theology), Schweitzer offered a Jesus who embodied an ethical faith. Thus, the Sermon on the Mount became for Schweitzer "the incontestable character of liberal Christianity. The truth that the ethical is the essence of religion is firmly established on the authority of Jesus...We are now at liberty to let the religion of Jesus become a living force in our thought, as its purely spiritual and ethical nature demands."[10] Thus, Schweitzer's Jesus proclaimed a transhistorical, pure religion that could be loosed from its historically mistaken moorings to live on for the duration of Christian faith. Therefore, though working differently with the category of history, both Strauss and Schweitzer believed in a pure Christian faith that could shake off its historical origins and live on into the future.

Of course, not everyone in New Testament studies has believed the search for the historical Jesus to be either valid or relevant. Some, like William Wrede, were far too skeptical of the historical value of the New Testament to promote the search at all.[11]

In addition to such historical skepticism, Martin Kähler in the late nineteenth century and Rudolph Bultmann a few decades later expressed strong theological objection to the premise that Christian faith and identity lay at all rooted in history. In his famous critique, *The So-called Historical Jesus and the Historic Biblical Christ,* Kähler characterized "the entire Life of Jesus movement as a blind alley."[12] Whereas historical research might have been able to situate Jesus historically, the New Testament documents were wholly inadequate to the task of reconstructing a biography of Jesus. In this sense, the historical Jesus was largely out of reach. But even more importantly for Kähler, it was the "historic, biblical Christ" that rendered Jesus significant at all. It was the Jesus *now,* who continually encounters the world, not the Jesus *then* that inspired and continues to inspire Christian proclamation. Beyond the measure of history and historical investigation, Kähler's Jesus was the one who continues to interact with the world in every age.

What Kähler signaled, Bultmann, of course, developed. Like other dialectical theologians, Bultmann not only argued that the historical yield of the canonical texts was minimal at best, he added that the aim of the gospel was to reveal how God judges all human history and knowledge. For Bultmann, history was more an obstacle than a vehicle for faith. Thus, he attacked the "pantheism of history" exhibited in life of Jesus research.[13] The pure faith that Bultmann sought to promote was not a distillation of the historical Jesus, but a thoroughgoing rejection of history as revelatory.

But no sooner had Bultmann declared the search dead, than his student, Ernst Käsemann, announced it reopened—arguing that revelation had in some way intersected with human history and that continuity between the historical Jesus and the living Christ remained central to Christian faith: "The question of the historical Jesus," he wrote:

> ...is, in its legitimate form, the question of the continuity of the Gospel within the discontinuity of the times and within the variation of the kerygma...The preaching of the Church may be carried on anonymously; the important thing is not the person, but the message. But the Gospel itself cannot be anonymous...[Jesus] cannot be classified according to the categories either of psychology or of the comparative study of religion or, finally of general history. If he can be placed at all, it must be in terms of historical particularity.[14]

Well beyond Käsemann's New Quest, and now deeply entrenched in the so-called Third Quest, the questions and implications of the initial quest remain, and with as much ambivalence as ever. Interpreters like John Dominic Crossan and Marcus Borg, following in the footsteps of Schweitzer and Käsemann, reinforce the notion of origins and historical particularity as authenticating.[15] Their search is for a specific paradigm of Jesus and Christian beginnings that can lend historical warrant and vitality to Christian self-understanding. In this regard, the search for Jesus is a quest not only for Jesus' identity but also for the identity of Christian faith and practice.

Like previous eras of Jesus research, so does this era, too, have its detractors. Luke Johnson sees the search for the historical Jesus as missing the mark. The question for Johnson is whether history and the recovery of an historical Jesus is really the stuff of revelation at all. For him, the identity of Christian faith and practice lies not in the historical past, but in the ongoing experience of Christ, shaped in part by Christian origins but not determined by it.[16]

Although the third quest has utilized new methodologies (especially those derived from the social sciences), new historical evidence (both textual—that is, the Dead Sea Scrolls and Nag Hammadi texts—and material—that is, the excavation of Sepphoris) and a new appreciation for (and better understanding of) Jesus as a first-century Jew, the motivations behind Jesus research and its accompanying debates persist along many of the same lines as did previous inquiry. Should we search? Can we ever really find the "real" Jesus? And what does it matter if we do? Yet no single theological or historical perspective dominates the current quest for Jesus. As N.T. Wright observes, "The current wave of books about Jesus offer a bewildering range of competing hypotheses. There is no unifying theological agenda; no final agreement about method; certainly no canon set of results."[17]

In his review of the history of life of Jesus research, Craig A. Evans argues that in the midst of similarities, a significant difference does distinguish the so-called Third Quest from previous searches for the historical Jesus. Evans demonstrates how, in contrast to earlier eras of research, current studies of Jesus ignore the question of myth and the place it formerly held in earlier studies. He observes:

> Myth has ceased to be an item of importance. In my judgment this has taken place primarily because the miracle tradition is no longer the stumbling block that it once was. The scholarly assumption now seems to be that a realistic, relatively myth-free historical picture of Jesus can, and does, emerge from the Gospels. What makes today's scholarship so different is that it does not find it necessary to formulate a theology or hermeneutic that deals with myth.[18]

Whereas earlier interpreters of Jesus, like Strauss and Bultmann, sought in myth that which would free liberal Christianity from all that historical investigation could not countenance, contemporary scholars, encouraged by new historical sources and methods, work without recourse to the language of myth. For those who have successfully severed historical investigation from explicit theological concern, much work awaits. John P. Meier succinctly summarizes the perspective:

> It is only in the light of this rigorous application of historical standards that one comes to see what was wrong with so much of the first and second quests. All too often, the first and second quests were theological projects masquerading as historical projects...Let the *historical* Jesus be a truly and solely *historical* reconstruction, with all the lacunae and truncations of the total reality that a purely historical inquiry into a marginal figure of ancient history will inevitably involve. After the purely historical project is finished, there will be more than enough time to ask about correlations with Christian faith and academic christology.[19]

Yet the scholarship that has come to regard the gospels' miracle accounts not as myth but as originating in the historical ministry of Jesus has not reached a consensus understanding of how to interpret or appropriate such history. As Paula Fredriksen queries:

> What about history and faith, or faith and theology, or Jesus and Christ? These categories still, after a century, stand in uneasy and

confused relation. A Jesus securely anchored in his first-century Jewish apocalyptic context–working miracles, driving away demons, predicting the imminent end of the world–is an embarrassment. Is it sheer serendipity that so many of our reconstructions define away the offending awkwardness? Miracles without cures, time without end, resurrection without bodies.[20]

What the search for Jesus reveals, amid the diversity of approaches, sources, and materials with which it works–is a deep ambivalence about the significance of origins that equals its drive for historical access and knowledge. Having arrived at an historical Jesus, what bearing, if any, does he have on the person who serves as the center of Christian faith and practice? Such ambivalence is at once familiar to those who know the experience of adoption, the question of searching for one's origins and any attempt to ground identity and self-understanding (whether individual or collective) in a previous, partially inaccessible, and largely unknown history.

Yet the urge for historical knowledge and grounding persists. Despite the age-old debate of whether we are formed by nature or nurture, blood or culture, it is neither biology nor culture that informs the adoptee's consciousness of an originating history. This is why responses to the Donaldson survey about racial/ethnic identity are so poignant–*it is our very history that Asian adoptees see inscribed in our bodies.* Here one's racial/ethnic identity becomes a means of owning and acknowledging a history to which we often have only very limited, if any, access.

And so many adoptees embark on "the search." Perhaps due to this sense of carrying history in one's body, many women begin when they are thinking about becoming pregnant and preparing to start families of their own. As Pertman notes, "Some indeterminable minority of adoptees say they're impervious to identity issues…they insist they have no desire to learn about their genetic backgrounds."[21] Of this group, most are men. Conversely, "Whatever the reasons, adoption professionals agree one unmistakable indication of this gender difference is that at least 80 percent of the hundreds of thousands of adoptees searching for their birthmothers (and, less frequently, their birth fathers) are women."[22] The end result of searching varies widely. Some adoptees seek reunion with birthmothers; others–wanting only historical data and a more complete narrative of beginnings–forgo any effort at making contact. Yet every year in the United States alone, thousands of adoptees attempt to locate a birth parent. Without knowing what they will discover, their journey lends itself to questions that parallel what scholars have asked in searching for and reconstructing the Jesus of history. What significance does my reconstruction of the past bear for the present and the future? How will a new narrative of my past shape my current identity? And what, after all, is the real meaning of origins?

My point here is not to argue for the equivalence of the search for the historical Jesus and the search for one's origins. Nor do I count myself among the manifold New Testament scholars researching the Jesus of history. Rather, what I hope to convey is that the drive to search for historical origins, replete with an abiding ambivalence about its precise significance, is a most persistent one. Once motivated by a commitment to proclaiming a mythic and more tenable Jesus, historical Jesus research is guided now more by scholars' convictions that history—which to them is neither optional nor a blind alley—is a compelling avenue for locating the identity and person of Jesus and a means of anchoring Christianity. Adoptees searching for birth parents are motivated by similar convictions about the function of origins, as well as the questions and confusion that accompanies them.

Feminist Criticism of Originating Stories

A second and related area of research, namely, feminist studies of early Christianity, provides important and helpful lessons for how adoptees, specifically those with minimal or no access to historical records detailing the circumstances of their births and adoptions, might respond to the very basic stories about their origins that adoption workers and adoptive parents relay to them. Here again, I am thinking of the situations of the thousands of Chinese girls who have been adopted in China by American parents. As Karin Evans, another journalist and adoptive parent, recounts in the critically acclaimed *Lost Daughters of China: Abandoned Girls, Their Journey to America and the Search for a Missing Past,* Chinese babies placed in adoption are denied any information about their birthmothers, families of origin, even their actual birth date. Rather, they are given new names that reflect the orphanages where they are placed while they await adoption. Evans writes:

> *Found forsaken.* The daughters of China come away with those two words, summing up their short lives. Our daughter, like so many other baby girls in China, was found with no note that we know of, no name, and no family clues. Once she arrived at the orphan- age, the people there guessed at her age and someone assigned her a birth date and name.[23]

In China, conditions such as very limited record keeping, the need for birth parents to "disappear" in order for their babies to qualify as bonafide "orphans" who can immigrate to the United States, and the fact that child relinquishment is against the law despite China's well-known one child policy, have conspired to substitute for real history only the most minimal sketch of a baby's origins. As Evans summarizes, "Overall, a mix of good intentions, legal hazards, fear, and shame has made birth parents elusive people to identify."[24] Hence, of her own Chinese daughter's origins she can only say, "Where did this wonderful daughter of mine come from? From whose flesh, I can't say. Nor at this point can I tell my daughter any more than a generalized story about her origins. Even the geography is a bit loose, vaguer than I used to think...the harder we poke at such information, the vaguer it can become."[25]

If the desire to discover one's origins is as strong as the adoption literature suggests, especially among female adoptees, then we may well wonder how entire generations of daughters of China will respond to such truncated beginnings as they mature into adulthood. What will they be able to make of the very brief and sketchy stories of origin which they have been allowed? How can one connect such historically unreliable stories to real history?

In order to begin exploring what can be learned from feminist studies of Christian origins, let us recall that much of this work has made of historical study and reconstruction what Elizabeth Castelli calls:

> ...[a] foundational tool for feminist interpretation of early Christianity. In pursuing this work, feminist scholars of early Christian history have attempted to enact European women's historian Joan Kelly's dictum that the project of women's history involves a "dual goal: to restore women to history and to restore our history to women." This process of double restoration is, of course, crucial to the political project of feminism and women's movements because it provides substance, texture and depth to our knowledge of the past, and therefore, *of ourselves in relation to the past* [emphasis mine].[26]

Here again, reconstruction of the past is intimately related to present identity and self-understanding, whether collective or individual. Yet the origins of Christianity that feminist studies have constructed are not a monolith. What Castelli observed about the study of women and Christian origins over a decade ago remains true today: feminist studies of early Christianity is best described in terms of "heteroglossia" and a "discursive diversity" that is "both individual and social."[27] The evolution of the field has yielded, and yielded to, increasingly diverse pictures of women in early Christianity and of ancient Christianity itself.

One of the lessons learned in the research that has been done since the late 1970s and early 1980s is one that could come only with time and some critical distance. As Elizabeth Clark has noted, a significant "offshoot of the quest for 'origins'" that emerged in the early decades of feminist inquiry was the way in which "scholars of religious history...looked back to 'origins' (often, of the religions to which they themselves give allegiance) to locate a golden era when women were accorded generous treatment by a prescient and charismatic founding figure."[28] Clark, of course, includes her own earlier work in this critique, as well as that of feminist pioneers in religion such as Elisabeth Schüssler Fiorenza.[29] Much has been learned, and, to the credit of feminist interpretation and as evidence of the consistency of its practice and theory, many of its methodological and historical assumptions have changed. For example, the field has moved away from its earlier and rather simplistic constructions of a feminist and frequently anti-Jewish Jesus. What have emerged in their place are contextualized readings of diverse texts and interpretations of material evidence that point toward a plurality of Christianities in antiquity.

The benefits of these lessons hard fought and won by feminist scholarship are clearly seen in Ross Kraemer's and Mary Rose D'Angelo's *Women and Christian Origins*.[30] In marked contrast to the kind of quest for origins illustrated by the long history of Jesus research, feminist work in Christian origins has moved beyond seeking a pure beginning and a single paradigm for authenticating and legitimizing women's place in early Christianity. The genealogy it has established is communal. Rather than constructing a family tree of sorts, it has set a family table at which women are invited to sit. It is not that women are asked to find in and among their foremothers their precise lineage, true origins, or selves. It is that at this table, a place has been set and an invitation extended to women who hear "you are one of us." The connection between past and present is established by neither conformity nor even continuity, but by the process of acknowledgement. It is not that the inauthentic is replaced by the authentic, it is that recognition is given to women both past and present; it is in this way, then, that "women are restored to history and history is restored to women."

In addition to shifting the goal of investigation from that of finding the "golden era" to which Clark alludes to making room for women's experience past and present, feminist studies of Christian origins have established a critical approach to the originating stories that the New Testament gospels provide. Feminist interpretation of Luke's gospel provides a helpful case in point.

Interpreters have long noted that Luke includes decidedly more women characters in his gospel than does any other gospel writer. Thus feminist interpreters initially turned to this gospel and Acts with an eye toward mining an anticipated egalitarian agenda in Luke's writing. However, increasingly nuanced gender analysis revealed a less-than-egalitarian story world that, in the words of Turid Karlsen Seim, "cannot be reduced either to a feminist treasure chamber or to a chamber of horrors."[31]

In her study of women in Luke, D'Angelo not only confirms what Seim has aptly coined Luke's "double message"–she also argues persuasively that "Luke's multiplication of representations of women is accompanied by a corresponding limitation of their roles. Luke is concerned not with changing the status of women, but with the appropriate deployment of gender."[32] She notes further:

> In Luke 6.12–16, the twelve were explicitly called, given the title "apostles," and associated with Jesus' ministry. In 8.1–3 the women are said to be with Jesus not as a result of a special call, but out of

gratitude for cures: they are not described as following (disciples), as the women in Mark 15.40–41 are, and they share in Jesus' ministry not by preaching and healing as the twelve do in 9.1–6, but by ministering *to*...Jesus and the twelve [emphasis mine].[33]

As D'Angelo shows, women *are* central to the Christian scene, but in a way that befits a Roman understanding of good social order.

Thus, probably owing to the public nature of his Gospel (remember that Luke dedicates it to one Theophilus), Luke appears to be expressly (and no doubt genuinely) invested in its public reception. Coupled with another public-relations effort "to tame and limit prophecy" that Luke shares with other early Christian evangelists, Luke's story promotes positive and very Roman-friendly images of Christian men and women.[34] As D'Angelo illustrates, feminist explication of women in the canonical gospels necessitates the interrogation of originating stories. Feminist interpretation inquires into both the stories that are told and the contexts and rhetorical agendas that gave rise to them. It is not just stories, then, but their function and the circumstances to which they were responding that fills out the history of women in earliest Christianity. Despite obvious gaps in our knowledge of women's history, we can examine critically and learn much from the context and function of the stories to which we do have access. This, too, is a recovery of history.

The methods and approaches to its subject that feminist interpretation of Christian origins utilizes are similar to those on which Evans draws in *The Lost Daughters of China*. Whereas she remains yet unable to offer her adopted daughter anything but the barest outline of what her life was prior to her adoption, she has provided for her and all recent Chinese adoptees a narrative of the conditions and contexts that have led to the phenomenon of mass American adoption of Chinese babies. She has also, mercifully, made sense of the rhetoric of abandonment and the penetrating silence that permeates Chinese adoption. None of these accomplishments replaces a more personal historical narrative, but her work does restore the daughters of China to Chinese history even as it restores their Chinese history to them. It is a gesture of acknowledgement that restores to tens of thousands of girls and women both dignity and identity.

Conclusion

A review of the study of origins in New Testament and early Christianity studies brings into view lessons that are relevant to the problem of origins with which many Pacific Asian North American adoptees contend. The drive to locate and examine origins is one that is both determined and persistent. The history of interpretation of the life and death of Jesus as well as adoption stories enable one to see that even the most well-meaning attempts to minimize or reframe the desire to uncover an originating history are unlikely to succeed. Furthermore, feminist historians of earliest Christianity have shown that even when obstacles to such historical investigation threaten to overwhelm the effort, the context and conditions that lead to the obscuring of origins can be meaningfully interrogated. Doing so is unlikely to yield more complete personal narratives, to be sure. But to interrogate the function and context, if not the content, of the generalized stories that adoptive parents take home from China will at least give to the "lost daughters of China" some historical grounding and acknowledgement of the larger political and social realities that prevented the recounting of more complete stories of their origins. Adoption professionals report how it is not unusual for adoptees to express a sense of rootlessness, of having no historical bearings and no real "beginning," as if they had been dropped from the sky into human history by the proverbial stork. When access to specific historical detail is denied, the historical context that served as the condition for such loss, perhaps the only avenue to the past that remains, becomes even more important to examine.

In short, literally thousands of Chinese North American girls will be asking their adoptive families about their origins and lost histories. It is my hope that we will recognize the drive behind their questions and acknowledge the validity of their need to ask them by helping them to learn all they can about the conditions and systems in China that set into motion their adoptions and the contexts that necessitated the rhetoric and content of their very abbreviated stories of origin. As Pertman says of the transformation of adoption in the United States from a lonely back road trip to a superhighway experience: "We should do all we can to make this a smooth ride."[35]

Living Past

A Hapa *Identifying with the Exodus, the Exile, and the Internment*

HENRY W. MORISADA RIETZ[1]

Grinnell College

Grinnell, Iowa

> *"Insofar as history comes alive for us, we become more alive in the present as well. For the sake of this vitality we risk the possibility of repeated pain. Time cannot become concrete unless it winds itself around the gritty details of our lives."*
>
> VERA SCHWARCZ[2]

I speak from experience; identifying one's self is not simple. My father was born in Hawai'i in 1927 to parents and grandparents who had immigrated from Japan.[3] My mother was born and raised in Nazi Germany in 1933, eventually emigrating to the United States in the early 1960s. Her mother was a French Jew. Her father was a Hungarian gypsy. I do not have the privilege of speaking from a generally recognized social location. My mixed, or what we call in Hawai'i *hapa*, heritage precludes me from claiming any one identity with integrity.[4] I am both Asian American and Euro-American, and yet I am neither. I am an "other" to the "Other."

I was conceived—though perhaps it was a more a misconception—in 1966. Even at that time in Hawai'i, it would have been shameful for a Japanese man, at least in *some* Japanese families, to marry a *haole* woman—a white woman.[5] But my father, being an honorable man, proposed to my mother, offering to sell his property and move with her to the mainland. My mother, however, refused. She would not allow him to abandon his family. My parents did not marry. For most of my life, my father's family did not know anything about me; they did not even know that I existed.

Although I was never ashamed, I did find it difficult growing up "without" relatives. I had no family heritage that I could claim. Or maybe, more accurately, there was no heritage that would claim me. The community of Hawai'i is small. Somehow, in some way, everyone's paths cross. When people meet for the first time, the conversation often turns to their extended families, and they discover how they are connected by their extended families. One's identity derives from the family one identifies with.

Moreover, I could not find a stable source of identity in the larger context of the United States either. I did not see myself in the images, histories, and experiences manufactured and presented by the dominant society, whether in the media of popular culture or the canons of academia. Nor was I seen by others for who I am. As I have experienced others encountering me, I find myself often alienated as different or assimilated as the same. My particularities are erased. A grant proposal writer at my college asked me why I was interested in programs for minority scholars–certainly I was not a person of color. A white relative once asked me why I had switched to round-rimmed glasses: "They make you look so oriental," he said. To identify merely with experiences I share with one group–whether Asian American or Euro-American–denies the differences that I have; it denies who I am.

Interpreting Identities

My experience leads me to emphasize particularity as the basis for community and communication, and thus identity construction and interpretation. As many poststructuralist and postcolonial theorists have pointed out, identity is constructed vis-à-vis an "other."[6] An individual or community is defined by differences from others. This is not that. We are not they. The identities of the self (especially as a community) and the other are then posited on the basis of similarities within each category with the internal differences being elided or ignored.[7] Moreover, the privileging of "sameness" also tends to ignore change, so that the categories and identities are seen as static, comprising unchanging essential essences. Identity thus becomes merely an intellectual construct, disembodied from living.

My lived experience, however, reveals to me some of the problems of privileging stasis over change, differences over similarities, as well as of valuing similarities over differences. In my search to find someone in a similar situation, I have yet to find another *hapa* person with the same story as mine.[8] But despite the differences, and even because of the differences, I have learned from listening to the stories of others. There is power in hearing and in sharing our *particular* stories, by maintaining both the similarities as well as the differences. When we maintain the particularities, we communicate, we are in relationship, not as stereotyped caricatures or abstractions, but as two distinct individuals, each with a rich nexus of relationships and experiences.

I would also suggest that the construction of identity and hermeneutics are two sides of the same coin. We do not exist in isolation. How one understands and constructs one's identity is affected by one's encounter and understanding of others—who one understands to be part of their community, and who is not. Moreover, how we encounter and interpret others—be they texts such as the Bible, historical experiences, or flesh and blood people—is also directly related to how we understand ourselves. Since identity is constructed vis-à-vis an "other," the identity of an individual or a community is constructed in relationship with others. More specifically, construction of the self involves interpretation of an "other"; thus, there is a related hermeneutic.

Just a Bit of B.S. (Biblical Studies, That Is)

"History has one task and one end what is useful…[that is] if ever again people find themselves in a like situation they may be able…from a consideration of the records of the past handle rightly what now confronts them."

Greek satirist Lucian writing in the second century C.E.[9]

Privileging particularity has implications not only for identity formation and communication, but also for interpreting texts, especially texts such as the Bible that are used to form the religious identity of various communities. Historically, biblical studies emerged as an academic discipline by differentiating itself from being merely the servant of the Christian Church, by producing knowledge that is not "theological," but, especially until the last few decades, "historical." Of course, the distinction between producing "theology" and "history" was not always maintained. As we are well aware, a lot of "theology" has been propagated as "history" and "history" is not reconstructed and told as a neutral project.[10]

In the eighteenth century, the usual products of theologians studying the bible were lists of proof texts used to support theological doctrines. G.T. Zachariae was one of the first to question the usefulness of these lists of biblical passages, isolated as they were from their literary and especially historical contexts.[11] Biblical studies emerged as an academic discipline in the eighteenth century as a project of the Enlightenment by presupposing an historical gulf between the reader's context and the original historical context of the texts. Up until the last few decades, various forms of historical criticism have dominated biblical studies. The biblical texts are studied within a reconstruction of their original historical contexts. However, within biblical studies, a sub-discipline of biblical theology emerged. Biblical theology—a Christian and predominately Protestant Christian project–traditionally seeks to overcome or bridge the historical gap that historical criticism sets up between the present historical context and the historical past of the biblical text.[12] So-called "biblical theology" is particularly interesting for my project of proposing a "hapa" hermeneutic. Unlike much of historical criticism, which espoused a naïve objectivity (at least as an ideal), so-called "biblical theologians" seek to produce interpretations that were meaningful to their historical present–that is, a sort of contextual interpretation. (Of course, many of them, especially the early European and Euro-American interpreters, were not cognizant of the import of race, ethnicity, gender, etc., on their interpretations).

As I survey the interpretations of biblical scholars, especially classical biblical theologians, I find a privileging of similarity as the marker of what is meaningful. If something is common or similar then it is meaningful.[13] Although European and Euro-American biblical theology is informed by historical criticism–which presupposes difference: a different time in history, a different location, a different culture–difference is often seen as the problem to be overcome, by the similarities that are discerned between "then" and "now."[14]

J.P. Gabler

The year 1787 is often identified as marking the beginning of biblical Studies as a discipline separate from dogmatic theology. In that year, J.P. Gabler gave his inaugural address entitled "On the Proper Distinction between Biblical and Dogmatic Theology and the Specific Objectives of Each." In this address, Gabler argued for a study of the individual books and authors of the Bible in their own historical contexts. Thus, he began recognizing not only the difference between his present and the time of the biblical writers, but also the historical differences among them. Gabler, however, wanted to do more than just historical study; he also wanted to produce something that was meaningful for his time. So, he proposed that once the various biblical books and authors were examined on their own, their "notions" and "ideas" would be compared to discern what was relevant only to a specific time from what is true for "all times and places."[15] Thus, Gabler posited similarities–"timeless truths"–as bridging the gaps of history.

Rudolf Bultmann

Writing a century and a half later, another European interpreter, Rudolf Bultmann, proposed another way of dealing with the historical gap between his present and the time of the biblical texts. The problem for Bultmann was that the Christian message, the "kerygma" or "proclamation," was imbedded in an obsolete worldview. Bultmann described the worldview of the Christian Scriptures as "essentially mythical in character. The world is viewed as a three storied structure, with the earth in the centre, the heaven above, and the underworld beneath…[T]he earth…is the scene of the supernatural activity of God and his angels on the one hand, and of Satan and his daemons on the other...Man is not in control of his life. Evil spirits may take possession of him."[16] For Bultmann, this mythical worldview is unbelievable to "modern man [*sic*]." He notes: "It is impossible to use electric light and the wireless and to avail ourselves of modern medical and surgical discoveries, and at the same time to believe in the New Testament world of daemons and spirits."[17] He rejected other interpretive strategies that explained away the miraculous and the supernatural aspects of the Bible, which he deemed had done irreparable harm to biblical proclamation. Instead, Bultmann proposed that the purpose of myth is "to express man's understanding of himself in the world in which he lives";[18] for him, what the myth of the Christian Scriptures ultimately expressed was the existential experience that "man is not in control of his life." This existential experience, for Bultmann, is shared by "modern man" and thus provided the similarity that bridged the gap between his present and the time of the biblical text.

Some "Others"

In the last several decades, voices other than European and Euro-American men have entered the conversation—voices of women, voices of people of a color other than white. Rather than beginning with the problem of historical difference from the text, these interpreters tend to be more self-conscious of their present location and identity, an identity that is often constructed by highlighting their differences from that of the dominant European and Euro-American male interpreters. They do not see themselves reflected in the abstract and supposedly universal terms such as "modern man," terms that they rightly see as masking a specific "white, European or American, upper middle class, traditionally educated straight male" identity.

Nevertheless, I would suggest that when interpreters of other colors turn to the biblical text, a privileging of similarity is often invoked. Many African American interpreters draw parallels between experiences of slavery and oppression depicted in the Bible with those experienced by African Americans; thus, the prominence of the exodus motif in African American interpretations. Delores Williams's womanist reading of the story of Hagar in Genesis provides just one example. For Williams, the story of the "slave woman Hagar...illustrates what the history of many African-American women taught them long ago; that is, the slave woman's story is and unavoidably has been shaped by the problems and desires of her owners."[19] Williams sees the story of Hagar as addressing and illustrating experiences that are similar to those in the history of African American women—experiences of enslavement and oppression, surrogate parenting, and homelessness. Similar to Bultmann, common experience provides the bridge across time between the story of the African Hagar and African

American women. However, in contrast to Bultmann, the experience is not necessarily that of all people, but an experience common to some. Nevertheless, what is found to be meaningful is what is similar.

The privileging of similarities is prevalent among other explicitly contextual interpretations.[20] The tendency may be seen in the first collection of explicitly Asian American interpretations of the Bible, *The Bible in Asian America*.[21] Uriah (Yong-Hwan) Kim, for example, insightfully draws our attention to Uriah the Hittite in 2 Samuel 11, a character often ignored by most interpreters who relate to and lift up David, and perhaps Bathsheba.[22] His close reading of the text shows Uriah to be the pivotal character in a story of struggle for identity. While Kim is sensitive to differences, his powerfully poignant hermeneutical payoff is explicitly based on the similarities between the contexts:

> Uriah's story is familiar to Asian Americans struggling for identity in the U.S. and echoes the tragic story of Vincent Chin. Vincent was a young Chinese American...[who] was killed as a "Jap" because two white auto workers thought that he was a Japanese and blamed him for the loss of their jobs...It could have easily been Uriah Kim, a Korean American, killed instead of Vincent Chin, a Chinese American, because...[a]fterall, we all look alike.[23]

Kim does not facilely appropriate the story, but provides a nuanced reading of the historical-literary context of Uriah the Hittite. Nevertheless, what is explicitly valued as meaningful for today are the similarities between the past and the present.[24]

This is not to say that strategies of discerning similarities are necessarily wrong. On the contrary, I have learned a lot from contextual interpretations that bridge the gap between the past and the present by discerning similarities between them. Nevertheless, my experience leads me to ask about the value of differences as well, because to me there is a power to be found in maintaining the differences, rather than merely treating difference as a problem to be overcome or perhaps put aside in creating meaning for today. In contrast, I am proposing a mode of interpretation that explicitly values both similarities as well as differences; that is to say, a mode that values particularity. Rita Nakashima Brock, I think, points us in that direction.[25] In her classic book, *Journeys by Heart,* Brock proposes a hermeneutic of "erotic power." For Brock, who is informed by psychoanalytic theory, which eschews emotional enmeshment as destructive, maintaining a distinction between oneself and another is important even when one is trying to understand others empathetically. She exemplifies the way that her hermeneutic enables her to understand and interpret the experiences of another with the story of hearing a friend talk about being abused as a child. Brock writes:

If I listen to a friend tell the story of a childhood molestation, her pain communicates itself vividly to me. But the pain I experience, triggered by hers, emerges from within me. It is not her pain, though it mirrors hers and enables me to take her pain into me. If I am oblivious to my own feelings and confuse mine with hers, I will experience my own pain through hers, making her uniqueness invisible. If I refuse my own feelings because I fear my own pain, my impassivity or my deflecting her pain by making it abstract or universal will reduce her presence to me. Maintaining my self-awareness, which allows my openness to her, allows me to respond in my own unique, creative way to her pain. Our empowerment comes not in her pain or in mine but in the space where the two meet inside us and between us. In that meeting, in the feelings underneath the speaking and listening, we are empowered to care and to heal. When I experience my own empowerment through connection, I know power emerges from my relationships.[26]

Familiar Myths

"I am the God of your father, the God of Abraham, the God of Isaac, and the God of Jacob."

EXODUS 3:6

The construction and maintenance of identities often involve the telling and retelling of meaningful stories–that is, "myths"–which are often ritually enacted. This is certainly true in the biblical traditions, in both the traditions that are recorded in the Bible as well as the religious traditions that draw on and interpret the Bible. The term "myth" does not imply that the stories are not historically accurate. Rather, myths are those stories that "bind groups of people, providing common reference points from which they may negotiate various facets of their lives."[27] Thus, the focus here is on the way that the stories are used and how they function in identity formation, rather than on their historicity.[28] So, for example, the ancestral narrative of Genesis 12–50 forms one of the first major sections of the biblical texts. In fact, as form critics have rightly discerned, fragments of earlier recitations of "history" preserved in the biblical text often begin with narratives about ancestors–stories about the patriarchs and matriarchs, and not, for example, creation accounts or flood narratives (e.g., Deut. 26:5b-9; Josh. 24:2b-13).[29]

The category of myth, developed in the study of religion, helps us to discern the ways that stories are used as the foundation for identity in a variety of different contexts, including the familial, ethnic, and political.[30] Stories about one's ancestors, the history of one's people and one's nation, are used to form and inform one's identity. My experience as *hapa,* however, always sounds a caution against the facile appropriation of such stories. I cannot easily appropriate them; I see differences as well as similarities.

Exodus, Exile, and Internment

February 19 has become a day of remembrance in the Asian American, and especially Japanese American, community.[31] On February 19, 1942, President Franklin Delano Roosevelt signed Executive Order 9066, resulting in the uprooting and detention of Japanese and Japanese Americans living on the west coast of the United States. Over 120,000 people of Japanese ancestry were removed from their homes, detained in special camps, and eventually relocated to concentration camps throughout the western interior of the United States: women, men, children, the elderly, as well as infants. Two thirds of these individuals were American citizens. Allowed only what they could physically carry, they lost their property and their possessions, many lost their homes and their farms. All were denied their freedom, their dignity, and their honor–all without due process, all without having committed a crime. Their sole offense was their ancestry: they were Americans of Japanese descent. Remembrance of the internment has become part of the Japanese American identity.

Remembrance of meaningful stories–myths–also lies at heart of worship and of rituals. Exodus 12 recounts the institution of the Passover celebration, the ritual remembrance of God's deliverance of the Israelites from bondage in Egypt: "This day shall be a day of remembrance for you. You shall celebrate it as a festival to the LORD" (Ex. 12:14). While the setting of the passage in the narrative is the night before the day of redemption, the temporal dimensions of the story–the juxtaposition of past, present, and future tenses–reveal the original setting of the passage in a ritual context. Note the future tenses: "For I will pass through the land of Egypt that night, and I will strike down every firstborn in the land of Egypt" (Ex. 12:12a). But notice also the past tense: "You shall observe the festival of unleavened bread, for on this very day I *brought* your companies out of the land of Egypt: you shall observe this day throughout your generations as a perpetual ordinance [emphasis mine]" (Ex. 12:17). The Passover event has been called "a moment frozen in time." Through the reading of the story, through the ritual reenactment of the Passover meal (the Seder), the reader, the audience, the worshiper is there, recreating and remembering God's mighty acts. Through ritual, the past comes alive; it becomes a living past. Such is the nature of ritual; such is the nature of remembrance.

According to the biblical text, the ritual remembrance of the exodus is to be celebrated "as a perpetual ordinance" by all who dwell in Israel. Through the ritual of Passover, the story of the exodus was to be passed down to future generations. The memory of the story was bequeathed to those who were not there: to the descendants of the people as well as to the aliens who dwelt in their midst. Remembrance of the exodus story by those who were not there serves to create and maintain identity–just as those of us in the United States ritually remember and celebrate that mythical first thanksgiving meal celebrated by the immigrant pilgrims, regardless of whether our ancestors were among that original band that landed at Plymouth Rock. My ancestors certainly did not come over on the Mayflower. I doubt many of yours did either. Neither was my father's family interned during World War II–there were too many Japanese Americans living in Hawai'i at that time for a broad internment policy to take effect there.[32] Nevertheless, we can still remember. Even though we may be Gentiles and our ancestors were not liberated from Egypt, even though our ancestors were not at that first mythical thanksgiving meal, even though our parents were not interned during World War II, we all can still remember:[33] "For seven days no leaven shall be found in your houses; for whoever eats what is leavened shall be cut off from the congregation of Israel, whether an alien or a native of the land" (Ex. 12:19; cf. 12:15). Those who do not remember the exodus are not part of Israel. Memory of the exodus is part of Israel's identity. So too, those of us in the United States, through the annual ritual of Thanksgiving, immigrants and their descendants regardless of their ancestry forge together an American identity.

Ritual remembrance, however, is not some nostalgic yearning merely to relive the past. We should not retreat from the present to some distant moment in the past; rather, ritual remembrance provides a context, a space in time for the past to impinge on the present. The memory of Israel's stories was appropriated and reappropriated throughout Israel's history to impact their present time. The richness of the biblical text, moreover, encourages readers and hearers not only to identify with the enslaved Israelites, but also with the enslaving Egyptians. Memory of the exodus story, for example, provided the basis for observing the Sabbath in the Deuteronomistic Decalogue:

> Observe the sabbath day and keep it holy, as the LORD your God has commanded you...You shall not do any work–you, or your son or your daughter, or your male or female slave...so that your male and female slave may rest as well as you. Remember that you were a slave in the land of Egypt, and the LORD your God brought you out from there." (Deut. 5:12–15 excerpted)

Memory of the experience of past suffering and oppression is to impact the people's actions in the present–how they treat each other, and those that they have authority over. We have multiple identities. In this way, we are *living past* the atrocities of history, making a better, more just, present.

Some of the most poignant and powerful remembrances of the exodus story come from the exilic period when Israel found itself once again in the midst of oppression. In 587 B.C.E., the Babylonians had conquered Judah–the Southern Kingdom had fallen–and Jerusalem and its magnificent temple had been destroyed. In order to control their conquered people, to prevent uprisings and revolts, the Babylonians engaged in a program of relocation. They took the leaders of the people, the priests and the royal families, and exiled them from the promised land: women, men, children, the elderly, as well as infants. "By the rivers of Babylon– / there we sat down and there we wept / when we remembered Zion," the psalmist sings. "How could we sing the LORD's song / in a foreign land?" (Ps. 137:1, 4). Allowed only what they could physically carry, they lost their property and their possessions; many lost their homes and their farms; all were denied their freedom, their dignity, and their honor.

We often think about the Babylonians' program of exile from the perspective of Judah–the people who were dispersed and relocated from the promised land. From the point of view of the Babylonians, however, the program of exile was an important measure to ensure their "homeland security." Rather than banishing the people, the Babylonian policy was to relocate their conquered subjects from the western margins of the empire toward the center. The Israelites were interned at the center of the empire as a means of controlling them.

Again, let us not engage in romantic nostalgia or sentimentality. The point of remembering the past, living past, is to affect our actions in the present: "Remember that you [too] were a slave in the land of Egypt." Whom are we interning today? I had a student in my Jewish traditions course recently who was passionate about inter-religious dialogue and its possibilities for reducing violence among Jews and Muslims. One day after class he approached me rather embarrassingly to tell me that he would have to miss the next class. He had to make a six-hour round trip to Omaha to register with the U.S. Immigration Service. He was embarrassed because, despite his love for the United States, his respect for human life, his efforts to reconcile Jews and Muslims and Christians, he was a suspect–he was being treated as if he were a potential criminal, as if he were a terrorist, all because he was born in Pakistan. In February of 2003, Representative Howard Coble from North Carolina, then chair of the Judiciary Subcommittee on Crime, Terrorism, and Homeland Security recalled the internment of Japanese Americans during World War II:

> We were at war. They [the Japanese Americans] were an endangered species. For many of these Japanese-Americans, it wasn't safe for them to be on the street...Some probably were intent on doing harm to us, just as some of these Arab-Americans are probably intent on doing harm to us.[34]

"Remember that you [too] were a slave in the land of Egypt."

In our academic, political, and theological discussions, it is in vogue to talk about marginality, liminality, multiculturalism, and inclusivity. While much of these discussions are important, and I am sympathetic to the sentiments, we must think more deeply about inclusivity. Indeed, minorities, foreigners, those who are somehow "other" are to be included, sometimes even brought into the center–but all too often they are included not on their own terms but on ours. Our policies and our rhetoric, our theories and our theologies, and our categories and our labels intern them. Some gays and lesbians want equal rights. So we will offer them civil unions while trying to pass amendments restricting marriage to one man and one woman. We include feminist, womanist, African American, Latin American, Asian American, queer and other so-called "adjectival" interpretations and theologies in our readings and in our sermons–sometimes even highlighting them at the center–but all on our own terms. All the while we neglect to recognize that Luther's, Calvin's, and Barth's theologies are no less perspectival, masking the ways that Reformed and Neo-Orthodox theologies also are affected by the race, ethnicity, gender, class, and sexual orientation of their proponents.

The internment reminds us that injustice occurs not only when we exclude people from discussion, from power, and from lands. Injustice can also occur when we intern people, force them into the center as a means of controlling them. Whom are we interning today? "Remember that you [too] were a slave in the land of Egypt."

In Particular

A mode of identity construction and a related hermeneutic based on particularity is intended to accomplish a number of goals. The conjoining of identity construction and hermeneutics is, in my opinion, a natural wedding. Inscribed in the notion of particularity is a relationship between oneself and an "other"–the multiple ways that the other is similar to or different from the self. Indeed, the intention is that by privileging, not just the similarities or the differences, but rather the particularities, the other would not be merely an object of study or a foil for identity construction, but would be a subject, an active participant in the relationship and construction, an "Other" with a capital "O." At the same time, however, the unavoidable–and indeed constructive–role of the interpreter in the process is not occluded. Rather, interpretation of the self and "Other"– that is, meaning–is constructed in the relationship between the two.

The complexity of the interpretive process, however, is seen to be even more difficult when one recognizes that there is often more than one "Other." Thus, in the reading above, there is a multiplicity of "texts" being interpreted. In addition to the various "texts" from the Bible speaking to different historical experiences, there are also the "texts" of Japanese American experiences of the internment, the post-9/11 United States, and even myself, among other things. The meaning that I am producing negotiates and values the similarities *and* differences–the particularities– not just between myself and an "Other," but between and among several "Others."

Maintaining particularities undermines assertions of "authenticity" and the imperialistic urge to *claim* the experiences of others while denying them to still others. The experiences of "Others" are just that, someone else's. Rather, the engagement with the stories of others expands our identities and allows us to grow critically. I can relate to the experiences of exile and internment, but all the while I recognize that those are also not my experiences, and thus I am also challenged to see how I am also complicit in policies and programs of exile and internment, by virtue of my education, gender, class, sexual orientation, physical ability, and citizenship, among other things. Living in the nexus of social relationships, both local and global, is complicated.

My privileging of particularity–of both similarities and differences–arises out of my struggle to construct my own identity, to own my *hapa* identity. While I argue that my proposal to emphasize particularity develops out of my *hapa* identity, I would also argue that it is applicable to those with a different perspective, a different identity. Indeed, I hope that my example of identifying with others whose stories are different from mine will assist others to do the same; we do not have to remember only the stories of *our* ancestors, *our* people, whoever that "our" may be and however constructed that "our" is. Since my identity is contested, I do not have the privilege of passively accepting a single or static identity. Change and difference for me is unavoidable.[35] It is not that only the interpretations of people of other colors are affected by their ethnicity, it is just that they are often more conscious of how. In my case, my experience of difference and the related conscious construction of my *hapa* identity sensitizes me to the multiplicity within individual identity. My perspective, however, is not ultimately privileged; rather, the benefit of my identity is merely heuristic. I find that by telling my story, others are then able to recognize the particularities of their identities. By remembering the stories of others and sharing our particular stories with each other, we may *identify with* one another, we may *live past.*

Living Past

In 1995, my father ended the silence surrounding my existence. He told his family about me. A month after my oldest daughter Maile was born, my father brought us to the family columbarium at the Soto mission, to the ashes of my grandparents. We brought flowers and offered incense. My father chanted the *okyo* and introduced us to his parents. The next month my parents were married. The wedding service was performed in the same Shinto shrine as my grandparents'. A friend of my mother's and I were the only witnesses. When I got divorced a few years later, my father's last name, Morisada, was legally added to my name. And so we *live past.*

Notes

Foreword

[1]Kosuke Koyama, *Waterbuffalo Theology* (Maryknoll, N.Y.: Orbis Books, 1974); Choan-Seng Song, *Third-eye Theology: Theology in Formation in Asian Settings* (Maryknoll, N.Y.: Orbis Books, 1979).

[2]See J.K. Kuan, "Asian Biblical Interpretation," in *Dictionary of Biblical Interpretation, A-J*, ed. John H. Hayes (Nashville: Abingdon Press, 1999), 70–77, especially the bibliography.

[3]While we use the term "Asian American" generically to refer to North Americans of Asian descent, we need to note that the North American context that the authors in this volume refer to is largely that of the United States of America.

[4]Gale A. Yee, "Inculturation and Diversity in the Politics of National Identity," *Journal of Asian and Asian American Theology* 2 (1997): 112.

[5]Gale A. Yee, *Poor Banished Children of Eve: Woman as Evil in the Hebrew Bible* (Minneapolis: Fortress Press, 2003), 165.

[6]Bharati Mukherjee, "American Dreamer," http://www.motherjones.com/commentary/columns/1997/01/mukherjee.html.

Chapter 1: Biblical Interpretation in India

[1]A.M. Mundadan, "Origins of Christianity in India," in *Christianity in India: A History in Ecumenical Perspective*, ed. H. C. Perumalil and E. R. Hambye (Alleppy, India: Prakasam Publications, 1972), 18. For a more elaborate treatment on the debate concerning the origins, see A.M. Mundadan, ed., *History of Christianity in India*, vol. 1 (Bangalore, India: Theological Publications in India, 1984), 9–66.

[2]Mundadan, ed., *History of Christianity in India*, vol. 1, 115. For a complete treatment of the period in question, see 67–115.

[3]C.P. Mathew and M.M. Thomas, eds., *The Indian Churches of St. Thomas* (Delhi: Indian Society for Promoting Christian Knowledge [ISPCK], 1967), 45.

[4]R.H.S. Boyd, *An Introduction to Indian Christian Theology* (Madras: Christian Literature Society [CLS], 1969), 12.

[5]D. Yesudas, "Indigenization or Adaptation? A Brief Study of Robert De Nobili's Attitude to Hinduism," *Bangalore Theological Forum* 1 (Sept. 1967): 39.

[6]Perumalil and Hambye, eds., *Christianity in India*, 74–75.

[7]Ignatius Hirudayam, *Christianity and Tamil Culture* (Madras: University of Madras, Dr. S. Radhakrishnan Institute for Advanced Study in Philosophy, 1977), 34–36.

[8]Henry Victor, "Tamil Translation of the Bible by the Danish-Halle Mission during the 18th century," *Indian Church History Review* 16/1 (1982): 72.

[9]Ibid., 77.

[10]E. Arno Lehmann, *It Began at Tranquebar* (Madras: CLS, 1956), 31.

[11]Victor, "Tamil Translation of the Bible," 81.

[12]R.H.S. Boyd, "The Use of the Bible in Indian Christian Theology," *Indian Journal of Theology* 22/4 (1973): 142.

[13]For Roy's doctrinal understandings, see Ram Mohan Roy, *An Appeal to the Christian Public in Defense of the Precepts of Jesus* (Calcutta: 1820); *idem, Second Appeal* (Calcutta: 1821); *idem, Final Appeal* (Calcutta: 1824). Among secondary literature see Manilal Parekh, *Rajarishi Ram Mohan Roy* (Rajkot, 1927); J.N. Farquar, *Modern Religious Movements* (London: ISPCK, 1918); and Boyd, *Indian Christian Theology*, 19–39.

[14]The normal spelling for the word is "Aryan," designating the people who came and settled in India. The spelling used by Banerjea is not to be taken as an adjectival form of Arius, of the fourth-century C.E. Arian controversy fame.

[15]Kaj Baago, *Pioneers of Indigenous Christianity*, Confessing the Faith in India Series No. 4 (Madras: CLS, 1969), 14.

[16]Ibid.

[17]Banerjea, *Arian* (sic) *Witness; idem, The Relation between Christianity and Hinduism* (Madras: CLS, 1880).

[18]W. Theodore de Bary, *Sources of Indian Tradition* (Delhi: Motilal Banarsidas, 1972), 15.

[19]Banerjea, *Christianity and Hinduism,* 11–17.

[20]G.V. Job et al., eds., *Rethinking Christianity in India* (Madras: CLS, 1938), 8.

[21]P. Chenchiah, "Who Is Jesus? A Study of Jesus in terms of the Creative Process." A series of articles published in *The Guardian* between July 29, 1943, to August 19, 1943. Excerpts are reproduced in D.A. Thangaswamy, *The Theology of Chenchiah* (Bangalore: Christian Institute for the Study of Religion and Society, 1966), 100–122.

[22]Chenchiah, "Who Is Jesus?" in Thangaswamy, *Theology of Chenchiah,* 156–64.

[23]V. Chakkarai, *Jesus the Avatar* (Madras: CLS, 1926), 112.

[24]Job et al., *Rethinking Christianity in India,* 75.

[25]Boyd, "Use of the Bible," 153. See also his *Indian Christian Theology,* 165–85.

[26]Boyd, "Use of the Bible," 154.

[27]M.P. John, "The Use of Bible by Indian Christian Theologians," *Indian Journal of Theology* 14/2 (1965): 48.

[28]A.J. Appaswamy, *Christianity as Bhakti Marga* (Madras: CLS, 1930).

[29]Ibid., 26.

[30]Ibid., 21.

[31]For a balanced look at the issue see John Webster, *The Dalit Christians: A History* (Delhi: ISPCK, 1992). Arguing for the antiquity of the Dalits in India is the work by James Massey, *Roots: A Concise History of Dalits* (Delhi: ISPCK, 1991).

[32]M.E. Prabhakar, ed., *Towards A Dalit Theology* (Delhi: ISPCK, 1988); Xavier Irudayaraj, ed., *Emerging Dalit Theology* (Madras: The Jesuit Theological Secretariate, 1990); Arvind Nirmal, ed., *Towards a Common Dalit Theology* (Madras: The Gurukul Lutheran Theological College and Research Institute, 1990); A.P. Nirmal, ed., *A Reader in Dalit Theology* (Madras: The Gurukul Lutheran Theological College and Research Institute, 1991).

[33]A.P. Nirmal, ed., *A Reader in Dalit Theology;* M. Azariah, *Witnessing in India Today* (Madras: United Evangelical Lutheran Churches, 1983); and *idem, Mission in Christ's Way in India Today* (Madras: CLS, 1989).

[34]Arvind Nirmal, "A Dialogue with Dalit Literature," in *Towards a Dalit Theology,* 64–82.

[35]Ibid., 77–78.

[36]Ibid., 79.

[37]Ibid., 80. For further theological discussion on dalit christology and pneumatology see also *idem,* "Towards a Christian Dalit Theology," in *Frontiers in Asian Christian Theology,* ed. R.S. Sugirtharajah (Maryknoll, N.Y.: Orbis Books, 1994), 27–40.

[38]Nirmal Minz, "A Theological Interpretation of the Tribal Reality in India," *Religion and Society* 34/4 (1987): 71–85. This is also reproduced in the anthology of essays *Frontiers in Asian Christian Theology,* ed. R.S. Sugirtharajah, 41–51.

[39]Ibid., 73.

[40]Ibid., 74.

[41]Ibid., 76.

[42]Ibid., 78.

[43]Aruna Gnanadason, "Towards an Indian Feminist Theology," in *We Dare to Dream: Doing Theology as Asian Women,* ed. Virginia Fabella and Sun Ai Lee Park (Maryknoll, N.Y.: Orbis Books, 1989), 117–26; *idem, No Longer a Secret: The Church and Violence Against Women* (Geneva: WCC, 1992); Prasanna Kumari, ed., *A Reader in Feminist Theology* (Chennai [Madras]: Gurukul Theological College and Research Institute, 1997); *idem,* ed., *Feminist Theology: Perspectives and Praxis* (Chennai [Madras]: Gurukul Theological College and Research Institute, 1999); Lalrinawmi Ralte and Evangeline Anderson-Rajkumar, eds., *Feminist Hermeneutics* (Delhi: ISPCK, 2002).

[44]Gnanadason, "Indian Feminist Theology," 120.

[45]Ibid., 125.

[46]Aruna Gnanadason, "The Holy Spirit Liberates and Unites," in *We Belong Together: Churches in Solidarity with Women,* ed. Sarah Cunningham (New York: Friendship Press, 1992), 117.

[47]Ibid.

[48]Ibid., 120.

[49]Of particular interest are articles found in Prabhakar, ed., *Towards A Dalit Theology;* Nirmal, ed., *Towards a Common Dalit Theology;* Nirmal, ed., *A Reader in Dalit Theology.*

[50]Samuel Rayan, "Jesus and the Poor in the Fourth Gospel," *Bible Bhashyam* 4/3 (1978): 213–28.

⁵¹G. Soares-Prabhu, "The Prophet as Theologian: Biblical Prophetism as a Paradigm for Doing Theology Today," *Asian Journal of Theology* 2/1 (1988): 3–11.

⁵²G. Soares-Prabhu, "Class in the Bible: the Biblical Poor as Social Class," in *Voices from the Margin: Interpreting the Bible in the Third World,* ed. R.S. Sugirtharajah (Maryknoll, N.Y.: Orbis, 1991), 141–71. For treatment of a variety of subjects pertinent to Indian biblical interpretation, see the collection of G. Soares-Prabhu's writings posthumously published in *Biblical Themes for a Contextual Theology Today* (Pune: Jnana-Deepa Vidyapeeth, 1999).

⁵³D.N. Premnath, *Eighth Century Prophets: A Social Analysis* (St. Louis: Chalice Press, 2003).

⁵⁴R.S. Sugirtharajah, ed., *The Postcolonial Bible* (Sheffield: Sheffield Academic Press, 1998); *Asian Biblical Hermeneutics and Postcolonialism: Contesting Interpretations* (Sheffield: Sheffield Academic Press, 1999); *Vernacular Hermeneutics* (Sheffield: Sheffield Academic Press, 1999); *The Bible and the Third World: Precolonial, Colonial and Postcolonial Encounters* (Cambridge/New York: Cambridge University Press, 2001); *Postcolonial Reconfigurations* (St. Louis: Chalice Press, 2003).

⁵⁵Sugirtharajah, *Asian Biblical Hermeneutics,* 101–2.

⁵⁶Joachim Jeremias, *The Parables of Jesus,* trans. S. H. Hooke (New York: Scribner, 1955).

⁵⁷Ibid., 103–4.

⁵⁸Jyoti Sahi, "Eve: The Ecological Voice of the Earth," *Vidyajyoti* 52/7 (1988): 341–45.

⁵⁹Ibid., 342.

⁶⁰Ibid., 343.

⁶¹Samuel Rayan, "The Earth is the Lord's," *Vidyajyoti* 54/3 (1990): 113–32.

⁶²Ibid., 122.

⁶³Ibid., 123.

⁶⁴R. J. Raja, "As it was in the Beginning…: Eco-Spirituality in the Book of Revelation," *Vidyajyoti* 55/12 (1991): 681–97.

⁶⁵Ibid., 685–86.

⁶⁶The proceedings of this seminar were published in *The Bhagavad Gita and the Bible,* ed. B.R. Kulkarni (Delhi: Unity Books, 1974).

⁶⁷The seminar papers were published under the title *India's Search for Reality and the Relevance of the Gospel of John,* ed. C. Duraisingh and C. Hargreaves (Delhi: ISPCK, 1975).

⁶⁸D.S. Amalorpavadoss, ed., *The Research Seminar on Non-Biblical Scriptures* (Bangalore: National Biblical Liturgical and Catechetical Center, 1974).

⁶⁹G. Soares-Prabhu, "The Inspiration of the Old Testament by the New and its implication for the possible inspiration of Non-Christian Scriptures," in *The Research Seminar on Non-Biblical Scriptures,* 99–115.

⁷⁰I. Vempeny, "An Approach to the Problem of Inspiration in the Non-Biblical Scriptures," in *The Research Seminar on Non-Biblical Scriptures,* 153–78.

⁷¹T.M. Manickam, "'Insight' as Inspiration and 'Anubhava' as Revelation in the Hindu Scriptures," in *The Research Seminar on Non-Biblical Scriptures,* 325–39.

⁷²Sam Bhajjan, "The Muslim Understanding of Scripture," in *The Research Seminar on Non-Biblical Scriptures,* 489–507.

⁷³Vandana, *Water of Fire* (Madras: CLS, 1981), xviii.

⁷⁴S.J. Samartha, *Living Faith* (Geneva: World Council of Churches, 1971); *The Hindu Response to the Unbound Christ* (Madras: CLS, 1974); *Courage for Dialogue* (Geneva: WCC, 1981); *One Christ, Many Religions: Toward a Revised Christology* (Maryknoll, N.Y.: Orbis Books, 1991).

⁷⁵S.J. Samartha, "The Cross and the Rainbow," in *The Myth of Christian Uniqueness,* ed. John Hick and Paul Knitter (Maryknoll, N.Y.: Orbis Books, 1987), 69–88.

⁷⁶Ibid., 78.

⁷⁷S.J. Samartha, "The Asian Context: Sources and Trends," in *Voices from the Margin,* 37. This is an excerpt from his earlier monograph entitled *The Search for New Hermeneutic in Asian Christian Theology* (Madras: CLS, 1987).

⁷⁸Ibid., 39.

⁷⁹Ibid., 40.

⁸⁰Ishanand Vempeny, *Krsna and Christ: In the Light of Some of the Fundamental Concepts and Themes of the Bhagavad Gita and the New Testament* (Pune, India: Ishvani Kendra, 1988).

⁸¹Ibid., 378–401.

⁸²Ibid., 402–43.

⁸³R.J. Raja, "The Gospels with an Indian Face," *Vidyajyoti* 55/2 (1991): 61–72; 121–41.

[84]Ibid., 139.
[85]Ibid., 140.
[86]Ibid.
[87]G. Soares-Prabhu, "Laughing at Idols: The Dark Side of Biblical Monotheism (an Indian Reading of Isaiah 44:9–20)," in *Reading from This Place, Social Location and Biblical Interpretation in Global Perspective, Vol. 2,* ed. Fernando F. Segovia and Mary Ann Tolbert (Minneapolis: Fortress Press, 1995), 109–31.
[88]Samuel Rayan, "Theology as Art," *Religion and Society* 26/2 (1979): 77–90.
[89]Ibid., 80.
[90]Ibid., 81.
[91]J.C. Winslow, *N.V. Tilak: The Christian Poet of Maharashtra* (Calcutta: YMCA, 1930), 85.
[92]A. Mariaselvam, *The Song of Songs and Ancient Tamil Poems* (Rome: Pontifical Biblical Institute, 1980).
[93]M. Lederle, "Christian Themes in Indian Paintings," *Vidyajyoti* 47/8 (1983): 390–97.
[94]Richard Taylor, "Jesus in Indian Paintings Revisited," *Religion and Society* 34/4 (1987): 52–54.
[95]Ibid., 53.
[96]Jyoti Sahi, "The Glory of God is Man (sic) Fully Alive," *Religion and Society* 34/4 (1987): 8.
[97]Sahi, "Glory of God," 8.
[98]Jyoti Sahi, "An Artist Looks at the Fourth Gospel," in *India's Search for Reality,* 78–79.
[99]Jyoti Sahi, "A Comparison between the Johannine Structure of the Image Sign and the Buddhist-Hindu Mandala," in *India's Search for Reality,* 84–92.
[100]Felix Wilfred, "Inculturation as a Hermeneutical Question," *Vidyajyoti* 52/9 (1988): 422.
[101]R.S. Sugirtharajah, "Postscript: Achievements and Items for a Future Agenda," in *Voices from the Margin,* 440–41.

Chapter 2: Chinese Biblical Interpretation

[1]For a history of mission in China, see K.A. Latourette, *The History of Christian Mission in China* (London: SPCK, 1929); Chih-hsin Wang, *Zhongguo jidujiao shigang* (*History of Christianity in China*), 3d ed. (Hong Kong: Chinese Christian Literature Council, 1979); R.R. Covell, *Confucius, The Buddha, and Christ: A History of the Gospel in Chinese* (Maryknoll, N.Y.: Orbis Books, 1986); Samuel Hugh Moffett, *A History of Christianity in Asia: Volume I: Beginning to 1500* (San Francisco: Harper, 1992), 287–323, 442–69.

[2]Shao-Jun Weng, *Hanyu jingjiao wendian quenshi* (*Sino-Nestorian Documents: Commentary and Exegesis*) (Hong Kong: Institute of Sino-Christian Studies, 1995); Charles F. Horne, ed., *The Sacred Books and Early Literature of the East, vol. 12, Medieval China* (New York: Parke, Austin & Lipscomb, 1917), 381–92; A.C. Moule, *Christians in China Before the Year 1550* (London: Society for Promoting Christian Knowledge, 1930); S.L. Lo, *Tangyuen erdai zhi jingjiao* (Nestorian Christianity in Tang and Yuen Dynasties) (Hong Kong: China Studies Press, 1966).

[3]C.E. Ronan and B.B.C. Oh, eds., *East Meets West: The Jesuits in China, 1582–1773* (Chicago: Loyola University Press, 1988); J. Gernet, *China and the Christian Impact: A Conflict of Cultures,* trans. J. Lloyd (Cambridge: Cambridge University Press; Paris: Editions de la Maison des Sciences de l'Homme, 1985).

[4]P.A. Varg, *Missionaries, Chinese, and Diplomats: The American Protestant Missionary Movement in China, 1890–1952* (Princeton: Princeton University Press, 1958); P.A. Cohen, "Christian Missions and their Impact to 1900," in *The Cambridge History of China,* ed. Denis Twitchett and John K. Fairbank, vol. 10 (Cambridge: Cambridge University Press, 1978); J.K. Fairbank, *The Missionary Enterprise in China and America* (Cambridge, Mass.: Harvard University Press, 1974); Zhi-ping Lin, ed., *Jidujiao ruhua baichishinian jinianji* (*An Anthology for the One Hundred and Seventieth Anniversary of the Coming of Christianity to China*) (Taipei: Cosmic Light, 1977); J.D. Whitehead, Y.M. Shaw, and N.J. Girardot, eds., *China and Christianity: Historical and Future Encounters* (Notre Dame: Notre Dame University Press, 1979); S.W. Barnett and J.K. Fairbank, eds., *Christianity in China: Early Protestant Missionary Writings* (Cambridge: Harvard University Press, 1985).

[5]Werner Kümmel, *The New Testament: The History of the Investigation of Its Problems,* trans. S. McLean Gilmour and H.C. Kee (Nashville: Abingdon Press, 1972; London: SCM, 1973).

⁶Stephen Neill, *The Interpretation of the New Testament, 1861–1961* (Oxford: Oxford University Press, 1964).

⁷Paul A. Cohen, *China and Christianity: The Missionary Movement and the Growth of Chinese Antiforeignism 1860–1870* (Cambridge: Harvard University Press, 1963).

⁸Jonathan D. Spence, *God's Chinese Son: The Taiping Heavenly Kingdom of Hong Xiuquan* (New York: Norton, 1997).

⁹Ka-lun Leung, *Fu lin zhonghua: zhongguo jindai jiaohuishi shijiang* (*Blessing Upon China: Ten Talks on the Contemporary Church History of China*) (Hong Kong: Tian Dao, 1988), 68.

¹⁰C.C. T'an, *The Boxer Catastrophe* (New York: Norton, 1955); S.C. Lu, *Zhongguo guanshen fanjiao zhi yuenyin* (*The Origin and Cause of Anti-Christian Movement Officials and Gentry, 1860–1874*) (Taipei: Institute of Modern History, Academia Sinica, 1966); L.T. Headland, *Chinese Heroes: Being a Record of Persecutions Endured by Native Christians in the Boxer Uprising* (New York: Eaton & Mains, 1902).

¹¹Leung, *Fu lin zhonghua*, 90.

¹²Wang, *Zhongguo jidujiao shigang*, 199.

¹³Paul A. Cohen: "Missionary Approaches: Hudson Taylor and Timothy Richard," in *Papers on China*, vol. 11 (Cambridge, Mass.: Harvard University East Asian Research Center, 1957), 29–62.

¹⁴Cf. Irene Eber, *The Jewish Bishop and the Chinese Bible: S.I.J. Schereschewsky (1831–1906)* (Leiden: Brill, 1999), 199–233.

¹⁵Cf. Fuk-tsang Ying, *Wenhua shiying yu zhongguo jidutu* (*1860–1911*) (*Cultural Accommodation and Chinese Christians [1860–1911]*) (Hong Kong: Alliance Bible Seminary, 1995).

¹⁶John Yieh, "Jia Yu-ming 'the Dean of Chinese Biblical Theology': A Hermeneutics of the Spirit and the Perfect Salvation," in *Papers for an International Conference on Religious Scripture and Interpretation* (Taipei: Graduate Institute of Religious Studies at National Chengchi University, 2000), 56–91.

¹⁷Ka-lun Leung, "Nee Tuo-shen zaochi de jiaohuiguan" ("Watchman Nee's Early Views on Church"), in *Papers for an International Conference on Religious Scripture and Interpretation* (Taipei: Graduate Institute of Religious Studies at National Chengchi University, 2000), 92–137.

¹⁸Za Shijie, *Minguo jidujiaoshi lunwenji* (*Essays on the History of Christianity in the Republic Period*) (Taipei: Cosmic Light, 1994); Fuk-tsang Ying, *Jidu xinyang yu jiuguo shijian—ershi shiji qienqi de gean yienjiu* (*Christian Doctrine and the Praxis of National Salvation: A Case Study of the First Half of 20th Century China*) (Hong Kong: Alliance Bible Seminary, 1997).

¹⁹Tse-tsung Chow, *The May Fourth Movement: Intellectual Revolution in Modern China* (Cambridge: Harvard University Press, 1960), 84–116; J.W. Israel, *Student Nationalism in China, 1927–1937* (Stanford: Stanford University Press, 1966).

²⁰Ka-che Yip, *Religion, Nationalism, and Chinese Students: The Anti-Christian Movement of 1922–1927* (Bellingham, Wash.: University of Washington Press, 1980).

²¹Wing-hung Lam, *Fengchaozhong fenqi de zhongguo jiaohui* (*Chinese Theology in Construction*) (Hong Kong: Tian Dao, 1980), 154–66.

²²D.W.Y. Kwok, *Scientism in Chinese Thought, 1900–1950* (New Haven: Yale University Press, 1965); Yu-ming Shaw, "The Reaction of Chinese Intellectuals toward Religion and Christianity in the Early Twentieth Century," in *China and Christianity: Historical and Future Encounters*, ed. J.D. Whitehead (Notre Dame: University of Notre Dame Press, 1979), 154–82.

²³Joseph Levenson, *Confucian China and Its Modern Fate: A Trilogy* (Berkeley: University of California Press, 1965), 123.

²⁴Wu Leichuan, *Jidujiao yu zhongguo wenhua* (*Christianity and Chinese Culture*) (Shanghai: Youth Association, 1936), 82–98.

²⁵Ibid., 56–59.

²⁶Wu Leichuan, "Lun zhongguo jidu jiaohui de qientu" ("On the Future of Chinese Christian Church"), *Truth Weekly* 1, no. 11 (1923).

²⁷Noteworthy is that his view was close to the historical-critical approach of D.F. Strauss, Albrecht Ritschl, and Adolf von Harnack and the demythologization of Rudolf Bultmann at about the same time.

²⁸Wu Leichuan, "Tienguo shi shenmo?" ("What is the kingdom of heaven?") (Parts I and II), *Truth Weekly* 3, nos. 9 and 11 (1925). John Yieh, "Cultural Reading of the Bible: Some Chinese Christian Cases," in *Text and Experience: Toward a Cultural Exegesis of the Bible*, ed. Daniel Smith-Christopher (Sheffield: Sheffield Academic Press, 1995), 130–36.

[29]Wu Leichuan, *Jidutu de xiwang* (*The Hope of Christians*) (Shanghai: Youth Association, 1940), 12–15. See also Tsai Yen-zen, "Jingdian quenshi yu wenhua huitong" ("Scriptural Interpretation and Cultural Exchange"), in *Papers for an International Conference on Religious Scripture and Interpretation* (Taipei: Graduate Institute of Religious Studies at National Chengchi University, 2000), 180–200, passim.

[30]Wu, *Jidujiao yu zhongguo wenhua*, 292; Yieh, "Cultural Reading of the Bible," 135.

[31]Tsai, "Jingdian quenshi yu wenhua huitong," 18; Ying, *Jidu xinyang yu jiuguo shijien*, 399–412.

[32]Winfried Glüer, *Christliche Theologie in China: T.C. Chao, 1918–1956* (Gütersloh: Gütersloher Verlagshaus Mohn, 1979); Wing-hung Lam, *Quigao Hegua: Chao Tzu-ch'en de shengping ji shenxue* (*The Life and Thought of Chao Tzu-ch'en*) (Hong Kong: China Graduate School of Theology, 1994).

[33]Chao Tzu-chen, "Religion and the Change of Circumstances," *Youth Progress* 30/2 (1920): 39. Cited in Wing-hung Lam, *Fongchozhong fengqi de zhongguo jiaohui* (*Chinese Theology in Construction*) (Hong Kong: Tian Dao, 1990), 41–42.

[34]Sze-kar Wan, "Paul the Mystical Sage: Chao Tzu-chen's Mystical-Ethical Hermeneutics of Character," in *Papers for an International Conference on Religious Scripture and Interpretation* (Taipei: Graduate Institute of Religious Studies at National Chengchi University, 2000), 1–55, esp. 8.

[35]Chao Tzu-chen, "Jesus as Christ: A Review of Wu Lei-chuan's *Christianity and Chinese Culture*," in *Issues of Chinese Christianity in the Twentieth Century*, ed. Y.M. Shaw (Taipei: Zhengzhong, 1980), 665–66.

[36]Sze-kar Wan, "The Emerging Hermeneutics of the Chinese Church: Debate between Wu Leichuan and T.C. Chao and the Chinese Christian Problematik," in *The Bible in Modern China: The Literary and Intellectual Impact*, ed. Irene Eber, Sze-kar Wan, Knut Walf (Sankt Augustin: Institut Monumenta Serica, 1999), 351–82.

[37]Wing-hung Lam, *Wang Ming-dao yu zhongguo jiaohui* (*Wang Ming-tao and the Chinese Church*) (Hong Kong: China Graduate School of Theology, 1982); *Shuling shenxue: Nee Tuo-shen sixiang de yianjiu* (*The Spiritual Theology of Watchman Nee*) (Hong Kong: China Graduate School of Theology, 1985).

[38]Leung, "Nee Tuo-shen zaochi de jiaohuiguan," 92–137.

[39]Wang Ming-dao, *Who Is Jesus* (1927; Hong Kong, Hongdao, 1962), 3–4.

[40]Wang Ming-dao, *Can Man Build the Kingdom of Heaven?* (1933; Hong Kong: Hongdao, 1962), 9–12.

[41]Watchman Nee, *Shulingren* (*The Spiritual Man*), 3 vols (New York: Christian Fellowship, 1968); *Zhengchang de jidutu shenhuo* (*The Normal Christian Life*) (Burlington, Ont.: Welch, 1961).

[42]Ka-lun Leung, "Huaren jiyaozhuyi jidutu de lingyi jiejing" ("The Spiritual Exegesis of Chinese Fundamentalist Christians"), in *Chaochien yu duohou: bentu shijing yu shenxue yienjiu* (*Far Ahead and Lagging Behind: Studies in Contextual Hermeneutics and Theology*) (Hong Kong: Alliance Bible Seminary, 2003), 1–58.

[43]Watchman Nee, "Shen huayu de zhishi" ("The Ministry of God's Word"), in *Nee Tuo-sheng zhushu quenji* (*Complete Collection of Watchman Nee's Writing*), vol. 10 (Hong Kong: Tien Liang, 1992), 139–40.

[44]Ka-lun Leung, "Wui lingyi jiejing bianwu," ("A Defense for Spiritual Interpretation of the Chinese Church"), in *The Role and Interpretation of the Bible in the Life of the Church in China* (Hong Kong: The Lutheran World Federation, 1997), 40–42. See also John Henderson, *Scripture, Canon, and Commentary: A Comparison of Confucian and Western Exegesis* (Princeton: Princeton University Press, 1991), 147.

[45]Ka-lun Leung, *Huaren chuandao yu fenxing budaojia* (*Evangelists and Revivalists of Modern China*) (Hong Kong: Alliance Bible Seminary, 1999).

[46]Yieh, "Jia Yu-Ming," 6–18.

[47]Jia Yu-ming, *Shen Dao Xue* (*Dogmatics*) (Taipei: Youth for Christ, 1971), 573–74.

[48]Sandra Schneiders, *The Revelatory Text: Interpreting the New Testament as Sacred Scripture*, 2d ed. (Collegeville: Liturgical Press, 1999); Yieh, "Jia Yu-ming," 17–18.

[49]Philip Wickeri, *Seeking the Common Ground: Protestant Christianity, the Three-Self Movement, and China's United Front* (Maryknoll, N.Y.: Orbis Books, 1988).

[50]Their sermons and writings can be found in *Tienfeng* and *Nanjing Theological Journal*. See, e.g., Ting Kuang-hsun, *Ting Kuang-hsun wen-ji* (*Writings of Ting Kuang-hsun*) (Nanjing: Yi Lin, 1998), 32, 108, 214.

[51]Ting Kuang-hsun, "Zai zhong-guo wei ji-du zuo-jien-zhen" ("To Testify for Christ in China"), *Union Theological Journal,* n.s. 1 (1984): 11–17; "Guanyu woguo de shenxue jiaoyu–wei yichi huiyi zhunbei de fayen" ("On theological education in my country–a prepared paper for a conference"), *Union Theological Journal,* n.s. 1 (1984): 46–49.

[52]A talk by Ji Jien-hong, chair of the Committee of the Three-Self Patriotic Movement, in Hong Kong, published in *Shidai luntan (Times Tribune),* issue 796, Dec 1, 2002.

[53]C.S. Song, *The Tears of Lady Ming: A Parable of People's Political Theology* (Geneva: World Council of Churches, 1981).

[54]Archie Lee, "Biblical Interpretation in Asian Perspective," *Asia Journal of Theology* 7 (1993): 38–48; "Reading Lamentations Cross-textually," a paper presented at the International Congress of Ethnic Chinese Biblical Scholars, Chung Chi College, The Chinese University of Hong Kong, May 25–28, 2004; K.K. Yeo, *What Has Jerusalem to Do with Beijing: Biblical Interpretation from a Chinese Perspective* (Harrisburg, Pa.: Trinity, 1998); *Chairman Mao Meets the Apostle Paul: Christianity, Communism, and the Hope of China* (Grand Rapids, Mich.: Brazos, 2002).

[55]Kwok Pui-lan, *Discovering the Bible in the Non-Biblical World* (Maryknoll, N.Y.: Orbis Books, 1995); ed., *Postcolonialism, Feminism and Religious Discourse* (New York: Routledge, 2002).

Chapter 3: Biblical Interpretation in Korea

[1]For a good reference on Korean history, see Ki-baik Lee, *A New History of Korea* (Cambridge: Harvard University Press, 1984).

[2]Stanley J. Samartha, *One Christ, Many Religions: Toward a Revised Christology* (Maryknoll, N.Y.: Orbis Books, 1991), 59.

[3]The Presbyterian Church in Korea has been very strong since the early period of its mission. Nowadays, it is believed that about 70 percent of Protestants in Korea are Presbyterians.

[4]Concerning the Nevius Mission Policy and its criticism, see L.G. Paik, *The History of Protestant Missions in Korea, 1832–1910* (Pyeng Yang: Union Christian College, 1929), 205–6.

[5]According to Tong-shik Ryu, Korean theology started with Byung-hun Choi: Tong-shik Ryu, *Hanguk Shinhak Ui Gwangmaek (The Treasure Veins of Korean Theology)* (Seoul: Chunmangsa, 1982), 53.

[6]This was published in the journal called *Shinhakuolbo.*

[7]He published these in theological journals such as *Shinhakuolbo* and *Shinhaksegye.*

[8]The communists took Yang into North Korea during the Korean War. He died there.

[9]During the Korean War, the communists also took Hyuk into North Korea, where he died.

[10]Song died in the hands of the communists during the Korean War, when he was a seminary professor.

[11]Higher criticism usually refers to historical or literary/source criticism. It is contrasted with lower criticism, which usually means textual criticism.

[12]Abingdon Press originally published the commentary in 1929. Its editors were F.C. Eiselen, E. Lewis, and D.G. Downey.

[13]On Kim, see Samuel Cheon, *Jae-joon Kim: Prophetic Conscience against Fundamentalism and Dictatorship* (Seoul: Salim, 2003) (in Korean).

[14]Concerning the reasons why it started in the 1960s, refer to Pong-nang Park, "A Theological Approach to the Understanding of the Indigenization of Christianity," *Northeast Asia Journal of Theology* 1 (1969): 107–8.

[15]Donghak is a new religion founded by Jae-woo Choi in 1860. Nowadays, it is called Cheondogyo.

[16]Tong-shik Ryu, "Poongryushinhak Uroui Yyro" ("Journey to Poongryu Theology"), in *Jongkydawonjooui Wa Shinhak Ui Mirae (Religious Pluralism and the Future of Theology)* (Seoul: Jongroseojuk, 1989), 31.

[17]"Minjung" is a Korean word, which literally means "the mass of the people." However, scholars of minjung theology have suggested several meanings. Concerning these, refer to Andrew Sung Park, "Minjung and Pungryu in Contemporary Korea: A Critical and Comparative Examination" (Ph.D. diss., Graduate Theological Union, 1985), 17–24. On page 24, he summarizes the term as follows: (1) the majority oppressed and exploited by the minority; (2) they as a historical reality will play a major role in establishing a new social order; they are the hope of history and the central theme for God's salvific work; (3) they are politically oppressed, socially marginalized, economically exploited, culturally despised, and religiously

condemned. On the other hand, the term "Minjung Ui Shinhak" ("Theology of Minjung"), among the published writings, was first used by Nam-dong Suh in his article "Theology of Minjung: A Response of Professor Hyonghyo Kim's Criticism," *Christian Thought* 203, no. 4 (1975): 85–90 (in Korean).

¹⁸Suh's articles on minjung theology were collected in his book: Nam-dong Suh, *Minjung Shinhak Ui Tamku* (*The Exploration of Minjung Theology*) (Seoul: Han Kil Sa, 1983).

¹⁹Suh took his concept of the *ochlos* from the Japanese theologian Tagawa Kensou, who considered it as the subject of the Mark's theology in his monograph, *Miracle et Evangile* (Paris: Presses Universitaires de France, 1966).

²⁰Nam-dong Suh, "Toward a Theology of Han," in *Minjung Theology: People as the Subjects of History*, ed. Commission on Theological Concerns of the Christian Conference of Asia [CTC-CCA] (Maryknoll, N.Y.: Orbis Books, 1983), 57–58. Originally presented in the CCA meeting of Oct. 1979.

²¹Nam-dong Suh, "Historical References for a Theology of Minjung," in *Minjung Theology*, 158–59. Originally published with the title "Theology of Minjung" in *Theological Thought* 24, no. 3 (1979): 78–109 (in Korean).

²²Suh, "Historical References," 162–63. Suh avoids using the term "the kingdom of God," because it has been understood as a heavenly place and ultimate symbol that the believer enters when he/she dies.

²³Byung-mu Ahn, "Jesus and the Minjung in the Gospel of Mark," in *Minjung Theology*, 138–52. Originally published in *Hyun-jon* 106, no. 11 (1979).

²⁴Ahn, "Jesus and the Minjung," 150–51.

²⁵Cyris Hee-suk Moon, "An Old Testament Understanding of Minjung," in *Minjung Theology*, 123–37. His study of the Old Testament for minjung theology is published in his book, *A Korean Minjung Theology: An Old Testament Perspective* (Maryknoll, N.Y.: Orbis Books, 1985).

²⁶Moon, "An Old Testament Understanding of Minjung," 123–24.

²⁷Yong-bock Kim, "The Bible and Social Biography of the Minjung," in *Messiah and Minjung: Christ's Solidarity with the People for New Life* (Hong Kong: CCA, 1992), 11–29.

²⁸Ibid., 24–25.

²⁹Though it mentions that it includes the Apocrypha, it actually has twelve apocryphal books that are considered the deuterocanonical books in the Catholic Church.

³⁰For a study on the North Korean Church's translation of the Bible, see Young-Jin Min, "The Bible Translation for the Reconciliation of Korean People," *Christian Thought* 363, no. 3 (1989): 52–71 (in Korean).

³¹Chan-kook Kim, "The Israelite History and Their Will for the Unification," *Christian Thought* 276, no. 6 (1981): 10–19 (in Korean).

³²Tae-soo Im, "The Chronicler's Unification Theology," *Theological Studies* 28, no. 9 (1987): 415–37 (in Korean); *idem*, "The Unification Theology of Israel," *Theological Thought* 71, no. 12 (1990): 877–98 (in Korean).

³³Yong-jin Min, "The meaning of the Jubilee," *Christian Thought* 283, no. 1 (1982): 16–25 (in Korean). See also his later work, *Peace, Reunification, Jubilee* (Seoul: CLSK, 1995), 197–228 (in Korean).

³⁴Ee-kon Kim, "Modern Meaning of the Jubilee Law," *Christian Thought* 337, no. 1 (1987): 113–33 (in Korean).

³⁵Sa-moon Kang, "Problems in the Application of the Jubilee Law upon the Fiftieth Year of the Liberation," in *The Fiftieth Year of the Liberation and the Jubilee of Korea* (Seoul: Gamsin, 1995), 47–82 (in Korean).

Chapter 4: Differences and Difficulties

¹Hans-Dieter Evers, "Group Conflict and Class Formation in South-East Asia," in *Modernization in South-East Asia,* ed. Han-Dieter Evers (London: Oxford University Press, 1973), 108–31.

²Some British, French, and Indian scholars called it Farther India, Greater India, *L'Inde Exterieure,* and the *Hinduized* or *Indianized* States. Chinese writings identified the region as Kun Kun or Nan Yang (Little China). Others have referred to the region between China and India as Indo-China, from French *Indochine,* which includes Laos, Vietnam, and Cambodia. "Indo-Pacific" is another suggested term. Cf. D.R. SarDesai, *Southeast Asia: Past and Present,* 2d ed. (London: MacMillan Press, 1989), 1.

[3]SarDesai, *Southeast Asia*, 5.

[4]The data are derived from the official Web site of ASEAN (http://www.aseansec.org), with the population figures dating to 2003: Brunei [363,000], Cambodia [13,798,000], Indonesia [213,494,000], Laos [5,618,000], Malaysia [23,050,000], Myanmar [53,515,000], Philippines [81,081,000], Singapore [4,185,000], Thailand [63,950,000], Vietnam [81,185,000].

[5]Ashok K. Dutt, "Perspectives on Southeast Asia," in *Southeast Asia: Realm of Contrasts*, ed. Ashok K. Dutt, 3d ed. (London: Westview Press, 1985), 258.

[6]SarDesai, *Southeast Asia*, 193.

[7]Ibid., 137.

[8]Ibid., 137–39.

[9]Frank Frost, "Introduction: ASEAN since 1967–Origins, Evolution and Recent Developments," in *ASEAN into the 1990s*, ed. Alison Broinowski (London: MacMillan Press, 1990), 1.

[10]China, Vietnam, and Thailand claimed all of the Nansha (Spratlys) islands and Malaysia, the Philippines, and Brunei claim some of the islands. Of the islands in the center of the archipelago, the Xisha (Paracels), thirty-seven of them are claimed by Vietnam, eight by the Philippines, and seven by China. Recently, there were also disputes between Indonesia and Malaysia on the rights to the oil rich Sipadan island, which lies between the furthest part of East Malaysia and the northeastern part of Indonesia's Kalimantan.

[11]Hans C. Rieger, "Towards the Making of an Asean Common Market: A Concrete Proposal," in *ASEAN at the Crossroads: Obstacles, Option and Opportunities in Economic Co-operation*, ed. Noordin Sopiee, Chew Lay See, and Lim Siang Jin (Kuala Lumpur, Malaysia: Institute of Strategic and International Studies, 1987), 73.

[12]Milton Osborne, *Southeast Asia: An Illustrated Introductory History* (Sydney: Allen & Unwin, 1988), 207–41.

[13]Dutt, "Perspectives on Southeast Asia," 256–58.

[14]Ibid., 258.

[15]Patrick Johnstone and Jason Mandryk, eds., *Operation World: When We Pray God Works*, 21st Century Edition (Carlisle, England: Paternoster, 2001).

[16]Itumeleng J. Mosala, "Reconstituting the Azanian *Mišpāḥôt* (Clans): Land, Class and Bible in South Africa Today," in *Text & Experience: Towards a Cultural Exegesis of the Bible*, ed. Daniel Smith-Christopher (Sheffield: Sheffield Academic Press, 1995), 238, states, "The Bible is inseparable from the modern history of South Africa. It was there at the founding of modern South Africa..." Cf. Gerald West, *Biblical Hermeneutics of Liberation: Modes of Reading the Bible in the South African Context*, rev. ed. (Maryknoll, N.Y.: Orbis Books, 1995).

[17]David J.A. Clines, "Possibilities and Priorities of Biblical Interpretation in an International Perspective," *Biblical Interpretation* 1 (1993): 73.

[18]Ibid., 74.

[19]Daniel Smith-Christopher, "Introduction," in *Text & Experience: Towards a Cultural Exegesis of the Bible*, ed. Daniel Smith-Christopher (Sheffield: Sheffield Academic Press, 1995), 16.

[20]Ibid..

[21]Clines, "Possibilities and Priorities of Biblical Interpretation," 74.

[22]Smith-Christopher, "Introduction," 19–20.

[23]Ibid., 22.

[24]SarDesai, *Southeast Asia*, 7.

[25]Jonathan Rigg, "Colonization, Decolonization, and the Impact of the Colonial Period in Southeast Asia," in *Southeast Asia: A Region in Transition: A Thematic Human Geography of the ASEAN Region*, ed. Jonathan Rigg (London: Unwin Hyman, 1991), 19–32.

Chapter 5: Reading the Bible as an Asian American

[1]This essay is an abridged and updated version of the paper, *History and Issues in Asian American Interpretation*, presented at the 1996 Annual Meeting of the Society of Biblical Literature in New Orleans, La.

[2]Gail Law, "A Model for the American Ethnic Chinese Churches," in *A Winning Combination: ABC/OBC*, ed. Cecilia Yau (Petaluma, Calif.: Chinese Christian Mission, 1986), 134. Also see Kenneth Uyeda Fong, *Pursuing the Pearl: A Comprehensive Resource for Multi-Asian Ministry* (Valley Forge, Pa.: Judson Press, 1999), 37–39, who identifies different types of Asian Americans drawing on the work of Harry H.L. Kitano and Roger Daniels, *Asian Americans: Emerging Minorities* (Englewood Cliffs, N.J.: Prentice-Hall, 1988).

³Yoshinobu Kumazawa, "Asian Theological Reflections on Liberation," *Northeast Asia Journal of Theology* 14 (1975): 1–2.

⁴See Jung Young Lee, *Marginality: The Key to Multicultural Theology* (Minneapolis: Fortress Press, 1995), 43, who is convinced that marginality holds the key to multicultural theology. He cites Everett Stonequist, *The Marginal Man: A Study in Personality and Culture Conflict* (New York: Russell and Russell, 1937), 8, who defines the marginal person as "one who is poised in psychological uncertainty between two (or more) social worlds, reflecting in his soul the discords and harmonies, repulsions and attractions of these worlds; one of which is often 'dominant' over the other; with which membership is implicitly based upon birth or ancestry (race or nationality); and cohere exclusion removes the individual from a system of group relations." The marginal person lives in two, at times antagonistic, worlds. Unable to belong fully to the dominant society due to race or nationality, the person cannot be completely accepted and is marginalized.

⁵*Liminality* refers to the in-between state of living between two worlds due to nonacceptance by the group that is dominant in society. See Sang Hyun Lee, "Pilgrimage and Home in the Wilderness of Marginality: Symbols and Context in Asian American Theology," *The Princeton Seminary Bulletin* 16, no. 1 (1995): 52.

⁶Sang Hyun Lee, "Asian American Theology in Immigrant Perspective: Called to be Pilgrims," in *Korean American Ministry,* exp. ed., ed. Sang Hyun Lee and John V. Moore (Louisville: General Assembly Council, Presbyterian Church, 1993), 52.

⁷Agnes M. Niyekawa, "Biliteracy Acquisition and Its Sociocultural Effects," in *Asian and Pacific-American Perspectives in Bilingual Education,* ed. Mae Chu-Chang (New York: Teachers College Press, 1983), 113. While the five-year rule is a generalization, I personally know individuals who were able to attain proficiency in less time even though they arrived in the United States as teenagers.

⁸Ibid., 114.

⁹J.Y. Lee, *Marginality,* 41. The issue of racism in the United States is integrally connected to the complex issue of the formation of race. For an excellent study, see Michael Omi and Howard Winant, *Racial Formation in the United States: From the 1960s to the 1990s,* 2d ed. (New York: Routledge, 1994).

¹⁰J.Y. Lee, *Marginality,* 45.

¹¹Ibid., 47.

¹²For further explanation see David J.A. Clines, "Images of Yahweh: God in the Pentateuch," in *Studies in Old Testament Theology: Historical and Contemporary Images of God and God's People,* ed. R.L. Hubbard Jr., R.K. Johnston, and R.P. Meye (Waco, Tex.: Word Books, 1992), 79–98.

¹³Justo L. Gonzalez, "Reading from My Bicultural Place: Acts 6:1–7," in *Reading from This Place, Volume 1: Social Location and Biblical Interpretation in the United States,* ed. Fernando F. Segovia and Mary Ann Tolbert (Minneapolis: Augsburg Fortress, 1995), 154.

¹⁴Jung Young Lee, *The Trinity in Asian Perspective* (Nashville: Abingdon Press, 1996), 35.

¹⁵Morris A. Inch, *Doing Theology Across Cultures* (Grand Rapids, Mich.: Baker Book House, 1982), 48.

¹⁶J.Y. Lee, *Trinity,* 31.

¹⁷Ibid., 32.

¹⁸Ibid., 34.

¹⁹Fumitaka Matsuoka, *Out of Silence: Emerging Themes in Asian American Churches* (Cleveland: United Church Press, 1995), 49–50.

²⁰This is a reference to John H. Elliot, *A Home for the Homeless: A Sociological Exegesis of 1 Peter, Its Strategy and Situation* (Philadelphia: Fortress Press, 1981).

²¹S.H. Lee, "Asian American Theology," 54–56.

²²Nicholas Iyoya, "Asian American Churches and Social Involvement," in *Church and Society* 64 (Jan.-Feb., 1974): 46. Also see J.Y. Lee, *Marginality,* 88.

²³Young Pai, "A Sociocultural Understanding of Korean American Youth 'Caught in the Web,'" in *Korean American Ministry,* ed. Lee and Moore, 266. Even Amy Tan and Maxine Hong Kingston, two highly successful Asian American writers, did not plan on being writers. Tan had plans to go to medical school. When that fell through she studied two years in a doctoral program at U.C. Berkeley before finally venturing out into creative writing. Kingston was originally expected to pursue a career as an engineer because of her skills in mathematics. Christina Chiu, *Lives of Notable Asian Americans* (New York: Chelsea House, 1996), 11, 38.

[24]Rudy V. Busto, "The Gospel According to the Model Minority?: Hazarding an Interpretation of Asian American Evangelical College Students," *Amerasia* 22, no. 1 (1996): 140.

[25]J.Y. Lee, *Trinity,* 22.

[26]Paul M. Nagano, "Search for Identity," in *Japanese American Christian Identity and Calling,* ed. Roy I. Sano (Berkeley: Pacific and Asian American Center for Theology and Strategies, 1978), 3–4.

[27]J.Y. Lee, *Marginality,* 8.

[28]Betty Lee Sung, *The Adjustment Experience of Chinese Immigrant Children in New York City* (Staten Island, N.Y.: Center for Migration Studies, 1987), 122–23.

[29]William A. Dyrness, *Invitation to Cross-Cultural Theology* (Grand Rapids, Mich.: Zondervan, 1992), 145.

[30]Matsuoka, *Out of Silence,* 59.

[31]William Shinto, "The Eccentric Ministry: A Style of Life in the Margin," in *The Theologies of Asian Americans and Pacific Peoples,* ed. Roy I. Sano (Berkeley: Pacific and Asian American Center for Theology and Strategies, 1976), 314.

[32]Pai, "Sociocultural Understanding of Korean American Youth," 259.

[33]For a series of Bible Studies on this theme, see Tom Lin, *Losing Face & Finding Grace: Twelve Bible Studies for Asian Americans* (Downers Grove, Ill.: InterVarsity Press, 1997).

[34]Unfortunately, the limitation of space for this essay does not permit examination of other elements. Two that come to mind are the areas of racial inclusion and feminism. The latter itself has long been recognized as another aspect of liberation theology. Two formidable Asian women writing in this field are Kwok Pui-lan, *Discovering the Bible in the Non-Biblical World* (Maryknoll, N.Y.: Orbis, 1995) and Gale A. Yee, *Poor Banished Children of Eve: Woman as Evil in the Hebrew Bible* (Minneapolis: Fortress Press, 2003).

[35]An essential publication is Tat-siong Benny Liew, ed., *The Bible in Asian America; Semeia* 90/91 (2002). There are two major sections in this double volume issue. The first consists of essays under the heading *Reading the Bible in Asian America,* the second, *Reading Readings of the Bible in Asian America.* The multifaceted nature of current Asian American interpretation is explored through the many contributors. Jeffrey Kuan presented a concise survey of Asian American writings in an unpublished paper presented in 2002 in Toronto, Canada, at the Consultation on Asian American Theology and Hermeneutics. He groups the literature into three categories—Cultural Hermeneutics, Liberation Perspectives, and Feminist Hermeneutics. Kuan identifies four issues that have emerged: culture and texts, colonial and diasporic experience, identity construction, and adoptee identity. Other articles by Kuan include: "Diasporic Reading of a Diasporic Text: Identity Politics and Race Relations and the Book of Esther," in *Interpreting Beyond Borders,* ed. Fernando F. Segovia (Sheffield: Sheffied Academic Press, 2000), 161–173; and "Reading Amy Tan Reading Job," in *Relating to the Text: Interdisciplinary and Form-Critical Insights on the Bible,* ed. T.J. Sandoval and C. Mandolfo, Journal for the Study of the Old Testament: Supplement Series [JSOTSup] 384 (London/New York: T & T Clark International, 2003), 263–74. For an example of colonial discourse, see R.S. Sugirtharajah, *Asian Biblical Hermeneutics and Postcolonialism: Contesting the Interpretations* (Maryknoll, N.Y.: Orbis Books, 1998).

[36]A survey of Asian American church leaders in the United States by the writer centering on themes in an Asian American theology produced twenty-three responses.

[37]Dennis Loo, "Why an Asian American Theology of Liberation?" in *Church and Society* 64 (Jan.-Feb., 1974): 51.

[38]Harry H.L. Kitano, *Japanese Americans: The Evolution of a Sub-Culture* (Englewood Cliffs, N.J.: Prentice Hall, 1969), 2–3.

[39]Ibid.

[40]This is not to say that they have completely forsaken their Asian heritage. For even the third-generation Sansei still struggle with the question of identity—whether they are Japanese Americans or Americans of Japanese ancestry. While retaining some "core" Japanese characteristics, they appear far more Caucasian than the previous two generations according to Fong (*Pursuing the Pearl,* 66–68). Interestingly enough, third- and fourth-generation Japanese Americans try to recall their ethnic identity, which the second generation does not do. See Kitano, *Japanese Americans,* 192. He cites the study of Marcus L. Hansen, *The Problems of the Third Generation* (Rock Island, Ill.: Augustana Historical Society, 1938).

[41]See Russell Jeung, "Evangelical and Mainline Teachings on Asian American Identity," *Semeia* 90/91 (2002): 211–36, as well as Antony W. Alumkal, "The Scandal of the 'Model

Minority' Mind? The Bible and Second-Generation Asian American Evangelicals," *Semeia* 90/91 (2002): 237–50.

[42]Busto, "Gospel," 137.

[43]Ibid., 138.

[44]Ibid., quoting Ada Lum, *A Hitchhiker's Guide to Missions* (Downers Grove, Ill.: InterVarsity Press, 1984), 139.

[45]Compare this attitude to that posed by Matsuoka (*Out of Silence*, 56): "Questions arise out of the profound anxiety of Asian Americans over our identities. Should ethnicity be a primary factor for our identities in this society? Do we look to another source in order to claim our identities? If it is not possible to ignore our ethnicities, what provides us with our primary anchoring points? Can we rely on our ancestral cultural heritages for our identity? What is the relationship between the particularity of being, for instance, Chinese American, and the commonality of being Asian American, or being a member of this society as a whole? What should one do in the situation in which a person says, 'I'm American,' while the rest of the society is saying, 'You are Asian'? How should we reconcile individual rights to identify ourselves with a sense of collective peoplehood? What is the glue that holds us together? These are the questions confronted by Asian Americans."

[46]Busto, "Gospel," 137.

[47]Ibid., 140.

[48]Loo, "Asian American Theology," 53–54.

Chapter 6: Neither Here nor There

[1]For example, The Congress of Asian Theologians (CATS) holds bi-yearly meetings in various countries in Asia: 1997 in Seoul, 1999 in Bangalore, 2001 in Yogyakarta, and 2003 in Chiang Mai, Thailand. The Program for Theologies and Cultures in Asia also holds annual conferences and publishes papers in the *Journal for Theologies and Cultures in Asia* (JTCA). The Asian Women's Resource Center provides a network for Asian women scholars through its journal, *In God's Image*. More than seventy ethnic Chinese scholars from around the world attended the first International Congress of Ethnic Chinese Biblical Scholars, May 25–28, 2004, held at Chung Chi College, Hong Kong Chinese University.

[2]Chan-Hie Kim, "Reading the Bible as Asian Americans," in *The New Interpreter's Bible*, ed. Leander E. Keck, et al., vol. 1 (Nashville: Abingdon Press, 1994), 163.

[3]Eviatar Zerubavel, *Social Mindscapes: An Invitation to Cognitive Sociology* (Cambridge, Mass.: Harvard University Press, 1997), 12. My sincere thanks to Dr. Jung Ha Kim, professor of sociology at Georgia State University, Atlanta, Georgia, for introducing me to the field of cognitive sociology and to the works of Professor Eviatar Zerubavel.

[4]Ibid., 15.

[5]All scripture translations in this essay are the author's own.

[6]See Robert Alter, *The Art of Biblical Narrative* (San Francisco: Basic Books, 1981); Adele Berlin, *Poetics and Interpretation of Biblical Narrative*, Bible and Literature Series 9 (Sheffield: Sheffield Academic Press, 1983); and Meir Sternberg, *The Poetics of Biblical Narrative*, Indiana Studies in Biblical Literature (Bloomington, Ind.: Indiana University Press, 1985).

[7]F.V. Greifenhagen, *Egypt on the Pentateuch's Ideological Map: Constructing Biblical Israel's Identity*, JSOTSup 361 (New York: Sheffield Academic Press, 2002), 6.

[8]E. Theodore Mullen Jr., *Narrative History and Ethnic Boundaries: The Deuteronomistic Historian and the Creation of Israelite National Identity* (Atlanta: Scholars Press, 1993), 7–14; idem, *Ethnic Myths and Pentateuchal Foundations: A New Approach to the Formation of the Pentateuch* (Atlanta: Scholars Press, 1997), 10–12; and Mark G. Brett, *Genesis: Procreation and Politics of Identity*, Old Testament Readings (London: Routledge, 2000), 4–5.

[9]John Bright, *A History of Israel*, 3d ed. (Philadelphia: Westminster Press, 1981), 343.

[10]Fredrik Barth, "Introduction," in *Ethnic Groups and Boundaries: The Social Organization of Culture Difference*, ed. Fredrik Barth (Bergen, Norway: Universitetsforlaget, 1969), 10–11.

[11]Lai Ling Elizabeth Ngan, "A Teaching Outline for the Book of Joshua," *Review & Expositor* 95 (Spring 1998): 161–64.

[12]E.A. Speiser, *Genesis: Introduction, Translation, and Notes*, Anchor Bible 1 (Garden City: Doubleday & Co., 1964), 117 n. 3.

[13]Cain Hope Felder, "Racial Motifs in the Biblical Narratives," in *Voices from the Margin: Interpreting the Bible in the Third World*, ed. R.S. Sugirtharajah, rev. ed (Maryknoll, N.Y.: Orbis Books, 1995), 201.

[14]George Steindorff and Keith C. Seele, *When Egypt Ruled the East,* rev. Keith C. Seele (Chicago: University of Chicago Press, 1957).

[15]Anthony D. Smith, *The Ethnic Origins of Nations* (Oxford: Basil Blackwell, 1986), 47.

[16]Sharon Pace Jeansonne, *The Women of Genesis: From Sarah to Potiphar's Wife* (Minneapolis: Fortress Press, 1975), 19. See also 1 Samuel 2:30; Nahum 1:14; and Job 40:4.

[17]John Van Seters, *Abraham in History and Tradition* (New Haven: Yale University Press, 1975), 193.

[18]Bruce Waltke and M. O'Connor state: "The cohortative expresses the will or strong desire of the speaker. In cases where the speaker has the ability to carry out an inclination it takes on the coloring of resolve ('I will…')." In the case of Genesis 21:16, the authors suggest the translation as, "I will not watch the boy die." Bruce K. Waltke and M. O'Connor, *An Introduction to Biblical Hebrew Syntax* (Winona Lake, Ind.: Eisenbrauns, 1990), 573.

Chapter 7: The *Realpolitik* of Liminality in Josiah's Kingdom and Asian America

[1]Martin Noth, *The Deuteronomistic History* (Sheffield: JSOT Press, 1981).

[2]F.M. Cross, *Canaanite Myth and Hebrew Epic: Essays in the History of the Religion of Israel* (Cambridge: Harvard University Press, 1973).

[3]Rudolf Smend, "The Law and the Nations: A Contribution to Deuteronomistic Traditional History," in *Reconsidering Israel and Judah: Recent Studies in the Deuteronomistic History,* ed. Gary N. Knoppers and J.G. McConville (Winona Lake, Ind.: Eisenbrauns, 1999), 95–110.

[4]Benedict Anderson, *Imagined Communities: Reflections on the Origin and Spread of Nationalism* (New York: Verso, 1991), 12.

[5]Ernest Gellner, *Nations and Nationalism* (Ithaca, N.Y.: Cornell University Press, 1983), 6.

[6]Anderson, *Imagined Communities,* 12.

[7]Ibid., 7.

[8]Gellner, *Nations and Nationalism,* 6.

[9]Ibid., 8.

[10]Ibid., 110.

[11]Ibid., 17.

[12]For example, Adrian Hastings, *The Construction of Nationhood: Ethnicity, Religion and Nationalism* (Cambridge: Cambridge University Press, 1997).

[13]Hastings represents the so-called revisionist view that critiques the modernist view represented by such writers as Benedict Anderson, Ernest Gellner, and Eric Hobsbawm.

[14]Patrick J. Geary, *The Myth of Nations: The Medieval Origins of Europe* (Princeton: Princeton University Press, 2002), 34.

[15]Homi K. Bhabha, "DissemiNation: Time, Narrative, and the Margins of the Modern Nation," in *Nation and Narration,* ed. Homi K. Bhabha (London: Routledge, 1990), 291–322.

[16]Ibid., 300.

[17]Ibid., 301.

[18]Henry Yu, *Thinking Orientals: Migration, Contact, and Exoticism in Modern America* (New York: Oxford University Press, 2001), xi.

[19]Robert Lee, *Orientals: Asian Americans in Popular Culture* (Philadelphia: Temple University Press, 1999), 8.

[20]Ibid., 12.

[21]Gary Okihiro, *Margins and Mainstreams: Asians in American History and Culture* (Seattle: University of Washington Press, 1994), 33.

[22]Ibid., xi.

[23]Ibid., 139–40.

[24]Lee, *Orientals,* 204.

[25]Ibid., 216.

[26]Ibid., 217.

[27]Gary Okihiro, *The Columbia Guide to Asian American History* (New York: Columbia University Press, 2001), xiv–xv.

[28]Ronald Takaki, *Strangers from a Different Shore: A History of Asian Americans* (New York: Penguin Books, 1989).

[29]Okihiro, *Margins and Mainstreams,* 150–51.

[30]Sucheng Chan, *Asian Americans: An Interpretive History* (Boston: Twayne, 1991), 14.

[31] Ibid., xiv.

[32] Hayim Tadmor, "World Dominion: The Expanding Horizon of the Assyrian Empire," in *Landscapes: Territories, Frontiers and Horizons in the Ancient Near East,* ed. L. Milano, S. de Martino, F.M. Fales, and G.B. Lanfranchi (Padova: Sargon, 1999), 55–62.

[33] Tadmor, "World Dominion," 55.

[34] Carlos Zaccagnini, "An Urartean Royal Inscription in the Report of Sargon's Eighty Campaign," in *Assyrian Royal Inscriptions: New Horizons in Literary, Ideological, and Historical Analysis,* ed. F.M. Fales (Rome: Instituto per l'Oriente, 1981), 262.

[35] K. Lawson Younger, *Ancient Conquest Accounts: A Study in Ancient Near Eastern and Biblical History Writing* (Sheffield: Sheffield Academic Press, 1990), 76.

[36] Eun Suk Cho, "Josianic Reform in the Deuteronomistic History Reconstructed in the Light of Factionalism and Use of Royal Apology" (Ph.D. diss., The Graduate Theological Union, 2002).

[37] Ibid., 229.

[38] Kong-hi Lo, "Cultic Centralization in the Deuteronomistic History: A Strategy of Dominance and Resistance" (Ph.D. diss., Chicago Theological Seminary, 2003), suggests this idea.

Chapter 8: Empowerment or Enslavement?

[1] It is believed that one source of inspiration for *Miss Saigon* was Puccini's 1904 tragic opera *Madame Butterfly.* See Nadine Goff, "The Pain of Vietnam: 'Miss Saigon' Revisits End of War," *Wisconsin State Journal* (Oct. 10, 2002): 3.

[2] Raymond E. Brown, *The Gospel According to John* (Garden City, N.Y.: Doubleday, 1966), 171.

[3] Craig R. Koester, "'The Savior of the World' (John 4:42)," *Journal of Biblical Literature* 109 (1990): 665–80.

[4] Sandra Schneiders, *The Revelatory Text: Interpreting the New Testament as Sacred Scripture* (New York: Harper SanFrancisco, 1991), 188–89; idem, "Women in the Fourth Gospel and the Role of Women in the Contemporary Church," *Biblical Theology Bulletin* 12 (1982): 40. Elisabeth Schüssler Fiorenza, *In Memory of Her: A Feminist Theological Reconstruction of Christian Origins* (New York: Crossroad, 1983), 327–28; Raymond Collins, "The Representative Figures of the Fourth Gospel," *Downside Review* 94 (1976): 38; Gail O'Day, "John," in *The Women's Bible Commentary,* ed. Carol Newsom and Sharon Ringe (Louisville: Westminster/John Knox Press, 1992), 296.

[5] Musa W. Dube, "Toward a Postcolonial Feminist Interpretation of the Bible," *Semeia* 78 (1997): 11–26; "Reading For Decolonization (John 4:1–42)," *Semeia* 75 (1996): 37–59. For postcolonial criticism and the Bible, see R.S. Surgirtharajah, ed., *The Postcolonial Bible* (Sheffield: Sheffield Academic Press, 1998).

[6] Richard A. Horsley, ed., *Paul and Empire: Religion and Power in Roman Imperial Society* (Harrisburg: Trinity Press International, 1997), 1; idem, "Messianic Figures and Movements in First-Century Palestine," in *The Messiah: Developments in Earliest Judaism and Christianity,* ed. James H. Charlesworth (Minneapolis: Fortress Press, 1987), 295.

[7] Regardless of its place of composition (e.g., Ephesus, Antioch, Alexandria, Palestine), the gospel of John was written under the inescapable influence of the Roman Empire, as the title "the Savior of the world" (Jn. 4:42), which was used for the Roman emperor, indicates.

[8] Even though *Miss Saigon* is an extremely successful musical play, it rarely mentions the miserable lives of military brides and their Amerasian children, the Bui Doi ("the dust of life"), who have been ostracized in their countries and not welcomed by the United States. For more information on Amerasian children, see Jean K. Kim, "Hybrid But Fatherless: Jesus for the 'Children of the Dust,'" *Ewha Journal of Feminist Theology* (forthcoming). Also, for the lives of the colonized women, see Jean K. Kim, *Woman and Nation: An Intercontextual Reading of the Gospel of John from a Postcolonial Feminist Perspective* (Leiden: Brill, 2004), 1–32.

[9] The outsider status of military brides in America is well researched in Ji-Yeon Yuh's *Beyond the Shadow of Camptown: Korean Military Brides in America* (New York: New York University Press, 2002).

[10] Jean K. Kim, "A Korean Feminist Reading of John 4:1–42," *Semeia* 78 (1997): 109–19. For the multiple marriages of the military brides, see the PBS broadcast, "The Women Outside," directed by J.T. Tagaki and Hye-jung Park, July 16, 1996.

[11]For a more detailed discussion, see Kim, *Woman and Nation*, 90–115.

[12]Homi K. Bhabha, "The Third Place," in *Identity: Community, Culture, Difference*, ed. Jonathan Rutherford (London: Lawrence and Wishart, 1991), 211.

[13]R. Schnackenburg, *The Gospel according to St. John*, vol. 1 (New York: Herder & Herder, 1968), 433; Barnabas Lindars, *The Gospel of John* (London: Oliphants, 1972), 185–87; Brown, *John*, 171; Birger Olsson, *Structure and Meaning in the Fourth Gospel: A Text-Linguistic Analysis of John 2:1–11 and 4:1–42* (Lund: Gleerup, 1974), 184–86; Calum M. Carmichael, "Marriage and the Samaritan Woman," *New Testament Studies* 26 (1979–1980): 338–39; Peter J. Cahill, "Narrative Art in John IV," *Religious Studies Bulletin* 2 (1982): 46–47.

[14]J. Duncan M. Derrett, "The Samaritan Woman's Pitcher," *The Downside Review* 102 (1984): 255; Jerome H. Neyrey, "Jacob Traditions and the Interpretation of John 4:10–26," *Catholic Biblical Quarterly* 41 (1979): 426; Koester, "The Savior of the World," 669–70.

[15]Brown, Derrett, and Olsson admit that Josephus might have simplified the number seven to five (*Jewish Antiquites* [*Ant.*] 9.288). Yet it is not clear if the five refers to the number of foreign nations or gods. See Hendrikus Boers, *Neither On this Mountain Nor in Jerusalem* (Atlanta: Scholars Press, 1988), 172.

[16]Koester, "The Savior of the World," 670.

[17]2 Kings 17:24–33; 18:15–20. Mordecai Cogan, "For We, Like You, Worship Your God: Three Biblical Portrayals of Samaritan Origins," *Vetus Testamentum* 38 (1988): 287–91.

[18]Koester, "The Savior of the World," 669–72.

[19]Ibid., 674–76.

[20]Leo F. Raditsa, "Augustus' Legislation Concerning Marriage, Procreation, Love Affairs and Adultery," *Aufstieg und Niedergang der römischen Welt: Geschichte und Kultur Roms im Spiegel der neueren Forschung [ANRW]* 2, no. 13: 307–10.

[21]Ibid., 310.

[22]Ibid., 314.

[23]Kim, *Woman and Nation*, 103–104; George R. Watson, *The Roman Soldier* (Ithaca, N.Y.: Cornell University Press, 1969), 134–35. There is no question about the native women held as slave-wives by the soldiers (*Jewish War* [*J.W.*] 3.301–2); Emil Schurer, *A History of the Jewish People: In the Times of Jesus Christ*, vol. 2 (Peabody: Hendrickson, 1994), 222; C. Bradford Wells, *Alexander and the Hellenistic World* (Toronto: A.M. Hakkert Ltd., 1970), 165–66; J. Brian Campbell, *The Emperor and the Roman Army 31 B.C.–A.D. 235* (Oxford: Clarendon Press, 1984), 300–303; idem, "The Marriage of Soldiers under the Empire," *Journal of Roman Studies* 68 (1978): 153–66.

[24]Marlene Epp, "The Memory of Violence: Soviet and East European Mennonite Refugees and Rape in the Second World War," *Journal of Women's History* 9 (1997): 67–68.

[25]Ahn Junghyo, *Silver Stallion: A Novel of Korea* (New York: Soho Press, 1990).

[26]Midday is a culturally wrong time for a woman to be at a well for a domestic purpose (Gen. 24:11; 29:7). Judith Gundry-Volf explains the unconventional behavior of the Samaritan woman by the hypothesis that she had been ostracized because of her unsavory marital history ("Spirit, Mercy, and the Other," *Theology Today* 51 [1995]: 511).

[27]Even after wars of conquest, the victorious side sets up military bases, which require women's sexual labor. A Roman city, Flavia Neapolis, was found at the foot of Mount Gerizim around 72 C.E., strengthening Roman control over the region (cf. *J.W.* 2.51–55; 3.307–315; *Ant.* 18.85–89). According to Koester, the Roman presence in Samaria would have been well known to Samaritan members of the Johannine community ("The Savior of the World," 679).

[28]A Hebrew prophet was prophesying when Israel was under the control of foreign powers such as Assyria, Babylon, and Egypt, whose military intrusions were not simply invasions of native land, but were quasi-automatically accompanied by the invasion of native women's bodies (cf. Jer. 3:1; 4:30; 13:20–21, 26–27). For an intimate relationship between a feminized city and whore metaphors, and sexually marginalized women's lives, see Jean K. Kim, "'Uncovering Her Wickedness': An Intercontextual Reading of Revelation 17 from a Postcolonial Feminist Perspective," *Journal for the Study of the New Testament* 73 (1999): 61–81.

[29]Cogan, "For We, Like You, Worship Your God," 288.

[30]David C. Greenwood, "On the Jewish Hope for a Restored Northern Kingdom," *Zeitschrift für die alttestamentliche Wissenschaft* 88 (1976): 382–83.

[31]The unyielding order regarding the prohibition of mixed marriage is strongly reflected in Ezra 10 and in Nehemiah 10.

³²Gary N. Knoppers, "Intermarriages, Social Complexity, and Ethnic Diversity in the Genealogy of Judah," *Journal of Biblical Literature* 120 (2001): 22, 28.

³³Shaye J.D. Cohen, "From the Bible to the Talmud: The Prohibition of Intermarriage," *Hebrew Annual Review* 7 (1983): 39.

³⁴Knoppers, "The Genealogy of Judah," 28.

³⁵Daniel L. Smith-Christopher, *A Biblical Theology of Exile* (Minneapolis: Fortress Press, 2002), 162.

³⁶Harold C. Washington, "Israel's Holy Seed and the Foreign Women of Ezra-Nehemiah: A Kristevan Reading," *Biblical Interpretation* 11 (2003): 430.

³⁷J. Blenkinsopp, *Ezra-Nehemiah: A Commentary*, Old Testament Library (Philadelphia: Westminster, 1988), 187–89. Jon Berquist argues that the list of men who divorced women "leans heavily toward the priest and leaders" (*Judaism in Persia's Shadow: A Social and Historical Approach* [Minneapolis: Fortress Press, 1995], 118). Tamara C. Eskenazi and Eleanore P. Judd interpret Ezra-Nehemiah's strict prohibition that marriage was declared invalid when a more conservative religious party gained power in society ("Marriage to a Stranger in Ezra 9–10," in *Second Temple Studies 2: Temple and Community in the Persian Period,* ed. Tamara C. Eskenazi and Kent H. Richard, JSOTSup 175 [Sheffield: JSOT Press, 1994], 266–85). Harold C. Washington, "The Strange Woman of Proverb 1–9 and Post-exilic Judean Society," in Eskenazi and Richards, *Second Temple Studies 2*, 235.

³⁸Kenneth G. Hoglund, *Achaemenid Imperial Administration in Syria-Palestine and the Missions of Ezra and Nehemiah* (Atlanta: Scholars Press, 1992), 205–40.

³⁹Ibid., 242–43.

⁴⁰Lisbeth S. Fried, *The Priest and the Great King: Temple-Palace Relations in the Persian Empire* (Winona Lake: Eisenbrauns, 2004), 201–9. Mary Douglas, "Responding to Ezra: The Priests and the Foreign Wives," *Biblical Interpretation* 10 (2002): 3–4.

⁴¹Fried, *The Priest and the Great King,* 220–21.

⁴²Hoglund, *Achaemenid Imperial Administration,* 241–44.

⁴³Douglas, "The Priests and the Foreign Wives," 2, 5.

⁴⁴For the native revolt during the Roman Empire, see Stephen L. Dyson, "Native Revolt Patterns in the Roman Empire," *ANRW* 2, no. 3:138–75.

⁴⁵Cf. Theudas (44 C.E.; *Ant.* 20.97–98); the Egyptian (55 C.E.; *Ant.* 20.169–72).

⁴⁶Bruce J. Berman, "Ethnicity, Patronage, and the African State: The Politics of Uncivil Nationalism," *African Affairs* 97 (1998): 305–41.

⁴⁷According to David Rensberger, there were two dominant attitudes toward Roman authority in John's time: "collaboration and resistance" (*Johannine Faith and Liberating Community* [Philadelphia: Westminster Press, 1988], 98); Koester, "The Savior of the World," 678–79.

⁴⁸Gary B. Miles, "Roman and Modern Imperialism: A Reassessment," *Society For Comparative Study of Society and History* 32 (1990): 629–30. Alan F. Segal, *Rebecca's Children: Judaism and Christianity in the Roman World* (Cambridge: Harvard University Press, 1986), 47–48. The relations between Jews and Samaritans were not so strained as to support the assumption that Jews had no dealings with Samaritans. A contemporary of Jesus, Agrippa I, managed to borrow the huge sum of a million drachmas from a man of Samaritan origin (*Ant.* 18.167). In the Samaritan woman's story, however, John seems to assert Jesus' superiority over the founding fathers of traditional Jewish religion by utilizing the betrothal type-scene (cf. 1:17–18; 5:38; 6:32; 8:53). For a discussion of Jacob tradition, see Neyrey, "Jacob Traditions and the Interpretation of John 4:10–26," 419–37; Stephen Grosby, "Category of the Primordial in the Study of Early Christianity and Second-Century Judaism," *History of Religion* 36 (1996): 141; Charles H.H. Scobie, "Johannine Geography," *Studies Religion/Science* 11 (1982): 77–84.

⁴⁹*J.W.* 3.307–315; Louis H. Feldman, *Studies in Hellenistic Judaism* (Leiden: Brill, 1996), 135–36.

⁵⁰Kim, *Woman and Nation,* 92–97.

⁵¹Cogan, "For We, Like You, Worship Your God," 289–91; James D. Purvis, "The Samaritan Problem: A Case Study in Jewish Sectarianism in the Roman Era," in *Traditions in Transformation: Turning Points in Biblical Faith,* ed. Baruch Halpern and Jon D. Levenson (Winona Lake, Ind.: Eisenbrauns, 1981), 323–50; P. W. Skehan, "Exodus in the Samaritan Recension from Qumran," *Journal of Biblical Literature* 74 (1955): 182–87.

⁵²The metaphorical usage of land/woman and seed/man has conceptualized a monogenetic creation throughout a long history. Carole Delaney, *The Seed and the Soil: Gender*

and Cosmology in Turkish Village Society (Berkeley: University of California Press, 1990); "Seeds of Honor, Fields of Shame," in *Honor and Shame and the Unity of the Mediterranean,* ed. David Gilmore (Washington, D.C.: American Anthropological Association, 1987), 38–39.

[53]Adeline Fehribach, *The Woman in the Life of Bridegroom: A Feminist Historical-Literary Analysis of the Female Characters in the Fourth Gospel* (Collegeville, Minn.: Glazer, 1998), 72, 56–58.

[54]When Judah fell to the Babylonians, Cyrus placed Gedaliah in charge of Judah, but under Samaria's supervision. Nehemiah's renewal of Judean independence caused the conflict between Judah and Samaria, since it threatened the power and wealth that Samaritans might have maintained through intermarriage. Cf. Fried, *The Priest and the Great King,* 187, 208.

[55]Fehribach, *The Woman in the Life of Bridegroom,* 78; Francis J. Moloney, *Belief in the Word: Reading John 1–4* (Minneapolis: Fortress Press, 1993), 170–71.

[56]Cf. Jeffrey L. Staley, *The Print's First Kiss: A Rhetorical Investigation of the Implied Reader in the Fourth Gospels* (Atlanta: Scholars Press, 1988), 102.

[57]Gayle Rubin, "The Traffic in Women: Notes on the 'Political Economy' of Sex," in *Toward an Anthropology of Women,* ed. Rayna R. Reiter (New York: Monthly Review, 1975), 172–74. For the life of bar women in U.S. military base areas, see Margo Okazawa-Rey, "Amerasian Children in GI Town: A Legacy of U.S. Militarism in South Korea," *Asian Journal of Women's Studies* 3 (1997): 71–86.

[58]Kim, *Woman and Nation,* 5–18; Saundra P. Sturdevant, "Okinawa Then and Now," in *Let the Good Times Roll: Prostitution and the U.S. Military in Asia,* ed. Saundra P. Sturdevant and Brenda Stolzfus (New York: New Press, 1992), 247; Bruce Cumings, "Silent But Deadly: Sexual Subordination in the U.S.-Korean Relationship," in *Let the Good Times Roll,* 171.

[59]Cynthia Enloe, "It Takes Two," in *Let the Good Times Roll,* 22–27.

[60]"Silence Broken: Korean Comfort Women," directed by Dai Sil Kim-Gibson, aired on PBS May 28, 2000.

[61]In his novel, Ahn portrays this triple jeopardy through Ollye's rage when she is directly confronted by the villagers' ostracism and ridicule: "Ollye hated the villagers, the Yankees, the children who scrawled the dirty insulting words, the boatman who must have passed the word around that she had become a Yankee princess, and everybody around her." As a vulnerable woman who had neither husband nor father to protect her from the intruding soldier, Ollye is triply stigmatized as a widow, a raped woman, and a sex worker. She is not like the other village women any longer because her body has been contaminated, and, finally, she is expelled from her native village (*Silver Stallion,* 149).

[62]Leslie Bow, *Betrayal and Other Acts of Subversion: Feminism, Sexual Politics, Asian American Women's Literature* (Princeton: Princeton University Press, 2001), 39.

[63]Yuh, *Beyond the Shadow of Camptown,* 2.

[64]Ibid., 2–3.

[65]Ibid., 199.

[66]Ibid., 188–96.

[67]Ibid., 202–14.

[68]Ibid., 216–18.

[69]Kim, "Korean Feminist Reading of John 4:1–42," 109–19.

[70]Yuh, *Beyond the Shadow of Camptown,* 220.

Chapter 9: A Light to the Nations

[1]Kenton Sparks, *Ethnicity and Identity in Ancient Israel: Prolegomena to the Study of Ethnic Sentiments and Their Expression in the Hebrew Bible* (Winona Lake, Ind.: Eisenbrauns, 1998).

[2]See Jeffrey Kuan, "Asian Biblical Interpretation," in *Dictionary of Biblical Interpretation, A-J,* ed. John H. Hayes (Nashville: Abingdon Press, 1999), 70–77.

[3]Chan-Hie Kim, "Reading the Bible as Asian Americans," *The New Interpreter's Bible,* vol. 1, ed. Leander E. Keck, et al. (Nashville: Abingdon Press, 1994), 161–66.

[4]Tat-siong Benny Liew, ed., "The Bible in Asian America," *Semeia* 90/91 (2002).

[5]Jong-Sun Noh, *Liberating God for Minjung* (Seoul, Korea: Hanul Academic, 1994).

[6]Nadav Na'aman, "Habiru-like Bands in the Assyrian Empire and Band in Biblical Historiography," *JAOS* 120 (2000): 621–24; "Habiru and Hebrews: The Transfer of a Social Term to the Literary Sphere," *JNES* 45 (1986): 271–88.

[7]Cyris Heesuk Moon, *A Korean Minjung Theology: An Old Testament Perspective* (Maryknoll, N.Y.: Orbis Books, 1985).

[8]Asian biblical interpretation is so extensive that it is difficult to sample all of South Asia, Southeast Asia, and East Asia. The following, perhaps, may be deemed as a minor sample among samples. Yeo Khiok-khng, *What Has Jerusalem to Do with Beijing?: Biblical Interpretation from a Chinese Perspective* (Harrisburg, Pa.: Trinity Press International, 1998); Fernando F. Segovia and Mary Ann Tolbert, eds., *Reading from This Place, Vol. 2: Social Location and Biblical Interpretation in Global Perspective* (Minneapolis: Fortress Press, 1995), see esp. "Part Two: Readings from Asia,"; R.S. Sugirtharajah, *Asian Biblical Hermeneutics and Postcolonialism: Contesting the Interpretations,* The Bible and Liberation (Sheffield: Sheffield Academic Press, 1999); idem, ed., *Voices from the Margins: Interpreting the Bible in the Third World,* rev. ed. (Maryknoll, N.Y./London: Orbis/Society for Promoting Christian Knowledge [SPCK], 1995); idem, ed., *The Postcolonial Bible* (Sheffield: Sheffield Academic Press, 1998); idem, ed., *Vernacular Hermeneutics* (Sheffield: Sheffield Academic Press, 1999); Jon R. Levison and Priscilla Pope-Levison, eds., *Return to Babel: Global Perspectives on the Bible* (Louisville: Westminster John Knox Press, 1999); Kwok Pui-lan, *Discovering the Bible in the Non-Biblical World* (Maryknoll, N.Y.: Orbis Books, 1995).

[9]George Koonthanam, "Yahweh the Defender of the Dalits: A Reflection of Isaiah 3:12-15," in *Voices from the Margin.* 105-16. The Brahmans (priests) developed a four-level, distinct caste system (Varnas) in Hinduism. At the top and foremost were the Brahmans (mouth) who controlled religion and society. Kshatriyas (arms), the warrior caste, followed; third were the Vaisyas (thighs), artisans and commercial class. Finally at the bottom of society were the Sudras (feet), farmers and peasant class. Beneath this four-fold cast system is a fifth group. They were and continue to be known as the untouchables or the Dalits–the oppressed, downtrodden, and exploited. Approximately 250 million Dalits, or approximately 25 percent of India's population is seen as untouchable. It should be noted that the Untouchability (Offences) Act of 1995 amended into the Protection of Civil Rights Act of 1976 has deemed it a criminal offense to keep the stratified caste system of marginalizing the "scheduled castes." See the endnotes of George M. Soares-Prabhu, "Exodus 20:1-17: An Asian Perspective," in *Return to Babel,* 53-54.

[10]Koonthanam, "Yahweh the Defender of the Dalits," 112.

[11]"Thirteen and Sold: Inside the Murky and Growing World of Trafficking in Minors," *India Today International,* October 13, 2003.

[12]George Koonthanam, "India's Untouchables," *National Geographic* (June 2003): 2-31.

[13]See Gary Y. Okihiro, *Margins and Mainstream: Asians in American History and Culture* (Seattle: University of Washington Press, 1994); Uma A. Segal, *A Framework for Immigration: Asians in the United States* (New York: Columbia University Press, 2002). See also *A Dream Unfinished: Theological Reflections on America from the Margins,* ed. Eleazar S. Fernandez and Fernando F. Segovia (Maryknoll, N.Y.: Orbis Books, 2001), esp. "Part II: Asian American Voices."

[14]Mary F. Foskett, "The Accidents of Being and the Politics of Identity: Biblical Images of Adoption and Asian Adoptees in America," *Semeia* 90/91 (2002): 135-44.

[15]Ibid., 141.

[16]Rainer Albertz, *Israel in Exile: The History and Literature of the Sixth Century B.C.E.,* trans. David Green (Atlanta: Society of Biblical Literature, 2003).

[17]See Robert P. Carroll, "Exile! What Exile?: Deportation and the Discourses of Diaspora," in *Leading Captivity Captive: "The Exile" as History and Ideology,* ed. Lester L. Grabbe, JSOTSup 278/ESHM 2 (Sheffield: Sheffield Academic Press, 1998), 74; James M. Scott, ed., *Exile: Old Testament, Jewish, and Christian Conceptions* (Leiden/New York: Brill, 1997); C.C. Torrey, *Ezra Studies* (Chicago: University of Chicago Press, 1910), 287-88; Peter Ackroyd, *Exile and Restoration,* Old Testament Library (Philadelphia: Westminster Press, 1968), 31, and especially 234-47; Ralph Klein, *Israel in Exile: A Theological Interpretation,* Overtures to Biblical Theology (Philadelphia: Fortress Press, 1979); Thomas L. Thompson, "The Exile in History and Myth: A Response to Hans Barstad," in *Leading Captivity Captive,* 101-18.

[18]Robert Wilson, *Sociological Approaches to the Old Testament,* Guides to Biblical Scholarship (Philadelphia: Fortress Press, 1984), 2.

[19]Ibid., 7.

[20]Stephen Cook, *Prophecy and Apocalypticism* (Minneapolis: Fortress Press, 1995). See also, Robert Wilson, *Prophecy and Society in Ancient Israel* (Philadelphia: Fortress Press, 1980).

[21]Robert D. Goette and Mae Pyen Hong, "A Theological Reflection on the Cultural Tensions Between First-Century Hebraic and Hellenistic Jewish Christians and Between

Twentieth-Century First- and Second-Generation Korean American Christians," in *Korean Americans and Their Religions: Pilgrims and Missionaries from a Different Shore,* ed. Ho-Youn Kown, Kwang Chung Kim, and R. Stephen Warner (University Park, Pa.: Penn State Press, 2001), 115–23, especially 122–23. In the appendix, Goette and Hong provide an important bifurcated model of American culture and Korean culture. Below is a modified and abridged appendix:

American Culture *(Individual centered)*	Korean Culture *(Relationship centered)*
Relationship: egalitarianism, equality	Hierarchical relationship (hegemonic at times)
Values individual's rights	Duties and responsibilities, self-appropriate function/assigned roles
Attitudes: assertive and self-expressive, standing up for self	Respect for authority, conformity to assigned role
Identity: personal ability and achievement, self-initiation	Status (position) in a group, success for the group
Socialization: active involvement, participatory decision making	Observation and emulation: watch, listen, do
Thinking style: analytic and detail-specific, objective vs. subjective, loosely structured teaching learning	Global and impressionistic, both objective and subjective, highly structured teaching learning

What needs to be highlighted is the fundamental variance between the first-generation Korean Americans and Americans. However, for the second-generation Korean Americans, the American and Korean cultures fuse as one—forming Americans who are of Korean origin. The conclusion in Goette and Hong is a call to first-generation Koreans who seek a narrow ministry as exemplified in the ministry of the apostle Peter (Jews only) to be more inclusive and have the apostle Paul's concept of ministry. They note that doubts remain regarding second-generation Korean American ministry, namely, Can they be fully encompassing?

[22]Anthony Giddens, *Modernity and Self Identity: Self and Society in the Late Modern Age* (Stanford: Stanford University Press, 1991), 52.

[23]Peter Berger and Thomas Luckmann, *The Social Construction of Reality* (New York: Anchor Books, 1966), 21.

[24]Ibid., 23.

[25]Sparks, *Ethnicity and Identity,* 309–19.

[26]Roy Melugin and Marvin A. Sweeney, eds., *New Visions of Isaiah,* Journal for the Study of the Old Testament: Supplement Series [JSOTSup] 214 (Sheffield: Sheffield Academic Press, 1996); Roy Melugin, *Formation of Isaiah 40–55,* Beihefte zur Zeitschrift für die alttestamentliche Wissenschaft 141, (Berlin/New York: W. De Gruyter, 1976); Marvin Sweeney, *Isaiah 1–39,* Forms of Old Testament Literature 16 (Grand Rapids, MI: William B. Eerdmans Publishing Company, 1996); Hendrik Carel Spykerboer, *Structure and Composition of Deutero-Isaiah with Special Reference to the Polemics against Idolatry* (Meppel: Krips Repro, 1976); Ronald e. Clements, *Isaiah 1–39,* New Century Bible Commentaries (Grand Rapids: William B. Eerdmans Publishing Company, 1980); "Beyond Tradition-History: Deutero-Isaianic Development of First Isaiah's Themes," Journal for the Study of the Old Testament 31 (1985): 95–113; Rolf Rendtorff, *The Old Testament: An Introduction* (Philadelphia: Fortress Press, 1986); Christopher Seitz, *Isaiah 1–39,* Interpretation Series (Louisville: John Knox Press, 1993); Brevard Childs, *Isaiah,* Old Testament Library (Louisville: Westminster John Knox Press, 2001); Rainer Albertz, *Israel in Exile: The History and Literature of the Sixth Century B.C.E.,* trans. David Green, Studies in Biblical Literature (Atlanta: Society of Biblical Literature, 2003), especially 376–433.

[27]Here, the syntax for the predicative phrases is conventional—the difficulty lies in the apposition of the nouns governed by the preposition ל. My translation will be given below.

[28]Sparks, *Ethnicity and Identity,* 310–11, especially note 82.

[29]Ibid., 317–18.

[30]John Oswalt, *The Book of Isaiah: Chapters 40–66,* New International Commentary on the Old Testament (Grand Rapids, Mich.: Wm. B. Eerdmans, 1998), 116.

³¹Joseph Blenkinsopp, *Isaiah 40–55,* Anchor Bible 19A (New York: Doubleday, 2002), 208.

³²Klaus Baltzer, *Deutero-Isaiah,* trans. Margot Kohl, Hermeneia (Minneapolis: Fortress Press, 2001), 124.

³³Here I take the preposition ל as the *lamed* of product to which a thing, person, is altered into. See §278 in Ronald J. Williams, *Hebrew Syntax: An Outline,* 2d ed. (Toronto: University of Toronto Press, 1992), 50.

³⁴Here the apposition is employed in a construct-like clause. See Bruce K. Waltke and M. O'Connor, *An Introduction to Biblical Hebrew Syntax* (Winona Lake, Ind.: Eisenbrauns, 1990), 226–234.

³⁵F. Brown, S.R. Driver, and C.A. Briggs, *A Hebrew and English Lexicon of the Old Testament* (Oxford: Oxford Univ. Press, 1907), 21: "the Messianic servant is אוֹר גּוֹיִם Isa. 42:6; 49:6; cf. אוֹר עַמִּים Isa 51:4; the advent of Messiah is shining great light Isa 9:1."

³⁶Ibid., 156.

³⁷Cf. Isaiah 2:4; 36:18; 37:12; and Isaiah 10:7; 11:10; 13:4; 14:6, 9, 12, 18; 16:8; 23:3; 25:3; 30:28; 33:3; 34:1; with 36:18; 37:12.

³⁸It should be noted that in chapters 42 and 49, this variance is even more lucid because we see the clear difference in the text and context where the definite article and the lack of the article are employed. I am bothered by the editors of the NRSV, RSV, NIV, ASV, NASV, etc., who have not paid close attention to this detail.

³⁹Isaiah 1:4; 2:4; 5:26; 8:9; 9:3; 10:6, 7, 13, 14; 11:10, 12; 12:4; 13:4; 14:2, 6, 9, 12, 18, 26, 32; 16:8; 17:12; 18:2, 7; 23:2; 24:13; 25:3, 7; 26:2, 15; 29:7, 8; 30:6, 28; 33:3, 4; 34:1, 2; 36:18; 37:12; (49:7; 51:4; 58:2; 60:12, 22; 66:8).

⁴⁰R.E. Clements, "A Light to the Nations: A Central Theme of the Book of Isaiah," in *Forming Prophetic Literature: Essays on Isaiah and the Twelve in Honor of John D.W. Watts,* ed. James W. Watts and Paul R. House, JSOTSup 235 (Sheffield: Sheffield University Press, 1996), 57–69.

⁴¹"Isaiah 40–55 has taken only a limited step beyond a traditional Jerusalemite theology in which the nations are merely servants of Israel, and in particular, Israel's king (cf. Ps. 2; 72:8–11), with the result that in Deutero-Isaiah the nations not only bow down before Yahweh and Israel but are also said to be given salvation." See Roy Melugin, "Israel and the Nations in Isaiah 40–55," in *Problems in Biblical Theology: Essays in Honor of Rolf Knierim,* ed. Henry T.C. Sun et al. (Grand Rapids, Mich.: Wm. B. Eerdmans, 1997), 261–62.

⁴²Don-chang Lee, "A Study of Social Networks within Two Korean Communities in America," in *The Korean Diaspora: Historical and Sociological Studies of Korean Immigration and Assimilation in North America,* ed. Hyung-chan Kim (Santa Barbara, Calif.: ABC-Clio Inc., 1977), 155–66.

⁴³S. Steve Kang, *Unveiling the Socioculturally Constructed Multivoiced Self: Themes of Self Construction and Self Integration in the Narratives of Second-Generation Korean American Young Adults* (Lanham, Md.: University Press of America, 2002).

⁴⁴Moon H. Jo, *Korean Immigrants and the Challenge of Adjustment* (Westport, Conn.: Greenwood Press, 1999). See also Tae-Hwan Kwak and Seong Hyong Lee, eds., *The Korean-American Community: Present and Future* (Seoul, Korea: Kyungnam University Press, 1991).

⁴⁵Luke I. Kim and Grace S. Kim, "Searching for and Defining a Korean American Identity in a Multicultural Society," in *Korean American Women: From Tradition to Modern Feminism,* ed. Young I. Song and Ailee Moon (Westport, Conn.: Praeger Press, 1998), 115–25.

⁴⁶Hyung-chan Kim, "Ethnic Enterprises among Korean Immigrants in American," in *The Korean Diaspora,* 85–126. See also the chapters entitled "Korean Ethnic Associations" and "Intergroup Relations" in Won Moo Hurh, *The Korean Americans* (Westport, Conn.: Greenwood Press, 1998), 105–39.

Chapter 10: Lot's Wife, Ruth, and Tô Thị

¹C.S. Song, *The Believing Heart: An Invitation to Story Theology* (Minneapolis: Fortress Press, 1999), 66.

²C.S. Song, "Context and Revelation with One Stroke of an Asian Brush," in *Lift Every Voice: Constructing Christian Theologies from the Underside,* ed. Susan B. Thislethwaite and Mary P. Engel (San Francisco: Harper & Row, 1990), 87.

³Quoted according to Song's translation.

[4]Song, *The Believing Heart*, 69.

[5]Fernando F. Segovia, "'And They Began to Speak in Other Tongues': Competing Modes of Discourse in Contemporary Biblical Criticism," in *Reading from This Place, Vol. 1: Social Location and Biblical Interpretation in the United States*, ed. Fernando F. Segovia and Mary Ann Tolbert (Minneapolis: Fortress Press, 1995), 28.

[6]Cf. Rita Nakashima Brock, "Interstitial Integrity: Reflections toward an Asian American Woman's Theology," in *Introduction to Christian Theology: Contemporary North American Perspectives*, ed. Roger A. Badham (Louisville: Westminster John Knox Press, 1998), 183–96; Kwok Pui-lan, *Introducing Asian Feminist Theology*, Introductions in Feminist Theology 4 (Cleveland: Pilgrim Press, 2000); Musa W. Dube *Postcolonial Feminist Interpretation of the Bible* (St. Louis: Chalice Press, 2000).

[7]All biblical citations are from the NRSV.

[8]Gordon J. Wenham, *Genesis 16–50*, Word Biblical Commentary 2 (Dallas: Word Books, 1994), 59.

[9]James Burton Coffman, *Commentary on Genesis the First Book of Moses* (Abilene: ACU Press, 1985), 257.

[10]Ibid., 256.

[11]Armstrong Black, *Ruth, a Hebrew Idyll: Twelve Short Studies* (London: Hodder and Stoughton, 1906), 6.

[12]E.g., Ibid.

[13]E.g., Edward Fay Campbell, *Ruth: A New Translation with Introduction, Notes, and Commentary*, Anchor Bible 7 (Garden City, N.Y.: Doubleday, 1975).

[14]Ibid., 3.

[15]Ibid.

[16]Ibid., 81.

[17]Ibid., 82.

[18]Ibid.

[19]Danna Nolan Fewell and David. M. Gunn, *Compromising Redemption: Relating Characters in the Book of Ruth*, Literary Currents in Biblical Interpretation (Louisville: Westminster John Knox Press, 1990), 11.

[20]Catherine Clark Kroeger and Mary J. Evans, *The IVP Women's Bible Commentary* (Downers Grove, Ill.: InterVarsity Press, 2002), 148.

[21]Ibid., 152.

[22]Julie L.C. Chu, "Returning Home: The Inspiration of the Role Dedifferentiation in the Book of Ruth for Taiwanese Women," *Semeia* 78 (1997): 47.

[23]Ibid., 49.

[24]Khiem Duy Pham, "The Mountain of Waiting," *Nimrod International Journal: Vietnam Revisited* 47, no. 2 (2004): 20.

[25]Some written versions inscribe a story of an unwitting marriage between a brother and sister that took place as ominously foretold by an astrologer. On discovering the wretched truth about the incestuous relationship, the horror-stricken brother/husband leaves his sister/wife and son under an invented pretext. To the end, the hapless sister/wife remains oblivious to the truth, steadfastly awaiting the return of her husband. See Pham's version, "The Mountain of Waiting," for instance.

[26]Black, *Ruth, a Hebrew Idyll*, 6.

[27]See, for instance, Que Thi Tran, Uyen Ngoc Vu, and Bang Thi Nguyen, *Nhung Khai Niem Co Ban Ve Gioi Va Van De Gioi O Viet Nam: Gender Basic Concepts and Gender Issues in Vietnam* (Ha Noi: Nha Xuat Ban Thong Ke, 1999).

[28]Claus Westermann, *Genesis 12–36: A Commentary*, trans. John J. Scullion, S.J. (Minneapolis: Augsburg Publishing House, 1985), 307.

[29]Wenham, *Genesis 16–50*, 59.

[30]Rose Sallberg Kam, *Their Stories, Our Stories: Women of the Bible* (New York: Continuum, 1995), 49.

[31]See Rebecca Goldstein, "Looking Back at Lot's Wife," *Commentary* 94 (1992). Elie Wiesel, "Lot's Wife," in *The Future of Prophetic Christianity*, ed. John Tully Carmody (Maryknoll, N.Y.: Orbis Books, 1993).

[32]Goldstein, "Looking Back at Lot's Wife," 41.

[33]Ibid.

[34]Danna Nolan Fewell and David M. Gunn, *Gender, Power, and Promise: The Subject of the Bible's First Story* (Nashville: Abingdon Press, 1993), 67.

[35]Ibid..

[36]C.S. Song, *The Tears of Lady Meng: A Parable of People's Political Theology* (Geneva: World Council of Churches, 1981).

[37]Ibid., 40.

[38]Andrew Sung Park, *The Wounded Heart of God: The Asian Concept of Han and the Christian Doctrine of Sin* (Nashville: Abingdon Press, 1993), 19.

[39]Hyun Kyung Chung, *Struggle to Be the Sun Again: Introducing Asian Women's Theology* (Maryknoll, N.Y.: Orbis Books, 1990), 42.

[40]This is my own crude translation of a Vietnamese song entitled "Ca Dao Me," original lyrics by the Vietnamese songwriter Trinh Cong Son. The term *ca dao* is Vietnamese for "folksong." *Me* is Vietnamese for "mother." It is inevitable that much of the flavor and meaning of the original expressions has been lost in the translation. What you see here—the terms and expressions chosen—are my preferences and constructs of the meaning of this stirring song.

[41]Fewell and Gunn, *Compromising Redemption.*

[42]Ibid., 13.

[43]Ibid., 14–15.

[44]Ibid., 32.

[45]Cf. Dube, *Postcolonial Feminist Interpretation.* In a lecture at Garrett-Evangelical Theological Seminary entitled "Finding a Home: Biblical Reflection on the Story of Ruth," Kwok Pui-lan employed a postcolonial feminist perspective to discuss the social location of Ruth as an immigrant woman. Emergent from this reading of Ruth are themes of "belonging," "assimilation," "marginalization," and "false inclusion," to name a few. Cf. also Chu, "Returning Home," 50.

[46]The questioning of "faith" and "redemption" are raised by Fewell and Gunn in *Compromising Redemption.*

[47]Gerhard Von Rad, *Genesis: A Commentary,* rev. ed. (Philadelphia: The Westminster Press, 1972), 221.

[48]Fewell and Gunn, *Compromising Redemption,* 30–31.

[49]Bonnie Honig, "Ruth, the Model Emigrée: Mourning and the Symbolic Politics of Immigration," in *Ruth and Esther: A Feminist Companion to the Bible,* ed. Athalya Brenner (Sheffield: Sheffield Academic Press, 1999).

[50]Ibid., 54.

[51]Ibid., 56–57.

Chapter 11: Betwixt and Between

[1]Peter C. Phan, "Betwixt and Between: Doing Theology with Memory and Imagination," in *Journeys at the Margin: Toward an Autobiographical Theology in American-Asian Perspective,* ed. Peter C. Phan and Jung Young Lee (Collegeville, Minn.: Liturgical Press, 1999), 113–33.

[2]Ibid., 128–29.

[3]David Tracy, *Plurality and Ambiguity: Hermeneutics, Religions, and Hope* (New York: Harper & Row, 1987,) 31; cited in Elisabeth Schüssler Fiorenza, "The Ethics of Biblical Interpretation: Decentering Biblical Scholarship," *Journal of Biblical Literature* 107 (1988): 13.

[4]See Hans-Georg Gadamer, *Truth and Method* (New York: Seabury Press, 1975); and Richard E. Palmer, *Hermeneutics: Interpretation Theory in Schleiermacher, Dilthey, Heidegger, and Gadamer* (Evanston, Ill.: Northwestern Univ. Press, 1969), 194–217.

[5]Schüssler Fiorenza, "Ethics," 13–14.

[6]Ibid., 14.

[7]Gadamer, *Truth and Method,* 325–41; Paul Ricoeur, "The Hermeneutical Function of Distanciation," in *Exegesis* (Pittsburgh: Pickwick Press, 1978), 297–320; David Tracy, *Analogical Imagination: Christian Theology and the Culture of Pluralism* (New York: Crossroad, 1981), 124–30, 259–65.

[8]This view of Gadamer's is succinctly summarized in Palmer, *Hermeneutics,* 198–201. See Rudolf Bultmann, "Is Exegesis without Presupposition Possible?" *Faith and Existence* (New York: Meridian Books, 1960), 289–96.

[9]Schüssler Fiorenza, "Ethics," 14.

[10]Ibid., 14.

[11]Ibid., 15.

[12]Ibid., 15-16. Schüssler Fiorenza sides with left-leaning scholars as a matter of course. This is evident in the following quote: "The growth of right-wing fundamentalism and of Biblicist literalism in society, religious institutions, and the broader culture feeds antidemocratic authoritarianism and fosters personal prejudice. In the light of this political situation, biblical scholarship has the responsibility to make its research available to a wider public" (p. 16). Schüssler Fiorenza wrote these lines in 1987, but her analysis is even more applicable today.

[13]Daniel Boyarin, *Radical Jew: Paul and the Politics of Identity* (Berkeley, Los Angeles, & London: Univ. of California Press, 1994), 228-60, but especially 242-46; Fernando Segovia, "Interpreting beyond Borders: Postcolonial Studies and Diasporic Studies in Biblical Criticism," in *Interpreting Beyond Borders,* ed. F. Segovia (Sheffield: Sheffield Academic Press, 2000), 9-32.

[14]In the sense that Peter Phan has defined "autobiographical"; see his "An Asian-American Theology: Believing and Thinking at the Boundaries," in *Journeys at the Margin,* xi-xviii.

[15]Here the notion of "cultural mimicry" is a helpful way of problematizing this Asian-American ambivalence; see Homi Bhabha, "Of Mimicry and Man," in *The Location of Culture* (London: Routledge, 1994), 85-92.

[16]Sze-kar Wan, "Does Diaspora Identity Imply Some Sort of Universality? An Asian-American Reading of Galatians," in *Interpreting beyond Borders,* 119.

[17]See Georgia Warnke, *Gadamer: Hermeneutics, Tradition and Reason* (Stanford: Stanford University Press, 1987), 91, 98-99, where she cites the criticisms of Emilio Betti and others.

[18]Gadamer, *Truth and Method,* 264; see Warnke, *Gadamer,* 95-96.

[19]Betti's criticism; see Warnke, *Gadamer,* 98.

[20]See the very helpful comparison of Asian-American theology to African-American and Hispanic-American theologies by Peter Phan, "Contemporary Theology and Inculturation in the United States," in *The Multicultural Church: A New Landscape in U.S. Church,* ed. W. Cenkner (New York: Paulist Press, 1996), 109-30.

[21]Phan, "Betwixt and Between," 113; reproduced in his "The Dragon and the Eagle: Toward a Vietnamese American Theology," in *Realizing the America of Our Hearts: Theological Voices of Asian Americans,* ed. F. Matsuoka and E. Fernandez (St. Louis: Chalice, 2003), 165.

[22]Phan, "Betwixt and Between," 113.

[23]Ibid., 114; cf. "Dragon and Eagle," 165-66.

[24]Phan, "Betwixt and Between," 127-30.

[25]Cited and critiqued by Jung Young Lee, *Marginality: The Key to Multicultural Theology* (Minneapolis: Fortress, 1995), 42-47.

[26]Jung Young Lee, *Marginality,* 50-51.

[27]Ibid., 59.

[28]Ibid., 60-61. Lee cites also from Charles Willie, whose new definition of marginality corresponds well to Lee's: "[The new concept of the marginal person is] the one who rises above two social or cultural groups, freeing the different groups to work together" (p. 61).

[29]Wesley Woo, "China and Chinese-American Identity," in *The Theologies of Asian Americans and Pacific Peoples,* comp. Roy Sano (Berkeley: Pacific School of Religion Asian Center for Theology and Strategies, 1976), 152.

[30]Turner and Terry Veling cited by Sang Hyun Lee, "Marginality as Coerced Liminality: Toward an Understanding of the Context of Asian American Theology," *Journeys at the Margin,* 14; his own view on 18.

[31]Sang Hyun Lee, "Marginality as Coerced Liminality," 19.

[32]Ibid., 25-26.

[33]Julia Ching, "House of Self," *Journeys at the Margin,* 41-61.

[34]Phan, "Dragon and Eagle," 165.

[35]Jung Young Lee, *Marginality,* 50.

[36]An account by Rey Chow in her *Writing Diaspora: Tactics of Intervention in Contemporary Cultural Studies* (Bloomington & Indianapolis: Indiana University Press, 1993). My personal experience and anecdotal accounts by other Chinese-Americans bear this out.

[37]Wesley Woo, "China and Chinese-American Identity," 152.

[38]Frantz Fanon, *Black Skin, White Masks,* trans. L. Markmann (New York: Grove Press, 1967).

[39]Homi Bhabha, "Remembering Fanon: Self, Psyche and the Colonial Condition," *Colonial Discourse and Postcolonial Theory: A Reader,* ed. P. Williams and L. Chrisman (New

York: Columbia Univ. Press, 1994), 117; emphasis his. An excellent example of such hybrid identity serving to subvert and transform the dominant culture is that of William Apess; see Laura E. Donaldson, "Son of the Forest, Child of God: William Apess and the Scene of Postcolonial nativity," in C. Richard King, *Postcolonial America* (Chicago: University of Illinois Press, 2000), 201-22.

[40]Mikhail Bakhtin, *Dialogical Imagination: Four Essays* (Austin, Tex.: Univ. of Texas Press, 1981), 360; cited in Robert C. Young, *Colonial Desire: Hybridity in Theory, Culture and Race* (London & New York: Routledge, 1995), 21.

[41]Young, *Colonial Desire*, 21.

[42]Ibid., 21–22; citation from Bakhtin, *Dialogic Imagination*, 361.

[43]Phrase found in Bill Ashcroft, Gareth Griffiths, and Helen Tiffin, *Post-Colonial Studies: Key Concepts* (London & New York: Routledge, 2000), 120.

[44]Young, *Colonial Desire*, 26–27.

[45]Warnke, *Gadamer*, 58.

Chapter 12: Yin/Yang Is Not Me

[1]Published in Gale A. Yee, "Inculturation and Diversity in the Politics of National Identity," *Journal of Asian and Asian American Theology* 2 (1997): 108–12.

[2]Some of what follows is explored more fully in Yee, "Inculturation and Diversity," 108–12.

[3]Maxine Hong Kingston, *The Woman Warrior: Memoirs of a Girlhood Among Ghosts* (1976; repr., New York: Vintage Books, 1977).

[4]Rey Chow, *The Protestant Ethnic & the Spirit of Capitalism* (New York: Columbia University Press, 2002), 95–87.

[5]Ibid., 104–5.

[6]Ibid., 107.

[7]Ibid., 117.

[8]Ibid.

[9]Ibid., 123–27. Also, Rey Chow, *Writing Diaspora: Tactics on Intervention in Contemporary Cultural Studies* (Bloomington: Indiana University Press, 1993), 1–26, where she lays out the problem of white male Western Orientalists describing the "disease of modern Chinese poetry."

[10]Henry Yu, *Thinking Orientals: Migration, Contact, and Exoticism in Modern America* (Oxford: Oxford University Press, 2001), 163.

[11]Ibid., 163–64.

[12]Gish Jen, "Racial Profiling," *Time Magazine (Asian Edition)* 162, no. 6, Aug 18–25 (2003): 68. See also the remarks of Chow, *The Protestant Ethnic*, 28–30 on the "Westernized" Chinese, for whom it is impossible to assume an unmediated access to Chinese culture.

[13]Explored fully in Lisa Lowe, "Heterogeneity, Hybridity, Multiplicity: Marking Asian American Differences," in *Asian American Studies: A Reader*, ed. Jean Yu-wen Shen Wu and Min Song (New Brunswick, N.J.: Rutgers University, 2000), 423–42.

[14]According to Mia Tuan, *Forever Foreigners or Honorary Whites: The Asian Ethnic Experience Today* (New Brunswick, N.J.: Rutgers University, 1998), 8, black Americans experience *racialization* processes differently. For Asians, the stain of foreignness further compounds racial marginalization: "Blacks may be many things in the minds of whites, but foreign is not one of them." White society usually does not ask African Americans, "Where are you from?" as it repeatedly does Asian Americans. Regarding Asian Americans as permanent outsiders or foreigners in American, see also Frank Wu, *Yellow: Race in America Beyond Black and White* (New York: Basic Books, 2001), 79–129; Yu, *Thinking Orientals*, 173–85; Kandice Chuh, *Imagine Otherwise: On Asian Americanist Critique* (Durham and London: Duke University Press, 2003), 20.

[15]The question posed by Amy Ling, "'Emerging Canons' of Asian American Literature and Art," in *Asian Americans: Comparative and Global Perspectives*, ed. Shirley Hune et al. (Pullman, Wash.: Washington State University Press, 1991), 195–96 in a literary context.

[16]W.E.B. Du Bois, "Krigwa Players Little Negro Theater,'" *The Crisis* 32 (1926): 134.

[17]Vincent L. Wimbush, ed., *African Americans and the Bible: Sacred Texts and Social Textures* (New York: Continuum, 2000).

[18]Tat-Siong Benny Liew, "Reading with Yin Yang Eyes: Negotiating the Ideological Dilemma of a Chinese American Biblical Hermeneutics," *Biblical Interpretation* 9 (2001): 309–35; "More Than Personal Encounters: Identity, Community, and Interpretation," *Union*

Seminary Quarterly Review 56 (2002): 41–44; Chan-Hie Kim, "Reading the Bible as Asian Americans," in *The New Interpreter's Bible, vol. 1,* ed. Leander E. Keck (Nashville: Abingdon, 1994), 161–66; Jeffrey Kah-Jin Kuan, "My Journey into Diasporic Hermeneutics," *Union Seminary Quarterly Review* 56 (2002): 50–54; "Diasporic Readings of a Diasporic Text: Identity Politics and Race Relations and the Book of Esther," in *Interpreting Beyond Borders,* ed. Fernando F. Segovia (Sheffield: Sheffield Academic Press, 2000), 161–73; Yee, "Inculturation and Diversity," 108–12.

[19]F. Bret Harte, *The Heathen Chinee* (Chicago: The Western News Company, 1870).

[20]Chow, *The Protestant Ethnic,* 106.

[21]Lowe, "Heterogeneity, Hybridity, Multiplicity," 429–31; Laura Hyun Yi Kang, *Compositional Subjects: Enfiguring Asian/American Women* (Durham and London: Duke University Press, 2002), 5; Chuh, *Imagine Otherwise,* 20.

[22]Jun Xing, *Asian America Through the Lens: History, Representations, and Identity* (Walnut Creek, Calif.: Alta Mira Press, 1998), 20–39; Lowe, "Heterogeneity, Hybridity, Multiplicity," 427.

[23]Lowe, "Heterogeneity, Hybridity, Multiplicity," 428–29.

[24]Xing, *Asian America Through the Lens,* 140–43.

[25]Stuart Hall, "Cultural Identity and Diaspora," in *Colonial Discourse and Post-Colonial Theory: A Reader,* ed. Patrick Williams and Laura Chrisman (New York: Columbia University Press, 1994), 394.

[26]See Xing, *Asian America Through the Lens,* 147, on the ways in which "becoming" an Asian American is reflected in Asian American filmmaking. See also Steve Fenton, *Ethnicity* (Cambridge, U.K.: Polity Press, 2003), 180, on the "contexts of ethnicity."

[27]My description, "hyphenated condition," is rhetorical. Within Asian American studies are discussions whether or not to use the hyphen in Asian (-) American. See David L. Eng, *Racial Castration: Managing Masculinity in Asian America* (Durham and London: Duke University Press, 2001), 211–25. Kang, *Compositional Subjects,* 2, prefers the slash, Asian/American woman, as a "diacritically awkward shorthand for the cultural, economic, and geopolitical pressures on the continental (Asian), the national (American), and the racial-ethnic (Asian American) as they come to bear on an implicitly more solid gendered ontology (woman)."

[28]For studies of this phenomenon, see Sheng-Mei Ma, *The Deathly Embrace: Orientalism and Asian American Identity* (Minneapolis: University of Minnesota Press, 2000); Yu, *Thinking Orientals;* Robert G. Lee, *Orientals: Asian Americans in Popular Culture* (Philadelphia: Temple University Press, 1999); Mari Yoshihara, *Embracing the East: White Women and American Orientalism* (New York: Oxford University, 2002); Yen Le Espiritu, "Ideological Racism and Cultural Resistance," in *Asian American Women and Men: Labor, Laws and Love* (Thousand Oaks, Calif.: Sage, 1997), 86–107; and Helen Zia, "Gangsters, Gooks, Geisha, and Geeks," in her *Asian American Dreams: The Emergence of an American People* (New York: Farrar, Straus & Giroux, 2000), 109–35.

[29]See Mari Yoshihara, "'Popular Expert on China': Authority and Gender in Pearl S. Buck's *The Good Earth,*" in *Embracing the East: White Women and American Orientalism* (New York: Oxford University, 2003), 149–69, for an analysis of the Orientalist bias in Pearl Buck's *The Good Earth.*

[30]Found in the comic strip *Terry and the Pirates.* For a discussion, see Ma, *The Deathly Embrace,* 12–20. Some Asian American feminists have recouped this icon. See Sonia Shah, ed., *Dragon Ladies: Asian American Feminists Breathe Fire* (Boston: South End, 1997).

[31]E.g., *The Chinese Maze Murders, The Chinese Nail Murders, The Emperor's Pearl, The Red Pavilion.* His classic Orientalist work on Chinese eroticism, *Sexual Life in Ancient China: A Preliminary Survey of Chinese Sex and Society From Ca. 1500 B.C. Till 1644 A.D.* (1961; repr., Leiden and Boston: Brill, 2003), is critiqued by Charlotte Furth, "Rethinking Van Gulik: Sexuality and Reproduction in Traditional Chinese Medicine," in *Engendering China: Women, Culture, and the State,* ed. Christina K. Gilmartin et al. (Cambridge, Mass.: Harvard University, 1994), 125–46.

[32]James Clavell, *Shogun* (New York: Dell, 1975), 692–96. This string of four round beads of white jade was pushed into the anus and pulled out by one's partner at the moment of "Clouds and Rain" (read: orgasm). For an analysis and critique of the American exoticization of Asian women, see Aki Uchida, "The Orientalization of Asian Women in America," *Women's Studies International Forum* 21 (1998): 161–74. The Asian woman fetish of white men has been explored in the novel by Mako Yoshikawa, *One Hundred and One Ways* (New York: Bantam

Books, 1999). "One hundred and one ways" refers to the number of ways a geisha was supposedly able to "unlock [men's] bodies with a groan" (9).

[33]Trevanian, *Shibumi* (New York: Ballantine Books, 1979). Another novel of the same ilk is Eric Van Lustbader, *The Ninja: A Novel* (New York: Fawcett Crest, 1980).

[34]Evidently the highest level of erotic proficiency involves the use of razor sharp knives in vulnerable places. In a textual note, Trevanian felt it was irresponsible for him to describe the procedure in detail, lest some mere mortals attempt it.

[35]From the introduction to Frank Chin et al., eds., *Aiiieeeee! An Anthology of Asian American Writers* (1974; repr., New York: Mentor, 1991), xi-xii. See also Gina Marchetti, *Romance and the "Yellow Peril": Race, Sex, and Discursive Strategies in Hollywood* (Berkeley: University of California Press, 1994); Peter X. Feng, ed., *Screening Asian Americans* (New Brunswick, N.J.: Rutgers University, 2002); Xing, *Asian America Through the Lens*, 53–86; Darrell Y. Hamamoto, *Monitored Peril: Asian Americans and the Politics of TV Representation* (Minneapolis: University of Minnesota, 1994).

[36]Kingston, *The Woman Warrior*, 6. For a helpful 60-minute video of clips of Hollywood depictions of Asians, see Deborah Gee, producer and director, *Slaying the Dragon* (San Francisco: NAATA Distribution, 1995).

[37]Ronald Takaki, *Strangers from a Different Shore: A History of Asian Americans* (New York: Penguin Books, 1989); Roger Daniels, *Prisoners Without Trial: Japanese Americans in World War II* (New York: Hill and Wang, 1993); Sucheng Chan, ed., *Entry Denied: Exclusion and the Chinese Community in America, 1882–1943* (Philadelphia: Temple University, 1991); Gary Y. Okihiro, *Margins and Mainstreams: Asians in American History and Culture* (Seattle: University of Washington Press, 1994); Helen Zia, *Asian American Dreams*; Wu, *Yellow: Race in America*.

[38]Karen D. Pyke and Denise L. Johnson, "Asian American Women and Racialized Femininities: 'Doing' Gender Across Cultural Worlds," *Gender & Society* 17, no. 1 (2003): 33–53.

[39]Ibid., 50–51.

[40]Kobena Mercer, "Skin Head Sex Thing" in *How do I look?: Queer Film and Video*, ed. Bad Object-Choices (Seattle: Bay Press, 1991), 206. Cited in Eng, *Racial Castration*, 138. See also Yu, *Thinking Orientals*, 201.

[41]Yu, *Thinking Orientals*, 199.

[42]See Tuan, *Forever Foreigners*, 5–8, 21–22, and Yu, *Thinking Orientals*, 202, on ethnicity as a matter of choice for whites.

[43]Eng, *Racial Castration*, 141–2.

[44]See Richard Delgado and Jean Stephanie, eds., *Critical White Studies: Looking Behind the Mirror* (Philadelphia: Temple University, 1997); Mike Hill, ed., *Whiteness: A Critical Reader* (New York/London: New York University Press, 1997); Ruth Frankenberg, ed., *Displacing Whiteness: Essays in Social and Cultural Criticism* (Chapel Hill, N.C.: Duke University Press, 1997); Maurice Berger, *White Lies: Race and the Myths of Whiteness* (New York: Farrar, Straus & Giroux, 1999); Joe L. Kincheloe, Shirley R. Steinberg, and Ronald E. Chennault, eds., *White Reign: Deploying Whiteness in America* (New York: St. Martin's Press, 1998); Matthew Frye Jacobson, *Whiteness of a Different Color: European Immigrants and the Alchemy of Race* (Cambridge, Mass.: Harvard University Press, 1998); Abby L. Ferber, *White Man Falling: Race, Gender, and White Supremacy* (Lanham, Md.: Rowman & Littlefield Publishers, Inc., 1998); George Lipsitz, *The Possessive Investment in Whiteness: Why White People Profit from Identity Politics* (Philadelphia: Temple University, 1998); Mason Stokes, *The Color of Sex: Whiteness, Heterosexuality, and the Fictions of White Supremacy* (Durham, N.C.: Duke University Press, 2001); Cynthia Levine-Rasky, *Working Through Whiteness: International Perspectives* (Albany, N.Y.: State University of New York Press, 2002); Vron Waren and Les Back, *Out of Whiteness: Color, Politics, and Culture* (Chicago: University of Chicago Press, 2002); Mary Elizabeth Hobgood, *Dismantling Privilege: An Ethics of Accountability* (Cleveland: Pilgrim Press, 2000); Karen Brodkin, *How Jews Became White Folks: And What That Says About Race in America* (New Brunswick, N.J.: Rutgers University Press, 1999); Louise Michele Newman, *White Women's Rights: The Racial Origins of Feminism in the United States* (New York: Oxford University Press, 1999); Robyn Wiegman, "Whiteness Studies and the Paradox of Particularity," *Boundary 2*, vol. 26, no. 3 (1999): 115–50; Jane Marcus, *Hearts of Darkness: White Women Write Race* (New Brunswick, N.J.: Rutgers University, 2003); Jennifer Guglielmo and Salvatore Salerno, eds., *Are Italians White? How Race Is Made in America* (New York: Routledge, 2003); Bridget T. Heneghan, *Whitewashing America: Material Culture and Race in the Antebellum Imagination* (Jackson, Miss.: University Press of Mississippi, 2003).

[45]Gale A. Yee, "'By the Hand of a Woman': The Biblical Metaphor of the Woman Warrior," *Semeia* 61 (1993): 99–132.

[46]Pending further study, I am assuming that Yael is a Kenite, although the only mention of ethnicity is about her husband, Heber the Kenite.

[47]Baruch Halpern, "Sisera and Old Lace: The Case of Deborah and Yael," in *The First Historians: The Hebrew Bible and History* (San Francisco: Harper & Row, 1988), 76–103.

[48]Roger Daniels, *Prisoners Without Trial: Japanese Americans in World War II* (New York: Hill and Wang, 1993), 24–25, 36–38; Wu, *Yellow: Race in America*, 95–103.

Chapter 13: Constructing Hybridity and Heterogeneity

[1]David Mura, *Turning Japanese: Memoirs of a Sansei* (New York: Doubleday, 1991), 124.

[2]For a discussion of the sociopolitical and historical context of the Asian American movement, see Glenn Omatsu, "The 'Four Prisons' and the Movements of Liberation: Asian American Activism from the 1960s to the 1990s," in *Asian American Studies: A Reader,* ed. Jean Yu-wen Shen Wu and Min Song (New Brunswick: Rutgers University Press, 2000), 164–96; and Yen Le Espiritu, "Panethnicity and Asian American Activism," in *Major Problems in Asian American History: Documents and Essays,* ed. Lon Kurashige and Alice Yang Murray (Boston: Houghton Mifflin, 2003), 442–49.

[3]Lisa Lowe, following Gayatri Spivak, uses the notion of "strategic essentialism" to speak about how it is possible to use essentialized notions of Asian American culture "for the purpose of contesting and disrupting the discourses that exclude Asian Americans, while simultaneously revealing the internal contradictions and slippages of Asian Americans so as to insure that such essentialisms will not be reproduced and proliferated by the very apparatuses we seek to disempower" ("Heterogeneity, Hybridity, Multiplicity: Marking Asian American Differences," in *Contemporary Asian America: A Multidisciplinary Reader,* ed. Min Zhou and James V. Gatewood [New York: New York University Press, 2000], 692). Lowe makes it clear that she does not seek to do away with the idea of "Asian American" culture. She argues, however, that problematizing the idea points us toward "the ongoing work of transforming hegemony."

[4]I understand "idealism" similarly to Rey Chow in *Ethics After Idealism: Theory-Culture-Ethnicity-Reading* (Bloomington: University of Indiana Press, 1998), xiii–xxiii. Chow argues that one must read complexity and contradiction into non-West literature in order to destabilize the discourse of otherness that constrains it. Idealism, according to Chow, infects not only the cultural characterizations that seek to reinforce the otherness of the non-West, but the "identity politics" of cultural studies.

[5]Lowe, in her discussion about Asian American intergenerational issues in literature, points to the strategic importance of notions such as hybridity. She says, "I stress heterogeneity, hybridity, and multiplicity in the characterization of Asian American culture as part of a twofold argument about cultural politics, the ultimate aim of that argument being to disrupt the current hegemonic relationship between 'dominant' and 'minority' positions" (Lowe, "Heterogeneity," 681).

[6]Chow, "Ethics After Idealism," xxi.

[7]Fernando F. Segovia, "Toward a Hermeneutics of the Diaspora: A Hermeneutics of Otherness and Engagement," in *Reading from This Place, Vol. 1: Social Location and Biblical Interpretation in the United States,* ed. Fernando F. Segovia and Mary Ann Tolbert (Minneapolis: Fortress Press, 1995), 57.

[8]See Frank M. Yamada, "Shibboleth and the Ma(r)king of Culture: Judges 12 and the Monolingualism of the Other," in *Derrida's Bible,* ed. Yvonne Sherwood (New York: Palgrave Macmillan, 2004), 119–34.

[9]For a brief summary of the context and themes within Asian American theology, see Seung Ai Yang, "Asian Americans," and Fumitaka Matsuoka, "Asian American Theology," in *Handbook of U.S. Theologies of Liberation,* ed. Miguel A. De La Torre (St. Louis: Chalice Press, 2004), 173–84; 218–29.

[10]Fumitaka Matsuoka, *Out of Silence: Emerging Themes in Asian American Churches* (Cleveland: United Church Press, 1995), 54.

[11]For examples of Asian American theology that use such themes, see especially Jung Young Lee, *Marginality: The Key to Multicultural Theology* (Minneapolis: Fortress Press, 1995); Sang Hyun Lee, "Pilgrimage and Home in the Wilderness of Marginality: Symbols and Context

in Asian American Theology," *Princton Seminary Bulletin* 16 (1995): 49–64; and Matsuoka, *Out of Silence.*

[12]Sang Hyun Lee argues that marginality, while forced upon Asian Americans by the dominant culture, is also simultaneously a place of creativity and redemption. He gives the example of Jesus' marginal status to reinforce his claim ("Pilgrimage and Home," 58).

[13]Some recent scholarship suggests that Asian American identity is more complicated and conflicted. See, for example, Uriah (Yong-Hwan) Kim, "Uriah the Hittite: A (Con)text of Struggle for Identity," *Semeia* 90/91 (2002): 69–85; Patrick S. Cheng, "Multiplicity and Judges 19: Constructing a Queer Asian Pacific American Biblical Hermeneutic," *Semeia* 90/91 (2002): 119–33; Mary F. Foskett, "The Accidents of Being and the Politics of Identity: Biblical Images of Adoption and Asian Adoptees in America," *Semeia* 90/91 (2002): 135–44; and Henry W. Reitz, "My Father Has No Children: Reflections on a *Hapa* Identity Toward a Hermeneutic of Particularity," *Semeia* 90/91 (2002): 145–57.

[14]Harry H.L. Kitano and Roger Daniels, *Asian Americans: Emerging Minorities* (Englewood Cliffs, N.J.: Prentice Hall, 1988), 71. In the second edition (1995), Kitano and Daniels add "Gosei," the fifth generation, along with Sansei and Yonsei. The tones of pervasive assimilation remain unchanged (78).

[15]Ibid., 73.

[16]See, for example, Stephen S. Fugita and David J. O'Brien, *Japanese American Ethnicity: The Persistence of Community* (Seattle: University of Washington Press, 1991); Jere Takahashi, *Nisei/Sansei: Shifting Japanese American Identities and Politics* (Philadelphia: Temple University Press, 1997); and Donna K. Nagata, *Legacy of Injustice: Exploring the Cross-Generational Impact of the Japanese American Internment* (New York: Plenum Press, 1993).

[17]Lowe, "Heterogeneity," 684.

[18]Michael Omi and Howard Winant, *Racial Formation in the United States: From the 1960s to the 1990s,* 2d ed. (New York: Routledge, 1994). See especially chapter 4, "Racial Formation," (53–76).

[19]Ibid., 55.

[20]Ibid., 99. In a note, Omi and Winant define "rearticulation" as "a practice of discursive reorganization or reinterpretation of ideological themes and interests already present in the subject's consciousness, such that these elements obtain new meanings or coherence" (99, n. 11).

[21]Takahashi uses Omi and Winant's work, especially their notion of rearticulation, to help explain shifting political practices between Niseis and Sanseis. See especially Takahashi, *Nisei/Sansei,* 8–10. For a work that considers Omi and Winant's ideas in the context of Asian American religion, see Antony W. Alumkal, *Asian American Evangelical Churches: Race, Ethnicity, and Assimilation in the Second Generation* (New York: LFB Scholarly Publishing, 2003). Within the context of Asian American literature, Patricia Chu has made similar arguments. She contends that Asian American authors transform the literary model of *bildungsroman* in that "they claim Americanness for Asian American subjects, and they construct accounts of Asian ethnicity that complicate, even as they support, the primary claim of Americanness by representing Asian Americans as grounded in highly specific ethnic histories in America" (Patricia P. Chu, *Assimilating Asians: Gendered Strategies of Authorship in Asian America* [Durham, N.C.: Duke University Press, 2000], 4).

[22]Homi Bhabha, *The Location of Culture* (New York: Routledge, 1994), 111.

[23]Ronald Takaki, *Strangers from a Different Shore: A History of Asian Americans,* rev. ed. (Boston: Little, Brown, and Company, 1998), 213–14.

[24]See, for example, Kitano and Daniels, *Asian Americans,* 66–75. However, the work of Takahashi (*Nisei/Sansei,* 1–13) and Nagata (*Legacy of Injustice,* 37–51) provide approaches that have more nuance in their cross-generational study of Japanese Americans.

[25]Lowe, "Heterogeneity," 680.

[26]In the 1970s, sixty percent of all new marriages among Sansei were interracial unions (Fugita and O'Brien, *Japanese American Ethnicity,* 131; citing data from Harry H.L. Kitano, Wai-Tsang Yeung, Lynn Chai, and Herbert Hatanaka, "Asian American Interracial Marriage," *Journal of Marriage and the Family* 46 [1984]: 179–90).

[27]For literature on mixed race Asian Americans see Cynthia L. Nakashima, "Asian American Studies Through (Somewhat) Asian Eyes: Integrating 'Mixed Race' into the Asian American Discourse," in *Asian American Studies After Critical Mass,* ed. Kent A. Ono (Oxford:

Blackwell Publishing, 2005), 111–20; Teresa Williams-León and Cynthia L. Nakashima, eds., *The Sum of Our Part: Mixed Heritage Asian Americans* (Philadelphia: Temple University Press, 2001); Paul R. Spickard, *Mixed Blood: Intermarriage and Ethnic Identity in Twentieth-Century America* (Madison: University of Wisconsin Press, 1989); "What Must I Be?: Asian Americans and the Question of Multiethnic Identity," in *Asian American Studies: A Reader,* ed. Jean Yu-wen Shen Wu and Min Song (New Brunswick, N.J.: Rutgers University Press, 2000), 255–69. For a perspective within the study of biblical hermeneutics see Reitz, "*Hapa* Identity."

[28]Lowe, "Heterogeneity," 681.

[29]R.S. Sugirtharajah has argued for a thoroughly interdisciplinary approach in postcolonial interpretation. He contends that postcolonial theory must seek to include various texts, religious traditions, and cultural experiences in his *The Bible and the Third World: Precolonial, Colonial and Postcolonial Encounters* (New York: Cambridge University Press, 2001), 262. I have argued elsewhere that his proposal, when read in light of Derrida's broader conceptualization of text, points to a broader notion of intertextuality—one that includes not only literary texts but historical and cultural experience (Frank M. Yamada, "Response to Sugirtharajah's *Asian Biblical Hermeneutics and Postcolonialism* and *The Bible and the Third World,*" a paper presented at the Society of Biblical Literature Annual Meeting, Denver, November 18, 2001).

[30]David Mura, *Where the Body Meets Memory: An Odyssey of Race, Sexuality, and Identity* (New York: Doubleday, 1996).

[31]Scholars such as Nagata have shown that the internment had a transgenerational impact on the Japanese American community. Reactions to the camps differed from generation to generation. However, the injustice had a profound effect, shaping the different response to the internment (Nagata, *Legacy of Injustice,* 75–218).

[32]I am not arguing that the internment is identical to the exile or Holocaust. Invasion by a foreign power, as was the case with the destruction of Judah, carries with it certain traumas that do not correspond to forced imprisonment. Moreover, the genocidal horrors of Auschwitz exceed the humiliations of Manzanar or Heart Mountain. My point is that these events share a functional similarity in relation to collective trauma. All these events are crucial historical moments from which identity construction emerges in future generations. For discussion, see Nagata, *Legacy of Injustice,* 37–51, where she examines the effects of the Holocaust on subsequent Jewish generations as a comparative framework for understanding the influence of the internment on Sanseis.

[33]For a good example of multidisciplinary work on the exile that takes into account the experience of dislocated peoples, including Japanese Americans, see Daniel Smith-Christopher, *The Religion of the Landless: The Social Context of the Babylonian Exile* (Bloomington, Ind.: Meyer Stone, 1989), 69–90.

[34]All translations are my own.

Chapter 14: Obscured Beginnings

[1]Adam Pertman, *Adoption Nation: How the Adoption Revolution Is Transforming America* (New York: Basic Books, 2000).

[2]The KAAN Web site is: http://www.kaanet.com.

[3]Karin Evans, *The Lost Daughters of China: Abandoned Girls, Their Journey to America, and the Search for a Missing Past* (New York: Jeremy P. Tarcher/Putnam, 2000).

[4]Madelyn Freundlich and Joy Kim Liberthal, *The Gathering of the First Generation of Adult Korean Adoptees: Adoptees' Perceptions of International Adoption* (New York: Evan B. Donaldson Adoption Institute, 2000). Online at http://www.adoptioninstitute.org/proed/korfindings.html.

[5]Freundlich and Liberthal, *The Gathering.*

[6]Ibid.

[7]David Friedrich Strauss, *The Life of Jesus Critically Examined* (Minneapolis: Fortress Press, 1972).

[8]Albert Schweitzer, *The Quest of the Historical Jesus: A Critical Study of Its Progress from Reimarus to Wrede,* trans. W. Montgomery (London: A.C. Black, 1954).

[9]Albert Schweitzer, *Out of My Life and Thought: An Autobiography,* trans. C.T. Campion, postscript 1932–1949 by Everett Skillings (New York: Henry Holt & Co., 1949), 55.

[10]Ibid., 58–59.

[11]William Wrede, *The Messianic Secret* (London: James Clarke and Co., 1971).

[12]Martin Kähler, *The So-Called Historical Jesus and the Historic Biblical Christ* (Minneapolis: Fortress Press, 1964), 28.

[13]Rudolf Bultmann, *Faith and Understanding*, ed. with an introduction by Robert W. Funk, trans. Louise Pettibone Smith (New York: Harper and Row, 1969).

[14]Ernst Käsemann, "The Problem of the Historical Jesus," in his *Essays on New Testament Themes*, trans. W.J. Montague (Philadelphia: Fortress, 1982), 213.

[15]John Dominic Crossan, *The Historical Jesus: The Life of a Mediterranean Jewish Peasant* (San Francisco: HarperSan Franciso, 1991); Marcus J. Borg, *Meeting Jesus Again for the First Time: The Historical Jesus and the Heart of Contemporary Faith* (San Francisco: HarperSan Francisco, 1994).

[16]Luke Timothy Johnson, *The Real Jesus: The Misguided Quest for the Historical Jesus and the Truth of the Traditional Gospels* (New York: HarperCollins, 1996).

[17]N.T. Wright, "Jesus, Quest for the Historical," in *The Anchor Bible Dictionary, Vol. 3*, ed. David Noel Freedman et. al. (New York: Doubleday, 1992), 800.

[18]Craig A. Evans, "Life of Jesus Research and the Eclipse of Mythology," *Theological Studies* 54 (1993): 34.

[19]John P. Meier, "The Present State of the 'Third Quest' for the Historical Jesus: Loss and Gain," *Biblica* 80 (1999): 463–64.

[20]Paula Fredriksen, "What You See Is What You Get: Context and Content in Current Research on the Historical Jesus," *Theology Today* 52 (1995): 94.

[21]Pertman, *Adoption Nation*, 87.

[22]Ibid., 87.

[23]Evans, *Lost Daughters of China*, 74.

[24]Ibid., 75.

[25]Ibid., 206.

[26]Elizabeth A. Castelli, "Heteroglossia, Hermeneutics and History: A Review Essay of Recent Feminist Studies of Early Christianity," *Journal of Feminist Studies in Religion* 10 (1994): 92.

[27]Ibid., 75.

[28]Elizabeth A. Clark, "Women, Gender and the Study of Christian History," *Church History* 70 (2001): 395–426.

[29]Elisabeth Schussler Fiorenza, *In Memory of Her: A Feminist Theological Reconstruction of Christian Origins* (New York: Crossroad, 1983).

[30]Ross Shepard Kraemer and Mary Rose D'Angelo, *Women and Christian Origins* (Oxford: Oxford University Press, 1999).

[31]Turid Karlsen Seim, *The Double Message: Patterns of Gender in Luke-Acts* (Edinburgh: T&T Clark, 1994), 249.

[32]Kramer and D'Angelo, *Women and Christian Origins*, 187.

[33]Ibid., 185.

[34]Ibid., 188.

[35]Pertman, *Adoption Nation*, 26.

Chapter 15: Living Past

[1]As this essay argues, my particular thoughts have been formed and informed in communities and in relationships. I am indebted to a number of them: the organizers and participants of the Asian Pacific Americans and Religion Research Initiative (APARRI); my colleagues at Grinnell College, especially Edmund Gilday; Sang Lee for the opportunity to speak at Princeton Theological Seminary's day of remembrance service; Frank Yamada; Peter Yuichi Clark; M. Eileen Burtle; and Sarah White. Most of all, I am grateful to my parents, Inge C. Rietz and Henry T. Morisada, and my daughters, Maile and Katherine Moriko, for their love and support.

[2]Vera Schwarcz, *Bridge Across Broken Time: Chinese and Jewish Cultural Memory* (New Haven and London: Yale University Press, 1998), 22.

[3]Versions of my family's story may be found in Henry Morisada Rietz, "My Father Has No Children: Reflections on a *Hapa* Identity Toward a Hermeneutic of Particularity," *Semeia* 90/91 (2002): 145–57; and idem, "My Father Has No Children," *Union Seminary Quarterly Review* 26 (2002): 59–63. For the importance of situating oneself in the process of interpretation, see the essays of Fernando F. Segovia in *Reading from This Place, Vol. 1: Social Location and Biblical Interpretation in the United States*, and *Reading from This Place, Vol. 2: Social Location and*

Biblical Interpretation in Global Perspective, ed. Fernando F. Segovia and Mary Ann Tolbert (Minneapolis: Fortress Press, 1995). For a brief discussion of the complexity of autobiography or "autoethnography," see Tat-Siong Benny Liew and Vincent L. Wimbush, "Contact Zones and Zoning Contexts: From the Los Angeles 'Riot' to a New York Symposium," *Union Seminary Quarterly Review* 26 (2002): 21–40, esp. 24–28.

⁴*Hapa* is short for *hapa-haole. Haole* is Hawaiian for "foreigner," and is popularly used in Hawai'i for people of European descent. *Hapa* is Hawaiian for "half." A person who is *hapa-haole* is "half-*haole.*"

⁵People of Japanese ancestry in Hawai'i usually identify themselves as simply "Japanese," rather than use a term such as Americans of Japanese ancestry, as is more common on the mainland United States. Japanese is not being used here to identify people born and raised in Japan. Some of the cultural distinctions between Japanese in Japan and Japanese Americans are nicely illustrated by David Mura's memoir of living for a year in Japan, entitled *Turning Japanese: Memoirs of a Sansei* (New York: Doubleday, 1991).

⁶For a recent brief summary, see "Introduction: Alien/Nation, Liberation, and the Postcolonial Underground," in *Postcolonial Theologies: Divinity and Empire,* ed. Catherine Keller, Michael Nausner, and Mayra Rivera (St. Louis: Chalice Press, 2004), 1–19, esp. pp. 8–13.

⁷See, for example, the discussion of the construction of the category "Asian" by Namsoon Kang, "Who/What Is Asian?: A Postcolonial Theological Reading of Orientalism and Neo-Orientalism," in *Postcolonial Theologies,* 100–117.

⁸For some published accounts of the experiences of other *hapa,* see Marie Hara and Nora Okja Keller, eds., *Intersecting Circles: The Voices of Hapa Women in Poetry and Prose* (Honolulu: Bamboo Ridge, 1999) and the film *Doubles: Japan and America's Intercultural Children,* produced and directed by Regge Life (1995). (I am grateful to Katya Gibel Azoulay for referring me to this film.)

⁹Adapted from "How to Write History," in *Lucian VI,* with an English translation by K. Kilburn, Loeb Classical Library (Cambridge and London: Harvard University Press), 15, 57, 59.

¹⁰In my opinion, Krister Stendahl's seductive distinction between "what it [i.e., the text] meant and what it means" is still functionally very influential in many ecclesial contexts (Stendahl, "Biblical Theology: A Program," in *Meanings: The Bible as Document and as Guide* [Philadelphia: Fortress, 1984], 11–44 [reprint of "Biblical Theology, Contemporary," in the *Interpreter's Dictionary of the Bible,* vol. 1, 1962]; and idem, "Method in the Study of Biblical Theology," in *The Bible in Modern Scholarship: Papers Read at the 100th Meeting of the Society of Biblical Literature, December 28–30, 1964,* ed. J. Philip Hyatt [Nashville and New York: Abingdon, 1965], 196–209). For a critique of Stendahl, see Ben C. Ollenburger, "What Krister Stendahl 'Meant'–A Normative Critique of 'Descriptive Biblical Theology,'" *Horizons in Biblical Theology* 8 (1986): 61–98.

¹¹John Sandys-Wunsch and Laurence Eldredge, "J.P. Gabler and the Distinction between Biblical and Dogmatic Theology: Translation, Commentary, and Discussion of His Originality," *Scottish Journal of Theology* 33 (1980): 133–58, see esp. 143, n. 2.

¹²See Jon D. Levenson, *The Hebrew Bible, the Old Testament, and Historical Criticism: Jews and Christians in Biblical Studies* (Louisville: Westminster/John Knox Press, 1993).

¹³The valuing of similarity is pervasive in all sorts of research. See, for example, the comments of Catherine Myser on bioethics: "Indeed, all too often, 'cultural differences' associated with research subjects in minoritized spaces–in or outside of the United States–are represented as 'obstacles,' 'difficulties,' and or 'challenges' for 'us' in the majority space of dominant U.S. bioethics and healthcare culture, requiring 'translation' or 'interpretation' by social scientists and others operating in (and ironically maintaining) that majority space" ("Differences from Somewhere: The Normativity of Whiteness in Bioethics in the U.S.," *The American Journal of Bioethics* 3, no. 2 [Spring 2003]: 9).

¹⁴I would suggest that the privileging of similarity pervades the way that people interpret texts–how often do we hear someone say, "I didn't like a book or a movie because I couldn't relate to any of the characters"? If people cannot discern similarity a subject is not considered to be interesting.

¹⁵Sandys-Wunsch and Eldredge, "J. P. Gabler," 138.

¹⁶Rudolf Bultmann, "New Testament and Mythology," in *Kerygma and Myth: A Theological Debate,* ed. Hans Werner Bartsch, trans. Reginald H. Fuller (London: Society for the Promotion of Christian Knowledge, 1957), 1.

¹⁷Ibid., 5.

¹⁸Ibid., 10.

¹⁹Delores Williams, *Sisters in the Wilderness: The Challenge of Womanist God-Talk* (Maryknoll, N.Y.: Orbis Books, 1993), 15.

²⁰Of course, all interpretations are contextual, whether the interpreter is explicit or not.

²¹Edited by Tat-siong Benny Liew, *Semeia* 90/91 (2002). This is a rich collection of essays to which my brief comments do not do justice.

²²Uriah (Yong-Hwan) Kim, "Uriah the Hittite: A (Con)text of Struggle for Identity," *Semeia* 90/91 (2002): 69–85. He insightfully articulates the dangers of readers identifying with David; see esp. 81.

²³Ibid., 82. Kim rightly begins his inquiry with the following questions: "Was Uriah the Hittite also in a similar (con)text as mine? Was he also a site/text of a struggle for identity in Israel? But first, who was Uriah the Hittite anyway?" (p. 72).

²⁴A similar strategy may be seen in the parallels that Jeffrey Kah-Jin Kuan draws between the book of Esther and the diasporic experiences of some Asian Americans (in fact, Kuan identifies his complex experience of being a third-generation Chinese Malaysian now living in the United States as being a "rediasporized person, a 'doubly' diasporic person"); see Kuan, "Diasporic Reading of a Diasporic Text: Identity Politics and Race Relations and the Book of Esther," in *Interpreting Beyond Borders,* ed. Fernando F. Segovia (Sheffield: Sheffield Academic Press, 2000), 165, n. 7.

²⁵Interestingly, Brock's own ethnic identity is complex; she was born in Japan to a Japanese mother and Puerto Rican father, emigrating from Okinawa when she was six to be raised in the United States by her mother and Caucasian stepfather. See her "On Mirrors, Mists, Murmurs and the Way toward Asian-American 'Thealogy,'" in *Weaving the Visions: New Patterns in Feminist Spirituality,* ed. Judith Plaskow and Carol P. Christ (San Francisco: Harper and Row, 1989), 235–43, esp. p. 237.

²⁶Rita Nakashima Brock, *Journeys by Heart: A Christology of Erotic Power* (New York: Crossroad, 1988), 37.

²⁷Craig R. Prentiss, "Introduction," in *Religion and the Creation of Race and Ethnicity: An Introduction,* ed. Craig R. Prentiss (New York and London: New York University Press, 2003), 5. Prentiss is dependent on Bruce Lincoln, *Discourse and the Construction of Society: Comparative Studies of Myth, Ritual, and Classification* (New York: Oxford University Press, 1989).

²⁸For a discussion of the ways that the term "myth" is used in religious studies, especially with regard to identity formation, see Russell T. McCutcheon, "Myth," in *Guide to the Study of Religion,* ed. Willi Braun and Russell T. McCutcheon (London and New York: Cassell, 2000), 190–208.

²⁹Note that both of these passages are set within a cultic context.

³⁰Of course, the sharp distinctions made between religious, familial, ethnic, and political are obliterated when one considers, for example, the formation and history of interpretation of Genesis 12–50.

³¹The commemoration of the internment of Japanese Americans functions "religiously" in a number of different ways. For an example, see Joanne Doi, "Tule Lake Pilgrimage: Dissonant Memories, Sacred Journey," in *Revealing the Sacred in Asian and Pacific America,* ed. Jane Naomi Iwamura and Paul Spickard (New York and London: Routledge, 2003), 273–89.

³²Of the 157,905 Japanese and Japanese Americans living in Hawai'i in 1940 (37.3 percent of the total population), only 1,037 (including 912 American citizens) were relocated to internment camps on the mainland of the United States. For a brief discussion of the deliberation whether to intern all people of Japanese ancestry, see David J. O'Brien and Stephen S. Fugita, *The Japanese American Experience* (Bloomington and Indianapolis: Indiana University Press, 1991), 48–51. My grandparents' house was searched several times by the F.B.I. and among the things confiscated were my father's Boy Scout manual. (It had a table of the Morse code.)

³³Of course, as an active member of the United Church of Christ who participates in Shinto and Buddhist rituals, and whose mother was born Jewish but was baptized Lutheran in Nazi Germany, my religious identity is a bit more ambiguous.

³⁴Anne Nakao, "Haunting Echoes of Japanese Internment," *The San Francisco Chronicle,* February 18, 2003. Online: http://www.sfgate.com/cgi-bin/article.cgi?file=/chronicle/archive/2003/02/18/DD160333.DTL.

[35]When I teach a course on contextual biblical interpretation, I have my students work through a survey that questions how aspects of their identity affect the way that they interpret the biblical text. Often it is the straight white male students who have the hardest time answering the survey. Since they are part of the dominant group, they have had the privilege of not having to construct their identity consciously. The survey that I use is adapted from Norman K. Gottward, "Framing Biblical Interpretation at New York Theological Seminary: A Student Self-Inventory on Biblical Hermeneutics," *Reading from this Place, Vol. 1: Social Location and Biblical Interpretation in the United States,* ed. Fernando F. Segovia and Mary Ann Tolbert (Minneapolis: Fortress, 1995), 251–61.

Selected Bibliography

Bhabha, Homi K., ed. *Nation and Narration*. London: Routledge, 1990.

Brock, Rita Nakashima. "Interstitial Integrity: Reflections toward an Asian American Woman's Theology." In *Introduction to Christian Theology: Contemporary North American Perspectives*, edited by Roger A. Badham, 183–96. Louisville: Westminster John Knox Press, 1998.

_____. *Journeys by Heart: A Christology of Erotic Power*. New York: Crossroad, 1988.

Chan, Sucheng. *Asian Americans: An Interpretive History*. Boston: Twayne, 1991.

Chow, Rey. *The Protestant Ethnic & the Spirit of Capitalism*. New York: Columbia University Press, 2002.

_____. *Writing Diaspora: Tactics of Intervention in Contemporary Cultural Studies*. Bloomington & Indianapolis: Indiana University Press, 1993.

Dube, Musa W. *Postcolonial Feminist Interpretation of the Bible*. St. Louis: Chalice Press, 2000.

Fabella, Virginia, and Sun Ai Lee Park, eds. *We Dare to Dream: Doing Theology as Asian Women*. Maryknoll, N.Y.: Orbis Books, 1989.

Fernandez, Eleazar S., and Fernando F. Segovia, eds. *A Dream Unfinished: Theological Reflections on America from the Margins*. Maryknoll, N.Y.: Orbis Books, 2001.

Kim, Chan-Hie. "Reading the Bible as Asian Americans." In *The New Interpreter's Bible*, vol. 1, , edited by Leander E. Keck et al., 161–66. Nashville: Abingdon Press, 1994.

Kim, Yong Bock. *Minjung Theology: People as the Subjects of History*. Singapore: Commission on Theological Concerns, Christian Conference of Asia, 1981.

Kitano, Harry H. L., and Roger Daniels. *Asian Americans: Emerging Minorities*. Englewood Cliffs, N.J.: Prentice-Hall, 1988.

Kuan, Jeffrey K. "Asian Biblical Interpretation." In *Dictionary of Biblical Interpretation, A-J*, edited by John H. Hayes, 70–77. Nashville: Abingdon Press, 1999.

_____. "Diasporic Reading of a Diasporic Text: Identity Politics and Race Relations and the Book of Esther." In *Interpreting Beyond Borders*, edited by Fernando F. Segovia, 161–73. Sheffield: Sheffied Academic Press, 2000.

_____. "Reading Amy Tan Reading Job." In *Relating to the Text: Interdisciplinary and Form-Critical Insights on the Bible*, edited by T. J. Sandoval and C. Mandolfo, 263–74. JSOTSup 384. London/New York: T & T Clark International, 2003.

Kwok, Pui-lan. *Discovering the Bible in the Non-Biblical World.* Maryknoll, N.Y.: Orbis Books, 1995.

———. *Introducing Asian Feminist Theology.* Introductions in Feminist Theology 4. Cleveland: Pilgrim Press, 2000.

———, ed., *Postcolonialism, Feminism and Religious Discourse.* New York: Routledge, 2002.

Lee, Archie C.C. "Biblical Interpretation in Asian Perspective," *Asia Journal of Theology* 7 (1993): 38–48.

Lee, Jung Young. *Marginality: The Key to Multicultural Theology.* Minneapolis: Fortress Press, 1995.

Lee, Sang Hyun. "Pilgrimage and Home in the Wilderness of Marginality: Symbols and Context in Asian American Theology." *Princeton Seminary Bulletin* 16 (1995): 49–64.

Levison, Jon R., and Priscilla Pope-Levison, eds. *Return to Babel: Global Perspectives on the Bible.* Louisville: Westminster John Knox Press, 1999.

Liew, Tat-siong Benny. "Reading with Yin Yang Eyes: Negotiating the Ideological Dilemma of a Chinese American Biblical Hermeneutics." *Biblical Interpretation* 9 (2001): 309–35.

———, ed. *The Bible in Asian America. Semeia* 90/91 (2002).

Lowe, Lisa. "Heterogeneity, Hybridity, Multiplicity: Marking Asian American Differences." In *Asian American Studies: A Reader*, edited by Jean Yu-wen Shen Wu and Min Song, 423–42. New Brunswick, N.J.: Rutgers University, 2000.

Matsuoka, Fumitaka. *Out of Silence, Emerging Themes in Asian American Churches.* Cleveland: United Church Press, 1995.

Matsuoka, Fumitaka, and Eleazar S. Fernandez, eds. *Realizing the America of Our Hearts: Theological Voices of Asian Americans.* St. Louis: Chalice Press, 2003.

Moon, Cyris Hee-suk. *A Korean Minjung Theology: An Old Testament Perspective.* Maryknoll, N.Y.: Orbis Books, 1985.

Okihiro, Gary. *Margins and Mainstreams: Asians in American History and Culture.* Seattle: University of Washington Press, 1994.

Omi, Michael, and Howard Winant. *Racial Formation in the United States: From the 1960s to the 1990s.* 2d ed. New York: Routledge, 1994.

Phan, Peter C. "Betwixt and Between: Doing Theology with Memory and Imagination." In *Journeys at the Margin: Toward an Autobiographical Theology in American-Asian Perspective*, edited by Peter C. Phan and Jung Young Lee, 113–33. Collegeville, Minn.: Liturgical Press, 1999.

Samartha, Stanley J. *One Christ, Many Religions: Toward a Revised Christology.* Maryknoll, N.Y.: Orbis Books, 1991.

Segovia, Fernando F., and Mary Ann Tolbert, eds. *Reading from This Place, Vol. 1: Social Location and Biblical Interpretation in the United States.* Minneapolis: Fortress Press, 1995.

_____, eds. *Reading from This Place, Vol. 2: Social Location and Biblical Interpretation in Global Perspective.* Minneapolis: Fortress Press, 1995.

Smith-Christopher, Daniel. *Text & Experience: Towards a Cultural Exegesis of the Bible.* Sheffield: Sheffield Academic Press, 1995.

Song, C.S. *The Believing Heart: An Invitation to Story Theology.* Minneapolis: Fortress Press, 1999.

_____. *The Tears of Lady Ming: A Parable of People's Political Theology.* Geneva: World Council of Churches, 1981.

Song, Young I., and Ailee Moon, eds. *Korean American Women: From Tradition to Modern Feminism.* Westport, Conn.: Praeger Press, 1998.

Sugirtharajah, R.S. *Asian Biblical Hermeneutics and Postcolonialism: Contesting Interpretations.* Sheffield: Sheffield Academic Press, 1999.

_____. *The Bible and the Third World: Precolonial, Colonial and Postcolonial Encounters.* Cambridge/New York: Cambridge University Press, 2001.

_____. *Postcolonial Reconfigurations.* St. Louis: Chalice Press, 2003.

_____, ed. *Frontiers in Asian Christian Theology.* Maryknoll, N.Y.: Orbis Books, 1994.

_____, ed. *The Postcolonial Bible.* Sheffield: Sheffield Academic Press, 1998.

_____, ed. *Vernacular Hermeneutics.* Sheffield: Sheffield Academic Press, 1999.

_____, ed. *Voices from the Margin: Interpreting the Bible in the Third World.* 2d ed. Maryknoll, N.Y.: Orbis Books, 1995.

Takaki, Ronald. *Strangers from a Different Shore: A History of Asian Americans.* New York: Penguin Books, 1989.

Wan, Sze-kar. "Does Diaspora Identity Imply Some Sort of Universality? An Asian-American Reading of Galatians." In *Interpreting Beyond Borders*, edited by Fernando F. Segovia, 119. Sheffield: Sheffield Academic Press, 2000.

Wu, Frank. *Yellow: Race in America Beyond Black and White.* New York: Basic Books, 2001.

Yee, Gale A. "Inculturation and Diversity in the Politics of National Identity." *Journal of Asian and Asian American Theology* 2 (1997): 108–12.

_____. *Poor Banished Children of Eve: Woman as Evil in the Hebrew Bible.* Minneapolis: Fortress Press, 2003.

Yeo, K.K. *What Has Jerusalem to Do with Beijing: Biblical Interpretation from a Chinese Perspective.* Harrisburg, Pa.: Trinity Press, 1998.

Yu, Henry. *Thinking Orientals: Migration, Contact, and Exoticism in Modern America.* Oxford: Oxford University Press, 2001.

Zia, Helen. *Asian American Dreams: The Emergence of an American People.* New York: Farrar, Straus & Giroux, 2000.